# VICTORY AT SEA

# Victory at Sea 1939-1945

*Written with the approval of the Admiralty by*

**Lieut.-Commander P.K. Kemp**

F.S.A., F.R.Hist.S., R.N.(Retd.)

*(Admiralty Archivist and Head of Historical Section)*

*With a foreword by*

**Admiral of the Fleet Viscount Cunningham of Hyndhope,**

K.T., G.C.B., O.M., D.S.O.

*"Believe me, I shall never more take my hat off for anything less than a British Seaman. It is easy to subscribe a million of money at Lloyd's, by putting your hand in your pocket; but it requires the hearts of lions, and the fortitude of untameable spirits, to attack the bold front of defiance . . . and bend it to your purpose."*

JOHN ECKSTEIN, writing from the Diamond Rock,
17th February, 1804.

WHITE LION PUBLISHERS LIMITED
London, Sydney and Toronto

First published in Great Britain by
Frederick Muller Ltd., 1957



White Lion edition 1976

ISBN 7274 0027 4

Made and printed in Great Britain
for White Lion Publishers Limited,
138 Park Lane, London W1Y 3DD
by Hendington Limited,
Lion House, North Town, Aldershot, Hampshire

# Contents

# List of Illustrations

*Between pages 192 - 193*

# List of Maps

# Foreword

By Admiral of the Fleet Viscount Cunningham of Hyndhope, K.T., G.C.B., O.M., D.S.O.

Immediately after the conclusion of the Second World War the Admiralty had intended to bring out a single-volume work, based on the official documents of the war, describing the naval effort between 1939 and 1945 in the struggle against Germany, Italy, and Japan. It had been hoped to have this book ready for sale to the general public in 1948. Owing to a variety of circumstances, however, this project never materialised. The proposal was resuscitated in 1956, when Lieutenant-Commander P. K. Kemp, R.N., the Admiralty Archivist and Head of the Historical Section, was invited to undertake the work.

Into this one volume the author has managed skilfully to compress the whole story of the war at sea during the Second World War. Those who may wish for a more detailed account of naval operations will find it in the official Cabinet Office history, in three volumes, by Captain S. W. Roskill, D.S.C., R.N., of which the first two volumes have now been published.

Wisely, in my opinion, the writer here has aimed to give the reader a broad and comprehensive picture of events and strategy, pausing now and again to describe more fully the actions and episodes of outstanding importance which illustrate the central strategic theme. This was a war in which, for the first time, the air arm made its appearance as a significant weapon, and Lieutenant-Commander Kemp makes clear how essential it is to pay full attention to its proper use at sea, and how smoothly it blends, when used with imagination and wisdom, in the art and exercise of command at sea. He also points out most graphically what may happen when, as in Norway and Crete and off Malaya, the enemy has unfettered use of air power. Throughout he stresses the absolute necessity of close co-operation between the three fighting Services and also between Allies. He also emphasises that in time of war the fighting ships and the merchant fleets, with their personnel, are interdependent and indivisible. All these points are well brought out at appropriate places in the narrative.

This book deserves a wide circulation among English-speaking people, and indeed among all people who value our way of life. The story it has to tell is a proud one. It is also a story with a moral, for on the day we forget what the sea has meant, and still means, to us, we lose our independence as a nation. It is argued sometimes that the advent of the aircraft, and even more the advent of nuclear warfare, has lessened the value of sea power. In my opinion Lieutenant-Commander Kemp, in this completely factual account of what sea power meant and achieved in this last war, makes quite plain its lasting influence in the life of any island nation. For my part, I would say that, from whatever angle the problem is approached, the fact remains that in 1957 we are as dependent upon the sea for our existence as we were a century or two centuries ago, or shall be a hundred years hence.

# Preface

The study of sea power in war, and its influence on campaigns and actions fought far distant from the oceans, is an exercise which has appealed to many historians. It is therefore with some trepidation that I venture to add yet one more volume to the many which have already appeared on this subject. There is, perhaps, some excuse for the present volume, in that it attempts to relate the study of sea power to the course of the last war, and to show the influence which it exerted both on the formulation of grand strategy and on the actual course of the land campaigns.

In its essence the story of British sea power is the story of the Royal and Merchant Navies. Of necessity, therefore, much of this book is concerned with the major naval operations of the war in an attempt to show how they fitted into, and in their outcome influenced, the major strategical pattern. The full story of the naval operations of the last war is being excellently told by Captain S. W. Roskill in his three-volume official history, *The War at Sea*, of which the first two volumes have now been published. In attempting to present, in a single volume of modest proportions, this overall picture of the naval war, I have been able to study the documentary evidence which exists in the Admiralty, the Service and some other Ministries, in addition to the captured enemy records. Numbered references to some of these official papers, which as yet are not available for public examination are made as unobtrusively as possible in the text. The purpose is the possible value they may have for the future historian in plotting some sort of a course through the mass of documentary evidence which will, presumably, find a permanent resting-place in the Public Record

Office after the lapse of the statutory number of years. Needless to say, all the opinions expressed and the inferences and conclusions drawn from my study of these papers are entirely my own.

It had been proposed by the Admiralty to produce some such book as this within three or four years of the ending of the war, but for various reasons it fell by the wayside. When, some five years later, the decision was taken to revive the project, though as a private and not an official venture, I was given the inestimable benefit of the work of my predecessors in this task, and to them I am most grateful. I am also deeply indebted to the staff of the Historical Section of the Admiralty, whose profound study of the last war, whose valuable advice, and whose willing co-operation in pointing out where I had gone astray in my facts made my task so much the easier. I have also had invaluable help from Admirals of the Fleet Viscount Cunningham of Hyndhope, Sir Charles Forbes, Lord Fraser of North Cape, and Lord Tovey of Langton Matravers, who have all been kind enough to read through the typescript and give me the benefit of their advice. Another to whom I owe an equal debt of gratitude is Viscount Alexander of Hillsborough, First Lord of the Admiralty during the greater part of the war, who also read the typescript and helped me with his advice. Captain S. W. Roskill was kind enough to let me see the typescript of his second volume and part of his third, before publication, which proved a great help in my task. To them all, and to many others too numerous to mention, my very grateful thanks are due.

P. K. K.

*Admiralty,*
15*th January*, 1957.

# Chapter 1

## THE DRIFT INTO WAR

THE four and a quarter years of war which came to an end in 1918 left many naval legacies. Of them all, perhaps the most important was a more vivid awareness that Britain was still an island nation, was still dependent on her merchant shipping for her existence in spite of modern weapons and modern methods of war. That shipping had been attacked during the war with a ferocity never before experienced, and at times to an extent where the ability to carry on fighting was brought to the razor's edge of decision.

It was not that this prime naval duty in war had been forgotten or was neglected during those four years of battle. Three hundred years of experience lay behind the Navy of 1914, and all of it told the same story. But in 1914 two new factors were at work. There had been radical changes since the earlier days in the weapons of sea power, and war had come before these new weapons had been fully mastered or, indeed, fully understood. The submarine, the torpedo, the aeroplane, all of them were virtually new, and there was no real background of experience or knowledge against which their performance in war could be judged. More important still was a change in the traditional national strategy. For the first time for centuries Britain no longer used her command of the sea as the basis for her war strategy. She fought this campaign mainly as a military power on the Continent, and in such a war the Navy could take little share.

So it was, at times, that there was a faltering in the prosecution of the chief naval duty in war. So it was, at times, that the nation's fate trembled on the brink.

It was not only on the naval side that unfamiliarity with the new weapons spelled near-disaster; the same story was being written on the blood-stained fields of Flanders.

With the new weapons had come a new ruthlessness in waging war. When victory finally crowned the concerted efforts of the Allied might, it rested on a slaughter unprecedented in the history of European civilisation. Across the wide floor of the Atlantic, amid the vast war cemeteries of France, Gallipoli, and Palestine, lay the bones of British youth. And with the victory came a revulsion of feeling against war as a means of settling international disputes. The public conscience was appalled by the astronomical losses of fighting men, and public feeling set the pattern of the uneasy years which were to follow. The war which Britain and her Allies had just fought came, in those early, hopeful years of peace, to be known as "the war to end all wars".

It was in this almost universal concept of no more major war that the Navy settled down to absorb the lessons of the conflict just over. One further factor arose to bedevil the scene, that of a financial stringency unexampled in its severity. It did not, of course, alter the lessons to be learned, but it made them infinitely more difficult to master.

Ageing ships were not replaced by new construction, arbitrary limits on the size and armament of ships were accepted under international agreements, and manœuvres at sea were carried out at slow speeds to economise in the expenditure of fuel oil. In such a setting it was difficult to achieve the realism so necessary in exercises if warlike experience was to be imbibed.

It was partly in this spirit of universal hopefulness and partly for reasons of financial economy that, at the Washington Naval Conference of 1921–2, Great Britain accepted a lower standard of naval strength than normally she would be prepared to consider. To all intents and purposes it was a one-power standard, and it became officially so three years later on a recommendation of the Committee of Imperial Defence. Under the terms of the Washington Treaty the Navy of Britain was limited, both in numbers and size of ships, to equality with that of the United States, while the navies of France, Italy, and Japan were all established on a lower maximum level. In those early years of peace it was only the Navy of Japan that could constitute any sort of a threat to our merchant ships at sea, for the other European navies were all in a state of serious decline and a war with the United States was unthinkable. The ratio of superiority over Japan as accepted at Washington was 5 : 3, and it was reasonably certain that, accepting the existing European navies at their face value, there was sufficient margin of strength to hold Japan in the event of a Far Eastern conflict while still retaining adequate naval strength in home waters.

For the first few years of peace the Navy was chiefly occupied with the normal run-down from wartime to peacetime strength. The rapid reduction in both ships and men which automatically follows a major war will always produce a period of unbalance, and the years from 1919 to 1923 were no exception. But while it could normally be expected that succeeding years would show a redressing of the balance, there were in 1923 political and economic factors which delayed that return to full naval health. In the interests of national economy a Cabinet assumption, made in August 1919, that for the purposes of framing the Service Estimates it could be assumed that there would be no major war for ten years, was given in 1923 the force of a Cabinet rule.

At that time it was a reasonable enough assumption, if taken with its corollary that, after the lapse of ten years, the fighting Services were to be ready again to play their parts in the event of war. But by decision of the Government this "Ten Year Rule" was renewed each year, so that any form of rebuilding or re-equipping the fleet on anything but a very minor scale was made impossible. Modern ships of war, with their complex equipment, cannot be built in a few weeks. Like the oak tree, the instrument of sea power grows slowly.

As the second decade of the century passed, the decline in the fighting strength of the Navy continued. As even the strongest castle will fall into ruins if neglected for too long, so also will a Navy, and the Navy of Great Britain was no exception to the rule. It was little consolation to know that, under the terms of the Washington Naval Treaty, the navies of other nations were equally hamstrung, for, unlike Britain, the integrity of their merchant shipping was not so vital a need.

One other political decision, though of an earlier year, also had its effect on the fighting efficiency of the fleet. This was the decision, taken in 1917, to amalgamate the air services of the Navy and the Army and to reconstitute them in a third, and independent, armed Service—the Royal Air Force. In its broader aspects, this denied to the Navy any effective control of its air arm, both in tactical development and in the provision of aircraft designed specifically for the purpose of sea battle. There was no lack of naval appreciation, even in those comparatively early days of aviation, of the vital part which air operations, in conjunction with a fleet at sea, would play in war, and this denial of Admiralty control had a naturally stultifying effect on the orderly development of naval aviation in what should have been its formative years. Its effect was to reduce still further the ability of the Navy to perform its essential tasks in war.

With governments all the world over pledged to peace, and moreover backed up by electorates still vividly aware of the dreadful slaughter of 1914–18, prospects of even a modest naval rearmament were singularly remote. Yet there were not wanting prophets in the wilderness. As early as 1925 the Committee of Imperial Defence were recommending the continuation of installation work at Singapore, so important a naval base for the maintenance of the communications by sea of Australia and New Zealand, and in 1931 the Service Ministries called attention to the terrible deficiencies caused by the "Ten Year Rule" under which our naval strength had now been so diminished as to render the Fleet incapable of affording efficient protection to essential trade in wartime. Their warnings fell on deaf ears.

In the following year the Service Chiefs of Staff, through the Committee of Imperial Defence, returned to the attack, and this time with slightly more success. The Cabinet, as a result, authorised the abandonment of the "Ten Year Rule", though at the time they laid down a new ruling that, in a period of financial crisis and industrial depression, any new expenditure on rearmament must inevitably be deferred. But in view of the Japanese aggression in Manchuria, which was launched in September 1931, the Government decided to go ahead with the development of Singapore as a fully equipped naval base.

The main naval preoccupation at the Admiralty during these years was the emergence of Japan as a potential enemy in the Far East. As far back as 1921, in deference to anti-Japanese feeling in the United States, Great Britain had not renewed her Treaty of Alliance with Japan and had thereby added profound problems to her Far Eastern naval strategy. In place of a friendly Japan there was now a brooding, restless Power athwart the routes used by the ships linking the home country with Australia and New Zealand, a Power, moreover, smarting under the fancied slight inflicted at Washington, where her naval strength had been limited to a lower ratio than that of Great Britain or of the United States. The emaciated state of the Royal Navy during these years, and the standstill of development work at Singapore, could hardly be expected to act as a deterrent to any Japanese thoughts of expansion. Japan struck at China, and a flaccid League of Nations condoned the aggression by its failure to act.

The days of Far Eastern preoccupation were numbered, however, for a new danger was arising nearer home which was largely to submerge the more distant threat. On 30th January, 1933, President Hindenburg called Adolf Hitler to the Chancellorship of Germany. Four weeks later the flames of the Reichstag acted as a beacon to Blackshirts and Brownshirts to round up and exterminate the political opponents of the new creed of Nazism. In a night of terror those unhappy men disappeared from human ken. The resulting elections, organised by Goebbels, swept the Nazis into power, and the gentler flame of German democracy flickered and went out.

Hitler did not take long to show his hand. His first international act was to sabotage, by his withdrawal, the Disarmament Conference of 1933, sitting in Geneva; his second was to walk out of the League of Nations; his third was to declare that Germany would tread the path of rearmament. All three had been accomplished by October 1933.

The British reaction was swift. The three Chiefs of Staff, studying the implications of these three German moves, came to the conclusion that Germany, under her new rulers and with her known capacity for rearmament should she press it to the utmost, could be ready for a major war by 1938. They recommended that a committee should be appointed to study and prepare for the Cabinet a detailed programme for making good the deficiencies of the armed forces. The Cabinet agreed and before the year was out a Defence Requirements Sub-Committee was set up for this purpose.

The members of this sub-committee were the three Service Chiefs of Staff, and a senior representative from both the Foreign Office and the Treasury. Their first report was in the hands of the Cabinet on 23rd February, 1934, and its naval recommendations were that all existing battleships should be modernised (under the Washington and London Naval Treaties no new capital ships could be constructed until 1937); naval bases and fuel depots should be brought completely up to date; a large expansion in anti-submarine equipment should be put in hand, including the fitting of trawlers with asdic apparatus; and finally that the Fleet Air Arm should be considerably augmented.

The financial implications of the report were not unduly arduous, even by the standards of 1934. The extra expenditure over the five years 1934–8 was estimated at £71,300,000, of which the Navy was to receive £21,000,000, while in addition the proposed naval replacement programme would cost a further £72,500,000. These sums, of course, were additional to the normal annual Service Estimates, but even at that it added no more than a further £144,000,000 to be spread over the five years in question.

Political and economic considerations in 1934 made even that relatively modest addition to the national expenditure unwelcome, and the Government was forced to look for means of reducing it. A proposal to limit the inevitable expansion, made necessary by German intransigence, to the Royal Air Force alone on the ground that the main danger to this country from a German declaration of war would lie in bombardment from the air, was not accepted by the Cabinet. But the Government was not prepared yet to put the case of British rearmament to the electorate, and the recommended expenditure was cut by one-third.

Even less happy was their decision to depart from the Committee's proposal for a co-ordinated strengthening of all three Services together and to allocate instead the major part of the money to rearmament in the air, for that was to force an unbalance in overall defensive strength. The Army bore the main brunt of the Cabinet's cuts, and it is against this decision of 1934 that the true background of the military débâcle of 1940 really lies.

So, in 1934, Britain took her first steps along the road of rearmament. That they were halting steps was not entirely due to the Government of the day, for behind it lay an electorate still unwilling to shoulder the rearmament burden. Speaking retrospectively about this period in the House of Commons in 1936, Mr. Stanley Baldwin said: "I asked myself what chance was there . . . within the next year or two of that feeling being so changed that the country would give a mandate for rearmament. Supposing I had gone to the country and said that Germany was rearming, and that we must rearm, does anybody think that this pacific democracy would have rallied to that cry at that moment? I cannot think of anything that would have made the loss of the election from my point of view more certain."[1] We may well consider as blameworthy a political party that places its own fortunes above the national need, but can the people of Britain be considered absolutely blameless themselves? It was they who, in the last resort, held the power.

The Navy's share in the 1934 rearmament was relatively modest. The estimates for that year made provision for the ordering of a new aircraft carrier, to be given the honoured name of *Ark Royal*, four cruisers, and the normal annual flotilla of one leader and eight destroyers, besides submarines and smaller craft. Only in the ordering of the *Ark Royal* was there any real sign of increased naval rearmament, for the other new construction was no more than sufficient for the usual annual replacement of obsolescent ships. But at least it was a start, and a start, too, in a significant direction.

Events in Europe and elsewhere, however, refused to stand still, overtaking with truly alarming rapidity the modest rearmament measures to which Britain had reluctantly committed herself. During the late summer of 1935 the United States, in a welter of nervous isolationism, passed her Neutrality Law, and thus effectively barred any reliance by Britain or any other belligerent, in the event of conflict, on the manufacturing resources for war material of that great nation. In the first week of October the Italian dictator let loose his army across the borders of Abyssinia, to confront Britain with a probably hostile power astride the Red Sea through which passed so much of her merchant shipping. And six months later, on 9th March, 1936, the German dictator matched his Italian friend by marching into the demilitarised Rhineland in contravention of the Treaty of Versailles and also of the later Locarno Treaty. Here was a deliberate challenge, and here, too, was a chance of confronting the growing military power of Germany with an armed strength that was still infinitely superior. For a week or two the fate of Europe hovered in the balance. But France, torn by internal political dissension, and Britain, mildly isolationist and still passionately desirous of peace, let the chance slip through their fingers. The Rhineland was occupied by Germany without the spilling of a drop of blood, and the German frontier with France was thereby advanced no less than 100 miles and to a river line that was more easily defensible. Almost equally important was the growth of Hitler's personal prestige in Germany in "getting away with it" against the counsel of his military advisers. The European stage was now being set for Hitler's *Drang nach Osten*, his advance to the East.

To the Service Chiefs of Staff the occupation of the Rhineland was the danger signal. The Committee of Imperial Defence set up a sub-committee, called the Ministerial Defence Plans (Policy) Committee, in order to examine the defence plans of the Chiefs of Staff in the light of Government policy, and to provide a nucleus for a War Committee or War Cabinet should a conflict develop. Its first act was to consider a memorandum from the Chiefs of Staff with the title "Planning for a war with Germany", in which it was assumed that the war would break out in the latter part of 1939. In the light of subsequent events the accuracy of the forecasted date was remarkable.

The material side of the memorandum was set out with startling detail and realism. In order to meet, with balanced forces, the threat of war by the second half of 1939, the Chiefs of Staff estimated essential expenditure over the next five years of a sum between £1,760,000,000 and £1,811,000,000.

Once more the Government intervened, reverting to the suggestion of 1934 that full priority need only be given to the Royal Air Force, with the other two Services lagging behind, the Navy only slightly and the Army considerably. The matter was referred to the new Minister for Co-ordination of Defence, Sir Thomas Inskip, whose office had been created in 1936, soon after the Rhineland occupation, in order to correlate the deficiency programmes of the three armed Services and to act as deputy for the Prime Minister in his chairmanship of the Committee of Imperial Defence. Sir Thomas Inskip, remarked that to maintain the security of the nation in war was the whole cornerstone of defence policy. He listed the resources of man-power, the industrial capacity, and the well-tried and well-known endurance of the British people as the mainstay of national security, and stated that unless they were maintained substantially unimpaired, especially during the shock of initial attack in war, the country would face ultimate defeat in a major war. This may have been a statement of the obvious, but at least it set out the fundamental basis of the problem. From it he went on to list four main objectives in the prosecution of a war with Germany:

(*a*) The protection of the United Kingdom against attack.
(*b*) The preservation of our merchant ships for the import of essential materials.
(*c*) The provision and maintenance of forces for the defence of British territories overseas.
(*d*) Co-operation in the defence of Allied territory.

It is to be presumed that these objectives were set out in order of merit, for the fourth objective was jettisoned by the Cabinet in deference to the view that all rearmament must be carried out within the limits of financial stability. The Chiefs of Staff remonstrated against the dropping of this objective, but without avail.

Under the Cabinet approvål of the earlier Defence Requirements Sub-Committee's report, the First Lord of the Admiralty had introduced a Supplementary Estimate in the Commons in 1936 to give effect to the first stage of naval rearmament. Parliamentary approval was given, now that the Washington Treaty ban on the construction of new capital ships had expired, to place orders for two new battleships of modern design, to be called the "King George V" class. At the same time contracts were placed for one more carrier, five cruisers, nine destroyers, four submarines, and six sloops, later to be given the generic name of convoy escorts. These were small ships of 1,250 tons and moderate speed, the forerunners of the frigates, sloops, and corvettes which were later to play so great a part in the task of convoy protection and U-boat killing throughout the years of war.

Cabinet endorsement of the Minister for the Co-ordination of Defence's memorandum of 1937, with its proposal to expand one Service (the Royal Air Force), at the expense of another (the Army), resulted in allocation of a total of £1,570,000,000 for defence over the next five years. Unfettered at long last by the financial curb of the Government, the Naval Estimates for 1937 reflected the effort to repair the damage caused by the years of complacency. Three more battleships of the "King George V" class, two more fleet carriers, seven cruisers, sixteen destroyers, seven submarines, and three convoy escorts, in future to be known as escort vessels, were ordered.

There was, however, still one fly in the ointment. On economic grounds it had been laid down by the Cabinet that the rearmament programme was to be implemented without interfering with normal trade. Inevitably that meant delays. It was not difficult to place the orders, but to get them carried through with reasonable speed in competition with the demands of industry was completely impossible. The nation's rearmament, which looked so impressive on paper, lacked reality in terms of ships, guns, and aircraft.

And all the time the enemies of Britain were arming. No consideration of normal trade held up German deliveries; for the entire country—social, industrial, and financial—had been geared to a war economy since 1934. Sprawled across the centre of Europe, effectively dividing the democracies of the West from those in the East, totalitarian Germany was erecting a barrier of steel behind which to carry out her barbaric aggrandisements. The three countries of the "Little Entente"—Rumania, Yugoslavia, and Czechoslovakia—with whom France maintained a treaty of alliance and on whose territorial integrity the balance of European power lay poised, were in the process of being isolated. Already the shadow of the crooked cross was to be seen in Austria and Czechoslovakia, in the former by the political clamour of the Austrian Nazi Party, succoured by Germany, in the latter by the claims of Henlein and his Sudeten Germans for incorporation into the Reich. It was the writing on the wall.

On 7th March, 1938, the German Army marched into Austria. The last tenuous link between France and Czechoslovakia, the mainstay of the "Little Entente", was severed. There could be no doubt now about Hitler's intentions. It was war, and whether it came now or later was a question only of political juggling. Equally apparent was Hitler's strategical concept. With the right bank of the Rhine in his hands and his fixed defences in the West, he could hold the Western democracies with a few divisions while he struck in the East. And almost before this strategy could be fully appreciated he implemented it with a demand for the cession of the Sudetenland, in which lay the Czech frontier fortifications and the great Skoda armament works.

In Britain the Chiefs of Staff reacted quickly. They urged the Cabinet to rescind the ruling that the rearmament programme must not be permitted to impede the course of normal trade. Under the new stress of European events the Cabinet agreed; indeed, they went further and instituted measures for working three shifts in the armament factories and for directing firms engaged in peacetime work into war production. The paper programme of rearmament began to show results, but they were coming too late.

Events in Europe now began to gather speed. From Germany,

heralding her next step, a clamour of abuse of Czechoslovakia arose. It was the typical Nazi prelude to a solution by intimidation or by force. In the light of this obvious and immediate threat to European peace—obvious because of France's treaty with Czechoslovakia and of Britain's solidarity with France—the Prime Minister, Mr. Neville Chamberlain, asked for a report from the Chiefs of Staff on the military implications of an alliance with France and other European States to resist by force any German attempt to attack Czechoslovakia. Their reply was categorical. They stated, without making any qualifications, that the country was not ready for war, that no measures of force, whether alone or in alliance with other European countries, could now stop Germany from inflicting a crushing defeat on Czechoslovakia, and that any involvement in war with Germany at this stage could well lead to an ultimate defeat, through her unpreparedness, of this country herself.

It is in this report by the Chiefs of Staff that we find the true background to Munich. In its essentials it informed the Prime Minister that, no matter what the cost, war must be averted until the rearmament programme began to bear substantial fruit. It placed him in a position from which there was no escape; national prestige, national honour, the obloquy of future generations, none of these could weigh against his overriding duty to his country, to gain time.

It was not on the naval side that the Chiefs of Staff based their fears, though the lack of adequate strength in escort vessels raised an ugly problem in the protection of merchant shipping. It was in the air that the weakness of Britain was most alarming. Intensive propaganda in the years between the wars had raised an unholy fear of the bomber and its powers of destruction. In the light of after-knowledge it is sometimes difficult to recapture those beliefs of 1930–40, fostered as they were by horror stories of mass slaughter and destruction; but at the time, with no background of experience as a guide, they were readily accepted as true. And from the figures there was no escape. Against an Air Ministry estimate of the German first-line bomber strength of 1,350 machines (the actual figure was 1,128),[2] Great Britain could pit no more than 100 eight-gun fighters

(Spitfire and Hurricane) and 500 obsolete fighters with insufficient speed to overtake the German bombers.[3]

So occurred Munich. For that unhappy betrayal of Czechoslovakia we are prone to blame the Prime Minister of the day, Mr. Neville Chamberlain, and his Government. The true blame, however, lies wider than that. It lies at the door of all those, of whatever political party, who opposed or neglected Britain's defences between 1919 and 1934.

On 30th July, 1937, came a decision for which the Navy had been waiting impatiently for years. This was to transfer from the Air Ministry to the Admiralty responsibility for the administration of the Fleet Air Arm. Its main, and most important, provision was the transfer to naval control of the training of pilots and observers from the point where specialisation in naval duties began. There could, at last, be true integration between sea and air in the realm of purely naval fighting, the welding of two strong weapons into one of greatly increased power. With the decision of the Government came an expansion of strength in the Fleet Air Arm, both in men and machines. One disability, however, remained. Responsibility for research, experiment, development, and supply of aircraft remained in the hands of the Air Ministry. In the press of their own air rearmament programme, the provision of aircraft for the Fleet Air Arm tended to take second place and to be no more than navalised versions of shore-based types. What were needed were machines individually designed and tested for the highly specialised duties which they would have to perform at sea.

In the quickening pace of rearmament the naval building programmes made good headway. The capital ships and the carriers ordered in 1936 and 1937 were, of course, comparatively long-term projects, but the smaller ships—cruisers, destroyers, submarines, and escort vessels—were beginning to reach the fleet in 1938 and 1939. At first a trickle, they increased to a moderate stream to swell the growing strength of the Navy. Yet, continually, events on the mainland of Europe overtook the pace of British rearmament. It seemed that the time which Mr. Chamberlain had bought so dearly at Munich was not to be sufficient for the nation's needs.

The agreement at Munich had been signed in the early hours of the morning of 30th September, 1938. Less than six months later the pledges which Hitler had given there had been thrown to the winds. On 14th March, 1939, German troops marched into an unresisting Prague, and the Czechoslovakian Republic was incorporated, through a German protectorate, into the Reich. Another bastion of defence against totalitarian aggression had fallen without a struggle.

The Chiefs of Staff, in their report of March 1938 to the Prime Minister on the implications of resistance to a German assault on Czechoslovakia, had envisaged the first brunt of an ensuing war falling on Britain. They expected to see a German attack on France held by the defences of the Maginot Line, with heavy air attack on Great Britain as the only German alternative in a Western war. Their report, naturally enough, was subjected to earnest study in the Admiralty, not only by the existing naval staff, but by the new First Sea Lord designate, Admiral of the Fleet Sir Roger Backhouse. One aspect of this study, of course, was that of existing and expected naval strength in relation to the major tasks of naval war, and for this purpose preliminary staff talks with the French Admiralty were begun in order to co-ordinate essential naval strategy as between the two navies in partnership.[4] Fuller staff talks were authorised by the Cabinet in the first week of February 1939,[5] and from them the broad lines of strategy emerged. It was agreed that in home waters Great Britain would station a fleet capable of defeating the German fleet as a whole, that the safety of ocean convoys should be a joint Franco-British responsibility, that French escorts should assist in the task of convoy in the Western Approaches, that a strong French force built round two battle-cruisers should be stationed at Brest to deal with the threat of armed raiders in the Atlantic, that the western Mediterranean should be under French naval control and the eastern Mediterranean under British.

To the First Sea Lord and the Naval Staff, this broad outline of agreed naval duties posed many concrete questions. They looked at them with the eyes of sailors, measuring up the duties to be performed in terms of ships required. The essentials were not difficult to work out. The first naval necessity in 1939 was still the same as it had been 250 years before, the maintenance of the regular flow of shipping in the face of enemy attack. That was still, as it had been all through history, the fundamental pedestal on which alone an overall war strategy could be securely built.

It was on this aspect of the combined staff talks, and especially on the particular problem of convoy, that the Sea Lords cast an anxious eye. On paper, the naval superiority of Britain and France over that of Germany was overwhelming, and even over Germany and Italy combined the margin was still impressive. But the figures on paper told only part of the story. Britain, as a maritime power, had essential commitments in every ocean in the world, and was dependent, moreover, for every facet of everyday life on the security of her merchant ships at sea. To her, and through her to France, the ability to fight, even to survive, rested on her ability to use the broad oceans for her merchant ships how and when she wished.

This vital requirement, studied in terms of ships, revealed a weakness that might well open the door to disaster. The convoy lessons of 1917 had never been fully digested, indeed to some extent had been forgotten, but in the number of ships that would be available for escort duties it was clear that there still lay a serious shortage. Sir Roger Backhouse sought the advice of his Deputy Chief of Naval Staff designate, Vice-Admiral Andrew Cunningham, a destroyer specialist of the previous war and with added experience in that arm as a Captain (D) between the wars. What was needed to fill the gap was a type of ship that was inexpensive, quick to build, and of reasonable endurance for convoy work. From his knowledge of the former war Admiral Cunningham brought forward the case of Admiralty "S"-class destroyers of 1917 and 1918, ships of about 1,000 tons displacement, of which quite a few were built and brought into commission in from nine to twelve months from the date of ordering. He suggested that, with the design brought up to date, this type of destroyer might help to fill the gap. So was born the "Hunt" class of fast escort vessel. Though they failed by four knots to reach their designed speed of twenty-nine knots and proved unsuitable for escort work in the North Atlantic, they were reasonably quick to build and went some way in redressing the adverse position in the Mediterranean. The first batch of them was ordered in the early months of 1939.

Another type of ship ordered in 1939 was the "Flower"-class corvette, a development of the whale catcher. A total of fifty-six of them was ordered before the outbreak of the war. Valuable as these corvettes, and also the "Hunt"-class, proved to be, they still could not make up for the lack of destroyers, of which none at all had been ordered in the 1938 programme. That was a shortage which was to make itself felt throughout the whole course of the war, for the losses among these invaluable ships were severe and never very far behind current production.

The German occupation of Czechoslovakia laid bare the next step to be taken in Hitler's march to the East. Poland was now effectively outflanked, and the preliminary chorus of abuse echoed loudly from end to end of the Reich. It was a signal only too well known. It had been heard before the rape of Austria, it had preceded the spoliation of Czechoslovakia. Now it presaged the downfall of Poland.

There was, in these early months of 1939, no love in Britain for Poland. The forced cession of the Czech Sudetenland to Germany under the Munich agreement had been followed by an unprincipled claim by Poland for the Teschen area of Czechoslovakia, and that dismembered country had been forced to accede to the Polish demand. But with the Germans now in Prague, Poland assumed a political importance which forced Britain to overlook her former aggression. It was time now—indeed, the time was long overdue—to serve notice on Germany that any further act of armed intervention in the affairs of a foreign State could be carried out only at the risk of a major war. The situation in which Poland found herself in March 1939 presented the opportunity. On the last day of the month the Prime Minister informed the House of Commons that Britain had given a guarantee to come to the aid of Poland should she be attacked. The guarantee was extended also to Rumania.

This was notice to Germany indeed, unmistakable and uncompromising. It threatened Hitler with war on two fronts should he continue his programme of expansion in the East, it upset completely his plans of conquest at the expense of the "Little Entente" powers. His basic strategy had lain on the assumption that he could hold the West at bay behind the recently constructed defences along the German frontier with France, while one by one he absorbed the smaller nations of the East and the rich plains of the Ukraine. Only when that vast meal had been properly digested had he contemplated full-scale war against the Western democracies, France and Britain.

The guarantee to Poland and Rumania could be implemented not by direct aid, for that was geographically impossible, but only by active war in the West, in Hitler's rear. Yet there lay to hand one key which might still be used to unlock the way to Poland's reinforcement. Along her eastern frontier lay Russia, whose enigmatic policies since the Revolution of 1917 had been the despair of Western politicians. There was, however, a gleam of light. Perhaps in anticipation of the hoped-for absorption of the Ukraine, the people of Germany were being conditioned to hatred of Russia by the familiar chorus of abuse. In that fact lay hope that Russia could be persuaded to join forces with the West in the stand against further German expansion in the East.

The efforts made to use this key were doomed to failure. There were many causes. Russia, though alive to the danger and in fear of the German expansionist drive towards her frontiers, still nourished bitterness against the Western powers for their failure to invite her to take part in the Munich conference. Poland, with a memory of past partitions at the hands of her neighbours, had no wish to see Russian troops on her soil, even if they came as allies. Both Britain and France had a fundamental distrust of Russia, based mainly on the democratic dislike of dictatorship. And looming in the background, casting a malignant shadow over all negotiations, was the military weakness of the Western nations, a weakness still not overcome by the slow pace of rearmament. For the Russian leaders, above all, were realists. They were concerned not so much with the moral obligations of the European set-up as with the numbers of divisions, tanks, aircraft, ships, and guns that Britain and France could throw into the struggle. "How many divisions," asked Stalin, "will France send against Germany on mobilisation?" "About a hundred." "How many will England send?" "Two, and two more later." "Ah," said Stalin, "two, and two more later. Do you know how many divisions we shall have to put on the Russian front if we go to war with Germany? More than three hundred."[6] It was in conversations such as this that hopes of alliances foundered, for it was useless to talk to Stalin of the part which British sea power could play in the struggle. The profound value of sea power in war was far beyond Stalin's comprehension.

The last hope of an accord with Russia disappeared on 3rd May when Litvinov was replaced as Foreign Commissar by Molotov, though the Western diplomats remained in Moscow for three more months in renewed attempts to bring about a last-minute compact. On 3rd May, too, the anti-Russian stream of abuse in Germany ceased abruptly. There could be only one meaning, though its very absurdity made it wellnigh unbelievable.

It burst upon an astonished and bewildered world during the night of 21st August with the announcement from Russia that the German Foreign Minister was flying to Moscow to sign a non-aggression pact. The declaration sealed the fate of Europe. Nothing now could stop the war, and its coming was likely to be counted in days, rather than in weeks or months. The last few grains of sand were running out through the hour-glass of history.

Thirty-six hours later, on the actual day that the German-Russian pact was signed, the Admiralty made its first preparatory move, taking over the control of all merchant shipping. On the following day, 24th August, all ships in commission at home were ordered to their war stations, and the ships of the Reserve Fleet were ordered to be manned up to full war complement. On the same day six submarines were sailed to maintain, at twelve-mile intervals, that part of the line of search across the North Sea which was beyond the range of Coastal Command's Anson aircraft. Two days later, on the 26th, four cruisers left Scapa to put into operation the Northern Patrol between the Faeroe Islands and Iceland and across the Denmark Strait. Finally, on the last day of August, the Commander-in-Chief Home Fleet, Admiral Sir Charles Forbes, sailed from Scapa with the fleet "to intercept and shadow"[7] any German ships that they might encounter at sea. On the morning of 3rd September, having seen no sign of enemy activity, the Commander-in-Chief turned for home. The fleet was still at sea when the signal to commence hostilities with Germany was sent out from Whitehall. A few hours after the declaration of war the destroyer *Somali* captured the first prize at sea of the war, a small German merchantman.

The German Navy, too, had been making its dispositions in anticipation of the actual declaration of war. On 21st August the pocket-battleship *Admiral Graf Spee*, under cover of darkness for her passage of the North Sea, slipped away northabout and reached her waiting position in the South Atlantic unobserved. Three days later the *Deutschland*, another pocket-battleship later to be renamed *Lützow*, followed her out with equal success, to take up her position in the North Atlantic. Their supply ships, *Altmark* and *Westerwald*, joined them out there, their departures also unobserved. At intervals between 19th and 29th August, seventeen ocean-going U-boats were despatched to their Atlantic war stations, and on the 21st seven of the smaller coastal type were sailed into the southern North Sea, to lay mines off the Channel ports as soon as the declaration of war was announced. Six more left their bases on the 25th for patrol areas in the central North Sea.

So, as the last hours of peace ticked remorselessly away, the rival navies faced each other across the oceans. It was turning out almost exactly as foreseen by the Chiefs of Staff in an appreciation submitted to the Cabinet in June, with one important exception. All that was to be expected in the initial stages of the war, said the Chiefs of Staff, was an enemy attack on merchant shipping, both by cruiser and by submarine, and as a result the first British and French dispositions at sea were made to counter it. In the known state of the German Navy, indeed, there was little else it could do. The one exception, however, was to have a considerable bearing on the first months of war. Pre-war naval planning had been based on the assumption that Mussolini would join his partner in the war without delay, and as a result much of the British and French naval strength was tied down in the Mediterranean. As the first months of war passed with no signs of Italian participation, the ships stationed there formed a useful pool in the early stages to sustain operations elsewhere.

The ocean stage was set with all the old hereditary skill. Up in the far North, blocking both the exits there into the Atlantic and the entrances into the North Sea through which the German merchant shipping would have to pass to reach their home ports, the cruisers of the Northern Patrol kept watch. From the Shetlands to the coast of Norway a line of search was stretched, partly air, partly submarine. At Scapa lay the main strength of the Home Fleet, more than capable of dealing with any surface threat that the enemy could produce. In the Channel, based on Portland, a strong squadron barred the southern exit into the Atlantic. The four home naval commands—Plymouth, Portsmouth, the Nore, and Rosyth—each had light forces of destroyers, anti-submarine vessels, and minesweepers for local defence and convoy duties, while at Blyth and Dundee flotillas of submarines were stationed to carry the naval war into German home waters. In the light of existing knowledge in 1939 it was a net strong enough to catch and hold any would-be marauders.

In the last few months before the sombre clouds of war settled over an embattled Europe, there had been important changes in the higher direction of the naval war. Since mid-April a serious illness had incapacitated Admiral of the Fleet Sir Roger Backhouse, and his duties as First Sea Lord had been carried out by the Deputy Chief of Naval Staff, Admiral Sir Andrew Cunningham. In mid-June, Admiral Backhouse resigned—he was to die a month later—and the Navy was shorn of its professional head at a most anxious moment. From the Mediterranean came Admiral Sir Dudley Pound to take over the post of First Sea Lord, bringing to the Admiralty, in which he had served for various periods as the Director of Plans and as a Sea Lord, a wide experience not only of high command at sea but also of Admiralty procedure. To the Mediterranean to relieve him as Commander-in-Chief went Admiral Sir Andrew Cunningham, who for the previous nine months had been in the centre of naval planning as Deputy Chief of Naval Staff. He, too, brought wide experience to his new appointment and, moreover, a reputation as a fighting seaman.

There was to be one more change. As the curtain rose to reveal the great drama of war the Prime Minister sent for Mr. Winston Churchill, already a Minister of the War Cabinet without a Department, and invited him to become First Lord of the Admiralty. Mr. Churchill accepted, and in the evening of 3rd September sat once more in the room in which he had set in motion, a quarter of a century earlier, the first naval moves in the previous war with Germany. The fact was announced to the fleet in a pregnant signal from the Board of Admiralty, "Winston is back".

# Chapter 2

## OPERATIONS OFF NORWAY

THE outcome of past wars had so frequently been decided in the final analysis by the exercise of sea power that the main strategical structure of the new war which faced the Admiralty on that September day of 1939 was not difficult to determine. The individual problems within the main structure, however, called for far more serious thought and study, and it was on their solution and their correct application that the success or otherwise of the first stage of the war would depend.

As a nation, Britain had emerged victorious from her wars of the past by winning for herself the undisputed use of the ocean highways of the world while at the same time denying them to her enemies. The power of Napoleonic France had perished through this British control of the seas; in earlier wars Holland and Spain had both been tumbled from their eminence by it. And within living memory was the plight of Germany in 1918, starved into surrender because the ships that could have kept her supplied with the essential food and war materials with which to carry on the battle had been driven from the seas. The formula of sea power had withstood the tests of time; could history be repeated in this new European struggle that had once again drawn the British people into its vortex?

An essential preliminary for the exercise of sea power in its dual role—the power to use the sea when and where you wish and to prevent the enemy from using it—lay in containing the German war effort, in so far as it was capable of containment by sea power, in the smallest possible space. A glance at the map of Europe gives the answer. The Baltic was a closed sea to the Allies in the face of modern naval weapons and air power, leaving open to German ships not only the invaluable Scandinavian iron-ore trade, but also such imports as could be smuggled down this central corridor. Although for five months of the year the ice of winter might close the Swedish ports engaged in this trade, the territorial waters of Norway presented the enemy with an alternative all-weather route in their place.

There was only one way in which sea power could operate to minimise this avenue of contact with the outside world, and that was by a system of contraband control of Scandinavian imports. Neutral ships at sea, bound to or from European ports, were intercepted by naval vessels on patrol and brought in to special anchorages where their cargoes were examined for contraband. Measures for this control had been worked out before the declaration of war,[1] and contraband control bases were set up on 3rd September at Kirkwall to cover the northabout route and at Ramsgate for the Channel route. It could have no effect on the iron-ore trade itself, of course, but it could prevent the import into Germany, via those Scandinavian countries, of valuable raw materials consigned to neutral sources for onward transmission to the enemy. Some estimate of the efficiency of this control of contraband can be gained from the fact that, in the four months of war ending in December 1939, 529,471 tons of commodities destined for Germany were seized and condemned in prize.[2] The German side door into the Mediterranean, through a friendly Italy, was closed by similar control bases at Gibraltar, Port Said, Haifa, and Malta, though only partially closed because of the political need to avoid alienating Italy so violently as to force her into the war straight away. The back door through Russia, opened by the Soviet-German Non-Aggression Pact of August 1939, was beyond the reach of the Allies. It remained open for many months until Hitler, victim of his own intuition, slammed it in his own face.

So, with the Navy blocking those German avenues of trade within its reach, the ring around the enemy was drawn. From the south of Norway, across and down the North Sea to the French frontier, and through the length of the Mediterranean Sea, Allied sea power held the ring. Allied land and air power filled the continental gaps. To the north, the west, and the south the strangulation of German trade began; to the east the open door remained.

It was outside this ring that the problems accumulated. Here again the lessons of former wars repeated themselves. In the vastness of the oceans even the most vigilant of past blockades had not been able to prevent the escape of privateers and occasional squadrons to harry, sink, and capture our merchant shipping. In the war of 1914–18, whose lessons had been so painfully learned, those same privateers, in their modern form of U-boat and armed raider, had found the way through the net, like their predecessors, without undue difficulty. It was equally certain that in 1939 the same sort of marauders would again slip through to cause destruction and delay on the trade routes. It was expected, too, in spite of the Anglo-German Naval Treaty of 1935 in which both nations had agreed to accept the rulings of the Hague Convention in the conduct of war at sea, that Hitler's U-boats would, as had the Kaiser's in 1917, honour those rules only in the breach.

In point of fact, both U-boats and raiders at the outbreak of war had been given orders to observe the principles of the Hague Convention in their attack on the Allies' shipping, for Hitler had high hopes of being able to persuade Britain and France to accept a *fait accompli* and to make peace on the defeat of Poland. The over-eagerness of Lieutenant Lemp, commanding *U.30* in the Atlantic, ruined these good intentions. On the evening of 3rd September, 200 miles west of the Hebrides, he torpedoed the 13,581-ton Donaldson liner *Athenia*, which sank an hour or so later with the loss of 112 lives. Not unnaturally the Admiralty assumed that unrestricted submarine warfare was already in force and took steps to accelerate as far as possible the provision of full convoy for the most threatened trade routes. At the same time, as a temporary stopgap until the convoy escorts could be organised, the three Home Fleet aircraft carriers, each with a destroyer screen, were formed into hunting groups to comb the Western Approaches for U-boats.

From Plymouth sailed the *Courageous* on 9th September and the

*Hermes* on the 14th, both with escorting destroyers. Although both groups were quickly in contact with U-boats through sightings from the air, their efforts were not crowned with success. From Scapa, up in the north, the *Ark Royal* and her destroyers put to sea on the 11th. U-boats were sighted and attacked on the 12th and 13th, again without success, but on the 14th a submarine attack on the *Ark Royal* herself led to swift retribution. The carrier had little difficulty in avoiding the torpedoes by the use of helm, and three of her destroyers quickly accounted for the assailant. She was *U.39*, and the whole of her crew were taken prisoner. Three days later, however, the *Courageous*, on her second cruise from Plymouth, was torpedoed and sunk 350 miles west of Land's End by *U.29*. It was the end of these hunting groups, for large carriers were too valuable to be risked in this fashion. They were at once withdrawn from this task, and for the next three years the answer to the Atlantic U-boats lay in the hands of the convoy escorts, both surface and air. That it was the correct answer was to be proved in the actual test of war.

Other blows also fell. Within twenty-four hours of the outbreak of war a U-boat laid nine magnetic mines in the contraband anchorage in the Downs. They were quickly followed by others, laid mainly by aircraft, and for a time they paralysed the movements of shipping up and down the coastal waters. The chance to learn their secrets came when one was dropped in the mud of the Thames Estuary, and they were laid bare by the technical skill and personal gallantry of a small band from the Torpedo School at Portsmouth, who dismantled the mine as it lay in the mud. It was a task in which one false movement meant instant death. There was no false move, and the dismantled mine provided the answer to the problem. Ships were girdled electrically to neutralise the magnetism of the mine, and special sweeps were quickly devised which exploded them in the main convoy channels without damage to the sweepers. A great force of minesweepers was rapidly built up and their gallant operations kept the merchant ships moving throughout the war.

Even more embarrassing was the penetration of a U-boat into the main fleet base of Scapa Flow and the sinking by her of the battleship *Royal Oak* with heavy loss of life. Here again was an example of the economic stringency which had so characterised those pre-war years. A survey of Scapa Flow in 1937 had revealed the gap in the defences through which Lieutenant Prien took *U.47* on the night of 13th/14th October. A suitable blockship had then been selected, but a government objection to its price resulted in the opportunity of purchase being missed. Under the stimulus of war that objection was at last removed and another suitable hulk purchased. It arrived at Scapa on 15th October, twenty-four hours too late to plug the gap in the defences which had cost the Navy one battleship and 831 valuable lives. It also cost the temporary withdrawal of the fleet from Scapa, partly to Rosyth and partly to Loch Ewe, on the west coast of Scotland, until a complete new survey of the Scapa defences could be made and much additional work done to them.

In the final planning for the war that had now fallen upon Britain it had been stipulated by the Chiefs of Staff[3] that the preliminary period must be conducted strictly on the defensive. To do otherwise, except in a limited degree on the naval front, would, they laid down, inevitably prejudice any chance of ultimate victory. This view was accepted by the War Cabinet. "Time," they said in effect, "is on our side," and instructions were given, and agreed to also by the French Government,[4] that planning should be based on the assumption that the war would last for at least three years. Here, indeed, was the result of neglect in the wasted years that had gone by. The chance to exert strong naval pressure in the Mediterranean against the weakest end of the Berlin-Rome Axis, where the odds were still favourable, had to be forgone. In its place was to be seen a relaxation of this legitimate pressure upon Italy in the hope of keeping her out of the war. The consequences, in loss of blood and treasure, of ships and aircraft and equipment, were to weigh very heavily in the final balance.

Out in the Atlantic the U-boats and the two German pocket-battleships were lying low. In spite of *U.30*'s blunder in sinking the *Athenia*—an attack which was hotly denied by the German propaganda machine—Hitler still had hopes that the end of the Polish campaign would bring a negotiated peace in its train. So, while it suited his plan, the rules of the Hague Convention were enforced. But as the weeks passed with no reply to the German approaches, the realisation that Britain and France at last meant business was forced into the German leader's mind. Step by step the restrictions of the Hague Convention were abrogated by the Nazi naval command, farther and farther west was extended the zone in which the Germans proclaimed unrestricted attack on merchant shipping, until by November, to all intents and purposes, attack without warning on the high seas was the rule against all Allied shipping. Neutral ships, too, were warned that they crossed the meridian of 20° West at their peril.

On 26th September the German Admiralty sent orders to the two pocket-battleships to begin operations against Allied merchant shipping. The *Deutschland*, roaming the North Atlantic, captured and sank two ships without trace, the first intimation of the cause of their loss not reaching the Admiralty until 21st October. The *Graf Spee*, operating in the South Atlantic, sank a ship off Pernambuco on 30th September. This was the s.s. *Clement*, and her raider distress signal was the first positive information at the Admiralty that enemy raiders were at sea. The nature of the signal—"RRRR"—indicated that the raider was a warship and not an armed merchant cruiser. From the operational state of the German Navy known to the Naval Intelligence Division in the Admiralty it was easy enough to deduce that the enemy was "either pocket-battleship or Hipper-class cruiser", and the information was signalled to all naval commands.[5]

To meet this threat to the widespread shipping, by no means unexpected, the Admiralty put into operation the plans already made to deal with such an emergency. Nine hunting groups were formed, each strong enough to destroy a *Deutschland*, and six were allocated to the Atlantic, two to the Indian Ocean, and one to the southward of the Cape of Good Hope. Four British capital ships, four carriers, and seven cruisers came from the Home, the Mediterranean, and the China commands, and the French Navy contributed two capital ships, one carrier, and five cruisers. As an additional safeguard, the two battleships of the Channel Force at Portland and three cruisers were despatched as a strong ocean escort force for the Halifax-Liverpool convoys.[6]

To search for one ship in an ocean as vast as the Atlantic is an immense task, calling into play resources infinitely more powerful than the quarry. The *Graf Spee* herself made the task even more difficult by her comparative lack of success, for accurate intelligence of a raider's whereabouts comes only from the positions of her victims. Four more ships sunk by her between Ascension Island and St. Helena drew the chase in that direction, but by the time it had arrived there the *Graf Spee* herself had doubled the Cape of Good Hope, to find her next victim south of Madagascar. In need of replenishment she returned to her tanker, the *Altmark*, in the central South Atlantic and re-advertised her position there on the 2nd December by sinking the *Doric Star* south-east of St. Helena. She claimed another victim on the 3rd, some two hundred miles to the south-west of the first.

To Commodore Harwood, in command of the South American Division of the South Atlantic Squadron, this course was a significant one. Prolonged across the South Atlantic it led almost directly to the focal area for shipping in and out of the River Plate. Estimating the raider's speed at fifteen knots, Commodore Harwood reckoned that the *Graf Spee* could arrive off the Plate in the evening of 12th December or the morning of the 13th. He made his dispositions accordingly. The 8-inch cruiser *Cumberland*, under self-refit at the Falkland Islands, was brought to short notice, and his three remaining ships, the 8-inch cruiser *Exeter* and the two 6-inch cruisers *Ajax* and *Achilles*, were ordered to concentrate in the area of maximum density of the River Plate shipping. The concentration was effected by 7.0 a.m. on 12th December, and the Commodore issued his orders. The enemy was to be attacked as soon as sighted, whether by day or night. If by day the squadron would act in two units, one on either quarter to permit flank marking; if by night the ships would remain in company in open order.[7] Every precaution had now been taken and all that remained was for the enemy ship to appear on the scene.

The *Graf Spee* was, in fact, making direct for the area suspected by Commodore Harwood. She was due to return to Germany early in the new year and Captain Langsdorff was hoping for a spectacular success before she left the area for home.[8] She arrived off the Plate, as Commodore Harwood had estimated, in the early hours of the morning of 13th December and began to search for possible victims. At fourteen minutes past six her smoke was sighted by the British squadron, at sixteen minutes past she was identified, and at eighteen minutes past she opened fire with her two 11-inch turrets. In accordance with the prearranged plan the *Exeter* hauled out of the line to port to form the second unit, and two minutes later the enemy's fire was being returned.

The *Exeter* was quickly hit, the 11-inch shells of the enemy bursting on board and causing considerable damage. In the face of great difficulties and with her bridge control wrecked she remained on her course, still firing from her after turret, the only one now left in action. But while she was bearing the brunt of the enemy's fire, both the *Ajax* and the *Achilles* were shooting well and their shells were hitting repeatedly.

The action had lasted half an hour when the *Graf Spee* began to use smoke to disguise her movements. This was a tribute to the accuracy of the cruisers' gunfire; it was also probably the turning-point of the action. From this time on the *Graf Spee* neglected the *Exeter* and appeared more intent on avoiding action with the *Ajax* and *Achilles* than on closing them to finish them off. Her course was taking her direct to the River Plate, and as the morning action faded it began to become apparent that she was seeking the sanctuary of neutral waters there. Commodore Harwood thereupon broke off the action and settled down to shadow her, ready at any moment to reopen the battle should she show signs of attempting to break back towards the open sea.

Throughout the day she held her course, and the two British cruisers hung on to her. The *Exeter*, too badly damaged now to play any further part in the battle, was detached to the Falkland Islands, and the *Cumberland* ordered up at full speed to take her place. Occasionally, when the shadowing cruisers approached too close, the *Graf Spee* opened fire, but in general her gunnery had begun to show signs of raggedness and her salvoes were probably intended only to keep her shadowers at a distance. Just before midnight the *Graf Spee* entered Uruguayan territorial waters and at 0050 on the 14th she anchored in Montevideo Roads, later entering harbour.

It was the end of the action, for the *Graf Spee* had no more fight in her. She had been hit twenty times and her captain was firmly of the opinion that to venture out again would mean inevitable destruction at the hands of the British.[9] Three days later, on 17th December, she steamed slowly out into the Roads. The British cruisers cleared for action, but they were to be denied a second chance of proving their mettle. The *Graf Spee* stopped in the estuary and scuttled herself. Commodore Harwood's ships steamed slowly past just beyond territorial waters to watch the flames reaching almost as high as the top of her control tower, "a magnificent and most cheering sight".[10]

The *Deutschland*, meanwhile, had been ordered home. Her only successes during her cruise had been two ships of a total of nearly 7,000 tons, a poor dividend, indeed, for the expenditure of so much effort and time. She slipped through the Northern Patrol during the second week of November and reached her base safely on the 15th of the month.

So ended the first wave of German raider warfare. The effort to break the ring had been beaten with a serious loss to the enemy. There was one further flurry of surface activity at the end of November when the battle-cruisers *Scharnhorst* and *Gneisenau* made a brief sortie as an attempted diversion to aid the *Graf Spee*. They encountered and sank the armed merchant cruiser *Rawalpindi* while she was on patrol in the Iceland-Faeroes sector of the Northern Patrol. As a diversion it failed, for the ship first sighted, the *Scharnhorst*, was reported by the *Rawalpindi* as the *Deutschland*, and by the time the *Gneisenau* joined the action the *Rawalpindi*'s wireless aerials had been shot away. The *Rawalpindi*'s sighting report quickly brought the cruiser *Newcastle* to the scene, but not in time to save the armed merchant cruiser. On the first sight of the *Newcastle* the two German battle-cruisers turned tail and fled. In the belief that this was in fact the *Deutschland* on the way back to Germany the Home Fleet sailed to the North Sea to intercept her.

The *Scharnhorst* and *Gneisenau*, however, got through unseen under cover of a full gale on the 26th which reduced visibility to little more than a couple of miles.

It was, therefore, on the U-boats alone for the time being that the attack on seaborne trade devolved after the sinking of the *Graf Spee*. After the inevitable opening successes against single, independent ships in September and October, while the convoy system was still being fully organised, the monthly totals of tonnage sunk dropped in the next two months to reasonably satisfactory figures, while nine U-boats paid the penalty. Although the Admiralty was not deluded by these facts into believing that the U-boat threat was being defeated, the figures did engender a sanguine hope that the ring round Germany, maintained at sea by the Royal Navy, was holding reasonably firm. And to buttress that hope there were our own submarine successes. On 13th September Lieutenant-Commander Bickford in the *Salmon* torpedoed the cruisers *Leipzig* and *Nürnberg*, damaging them both, and two days later Lieutenant-Commander Phillips in the *Ursula* sank one of the destroyers that was escorting the damaged *Leipzig* home.

The first signs of a threat to the security of the sea ring in the north came, curiously enough, with the local war between Russia and Finland. The Russian attack was launched on 30th November, 1939, and in Britain and France—indeed, throughout the neutral world—a wave of sympathy arose for a small and weak nation subjected to wanton aggression by a large and powerful neighbour. In belligerent Britain and France there was more than sympathy; there was the opportunity, through the provision of material help to Finland, of obtaining an additional dividend by gaining control of the Swedish iron-ore trade, almost all of which went to Germany by means of her Baltic sea routes. There was also the risk that a Russian victory in Finland might be followed by demands on Sweden and Norway such that Germany might feel impelled to intervene in her own interests. And any intervention by Germany in Norway, leading to any sort of German control of the Norwegian west coast, would inevitably raise naval problems of an uncomfortable magnitude.

It was a situation that, politically, was fraught with danger. The road to Finland was barred by Scandinavian neutrality, and any large-scale violation of it would almost certainly provoke strong German reaction. Moreover, the Chiefs of Staff had already pointed out the grave disadvantages of incurring any further commitments in Scandinavia.[11] Yet the lure of this iron-ore trade, with the economic damage it could do to the enemy, was wellnigh irresistible to the War Cabinet. On 19th December the Supreme War Council decided as a first step to take diplomatic action in Norway and Sweden with a view to facilitating the passage of men and arms to Finland and to bolstering the determination of those two countries actively to resist any German aggression.[12] In Norway and Sweden, however, the fear of German might and of the almost inevitable retaliation which would follow effectively stopped any hope of organised Allied support for Finnish resistance to the Russian threat. Britain and France were reduced to the sending of small, clandestine shipments of arms and a few "volunteers".

The potential value of the Norwegian bases to Germany in her conduct of the U-boat war had, naturally, been appreciated as much by the German Chiefs of Staff as by the British. As early as 10th October the German naval Commander-in-Chief, Admiral Raeder, had sent a memorandum to Hitler pointing out the importance of Trondheim as a base for submarines.[13] Rosenberg, the apostle of the Nazi faith, was thereupon sent to Norway to mobilise opinion in favour of a German coup and he found ready listeners in the persons of two Norwegian politicians with Nazi sympathies, Quisling and Hagelin. On his recommendation Raeder received the two renegade Norwegians on 11th December, when plans for a German occupation of that country were discussed. On the following day these plans were submitted to Hitler, and he gave the order to start preparations immediately.[14]

So it was that all the belligerents began to cast envious eyes on the obvious strategic possibilities of the Norwegian ports. To the British and French it meant the denial to Germany of much of the vital Scandinavian iron ore, to the Germans it meant not only an advanced U-boat base for operations against Allied trade but also a useful breach in the Allied sea blockade. But while both sides desired the use of Norway's coastline, their approaches to the fulfilment of these desires differed radically. The German plan envisaged invasion and forcible occupation, that of Britain and France followed the more tortuous path of diplomatic persuasion and was foredoomed to failure from the start, periodically wrecking itself on the rock of Scandinavian neutrality.

The British and French problem was twofold, whether to attempt the major task of stopping the whole of the iron-ore trade, which included that of Sweden, or of trying to halt only the Narvik traffic. The Chiefs of Staff were in favour of the major operation, even if it involved the despatch of an expeditionary force to occupy Narvik and military operations in southern Scandinavia against probable German retaliation. In their view this could be achieved only with Norwegian and Swedish co-operation, for in the then state of Allied military strength they could not risk the added and active enmity of those two countries which unilateral action would ensure. To the War Cabinet, however, the chance of such Scandinavian co-operation appeared minute, and it was decided to take instead the lesser step of trying to stop the Narvik traffic only. It was thought that this step by itself would be unlikely to precipitate a German counter-invasion. Using as an excuse the fact of German violation of Norwegian territorial waters, the Government of Norway was informed that the Allies proposed to act in the matter by stopping the iron-ore ships with a flotilla of destroyers.

The Scandinavian reaction was immediate. Both Norway and Sweden sent official protests and the King of Norway backed them up with a personal appeal to King George VI to use his influence in preventing any such action. In the face of so strong an objection the War Cabinet dropped the proposal.

Yet this Scandinavian-German iron-ore traffic remained a powerful irritant, both in Britain and in France. In Britain the main objective was the deprivation to Germany of this vital war commodity, in France there was also a desire to reduce the German menace to the French defences by opening up another front elsewhere.[15] The Russo-Finnish war still seemed to offer an opportunity of peaceful penetration into the vital areas of Norway, and on 5th February the Supreme War Council decided once more to make an attempt to secure Norwegian and Swedish agreement to the passage of troops to Finland through Narvik, invoking the Covenant of the League of Nations as an excuse.[16] But at this precise moment diplomatic relations were prejudiced by the *Altmark* episode, in which a British destroyer, H.M.S. *Cossack*, on 16th February, entered Norwegian territorial waters and forcibly removed British Merchant Navy men, captured by the *Graf Spee* during her cruise, from the German tanker *Altmark* which was sheltering in a Norwegian fjord. Both Norway and Sweden again refused the Allied request. In the end, all these negotiations died a natural death when Finnish resistance collapsed at the beginning of March.

It is necessary at this stage to take a quick look back at the Allied grand strategy. It had been agreed between Britain and France at the start of the war, as related earlier, that the Western Allies should remain strictly on the defensive while they built up their war potential. It had been laid down that "time was on our side".[17] In war, however, and especially in naval war, the defensive inevitably brings disadvantages in its train. The collapse of Finland was a case in point. Neutral opinion throughout the world accepted it as a moral and diplomatic defeat for the Allies, and as a similar victory for Germany, since Britain and France had so publicly associated themselves with the Finnish cause. It was time, therefore, for the Allies to make a revaluation of their essential guiding strategy and to initiate some action rather more positive.

The Chiefs of Staff set the ball rolling with a report that time was only on the Allied side provided that they took the fullest advantage of it.[18] In the light of that report the War Cabinet decided to adopt a more offensive policy in the economic field, a policy with which the Chiefs of Staff expressed their agreement.[19] Almost automatically it was the suppression of the Narvik iron-ore traffic which came first on the list for discussion to implement the new policy. In the absence now of the Finnish excuse, the Supreme War Council came to the conclusion that the best way to do this was by forcing the German carrying trade out into international waters by the laying of minefields in territorial waters, regardless of Norwegian susceptibilities.[20] The date for the operation was fixed for early April.

Allied planning, however, though possibly adequate in broad outline, left at this stage of the war much to be desired in its attention to detail. It should have been reasonably obvious that, by themselves, minefields in territorial waters could never provide more than a very temporary solution to the problem and that they would need to be backed up by some more permanent force if serious economic damage to Germany was to ensue. In the long run Allied occupation of Narvik was the only true answer to the problem of the Norwegian iron-ore trade, and for that a field force of reasonable size must inevitably be required. In March of 1940, when the decision to lay the minefields was taken, such a force existed. It had been assembled as aid for Finland, and warships and transports had been allocated for its carriage to Norway. But with the collapse of Finland the force had been disbanded and the ships dispersed. Instead, small forces of battalion strength were earmarked for occupation of all the main Norwegian ports on the west coast; but to be used only to forestall German landings should they be threatened.

In comparison with the vacillations of Allied policy over Norway, the enemy's policy was clear-cut and positive. As soon as Hitler, on 12th December, 1939, had agreed to consider the occupation of Norway, planning had begun in meticulous detail. On 1st March, 1940, Hitler finally took the decision to occupy Denmark and Norway by force, and the necessary operational directives were issued. By the 26th it was possible for the German Chiefs of Staff to report that they would be ready to carry out the invasion during the new moon period of April (7th–15th), and on 1st April the final date was fixed. It was to be 9th April at 5.15 a.m.[21] All preparations, down to the last man and the last round of ammunition, were complete.

The small minelaying operation in Norwegian waters planned by the Allies was first fixed for 5th April. It was then postponed, on account of French objections, but agreed again for the 8th. Three fields were planned for laying in the approaches to the Inner Leads, one in the north off Bodo, one off Stadlandet, and an imaginary one (to be declared as a dangerous area) off Bud. The destroyers and minelayers detailed to lay the fields sailed from Scapa on 5th April. As cover for the minelayers the Commander-in-Chief ordered Vice-Admiral Whitworth in the battle-cruiser *Renown*, with a screen of destroyers, to accompany them. Behind them, at Rosyth and in the Clyde, lay cruisers and transports with the battalions earmarked for Norway already on board. They were to sail only if the laying of the minefields were to provoke active German reactions. This operation for forestalling German landings in Norway was known as Plan R.4.

The enemy plan, fixed for 9th April, entailed the use of almost the entire German Navy. The Norwegian coast, as far north as Vest Fjord, came within the purview of these operations, and the occupation force for Narvik sailed in ten destroyers. That for Trondheim was embarked in four destroyers, and these two forces, having the farthest to go, sailed in company. The *Scharnhorst* and *Gneisenau* sailed at the same time as cover for the Narvik destroyers, the 8-inch cruiser *Admiral Hipper* as cover for the Trondheim party. All these ships left their German North Sea ports early in the morning of 7th April.

They were sighted by British reconnaissance aircraft as they were making their way up the Jutland coast. A force of bombers sent to attack them from the air failed to do any damage, and the Home Fleet, under Admiral Sir Charles Forbes, flying his flag in the *Rodney*, sailed from Scapa in the evening of the same day. As more and more reports of movements of enemy ships came in, other vessels were ordered to sea by the Admiralty to augment Admiral Forbes's forces. They included the four cruisers at Rosyth in which the troops for Norway had been embarked. The soldiers were all hastily put ashore before the four ships sailed.

This sudden abandonment of Plan R.4 came as a surprise to the Commander-in-Chief. From the many sighting reports of the enemy which had reached the flagship he was convinced that a German assault on Norway was in progress and that the very conditions for which the plan had been devised now held good. It seemed that in

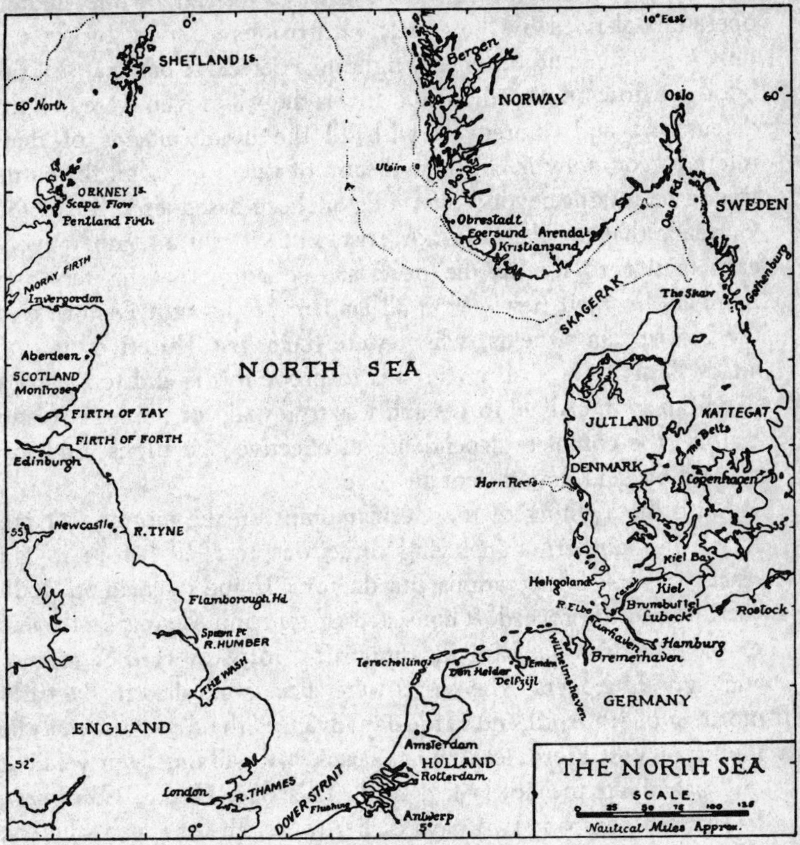


the Admiralty, in spite of the accumulating evidence, the whole German operation was thought to be one of passing the *Scharnhorst* and the *Gneisenau* out to the Atlantic trade routes. It is always easy to be wise after the event, but if in fact Plan R.4 had been at once put into operation, it might have brought considerable advantages, particularly when allied to the flexibility which sea power confers. It would not have been difficult to switch the destination of the troops even after sailing, and as events turned out they could have arrived at Narvik just at that crucial moment when the town was ripe for seizure.

So began the campaign for Norway. Instead of the limited operation planned by the Allies, with troops standing by for use only if required and the enemy fighting a defensive battle at sea, the boot was now on the other foot. It was the Allies who were to fight defensively and, moreover, with all the disadvantages of their inferior geography in this new theatre of war. For them, the battle was to be fought beyond the range of shore-based aircraft; for the Germans that problem did not exist, since it was a comparatively easy matter to fly up the necessary squadrons of fighters and bombers by their newly-won all-land route through Denmark to the Norwegian airfields, which were their first objectives in the attack. This lack of air cover was to prove in the end too great a handicap to the Allied forces and was to reveal, for the first time in history, the complete dependence of effective operations, both by sea and by land, on efficient air cover.

With the sighting of the German ships on the morning of 7th April the southern minelaying force was recalled before it had reached its area of operations, but the force laying the field off Bodo was allowed to proceed. It consisted of four minelaying destroyers of the 20th Flotilla, with its supporting force of H.M.S. *Renown* and eight destroyers. The mines were successfully laid in the early morning of 8th April, and as the day advanced the *Renown* lay off the mouth of Vest Fjord, leading to Narvik, with all the destroyers but one patrolling the newly-laid field. This one, H.M.S. *Glowworm*, had parted company two days earlier to search for a man who had fallen overboard. Having recovered him, she was now on her way to rejoin, but the heavy seas had slowed her down and she was approximately abreast of Trondheim. Shortly before eight o'clock she sighted two enemy destroyers, of which one was the *Berndt von Arnim*, one of the ten ships detailed for the German occupation of Narvik. The *Glowworm* engaged her in a running fight, only to meet later the overwhelming power of the *Hipper*'s guns. She met her end gloriously and heroically by ramming and damaging her huge adversary. It was not until the few men who survived were released from their prison camp after the war that the whole story became known and the gallantry of her commanding officer,

Lieutenant-Commander G. B. Roope, rewarded with a posthumous Victoria Cross.

Her sighting signals, the last of which was faded out and indicated her probable fate, were to have a considerable effect on the operations which followed. Admiral Whitworth had first steered to her assistance, then assuming that the *Glowworm*'s adversaries were bound for Narvik, sailed to take up a position where he might cut them off. Admiral Forbes detached the battle-cruiser *Repulse*, the cruiser *Penelope*, and four destroyers to the *Glowworm*'s aid, and the Admiralty, by signal from Whitehall, ordered all the destroyers in the Narvik area to join the *Renown*. By doing this, the way to Narvik was left unguarded and the ten German destroyers, carrying the occupation forces, slipped in unchallenged and unnoticed.

Early in the morning of the 9th the first contact between major units took place. Admiral Whitworth, in the *Renown*, sighted the *Scharnhorst* and *Gneisenau* as they were withdrawing to the north on completion of their task of covering the ten German destroyers for Narvik. She opened fire at 4.5 a.m. and twelve minutes later hit the *Gneisenau*, putting her main armament control out of action. In spite of a very heavy sea which prevented the destroyers from keeping up, and of occasional snow showers which blotted out all sight of the enemy, she hit the *Gneisenau* twice more before the two enemy ships, taking advantage of their superior speed, ran out of sight to the northward. This lack of enterprise on the part of the German Admiral Lütjens is difficult to understand in this isolated action. Both his ships were modern and well-found, while the *Renown* was old, was out by herself ahead of her destroyers, and but lightly protected with armour. Had Admiral Lütjens turned and fought there could have been but one result and Germany could have claimed a major success at sea.

Later that evening the Admiralty ordered Admiral Whitworth to return to Vest Fjord and to patrol off the entrance. His task was to prevent any enemy ships from entering the fjord. The order came, of course, too late, for by this time the German destroyers were there, their troops ashore, and the town captured. At about the same time the Commander-in-Chief ordered Captain (D) 2nd

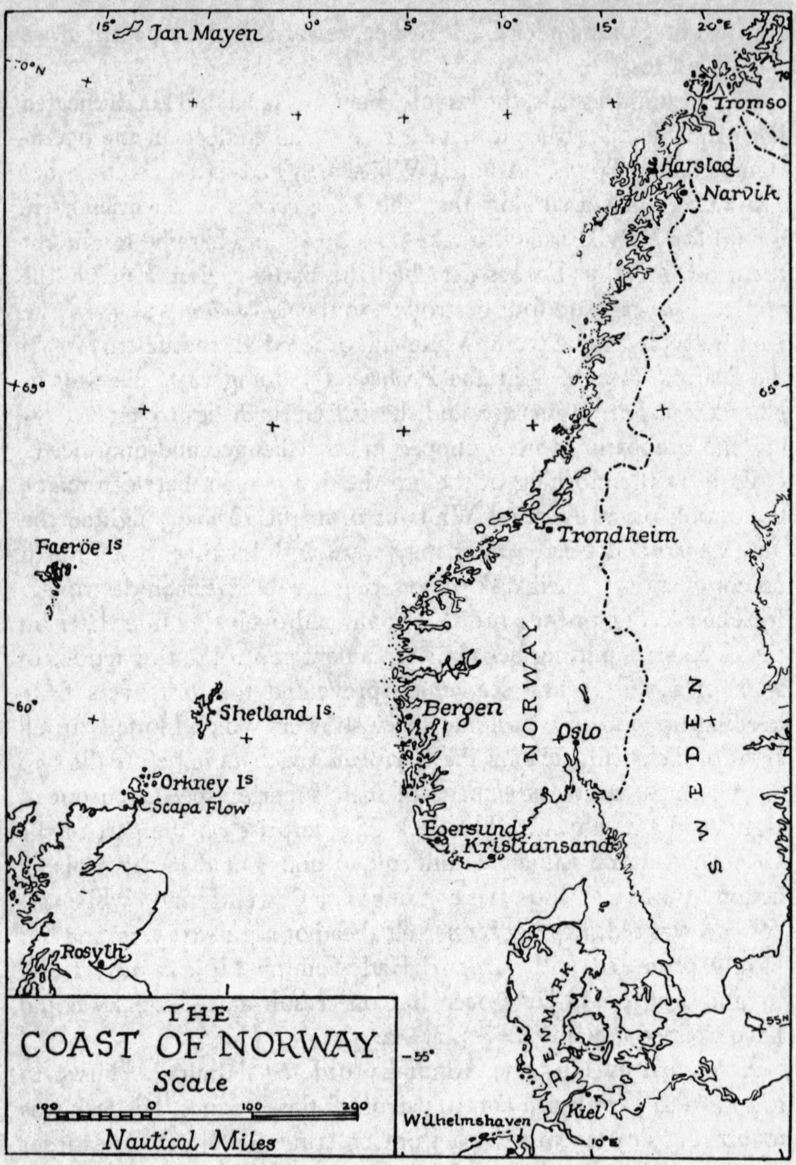
Jan Mayen
Tromso
Harstad
Narvik
Faeröe Is
Trondheim
NORWAY
Bergen
Oslo
SWEDEN
Shetland Is.
Orkney Is
Scapa Flow
Egersund
Kristiansand
Rosyth
DENMARK
Kiel
Wilhelmshaven
THE
COAST OF NORWAY
Scale
Nautical Miles

Destroyer Flotilla "to send some destroyers up to Narvik to make certain that no enemy troops land".

Thus the stage was set for the two battles of Narvik which followed, the first on 10th April, the second three days later. In the first, Captain Warburton-Lee with five destroyers—his own ship H.M.S. *Hardy*, the *Hotspur*, *Havock*, *Hunter*, and *Hostile*—entered the fjord at dawn high water on the 10th. After a difficult passage through continuous snowstorms the ships ran into clear weather as they arrived off the town. They had made the passage unobserved and their appearance was a complete surprise to the enemy. By gun and torpedo attacks inside the harbour they sank two of the enemy—the destroyers *Wilhelm Heidkamp* and *Anton Schmidt*—and damaged three others, as well as several merchant ships. On their withdrawal, however, they ran into five more of the enemy and, caught between two fires, the *Hunter* was sunk and the *Hardy* so damaged that she had to be beached. Captain Warburton-Lee lost his life in the course of the action and his gallantry in pressing home his attack was later recognised by the award of a posthumous Victoria Cross.

The second battle of Narvik, fought on the 13th, sealed the fate of the remaining enemy destroyers. Admiral Whitworth, reinforced by now by the battleship *Warspite*, transferred his flag to her and, with nine destroyers in company, entered the fjord during the forenoon. He achieved complete success, sinking the remaining eight destroyers and one U-boat, discovered and bombed by the *Warspite*'s reconnaissance aircraft. Their destruction effectively opened the way for the capture of Narvik itself, but by now there was no military force available. That hurried disembarkation of the soldiers already earmarked and on board at Rosyth was to be sadly regretted. As it turned out, Narvik itself was not finally occupied for another six weeks, and by that time the progress of events in another and more vital sphere of action had made its capture completely unimportant.

While these events were taking place in the north, there had been isolated successes farther south. Naval aircraft from the Orkneys attacked and sank the cruiser *Königsberg* at Bergen, the submarine *Truant* torpedoed and so badly damaged the cruiser *Karlsruhe* that she had to be sunk by her own forces, and the submarine *Spearfish* caught the pocket-battleship *Lützow* (formerly the *Deutschland*) on her way home from Oslo and torpedoed her, causing very severe damage. But these successes had little bearing on the campaign as a whole. The enemy had succeeded in gaining his main objectives with, on the whole, surprising ease. His troops were ashore and in occupation of all the main ports and airfields on the Norwegian coast. Oslo, the capital, was in his hands, and reinforcement of his Norwegian troops was a comparatively simple matter by virtue of his occupation of the whole of Denmark. Only at Narvik had he received a really crushing defeat, and even there his soldiers still held the port.

The task now facing the Allies was that of recovering not only the ground but also the initiative lost through the swiftness and unexpectedness of the German attack. All such operations, especially when carried out at a long distance from main supply bases, are among the most difficult and hazardous in war, and those in Norway were no exception to the rule. It was by no means beyond the power of the Navy to transport troops and equipment to the various scenes of operations and put them ashore, for that is one of the essentials of sea power in which the Navy excelled, but for the troops to consolidate themselves there was a very different matter. Not only was this campaign now being fought on exterior lines of communication, but there were also conflicting priorities amongst the three Services themselves which made the task even more difficult. While the most pressing immediate need in Norway was for anti-aircraft guns, to provide protection from incessant air attack, it was pointed out that Anti-Aircraft Command at home, far from being able to release any of its own supplies, was still itself short by 12,000 guns of the number considered necessary for home defence. Because of that, the operations in Norway were sadly hampered. There were other, similar, cases too.

Yet more important still to the outcome of the campaign was the need for speed in the despatch of troops. When the four and one-half divisions originally designed for aid to Finland were disbanded, there remained no more than the few battalions available which had been earmarked for use in Norway under Plan R.4. These were ill-equipped, insufficiently trained, and inadequately protected against the rigours of the Norwegian climate. Moreover, their role now was a very different one from that originally envisaged. Instead of occupying the main Norwegian ports, with local help and acquiescence, and disputing their possession against an invading enemy, they were now themselves in the position of being invaders, to fight a totally different kind of war against an enemy already in possession.[22] It was a most severe handicap and the wonder is, not that the campaign in Norway eventually ended in failure, but that the few British and French troops who were landed succeeded in making a fight of it for so long.

On the morning of 9th April, when confirmation of the German landings was received, London was the scene of great activity. The three Chiefs of Staff were called early from their beds and, meeting at 6.0 a.m., decided that the first objectives to be secured were the ports of Bergen and Trondheim. At the time of their meeting it was not known that Narvik had also been occupied; it was thought still to be clear of the enemy. Two and a half hours later, at the Chiefs of Staffs' request, the War Cabinet met and, while confirming the importance of capturing Bergen and Trondheim, laid down that no troops were to be moved until the naval situation had become clearer. Later that same morning the Chiefs of Staff met for a second time, and by then news of the German occupation of Narvik had been received. But beyond ordering the move of the available battalions to new ports of embarkation (Scapa and the Clyde), no further firm decisions were reached.

In the afternoon the Supreme War Council met and called for attacks on Narvik, Bergen, and Trondheim. Plans for these were left to the Military Co-ordination Committee, which met at 9.30 p.m. There it was decided that small landings were to be made at Namsos and Aandalsnes, north and south respectively of Trondheim, in order to hold the ground while the main attack was directed to the capture of Narvik. Thus, with the meetings of the various committees concerned, one vital day had been lost to the Allies and one vital day presented to the enemy in which to consolidate his gains. Not one Allied soldier was yet on the high seas *en route* for the battlefield.

The day of the 10th was similarly occupied with the making of plans and the briefing of the various theatre and area commanders. It had been hoped, and expected, that half of one battalion, designed for Narvik, would be able to sail from Scapa before noon on the 11th, the second half, together with further troops from the Clyde, following two days later. In fact, the first half, embarked in the cruiser *Southampton*, did not clear Scapa until 1.0 p.m. on the 12th. Had they sailed on the previous day they would have reached the latitude of Narvik on the 13th, the day of the second battle in which the *Warspite* and her nine destroyers had shattered the entire German naval force and whose guns now dominated the town.

At home, in the light of the supposed strength of the German grip on Narvik, the military plans had stipulated landings in Vaagsfjord, to the north of the Vest Fjord, in which lay Narvik itself. After the second battle, Admiral Whitworth had signalled more than once[23] that in his view direct occupation of the town would be a relatively simple matter, but by the time this opinion had passed through the various channels and had been digested it was too late to divert the soldiers. They were already ashore near Sjovegan, on the northern shore of Vaagsfjord, and forty miles of deep snow lay between them and their objective. So was another good chance missed.

The small landings to hold the ground at Namsos and Aandalsnes, as envisaged by the Military Co-ordination Committee at its meeting on 9th April, were made by naval parties of seamen and marines on 14th April at Namsos and 17th April at Aandalsnes. Both were unopposed and both in due course were relieved by Regular troops from Britain who were to conduct the land operations for the capture of Trondheim.

It was in the support and maintenance of these military operations that, for the next four to eight weeks, the main strength of the Navy was to be chiefly engaged. There were no delusions at the Admiralty as to what the acquisition by the enemy of these forward bases would mean in terms of naval endeavour. There had been British readers, as well as German, of Admiral Wegener's thesis on German naval strategy, *Die Seestrategie des Weltkrieges*. On the merits of Danish or Norwegian bases for the purpose of maintaining access with the oceans, Admiral Wegener had written: "The Norwegian position was certainly preferable. England could then no longer maintain the blockade line from the Shetlands to Norway but must withdraw approximately to the line of the Shetlands—the Faeroes—Iceland. But this line was a net with very wide meshes. . . . Moreover [it] was hard for England to defend; for in the first place it lay comparatively near to our [new] bases, and, above all, as the map shows, we should considerably outflank the English strategic position to the north."[24] This paragraph in Admiral Wegener's book was beginning now to have an ominous ring of prophecy.

Almost at once the naval, equally with the military, side of the campaign ran into difficulties. It was easy enough for the Navy to carry the Army and its supplies across the North Sea, to put it ashore at its appointed landing-places, and to improvise the necessary base installations. That was a traditional task, carried out with all the customary skill and accuracy and, moreover, without loss apart from one small storeship which fell victim to a U-boat's torpedo. Only then, however, did the real difficulties start. From the captured Norwegian airfields the German aircraft operated with telling effect. They had, in the main, little opposition, and a frightening foretaste of the future was the vast amount of anti-aircraft ammunition that had to be expended for even the smallest successes. The special anti-aircraft cruisers employed in the defence of these landing-bases—the *Cairo*, *Carlisle*, and *Curaçao*—used up practically their entire stock of special shell in defending themselves from almost continuous air attack, leaving but little over for the defence of the bases.

Both these main bases—Namsos and Aandalsnes—were quickly reduced to blazing wrecks by the bombers of the Luftwaffe. Any attempt to disembark troops and stores by daylight was tantamount to disaster, but by night the work went on. The cruisers and destroyers, both British and French, continued to bring in troops and stores, to put them ashore under cover of darkness, and to return for more. But even as the troops landed the writing was already on the wall. An effort to neutralise the German air supremacy by the formation of a Royal Air Force fighter station ashore ended in catastrophe. The frozen lake at Lesjeskog was selected as a landing-ground and a squadron of Gladiator fighters flown off from the deck of H.M.S. *Glorious* to land there, in order to operate as fighter cover for the troops ashore. By the end of their first day only four Gladiators remained to transfer to a more distant lake; thirteen had to be left behind, wrecked and burned. Such an experience signed the death warrant of the operation.

Inevitably, evacuation of the Allied forces followed. There was no other answer in the face of the air threat. Earlier attempts to provide fighter cover from carriers had not solved the problem, firstly, because there were not sufficient carriers to operate their aircraft continuously and, secondly, because their aircraft were needed to provide cover for themselves and the other naval forces operating in the area. Much, probably far too much, had been hoped for from the Gladiators at Lesjeskog, but they had proved, in spite of great efforts and great gallantry, a broken reed. At their meeting on the morning of 26th April the Military Co-ordination Committee decided that there was no alternative but to evacuate central Norway. It was the only possible decision that could be made.

Once more the Allied navies came in force into the derelict harbours of Namsos and Aandalsnes, this time to bring away the men they had landed there ten days or so earlier. The operations were planned for the nights of 30th April and 1st May at Aandalsnes, and 1st and 2nd May at Namsos. But before those operations took place there appeared, for the Norwegian nation, an even unhappier omen. In the darkness of late evening of 27th April, H.M.S. *Glasgow* and two destroyers arrived at Molde. There they embarked the King of Norway and the Crown Prince, members of the Norwegian Government, and the Bank of Norway's gold reserve. Sadly they left the southern half of their stricken country for a safer haven in the far north. It was the first, bitter taste of defeat.

The evacuations at Aandalsnes and Namsos were carried out with skill, speed, and precision. There were some fears at first of the outcome at Aandalsnes, for on the night of the 29th the port was, for the first time, bombed throughout the dark hours and evacuation was, of course, possible only at night. It was a risk, however, that had to be accepted, and at 10.30 p.m. on the night of 30th April, Vice-Admiral Sir Frederick Edward-Collins entered the port with the cruisers *Galatea*, *Arethusa*, *Sheffield*, and *Southampton*, six destroyers, and one transport. Nearly 2,200 men, a little less than half the total military force, were embarked and the ships were clear of the fjord before the sun rose the next morning. On the following night the same task fell to Vice-Admiral Sir Geoffrey Layton, with the cruisers *Manchester* and *Birmingham*, five destroyers, the sloop *Auckland*, and the anti-aircraft cruiser *Calcutta*. They entered Aandalsnes at 11 p.m., the destroyers going alongside the quay and ferrying out the men to the cruisers, which sailed as soon as they were full. When all but the rearguard were embarked the force sailed for home, leaving the *Auckland* and *Calcutta* to take on board the last 200 men who had guarded the retreat. Instead of the 200 expected, over 700 men turned up. The remaining darkness was to be counted in minutes now, instead of hours, but with the aid of naval shore parties the tired men were safely brought on board in fifteen minutes and the two ships sailed, to reach the open sea unmolested. Every man was accounted for and not a single casualty incurred in this hazardous operation.

At Namsos the risks were even greater. It was unlikely that all knowledge of the withdrawal could be completely denied to the enemy; it was equally certain that when he realised what was happening he would dispute it to the utmost of his power. There were 5,400 troops ashore in the Namsos area, and to Vice-Admiral J. H. D. Cunningham, in command of the naval force, it appeared essential to complete the evacuation in one night instead of two, as originally planned. General Carton de Wiart, in command ashore, declared this to be impossible; nonetheless Admiral Cunningham was determined to attempt it.

On the night of 1st May his ships, the British cruisers *Devonshire* and *York* and the French cruiser *Montcalm*, with nine destroyers and three transports, approached the Norwegian coast only to find extensive fog patches which prevented the entry of the larger ships into pilotage waters. Some of the destroyers, under Captain Lord Louis Mountbatten and on his suggestion, managed to grope their way in, to find the fjord clear. Admiral Cunningham then sent Captain P. L. Vian, in the destroyer *Afridi*, to lead the transports in through the fog. H.M.S. *York* and the destroyer *Nubian* followed.

Embarkation proceeded apace. Two of the transports secured alongside the quay and were quickly filled, while the destroyers ferried other parties to the *York* and the third transport lying out in the small harbour. As the hours of darkness shortened, so too did the long lines of men ashore awaiting embarkation. Early in the morning, while it was still dark, the first group of ships sailed with the greater portion of the troops. They reached Scapa undetected by the enemy. Later, as the first tinges of dawn were beginning to light the eastern sky, the rest of the ships sailed, and in them they carried the whole of the remaining soldiers. As at Aandalsnes, all were accounted for.

It was then that the fog off shore, which had earlier held up the larger ships off Namsos, could have proved its value. Alas, it had lifted and the sky was clear. Enemy bombers soon discovered the second group of ships as they steamed across the North Sea and their attacks were continuous. They hit and sank the *Afridi* and the French destroyer *Bison*. In the latter was embarked a small part of the Namsos rearguard, and they were the only losses suffered by the Army.

There remains to be recorded one comment on the conduct of this operation. It comes from General Carton de Wiart, commanding ashore at Namsos. "In the course of that last, endless day," he wrote, "I got a message from the Navy to say that they would evacuate the whole of my force that night. I thought it was impossible, but learned a few hours later that the Navy do not know the word."[25]

Narvik remained. The first landing, it will be remembered, had been made in Vaagsfjord on 14th April. In command ashore was Major-General Mackesy, afloat was Admiral of the Fleet Lord Cork and Orrery with the title of Flag Officer, Narvik. When the two met at Harstad, which had been selected as the main base for the operations, they discovered that they had received totally different instructions and consequently held "diametrically opposed views".[26] General Mackesy maintained that his force was not ready yet for fighting, that its stores required sorting before it could move, that it must await the arrival of its artillery before it could undertake any active operations. Lord Cork, vitally alive to the implications of the second battle of Narvik fought the previous day and also to Admiral Whitworth's signal which had stated: "I am convinced that Narvik can be taken by direct assault now without fear of meeting serious opposition on landing", wanted an immediate assault on the town. The General, however, was adamant and the fleeting chance of an important success, if chance it were, was missed. Lord Cork was appointed in supreme command of the expedition on 20th April, but by that date the morale of the Germans in Narvik had recovered after its severe drop following the two naval battles.

The military build-up in the Narvik area was slow at first, but gained momentum after the evacuations farther south. By the first week in May the concentration was complete and Lord Cork proposed to attack the town on the 8th. The operation, however, was postponed, and instead a landing was made at Bjerkvik, at the top of Herjangs Fjord. Covered by aircraft from H.M.S. *Ark Royal*, it was completely successful.

There was, nevertheless, still the problem of the attack from the air. Successes ashore could be maintained only under an air cover sufficiently incisive to discourage the German bombers, which were by now beginning to arrive in the area in increasing numbers. Airfields ashore had been laboriously prepared for the Royal Air Force, and after the Bjerkvik operation the *Ark Royal* was sent home to ferry across Royal Air Force Hurricanes. Her departure from the area coincided with a steep rise in German air attacks on the ships supporting the shore operations, and losses began to mount alarmingly, culminating in the sinking of H.M.S. *Curlew*, one of the special anti-aircraft cruisers whose value was becoming increasingly apparent.

By the end of the third week in May the first of the Royal Air Force fighters—Hurricanes and Gladiators—were flown off from the *Furious* and *Glorious* and landed safely on their airfields. The assault on Narvik could now go forward assured at last of adequate fighter protection from the enemy bombers. But already it was too late. Across France were pounding the German armoured divisions, making for the Channel ports, and for the first time for 140 years there was serious talk of an invasion of Britain. In the threat of that danger the occupation of Narvik was no longer practical politics.

On 24th May the War Cabinet, under the shadow of the grave news from the French battlefield, decided on the total evacuation of Norway. The orders reached the naval and military commanders, Admiral of the Fleet Lord Cork and Lieutenant-General Auchinleck, who had by then superseded General Mackesy, on the 26th, but were later modified to include the striking of one last blow at the enemy in Norway. Narvik was to be captured before the final evacuation to permit destruction of the railway and the harbour facilities for loading ore. Its capture presented no difficulties. By the morning of the 28th the town was in Allied hands and demolition work was in progress. Unfortunately, the R.A.F. fighter airfield was fogbound and the consequent lack of air cover enabled the enemy bombers to operate unopposed. H.M.S. *Cairo*, yet another of our valuable anti-aircraft cruisers, was hit and damaged.

There remained but one final act in this unhappy campaign. This was the last, and also the largest, of the evacuations. Some 25,000 troops were ashore in the area and their safe removal was something of a major operation. There had, so far, been little or no German naval reaction at sea to the whole of the Allied campaign in North Sea waters and, so far as was known, no enemy units were at sea to dispute this final withdrawal. Yet Admiral Forbes, correctly as it turned out, was not satisfied over this apparent quiescence on the part of the German Navy, and sent H.M.S. *Valiant* and four destroyers from the Home Fleet to cover the homecoming convoys. It was as well that he did, for the enemy had planned an operation to harass the naval forces in the Harstad area, though without knowledge, of course, of the evacuation plans.

The evacuation itself was covered by naval aircraft from the *Ark Royal* and *Glorious*, whose duty, after the completion of that task, was to embark the shore-based fighters and bring them home. For five nights the soldiers were ferried out to the troopships, which sailed for home in two groups. Both arrived in the Clyde in safety, a total of 25,000 men brought home without loss. Most of their stores and all their transport had to be left behind, and it is, perhaps, an example of the hurried planning for the whole campaign that the trucks for one of the first battalions to land at Harstad were received on the day of their final embarkation, just in time to be pushed, unused, into the sea. It could hardly be called planning at its best.

The *Ark Royal*, after embarking her quota of shore-based aircraft, sailed for home in the last convoy. The *Glorious*, with two escorting destroyers, had been ordered to proceed independently because of shortage of fuel. She had, on the morning of the 8th, received her complement of shore-based fighters, who had landed on in most spirited and gallant fashion. With no arrester hooks, and with no former experience of deck landings, the Royal Air Force pilots had flown their Hurricanes out to sea to attempt this difficult task with no additional braking device beyond semi-deflated tyres on their landing wheels. Each landing on was successful beyond all hopes, and the carrier, escorted by the *Acasta* and *Ardent*, set course for home.

Their passage across the North Sea synchronised with the harassing operations planned by the enemy. Up towards the north steamed the *Scharnhorst*, *Gneisenau*, *Hipper*, and four destroyers, with the intention of a raid into the waters round Harstad. On his way north Admiral Marschall, in command of the German force, began to receive reports from shore-based reconnaissance aircraft. On the evening of the 7th an Allied convoy was reported off Ard Fjord; a few minutes later there was another sighting from the air, reporting two carriers about forty-five miles north of Andenes.[27] From these two reports Admiral Marschall correctly assumed that an evacuation was taking place and abandoned his previous orders, steering to intercept. Early in the morning of the 8th he ran into his first victims, a small group of ships homeward bound and comprising a tanker, an empty transport, a hospital ship, and an escorting trawler. Only the hospital ship was allowed to proceed; the other three were sunk. Then, detaching the *Hipper* and the destroyers to Trondheim, Admiral Marschall took his two big ships up into the northern wastes of the North Sea in search of bigger prey.

During the afternoon of the 8th smoke was sighted from the *Scharnhorst*'s foretop. The two battle-cruisers closed to investigate, and soon recognised the unwieldy bulk of an aircraft carrier. She was the *Glorious*, and a few minutes later the first 11-inch shells struck her, wrecking her hangars and setting her on fire. Strenuous efforts were made to get her Swordfish aircraft up on deck, armed with torpedoes, and into the air, but it had been left too late and not one was able to take off.

It was left to the *Ardent* and *Acasta* to make what defence was possible. And gloriously they did it in the very finest tradition of their Service. Laying a smoke screen to protect the *Glorious* from the worst of the gunfire, both sped at their maximum speed towards their giant adversaries. Lieutenant-Commander J. F. Barker, of the *Ardent*, as he narrowed the gap between himself and the enemy, turned on to a parallel course and fired a full salvo of torpedoes. The *Ardent* was overwhelmed by gunfire and sank a minute or two later.

Commander C. E. Glasfurd, in the *Acasta*, making use of the covering smoke-screen, carried on the battle. She was alone now, for the *Glorious*, badly holed by the plunging fire of the two German battle-cruisers, had rolled over and sunk. As the *Acasta* came out of the smoke for her attack she was hit again and again, but with all her guns firing she continued to close the enemy. Finally, low in the water now and near her end, she too turned and fired her torpedoes. One of them hit the *Scharnhorst* aft, damaging her starboard propeller shaft and flooding an engine room and the after-turret magazine. A shell from one of her guns hit one of the forward turrets, but was too small to do any damage. Then, having struck her blow, the *Acasta*, too, met her end in the concentrated gunfire of the two German ships. She had done even better than she knew, for without her torpedo hits the *Scharnhorst* and *Gneisenau* would almost certainly have fallen in with Lord Cork's main convoy.

This final act in the ill-fated campaign was all the more tragic in that it was largely unnecessary. Three separate precautionary moves might have saved the *Glorious*. Captain d'Oyley-Hughes, commanding the carrier, considered that the only danger he had to face was from U-boats, and that his speed and that of his escorts was a sufficient defence. All the ship's Swordfish were therefore down below in the hangar. Had they been on deck, and air patrols flown from the ship, the *Glorious* would have had sufficient warning of the enemy's presence possibly to keep clear of their track.

A second precautionary move would have been for Coastal Command to send out reconnaissance flights over the area during the period covering the return of these convoys from northern Norway. These, too, could have given adequate warning of the approaching German ships. But such was the degree of secrecy covering these homeward-bound convoys from Norway that Coastal Command had never been officially informed of them.

Finally, there was the Home Fleet, and it may be asked why it was not out in force to cover these valuable convoys. The answer lay in part in the invasion "scare", for Admiral Forbes had been ordered by the First Sea Lord to keep two heavy ships at Scapa in case invasion should become a reality. Admiral Forbes had, as has been recorded, sent out the *Valiant* and four destroyers to cover the first group of the returning transports. The second and final group provided its own escort in the shape of the two cruisers, *Southampton* and *Coventry*, and the five destroyers which had been operating in Norwegian waters. Later this group was joined by the *Ark Royal* and her escorting destroyers. Unfortunately, on 5th June, a "Q-ship" had reported sighting two unknown ships, possibly raiders, north-east of the Faeroes, and Admiral Forbes had despatched a strong force, including the battle-cruisers *Repulse* and *Renown*, to intercept them. The report, however, was a false one and, too late, the *Repulse* and her fellow-ships were ordered to join the home-coming convoy. Too late, too, the *Rodney* raised steam and sailed from Scapa, but by then the damage had been done. She had been one of the two heavy ships retained at Scapa on the First Sea Lord's instructions.

Yet it was not all on the one side of the balance. Grievous as was the loss of the *Glorious* and her valuable crew—the more so since so many of them were trained pilots, both of the Royal Air Force and the Fleet Air Arm—there had been the severe damage caused to the *Scharnhorst* by the *Acasta*'s torpedo. And there was more to come. Back in Norwegian waters lay the British submarine *Clyde*. On the night of 20th June she sighted a darkened ship and, in spite of heavy weather, managed to hit her with one torpedo. It was the *Gneisenau*, and the *Clyde*'s success put her out of action for another six months.

There was, too, one other aspect of the campaign which, if not belonging strictly to the profit side, yet gave promise of better things to come. In spite of every drawback, of conflicting orders, of shortage of equipment, of serious reverses that ended in defeat, and of continuous and paralysing attack from the air, the morale of the men of all three Services remained proud and high. In the Navy the exemplary courage of its young men, of its destroyer captains and crews who died gloriously against great odds, of its pilots and observers whose "honour and courage remained throughout as dazzling as the snow-covered mountains over which they so triumphantly flew",[28] stands out as a splendid example of traditional naval gallantry.

The whole of the Norwegian coast was now in German hands. Its fine harbours, its airfields, its favourable geographical position, could now all be used in the battle against Britain. Admiral Wegener's prophecy had come to pass and his words, "we should considerably outflank the English strategic position to the north",[29] were now a concrete fact. The sea ring round Germany, held by the Allied command of the oceans, had been pierced.

Re-establishment, in the face of German shore-based air power, was impossible. The operations so recently concluded had proved that navies, no matter how overwhelmingly strong on the surface of the sea, could not live with the air above them dominated by the enemy. The carrier strength of the Navy, insufficient for its needs even at the start of the war, had been still further reduced by the losses of the *Courageous* and the *Glorious*, and there was no hope of providing the necessary air superiority in the North Sea through that means. One answer alone was possible, to hold the enemy farther out and to re-establish the sea blockade on a new line. It was to make the task infinitely more difficult, yet no possible alternative presented itself.

The German occupation of Denmark had, in fact, facilitated the necessary operations. To the north and north-west of Britain lay Danish possessions in the shape of the Faeroe Islands and Iceland, and in the German invasion of their motherland had lain the excuse for British occupation. Small British forces were already ashore in both places securing them against German attack. With their occupation the sea ring round Germany was once more held. But, as Admiral Wegener had said eleven years earlier, "this line was a net with very wide meshes. . . . Moreover, it was hard for England to defend."

# Chapter 3

## DUNKIRK AND THE ITALIAN INTERVENTION

If the result of the Norwegian campaign had been a strategical calamity, worse was to follow hard upon its heels. Even as the decision to evacuate Norway was taken by the War Cabinet on 24th May, urgent orders were sent to the Home Fleet to detach cruisers and destroyers to the Channel. The course of the war in north-west Europe was even at that early stage beginning to take an ugly turn.

The German attack in the west had been launched on 10th May, 1940, and almost at once the defence had begun to crumble with a speed that became progressively more alarming. The main enemy thrust through the Ardennes Forest struck at the "hinge" of the Maginot Line near Sedan and, bursting through, swept onwards to the north-west. At a single bound, as it were, this great armoured Maginot Line, constructed through the years with so much effort and at the cost of such vast treasure, was outflanked. It was to fall a few days later, with its great guns silent and unused, its vast accumulation of stores and ammunition unexpended and useless.

The German divisions swept onward. On 24th May Boulogne fell, and two days later Calais succumbed after a valiant stand. One by one the Channel and Biscay ports were to fall to the enemy as the westward sweep continued: Le Havre, Cherbourg, St. Malo, Brest, St. Nazaire, La Pallice; until by 25th June the German grip extended as far south and west as Bordeaux. All through the smiling French countryside, basking in the summer sunshine of a warm and benign June, "the echo of musketry and the beat of marching boots" proclaimed the defeat of a nation. Great Britain, shorn of the support of an ally, faced a situation as desperate as any in all her long history.

It was in this swift reversal of fortune, a short six weeks of dramatic tragedy, that command of the sea once more revealed its incalculable power, and also its influence on the land battles fought far from its shores. Sea power had landed the armies unscathed on the European battlefield; it was now to withdraw them again to the haven of their homeland. Sea power, too, was to hold inviolate the narrow waters which still made Britain an island, to deny to a victorious enemy the final prize which hung, so tantalisingly, almost within his grasp. To the Navy, as to all the citizens of Britain, was to dawn its "finest hour".

Seven days before the Germans launched their attacks on Holland, Belgium, and France, the Admiralty had begun to concentrate ships in the southern ports of Britain. It was not foreknowledge of the coming event which dictated these moves so much as an intelligent supposition that some such attack must come soon, combined with anxiety for the fate of Holland and Belgium when the expected blow should fall. Both these countries had refused to enter into any staff talks with the Western Allies in advance of a German onslaught, and when that onslaught came the opportunity to coordinate any plan of defence had passed beyond recall.

On 3rd May two cruisers, the *Galatea* and *Arethusa*, were ordered down from Rosyth to augment the Nore Command,[1] and four days later the Commander-in-Chief was ordered to detach a cruiser (H.M.S. *Birmingham*) and eight modern destroyers from the Home Fleet to concentrate at Harwich.[2] These were to be ready for immediate operations in aid of the Low Countries should the need arise.

It was at this anxious time, with the naval forces of Britain concentrating for what was to develop into one of the fiercest battles of the war, that the Admiralty lost its dynamic First Lord. On 8th May, after a two-day debate in the House of Commons, an adverse vote indicated that confidence in Mr. Chamberlain's leadership had waned. On 10th May he tendered his resignation, and Mr. Winston Churchill left Admiralty House to take up a new residence at 10 Downing Street as the nation's chosen war leader. And two days later, on 12th May, the Admiralty opened its doors to Mr. A. V. Alexander as the new First Lord, to reoccupy the chair in which he had last sat in 1931.

As the enemy struck westwards in the small hours of 10th May, naval forces were already at sea. H.M.S. *Kelly*, a destroyer leader, had been torpedoed in the North Sea by a German motor torpedo-boat on the 9th and in the force covering her withdrawal was H.M.S. *Birmingham*. She was at once ordered to Terschelling at full speed to render such help to the hard-pressed Dutch as was possible. Four destroyers—the *Wild Swan*, *Wivern*, *Hyperion*, and *Havock*—were sent to Waalhaven, where it was reported that the airfield had been captured by 1,200 German soldiers in Dutch uniforms, and a Royal Marine force of 200 men was sent in the destroyers *Verity* and *Venomous* to the Hook. Other ships followed as quickly as they could be got ready for sea.

Eager and swift as was the help offered by the Navy to the hapless Dutch, it came too late to affect the issue in Holland. The speed of the German land advance and the overwhelming weight of the attack from the air broke the back of Dutch resistance with almost unbelievable swiftness, and long before more substantial British aid could arrive across the sea. On 15th May, just five days from the first crossing of the frontier by German troops, the Dutch nation laid down its arms in total surrender.

The naval aid, tendered with such speed, was thus forced to become instead a means of evacuation. To augment the ships already diverted to Dutch waters the Admiralty ordered others, cruisers and destroyers, to assist in the removal of Dutch officials and British refugees. Some thousands were thus brought to safety, and at the same time landing-parties from the ships went ashore to carry out demolition work on the coast defences, power stations, dock gates, oil storage tanks, and other installations which might be of value to the enemy. H.M.S. *Codrington* brought Princess Juliana and her children to Britain on 12th May, and the Queen of the Netherlands, evading an attack by German parachute troops designed expressly to capture her, embarked in H.M.S. *Hereward* on the 13th and was brought safely to Harwich. By midnight on 14th May all further evacuation from Holland ceased, the Dutch Army having capitulated, and those who had, perforce, to be left behind were told to try to make their way towards Belgian ports where the Navy would attempt to continue the work of rescue.

On 14th May a new hint of danger was in the air. At their meeting on that day the Chiefs of Staff received a note from the War Cabinet to the effect that the French Prime Minister had telephoned to Mr. Churchill stating that the Germans had crossed the River Meuse and broken through south of Sedan. As a result the First Sea Lord signalled to Admiral Forbes at Scapa that the danger of an invasion of Britain was "very real". The Commander-in-Chief, however, refuted the suggestion and backed up his opinion with powerful arguments. As a sailor he knew well that a successful invasion would have to be preceded by the defeat of the Navy, and the Navy was still a very long way from defeat.

At their meeting on the following day, the Chiefs of Staff were told, again by M. Reynaud, "that the battle was lost and the road to Paris open".[3] Thoughts and fears that France might prove to be an unstable partner in the Western Alliance, hitherto vague and uncertain, now began to assume substance and reality, and the Chiefs of Staff devoted their collective wisdom to the formulation of a strategy designed for a Britain fighting alone.

As the battle in northern France progressed, a possibility even more urgent and more immediate than a consideration of strategy emerged from the growing tale of disaster. On the evening of 20th May German armoured forces reached Abbeville, and the British Expeditionary Force's main lines of communication with its home base were cut. Three or four days later the subsidiary lines, too, were cut by the loss of the Channel ports, and the Army was faced either with a large-scale and largely improvised withdrawal through inadequate ports or with surrender. One thing alone could decide their fate. It lay in the ability or otherwise of the Navy to hold the French inshore waters long enough to make a withdrawal possible and, though to a lesser extent, the ability of the Royal Air Force to hold the skies above the beaches. On those alone depended the life or death of the B.E.F.

On 20th May the first meeting was held of those who were to direct what later was to become known as Operation "Dynamo". So little of the true military situation in France was known in London at that date that, even though this initial meeting was held in the War Office, the possibility of a "hazardous evacuation of very large forces" was considered as "unlikely".[4] But on the following day, at Dover, the necessity was already looming larger and the first definite orders were issued, including one to concentrate in south coast waters as many personnel ships and small craft as could be made available.[5] Steps were taken at the same time to integrate the operations of Fighter and Coastal Command squadrons with the overall plan of the Flag Officer Dover, Vice-Admiral B. H. Ramsay. Five Fleet Air Arm squadrons were also placed under the operational control of Coastal Command in order to augment the available numbers.

By 22nd May the preliminary plans were complete. The Admiralty had been assiduous in the collection of available small craft for the operation, in equipping them with the necessary gear and instruments, and in the provision of naval crews where possible. All these preliminary steps were co-ordinated by the Vice-Admiral Dover, and at 7.44 p.m. on that day a signal from the Admiralty informed all the authorities concerned that "the operation for which these ships are being prepared will be known as Dynamo".[6] It was the first mention of a name that was later to become famous all over the world.

But before the evacuation of the B.E.F. was to start from Dunkirk and its neighbouring beaches there was a smaller operation at Boulogne which gave some foretaste of the difficulties in store in the major withdrawal. Early on the 23rd a naval demolition party under Lieutenant-Commander A. E. P. Welman was landed from the destroyer *Vimy*, together with a force of seamen and marines to cover the demolitions. They were given the somewhat unwarlike name of "Force Buttercup".

On their arrival they found the town under attack by tanks and infantry and also subjected to observed shellfire. Two battalions of the Irish Guards, the Welsh Guards, and other troops were still fighting a desperate rearguard action for the town, but by mid-afternoon almost the whole of Boulogne, except for a small bridge-head round the harbour area, was in the hands of the enemy. The destroyers *Keith* and *Whitshed* arrived in the early evening to carry out the evacuation as soon as the demolitions were completed, and they were subjected to a heavy air attack as well as to close-range mortar, machine-gun, and rifle fire which caused some damage and casualties, including Captain D. J. R. Simson of the *Keith* (D.19), who was killed. The destroyers, which were at the time evacuating wounded, were forced to leave harbour with their task uncompleted, but an hour and a half later were both back and continuing the work of rescue. They were joined later by the *Venetia*, *Venomous*, *Vimiera*, *Wild Swan*, and *Windsor* to assist with the evacuation of British and French soldiers. While the last of the demolition charges were being placed and fired, German tanks towing field guns appeared over the brow of the hill before the harbour and opened a heavy fire. The destroyers replied in a close-range action described by eye-witnesses ashore as "magnificent", and even as they fought back the work of embarkation went on undeterred by the falling shells. The *Venetia* was hit while she was in the narrow entrance channel, but she was swiftly brought under control and emerged safely. The *Venomous* had her rudder jammed while she steamed astern down the Channel, but steering with her engines, reached the open sea. The *Wild Swan*, following her out, grounded momentarily in the harbour, but got off and she, too, reached safety.

With all the destroyers loaded and gone, there still remained an estimated 1,000 troops in Boulogne. Admiral Ramsay therefore sent the *Vimiera* back for a second trip to the beleaguered port. She entered in darkness, to find all silent in the port area. After hailing the shore many times, her Commanding Officer received an answer and, going alongside the jetty, found not 1,000 but over 1,400 troops still awaiting evacuation. For an hour she lay there, the soldiers crowding aboard until only a small space around the guns had been left clear. As she slipped anchor and proceeded she was attacked from the air, one bomb exploding no more than twenty yards away. She reached Dover and landed over 1,400 men, to bring the total evacuated from Boulogne up to 4,500.

The *Keith*, *Venetia*, *Venomous*, *Whitshed*, and *Wild Swan* were all damaged in this small operation, and the naval casualties amounted to eighty-three officers and men. It was a taste, and not too palatable a one, of what the major operation at Dunkirk might bring.

By Sunday, 26th May, all hopes of a military counter-attack southwards, to link up the B.E.F. once more with the main French armies around the Maginot Line, had faded. One hope alone remained now, retirement to the coast and the establishment of a defensive perimeter while some, at any rate, of the troops ashore were withdrawn by sea. Lord Gort, in command of the B.E.F., telegraphed to the Secretary of State for War on the implications of this decision and wrote: "I must not conceal from you that a great part of the B.E.F. and its equipment will inevitably be lost, even in best circumstances."[7]

In the afternoon of that same Sunday the Admiralty, in the knowledge that withdrawal was now imminent, informed Vice-Admiral Ramsay that "it was imperative for 'Dynamo' to be implemented with the greatest vigour, with a view to lifting up to 45,000 of the B.E.F. within two days". And four hours later there went out from the Admiralty the historic signal, "Operation Dynamo is to commence".[8] It was three minutes before 7.0 p.m. Thirty-three minutes later the destroyer *Wolsey* left Dover to act as wireless link ship between the Admiral's office at Dover and the naval beach parties ashore at Dunkirk. And at 9.15 p.m. the armed boarding vessel *Mona's Isle* sailed from the Downs, the first of an armada of miscellaneous small ships which were to snatch an army from the encircling grip of the enemy. In spite of a fouled propeller in Dunkirk Harbour, near misses from shore-based enemy guns, and a machine-gun attack from the air which caused eighty-three casualties, the *Mona's Isle* reached Dover at noon on the 27th and disembarked 1,420 troops. It was a hopeful start.

Of the eight days of endeavour, which is now known universally by the all-embracing name of "Dunkirk", it is not possible to write in detail, for the number of ships which eventually made their way to those historic beaches is almost legion. The main problem which faced the Navy when the operation began was a twofold one: first, how best to use a port that was already heavily damaged and under almost constant attack from the air, and second, how to lift men off the ten miles of beaches which lay to the east of the town and to which no ship of any size could approach nearer than half a mile. As viewed from Admiral Ramsay's headquarters at Dover, these problems could only be solved by a combination of three factors: the local decisions of naval officers in charge ashore in the main embarkation areas as to the best use to which available ships and boats could be put, the ability of the Royal Air Force to provide some degree of protection from air attack for the ships engaged, and the orderly discipline of the men awaiting embarkation. And even given all three it was thought at Dover that the Admiralty's target figure of 45,000 men was unduly optimistic.

The experiences of the first full day of evacuation, 28th May, were not particularly hopeful, though they contained one useful lesson. Of the total of 17,804 men brought home, nearly 12,000 had been embarked from a single damaged breakwater in Dunkirk harbour, and only some 6,000 from the ten miles of beach which lay to the eastward of the town. It was at once apparent that the main volume of the evacuation must come through the port, with the beaches playing a subsidiary, though still extremely valuable, part. During the 29th the naval build-up of ships increased considerably as more destroyers, sloops, minesweepers, and patrol craft reached the Dover area from more distant stations. And at the same time the Admiralty cast their net far and wide for small boats to swell the numbers taken off the beaches. As a result of the increase in the number of ships, the day's total reached the satisfactory figure of 47,310, which might have been even larger had not false reports reached Dover in the evening that the harbour entrance at Dunkirk was blocked. As a result, ships were diverted to the beaches and a good opportunity was lost.

The total figures for the day, good as they undoubtedly were, had been achieved only at the cost of severe loss in the ships involved. German E-boats, lying off the shipping routes, had sunk two destroyers, the *Grafton* and *Wakeful*, and two more, the *Montrose* and *Mackay*, had been in collision and were badly damaged. A magnetic mine, of which large numbers were being laid by the enemy in the shallow waters around Dunkirk, had exploded under the personnel ship *Mona's Queen*, sinking her in less than two minutes. But worse losses still had come from the repeated enemy attacks from the air. Ships sunk by bombing attacks were the destroyer *Grenade*, the personnel ships *Normannia*, *Lorina*, and *Fenella*, the merchant ship *Clan Macalister*, the boarding vessel *King Orry*, and the special service vessel *Crested Eagle*, together with many small craft. And among the large number damaged by air attack were the destroyers *Gallant*, *Jaguar*, *Greyhound*, *Intrepid*, and *Saladin*, the sloop *Bideford*, and the personnel ship *Canterbury*.

For the next three days Operation "Dynamo" continued to run at full power, and the figures of men lifted from the port and the beaches reached impressive totals: 53,823 on 30th May, 68,014 on the 31st, and 64,429 on 1st June. On each of those three days it was the destroyers which brought home the bulk of the men, their great speed enabling them to cut many hours off the average time taken on a round trip. Losses, as on the 29th, were still grievously heavy, but the urgency of the problem, its importance to the whole future of the war, and, above all, the natural reluctance of one Service to let another one down, permitted a scale of losses to be accepted that might, in less vital circumstances, have caused an abandonment of the whole operation.

By midnight on 1st June the major part of the British Expeditionary Force was home, though as yet the operation was by no means concluded. Substantial numbers still remained, swelled daily by French and Belgian soldiers converging into the ever-narrowing bridgehead held around Dunkirk. On 2nd and 3rd June the great majority of men were embarked over the harbour jetty, the beaches contributing only 6,695 and 1,870 on the two days respectively. It was a measure of the contracting perimeter around Dunkirk, with all that it meant to the ships in the increased numbers of shore-based guns which the enemy could bring to bear.

By 3rd June the destroyer crews were approaching a state of exhaustion. With their speed, their endurance, and their guns to provide for themselves a measure of defence against attack, they were the best type of ship to use for the purpose, and naturally they were used to the utmost. One spare destroyer crew had been mustered at Dover to provide temporary reliefs and a chance of some rest to the exhausted men, but one spare crew among the forty-one destroyers engaged was not sufficient to give to them all the few hours of physical recuperation they needed. The normal exhaustion expected from prolonged operations was accelerated both by the additional hazards of the operation—the bombing attacks of unprecedented violence, the constant working in mined waters, the embarkation of troops in conditions of great difficulty and danger, the rescue of men from the sea often in a state of unbelievable physical distress, and the evidence of major defeat that surrounded the scene—and also by the fact that their ships were always so crowded with soldiers that even in their normal living spaces there was no room for them to lie down.

The last five destroyers to enter Dunkirk on the night of 2nd/3rd June returned to Dover almost empty. The reason was not, as Admiral Ramsay first thought, that all the available troops had been brought back, though it was true so far as British soldiers were concerned. There were many French troops still to come, but they had failed to make their appearance as originally arranged. This was not, in fact, the fault of the French, for they had had to mount a counter-attack to hold the perimeter east of Bergues.

Admiral Ramsay's belief that the operation was over, and far more successfully completed than anyone had dared to hope, was shattered by a signal from the Admiralty that evacuation from Dunkirk was to continue over the night 3rd/4th June. This led the Admiral to bring to the notice of the Admiralty the conditions of strain under which his ships' crews were working and to press that this extra night of evacuation should be the last, at least so far as the

Dover forces were concerned. His signal, which was sent during the afternoon of the 3rd, read:

"After nine days of operations of a nature unprecedented in naval warfare, which followed on two weeks of intense strain, commanding officers, officers, and ships' companies are at the end of their tether.

"I therefore view a continuance of the demands made by evacuation with the utmost concern as likely to strain to breaking-point the endurance of officers and men.

"I should fail in my duty did I not represent to Their Lordships the existence of this state of affairs in the ships under my command, and I consider it would be unfortunate, after the magnificent manner in which officers and men of the surviving ships have faced heavy loss and responded to every call made upon them, that they should be subjected to a test which I feel may be beyond the limit of human endurance.

"If therefore evacuation has to be continued after tonight I would emphasise in the strongest possible manner that fresh forces should be used for these operations, and any consequent delay in their execution should be accepted."[9]

But the Admiral knew that he could count on his ships' companies for this one last effort. In a signal to all the ships concerned he said:

"I hoped and believed that last night would see us through, but the French, who were covering the retirement of the British rearguard, had to repel a strong German attack and so were unable to send their troops to the pier in time to be embarked.

"We cannot leave our Allies in the lurch and I must call on all officers and men detailed for further evacuation tonight to let the world see that we never let down our Ally."

Admiral Ramsay did not call in vain. During the afternoon he learned that the estimated figure of those still awaiting evacuation was about 30,000, a total that was almost exactly the full lifting capacity of all his available ships, though to get them all on board during the hours of darkness would call for organisation ashore of a very high order. A number of French officers and ratings were added to the British pier parties in order to speed up the embarkation on the other side.

Of the forty-one destroyers which Admiral Ramsay had had under his command during the withdrawal, only nine now remained. It was, of course, these destroyers which would form the spearpoint of the night's evacuation, in spite of the fact that they, alone of all the ships engaged, had been employed on this work without a break from the start. With them went nine personnel ships, eleven minesweepers, and such other smaller ships and boats as could conveniently make the crossing in the time available. At the last moment Admiral Ramsay's plans for providing sufficient ships were nearly jeopardised when one of the personnel vessels, the *S.S. Manxman*, which had already made several trips to Dunkirk, refused to sail. Her place was gallantly taken by another, the *Royal Sovereign*.

Shortly after 10 p.m. the first ships arrived, the destroyer *Whitshed* leading them in. The harbour was very crowded and, moreover, made more dangerous by the large number of wrecks, many of them in the fairway. As the fifty or more ships arrived for this final lift there was a fresh easterly wind blowing which caused a choppy, confused sea off the entrance. Fortunately the ships were spared the added difficulty of fog, which was thick off the English coast at the time of their departure.

Inevitably there were a number of casualties from collision and grounding, but in the main this last night's effort went smoothly and quickly. Encouraged by the French contingents in the pier parties, the troops followed one another down to the two piers in a continuous stream and marched aboard quickly, enabling the ships to get away without waste of time.

The night's evacuation was due to end at 3.0 a.m., and when the last ship sailed five minutes after this time some 26,000 men had been embarked. The British pier party was brought home by the destroyer *Express*, which arrived at 2.30 a.m., and she made it the occasion to bring back 611 troops in addition to the pier party she had been sent to collect. As she left, enemy shells began to fall in the harbour area. The German guns were now within three miles of the port and the end had come.

There was, however, one final act before Dunkirk was abandoned to the enemy. From the Downs, at 8.30 p.m. on the 3rd, three specially prepared blockships had sailed for Dunkirk, their mission being to scuttle themselves in the fairway between the breakwater heads. They were led over by the destroyer *Shikari*. One, the *Gourko*, was sunk outside Dunkirk by a magnetic mine, but the other two scuttled themselves in the channel, though not completely blocking it. The *Shikari* improved the occasion by bringing back the French General Barthelémy and 382 troops. She was the last ship to leave Dunkirk.

In all, 338,226 men were brought back from Dunkirk. When the operation was begun the Admiralty had hoped for 45,000, and Admiral Ramsay, the man on the spot in command, had thought that an ambitious estimate. It was the ability of the Navy to control the waters of the Channel and of the Royal Air Force to keep back the worst of the German air power that had made it possible so greatly to improve upon the hoped-for figure. In spite of every threat to those narrow sea communications between England and the coast of France, threats by enemy E- and U-boats, by magnetic mine, by devastating attacks from the air, by the gunfire of shore-based batteries, those sea routes were held long enough to rescue an army from annihilation.

The cost in ships had been grievous, and the more so when it was realised, as it so quickly was, that it was just those types of ships which were to be so desperately required in the struggle ahead. Of the forty-one destroyers engaged, six were sunk and nineteen damaged, and the losses in other types of ships were in only slightly less proportion. Yet the cost was borne willingly and cheerfully, for it was an occasion that demanded none but heroic measures. And it was in the light of that national heroism in emergency that the sea around Dunkirk was thronged not only by naval ships and the vessels of many public authorities under naval control, but also by large numbers of small craft whose private owners, anxious to help, had taken their boats over unheralded into those danger-strewn waters. There was an echo of that private heroism in the award later, by the yachtsmen of America, of the Blue Water Medal, given only for deeds of outstanding courage, to the yachtsmen of Britain for the part they played in this great battle.

The evacuation of Dunkirk was widely hailed as a miracle. But the word too easily obscures the fact that it was a superb combined operation of all three Services carried through with tenacity, skill, and exemplary courage. To the hard fighting of the Army which held the enemy at bay on the ground, to the gallant way in which the Royal Air Force did continuous battle against heavy odds in the sky, and to the skill and fortitude of the Navy which fought its ships across to the other side and held the sea lanes open was due the success of Operation "Dynamo".

The successful withdrawal from Dunkirk, however, was not as yet the end of the land campaign in Europe. Even as the last troops were embarking at that shattered port, the War Cabinet was deciding to send three more divisions to France in an attempt to hold a new front on the Somme. This movement, in fact, started on 7th June with the passage of troops to Le Havre, but the rapidity with which the land situation deteriorated almost overtook the intention, and the troops were withdrawn again through that port and Cherbourg on the 11th.

The enemy advance, with Dunkirk now in their hands, gathered a fresh momentum. On 14th June the Germans were in Paris, on the 15th they crossed the Rhine at Strasbourg, on the 16th they broke through in Champagne, raced down behind the Maginot Line, and crossed the Loire. By dusk of the 17th they had occupied Orleans and Metz and had reached the Swiss frontier near Basle. All was over in the west, and the stillness of shattering defeat lay over the tortured land of France. A chapter in French history, and in the history of the war, was closing.

In the face of this swift and sudden onslaught there was no more that could be done than to accept the bitter fact that the campaign was over and to bring home as many more men as possible. The retreating British troops were directed on to the western Channel and Biscay ports, and thither again went the destroyers and the personnel ships, and also the liners *Otranto*, *Arandora Star*, *Strathaird*, *Georgic*, *Duchess of York*, *Batory*, *Sobieski*, *Franconia*, and

*Lancastria.* The evacuations from Cherbourg and St. Malo went smoothly, just over 52,000 men being brought home by the 17th, but those from the Biscay ports, being largely beyond the range of air cover from home, did not fare so well. In numbers of men brought home the figures were certainly impressive, 32,584 from Brest and 57,235 from St. Nazaire, but some heavy losses had to be accepted from German bombing attacks. The most grievous was that of the liner *Lancastria*, bombed and set on fire off the mouth of the River Loire. She was fully loaded at the time with nearly 6,000 troops, and some 3,000 of them lost their lives when she sank.

On the overall view, these evacuations were every bit as successful as those from Dunkirk and its beaches, though perhaps less spectacular. They owed their success very largely to the initiative and leadership of the destroyer captains. These young men, arriving usually without precise orders since precision was impossible in the unstable and constantly changing situation, had to take their own decisions in the light of local conditions as they found them. Throughout this difficult time their steadiness and general sagacity was admirable, their skill and enterprise beyond praise. To them many soldiers owed their lives and their liberty.

During the course of these Biscay port evacuations, another immediate problem was taxing the attention of the Board of Admiralty. This was the future of the French Fleet. To let it fall into the hands of the advancing Germans would be to present a hostage to fortune of incalculable magnitude. In Brest the great battleship *Richelieu* was in the last stages of completion, at St. Nazaire her sister-ship, the *Jean Bart*, was not so far advanced. These were but two units of a considerable fleet; the future employment by the German Navy of them or of the many other fine French ships did not bear contemplation for a moment.

At a meeting of the Supreme War Council held in France on 12th June, with the reality of defeat already casting its shadow before it, Admiral Darlan, the French Naval Commander-in-Chief, had stated categorically that the French Fleet would never be surrendered and that in the last resort he would send it to Canada. On the following day, at the 16th and last meeting of the Supreme War

Council to be held, it was reported by General Weygand that organised resistance was at an end and that the French Army was disintegrating into disconnected groups. The moment of Admiral Darlan's "last resort" had come and it was important now, before the final chance slipped away, to remove the French Fleet away from the German danger.

It was to hold Admiral Darlan to his word, expressed at the Supreme War Council meeting of 12th June, that Mr. A. V. Alexander, First Lord of the Admiralty, and Admiral Sir Dudley Pound, First Sea Lord, flew to Bordeaux on 18th June. They were met there with a complete reversal of French naval opinion, the Admiral declaring that his fleet must remain in French waters. All, however, was not lost, for there were French colonial waters still beyond the immediate reach of the enemy and it was thought that, for the time being and failing a more positive removal, there must be some reasonable grounds for belief that the ships would be safe enough there. Mr. Alexander, requiring an assurance to this effect from the highest authority, sought an interview with M. Lebrun, the President, to find only an overwrought man whose only words were, "Ma pauvre France, ma pauvre France," while the tears ran down his cheeks.

In the meantime the French defeat had been followed by repercussions in the political field. The French Prime Minister, M. Reynaud, had resigned on 16th June and his place was taken by Marshal Pétain, who by the following day had opened negotiations with the German leaders for an armistice. In Britain, as the anxious days followed, there was no knowledge of the terms which the Germans had imposed, though on 24th June, President Lebrun telegraphed to King George VI in London that, according to the armistice terms, the French Fleet could not be employed against Great Britain. And by this time the major French units were, in fact, beyond the enemy's reach. The *Richelieu* was at Dakar, the *Jean Bart* at Casablanca, the *Strasbourg* and *Dunkerque* at Oran and Mers-el-Kebir, while the main cruiser strength was divided between Toulon, Algiers, and Sfax.

Nevertheless, the War Cabinet was still worried. So much

depended on the French Fleet; the whole balance of sea power, now the only hope left to Britain of winning the war, hung poised precariously on the integrity of the German assurances to France. And there was no lack of evidence as to the value of a German assurance. The events of 1937, 1938, and 1939 were still of too recent occurrence to permit of much reliance on a Nazi promise. Even as the War Cabinet deliberated on this thorny problem events in the French Empire took a sinister turn. Mr. Duff Cooper and Lord Gort, who had been sent to North Africa to try to persuade former French ministers to set up an émigré government, were rebuffed by General Noguès, who refused to receive them, and Lord Dillon, of the British Mission in Algeria, reported that there was no hope of any resistance there and that the general attitude of the French Fleet in Algerian harbours was uncertain.

The stage was being set for the inevitable climax. The Chiefs of Staff, at a meeting on 30th June, set out five alternative courses of action with regard to the French Fleet. They discarded the first four and adopted the fifth, recommending that if concrete guarantees could not be obtained on agreement to demilitarise the ships or to sail them to transatlantic ports, action should be taken against the French Fleet at Oran. This decision was taken against a background of stark realism. Already there were obvious thoughts of invasion in the air, and the possible employment by Germany of French warships to support an assault across the Channel was to tip the balance of sea power decisively against Great Britain in that area. And in the longer view of attack against seaborne trade the possibility was equally unthinkable.

The War Cabinet, in fact, had itself come to the same conclusion as the Chiefs of Staff, though in deference to French susceptibilities the proposed action had been delayed. But with the publication of the Armistice terms all doubt came to an end. Clause 8 of the Armistice read: "Except for that part of the Fleet destined for the protection of colonial interests, all ships outside French territorial waters must be recalled to France." That requirement, it is true, was accompanied by a declaration that Germany had no intention of using those ships for her own purposes "except for supervision and minesweeping", but no one in Britain was prepared to place much reliance in such a declaration. Clause 8 was later modified by Hitler to allow of the French ships being disarmed in North African ports, though whether this information reached the British Government in time is in doubt. There was evidence, too, that the Germans had captured the French naval codes and ciphers and were already issuing orders in the name of the French Commander-in-Chief.[10] So the die was cast, and orders issued for action against the ships of our former ally.

On the morning of 3rd July all French ships in British ports were boarded and occupied, with on the whole only minor resistance. The French squadron at Alexandria, after anxious deliberation, accepted a demand to immobilise itself. But at Oran the British demands were refused and force became necessary. Vice-Admiral Sir James Somerville, in command of Force H, based at Gibraltar to guard the western Mediterranean, was compelled to open fire and, at a range of 15,000 yards, did considerable damage. The *Dunkerque*, attempting to escape, was damaged and ran aground, the old battleship *Bretagne* was sunk, the *Provence* was hit and beached, and some smaller ships damaged. But the *Strasbourg*, accompanied by five destroyers, succeeded in escaping and reached Toulon in safety.[11] Five days later action was taken against the *Richelieu* at Dakar.[12] In two separate attacks, one by the Fleet Air Arm operating from the *Hermes*, and one by depth charges dropped by a motor-boat, she was damaged aft and put temporarily out of action.

These unhappy operations at Oran and Dakar, as painful and unpleasant to the British Navy as to the French, left behind them an unpleasant legacy of suspicion and distrust. It was, perhaps, epitomised in the action of M. Cambon, the French Ambassador in London. After the attack on Oran he called on the Foreign Secretary to say that he was resigning his post since he feared he might have to make a communication on behalf of his Government which, after having lived in England for twenty-five years, he would not wish to make.

The collapse of France and all that it meant to the security of Great Britain was not, of course, the only problem facing the War

Cabinet and the Chiefs of Staff Committee. On 10th June, stimulated by the startling success of the other end of her Axis, Italy declared war on France and Britain. Her intervention had long been expected and a general plan of operations in such an event had been formulated in the Anglo-French staff conversations of May 1939. But whereas that general plan had envisaged a France strong and active in the western Mediterranean, the situation in those waters was now very different. It was in the light of this French naval vacuum in the new area of hostilities that the Chiefs of Staff presented to the War Cabinet a memorandum[13] covering the essential strategy required to safeguard the vital Middle East area. The minimum requirement for the successful prosecution of the war, they laid down, was the complete denial to the enemy of Egypt and the Sudan, from whose territories the Suez Canal could be controlled; the successful defence, if attacked, of Iraq for the control of oil supplies in Iraq and Persia; of Palestine, which controlled the terminus of the oil pipeline at Haifa; of Aden, essential for the control of the Red Sea route for shipping; and of Kenya, as a second line of defence in Africa should Egypt fall.

The naval implications of this strategical outline, apart from the essential maintenance of capital ship fleets based on Gibraltar and in the eastern Mediterranean, rested firmly on the ability of the Navy to guarantee the passage of merchant ships across the oceans necessary to maintain the requisite British forces in the vital Middle Eastern area. The Italian intervention had automatically made the Mediterranean untenable as an ocean highway for normal merchant shipping, and although both ends of that inland sea were firmly held by British naval might, every movement of ships to reinforce the eastern end, except for a few fast merchant ships, heavily escorted, and, of course, naval reinforcements, had inevitably to take the long journey around the Cape. This was to strain the resources of the Navy almost beyond breaking-point, yet there could be no alternative. The only hope of a successful outcome to the conflict depended in the final analysis on the ability of Britain to keep her Merchant Navy sailing, and it rested on that alone.

The task, in those anxious days, was stupendous. At home,

across the Channel and apparently preparing to spring, lay the German military might, a force so powerful, so wonderfully integrated, that it had swept the Army of France into the dust in a single month of fighting. Absolute priority at home was given to operations necessary to resist the expected invasion,[14] a priority that called for substantial naval forces, especially in cruisers, destroyers, and small coastal craft. Four flotillas of destroyers, based on the Humber, Harwich, Sheerness, and either Dover or Portsmouth, were to form the spearhead of attack on any seaborne invasion fleet, and behind them, in immediate support, eight cruisers were disposed along the east, south, and west coasts. Much of this anti-invasion force had to come from the Home Fleet and, indeed, the heavy units of that fleet were ordered to accept any risk from air attack, U-boat, or E-boat, in order to close the scene of action should invasion forces actually attempt the sea crossing.[15]

Responsible naval opinion remained unconvinced of the necessity for all these measures. In spite of the German concentration on the opposite shore, in spite of the heavy enemy air attacks across the Channel, it was, as the Navy well knew, in command of the sea that the ultimate decision lay. It was this knowledge, so deep and so fundamental, that enabled naval confidence to remain quite unshaken by enemy threats. Admiral Forbes protested, though in vain, against this immobilisation of his cruisers and destroyers, so urgently needed about their proper naval business of dealing with the armed raiders and the U-boats. The War Cabinet and the Chiefs of Staff, however, remained adamant, and these naval preparations to repel the invasion held the day.

There were, too, the problems of the Atlantic and the home trade to add to the Admiralty's preoccupations. The acquisition by Germany of additional U-boat and air bases in Norway was bad enough, shortening the U-boats' passage to their operational areas by some 1,200 miles and more, but the new bases acquired by the Dutch, Belgian, and French collapse made the problem infinitely more serious. While France still stood, the passage of the English Channel had been effectively denied to the enemy, partly by surface patrols and fixed shore defences and partly by a mine barrage across the Dover Straits. Three U-boats had already come to grief in an attempt to force this barrage. But the Channel was now open to German ships, for they could rely on continuous air cover throughout, provided from the fine French airfields which had fallen into German hands. The coastal convoys along the eastern and southern coasts of Britain were now easier to attack, both by German E-boats, operating from Dutch, Belgian, and French bases, and by the German Air Force, whose new French airfields so greatly increased the range of action of their aircraft into British waters.

In the Atlantic, too, the intensity of the battle was certain to increase. During the campaign for Norway and for France the U-boats had been largely withdrawn from their Atlantic areas to support those operations. But now they were beginning to stream back, and from new bases that offered them incalculable advantages. There was a slight delay in the German operational use of the Biscay ports, due to the Allied demolitions, but Lorient was ready early in July[16] and the first U-boat entered it on the 7th of that month. Brest and La Pallice quickly followed, and a long-range air reconnaissance unit, to co-operate in the attack on Atlantic shipping, was established at Lorient in the first week of August. A measure of the increasing U-boat onslaught was the steep rise in the shipping loss for June (58 ships of 284,113 tons) and July (38 ships of 195,825 tons), nearly all of them in the Atlantic. These were casualties due to the U-boats alone; other causes almost doubled these figures.

Inevitably, this increasing pace of attack on shipping resulted in urgent calls for more escorts, the smaller warships whose presence alone could add to the security of the ocean and coastal convoys. These calls came at an impossible time. Not only was the absolute priority given to anti-invasion duties necessarily tying up large numbers of destroyers in a vital role, but the losses suffered in Norwegian waters and in the evacuations from the French coast had already seriously reduced the number available. Out of a total strength of 178 destroyers, no fewer than 66 were still under repair. By a severe cutting of commitments elsewhere the anti-invasion forces were provided, but the resulting margin of defence was desperately slender. That the anti-invasion destroyers played a vital, and even decisive, part in persuading Hitler first to postpone and finally to abandon the proposed invasion of Britain can be discovered from the German archives,[17] even though, indeed, they fought no battle in their anti-invasion role.

And in the meantime, with the naval forces at home stretched to their ultimate limit, war in the Mediterranean had been a reality since 10th June. In their appreciation of future strategic policy formulated by the Chiefs of Staff at the beginning of July,[18] it was stressed that our general strategy must remain defensive until two main objectives were achieved, the first to expand all our forces with the greatest possible speed in order to prevent the enemy from gaining a decision in the near future, the second to reach the production totals of war equipment aimed at as necessary before the French collapse. This, indeed, was a far more formidable task than it might appear, for it meant that the French quota of production was now to be added as an additional burden on British factories. What made the task of even more gigantic proportions was that to the war against Germany in the Atlantic and the nearer seas was now added the burden of war against Italy in the Mediterranean.

Yet there were rays of light in the darkness. Great Britain did not at this anxious hour, as so many have described, stand alone against the enemy. The Dominions were still in the fight with growing forces of men and ships. And in Britain herself were substantial forces of Poles, Norwegians, Dutch, Belgians, and French, with parts of their navies which had escaped from the Nazi onslaught, and a large proportion, too, of their merchant navies to swell the Allied shipping pool. They, too, were standing firm in the hour of danger. An even brighter ray of light shone out on 4th July when the President of the United States agreed to technical naval discussions between the two countries taking place in London. It was a gesture which showed the direction in which American sympathies lay.

Although, through force of circumstances, British major strategy was now based on strict defence, it did not mean that no offensive action could be taken. Pure defence could well prove dangerous in the psychological atmosphere it generated, as well as being an invitation to Germany to hit us when and where she could. Under the instigation of Mr. Churchill measures were put in hand to make the enemy "wonder when they were going to be struck next instead of enforcing us to wall in the island and roof it over".[19] Steps were taken to train forces especially suitable for raiding operations and instructions issued to press on with the development and production of special landing-craft. The organisation of a separate Combined Operations Headquarters was also set up, with general instructions to plan raids on enemy-occupied coasts.

The same spirit of offence within the general defensive strategy was plainly apparent in the naval war against Italy. The initiative in the central and western Mediterranean lay inevitably in the hands of the Italian Fleet, supported as it was by reasonable air cover from shore-based airfields. It might well have been theirs in the eastern Mediterranean as well had the spirit been willing. The necessary offensive spirit, however, was not there. Although Mussolini had issued a directive that the Italian Navy was to assume "the offensive at all points in the Mediterranean and outside", Admiral Cavagnari, the Italian Chief of Naval Staff, had already decided that discretion was the better part of valour and that his Navy's strategy must be defensive in view of the importance of Italian communications to North Africa. Only in the disposition of his U-boats did the Italian Admiral show any desire to assume the offensive spirit. As an opening gambit he had some fifty out on patrol, but these suffered such severe losses in the first few days of the Mediterranean war that the numbers, and their patrol areas, were both speedily curtailed. Nine of them were sunk before the end of June and a tenth had stranded on a reef in the Red Sea and become a total loss.

Admiral Cunningham's main preoccupation during these early weeks of the Mediterranean war was to keep the Italian Fleet out of the eastern Mediterranean and the Ægean, and thus to secure for British ships the ability to carry essential supplies for the fighting forces in that area, as well as to cut off seaborne supplies to the Italian Dodecanese islands. With his limited forces, especially in flotilla ships and aircraft, there was little else that he could do. So much of Britain's potential for waging war was locked up in the

Middle East in the shape of the oilfields of Iraq and Persia that it had become an area of paramount importance to the whole prosecution of the war. Its integrity from Axis attack or infiltration depended on the few British troops and aircraft scattered thinly over its wide area, backed by the strength and the resolution of the Mediterranean Fleet. If that failed, all was lost.

But Admiral Cunningham had also another problem, even less easy of solution. In the central Mediterranean, less than half an hour's flying time from Italian airfields, less than twelve hours' steaming from the Italian naval base at Taranto, lay Malta. Almost the first warlike act of the Italians was to raid the island, and Italian aircraft were dropping bombs there only five hours after the declaration of war. Pre-war neglect and wartime priorities in other spheres had left Malta virtually defenceless, and supplies were now an urgent necessity. Their passage to Malta and the corresponding evacuation of unrequired personnel and stores from Malta gave to the Commander-in-Chief the opportunity to strike offensively in the central Mediterranean while still remaining within the general defensive strategy enjoined by the Chiefs of Staff. Admiral Cunningham was quick to seize the chance.

The first brush with the enemy fleet came on 9th July, when both navies were covering the passage of convoys, the British to Malta, the Italian to North Africa. An air reconnaissance report from Malta provided the first intimation that the Italians were out, and the two fleets sighted each other during the course of the afternoon. The engagement was at long range and indecisive, with the Italians turning away at high speed under cover of smoke after the battleship *Giulio Cesare* and the cruiser *Bolzano* had been hit.

The action was of importance not only in the indication it gave to Admiral Cunningham of the probable Italian reactions in future encounters between surface ships but also as the first step in the establishment of moral ascendancy over the Italians at sea. In general, the British ships were slower than the Italian, type for type, by from two to five knots, and any Italian unwillingness to stand and fight would need to be overcome by other means. An obvious answer to that was the carrier, with the ability of her aircraft to reach out ahead of the fleet and slow down the enemy by torpedo attack.

At the time of this action Admiral Cunningham had only the obsolescent *Eagle* as a carrier, though he was shortly to be reinforced by the new *Illustrious.* She arrived in the Mediterranean in September, and in November came the opportunity to put into practice a plan that the Commander-in-Chief had long wished to try. This was an attack by naval aircraft on the Italian Fleet as it lay at anchor in its base at Taranto. Before this operation could be carried out the Italians were to experience once more the mettle of Admiral Cunningham's ships when the cruiser *Colleone* was sunk off Crete by H.M.A.S. *Sydney* and the 2nd Destroyer Flotilla.

The opportunity to attack the Italian Fleet at Taranto was presented partly by the arrival at Gibraltar of further reinforcements for the Mediterranean Fleet and partly by a diversionary air attack from the carrier *Ark Royal*, of Force H, on enemy airfields in Sardinia. Accompanied by Admiral Sir James Somerville's Force H, based on Gibraltar, the reinforcements steamed east through the Mediterranean to Malta, where guns and men were disembarked, while the *Ark Royal* was detached to carry out her part in the programme. The reinforcements then steamed on towards Alexandria with part of the Mediterranean Fleet in company. Meanwhile the *Illustrious*, screened by four cruisers (which later carried out an operation of their own in the Adriatic in which they destroyed an enemy convoy) and four destroyers, proceeded to a position off the west coast of Greece and from there flew off on the evening of 11th November two striking forces of Swordfish, one of twelve aircraft and one of nine. The late evening weather was ideal, with the moon nearly at the full and extensive thin cloud at about 8,000 feet. The two striking forces left the *Illustrious* at about 8.30 p.m. and 9.30 p.m. respectively.

An hour and a half after take-off they were over Taranto. Surprise was complete, and although the port was strongly defended with balloons, anti-torpedo nets, and anti-aircraft guns, the twenty-one Swordfish scored a resounding success. The new battleship *Littorio* was hit by three torpedoes and put out of action for five months, the older battleships *Cavour* and *Duilio* each received one torpedo hit and the former was sunk. A cruiser and a destroyer were hit by bombs and in addition damage was done to port installations. Only two aircraft failed to return from this daring and well-conceived raid, which was, in the words of Admiral Cunningham, probably unsurpassed in history as an example of economy of force.

Although only one of the three Italian battleships was permanently disabled, the temporary loss of the other two from the active fleet had a profound effect on the balance of naval power throughout the Mediterranean as a whole. The vigorous action by Admiral Somerville's ships from Gibraltar and by Admiral Cunningham's from Alexandria was driving the enemy back to such an extent that there were sanguine hopes of being able to reopen the Mediterranean route for special convoys. The success at Taranto added to those hopes. Such a convoy did, in fact, get through during the last week in November, and its passage led to another brush with the Italian Fleet, this time by Admiral Somerville's forces, off Cape Spartivento, the southern tip of Sardinia.

The result, as in Admiral Cunningham's action of 9th July, was completely inconclusive. After a brief action at very long range the Italian force retired at full speed, and torpedo bombers from the *Ark Royal*, as had their brothers from the *Eagle* in the former action, failed to stop them. Rather than continue a chase that would lead him not only unduly close to enemy coastal waters but still farther from the convoy whose safety was his prime object, Admiral Somerville called off the hopeless pursuit and rejoined the merchant ships. For this he was criticised in London, but an investigation by Admiral of the Fleet Lord Cork and Orrery found that his action was not only fully justified by the circumstances but the only correct one in view of the failure of the *Ark Royal*'s aircrews to hit their targets. As yet, mainly because of the very rapid expansion of the Fleet Air Arm, pilots and observers had not reached the high degree of training and experience so necessary for sea operations of this nature. It was another legacy of that unhappy pre-war policy which had denied to the Navy control of its own air arm.

In the meantime, around the coasts and over the mainland of

England had been fought the Battle of Britain. In its essentials it was an air war, fought for the mastery of the skies as a prelude to invasion. To the Royal Air Force as a whole, to Fighter Command in the main, and to No. 11 Group of that Command in particular, must go the major credit for that astounding victory. The odds they faced were tremendous, their losses were heavy and grievous, the courage and tenacity with which pilots again and again hurled themselves at the invading aircraft was beyond all praise. But while the losses of fighters themselves could be replaced from stock and from an expanding production, the losses among the pilots themselves was a far more serious matter. The loan of fifty-eight pilots from the Fleet Air Arm, some of them straight from the naval fighter school at Yeovilton, to help fly the Spitfires and Hurricanes was little more than a drop in the ocean, and it required the drastic switching of pilots from Bomber and Coastal Commands, a wider use of trained pilots from among the Poles, Czechs, Norwegians, Belgians, Dutch, and French forces who had escaped to Britain, and the great-hearted endeavour of some American volunteers who banded themselves together into an "Eagle" Squadron to fight for Britain, to keep up the number.

Below this battle in the skies was fought the battle of the coastal waters. Hitler's plan to defeat Britain lay not so much in invasion, which in fact was to be the last resort, but in the strangulation of trade and the obliteration of war production by bombardment from the air. In the wake of the German armies came the E-boats, pushing their bases farther and farther west until they reached Cherbourg during the second half of June. They coupled attacks on merchant shipping with offensive minelaying in the Thames Estuary, and they became a thorn in the side of the coastal convoy system. Heavy air attacks on ports and shipping also claimed their victims, and the calls for naval protection increased considerably. Nor was pure offence neglected, and during these anxious months the German "invasion" ports in Europe between Delfzijl and Le Havre several times suffered from the weight and accuracy of naval bombardment.

This was the traditional naval defence against invasion, tried and proved through centuries of experience. It was based on the close watch on the invasion forces by flotilla vessels; in the old days by sloops, cutters, and gun-vessels, in 1940 by destroyers, motor torpedo boats, and gunboats. Behind them lay the immediate stiffening of the defence by more powerful ships; in earlier years by fourth and fifth rates, today by cruisers. And behind them again lay the final safeguard of all, the immense strength of the battle-fleet to be called into action when the invasion forces sailed. Here, in 1940, across the waters, stood the army of Hitler, as before them had stood the armies of Napoleon, of Louis XIV, of Philip II of Spain. Between them all and their hearts' desire had stood the Navy of Britain. Between Hitler and his it still stood. As the days and the weeks passed, as the barges and the transports, collected with so much dislocation of normal trade, still remained stationary in their ports, the Lords of the Admiralty could say, in the words of the Earl of St. Vincent, a former First Lord of 150 years ago, that being a military question he hesitated to express an opinion about invasion as such. All he knew was that an invasion could not come by sea.

But beyond the drama being played out across the waters of the English Channel and the southern North Sea there still remained the major task of the war, the crux on which rested the whole war strategy of the nation. Two vital requirements dictated the broad pattern of naval endeavour, the need to re-establish the ring of sea power around a Germany now vastly swollen by her dramatic conquests and by the entry into the war of Italy, and the vital need to maintain the regular flow of merchant shipping on which the whole ability of the nation to continue the fight depended. Both were made immeasurably more difficult by the collapse of the European campaign.

Far out in the Atlantic the line of sea power had now to be re-established. With the ports of Norway at his disposal, Hitler could now command the eastern North Sea up to the Arctic Circle, a wide corridor of ingress and egress for U-boats, armed raiders, and the occasional blockade runner. From the ports on the Biscay coast the U-boats could reach farther out into the Atlantic, and the raiders and blockade runners could penetrate in comparative safety deep into the oceans before they reached waters in which British sea power could stretch out its long arm to seize them. And from the Biscay airfields the German long-range Focke-Wulfs could search the Atlantic waters for convoys and report their positions to the hungry U-boats.

The lesson of Norway, the lesson of Dunkirk, the lesson of the anti-invasion operations all pointed towards one inescapable fact, that ships at sea could not operate in waters dominated by enemy air power. Thus the ring around the central powers must needs be drawn beyond the range of their aircraft. Britain, outflanked now to south and east, had need to guard well the north and west if she were not to perish. So, northward, British sea power stretched out to Iceland and across the Denmark Straits to the coast of Greenland. Westward, it reached from Northern Ireland out into the Atlantic, sweeping widely down to the south, to Gibraltar, and to Freetown in Sierra Leone. And to complete the circle the sea communications of the eastern Mediterranean were held by the Mediterranean Fleet, stretching up from Malta to the western coast of Greece.

Within this tenuous circle were held the Axis powers. It was the barrier through which they must break if they were to reach the raw materials of the outer world. It could not as yet be held strongly enough to prevent the raiders slipping through, nor would it ever stop the U-boats. But it could, and did, effectively cut off the vast majority of the seaborne trade without which Hitler and Mussolini could not win their war. This was a task as old as the Navy itself, a task for which the fund of knowledge and experience reached back through history as far as the Dutch wars of Cromwell and Charles II. It had in turn defeated the Dutch, the Spanish, the French, and more recently the Germans themselves in the previous war. Though the weapons of sea power had changed, the principles still remained the same, and the Navy could face this new task with a confidence born of intimate knowledge and experience.

This was the barrier which had to be held at all costs, for if victory were to come it had to serve a dual purpose. It had to do more than stop the seaborne trade of Germany and Italy; while containing them it had to make possible the slow build-up of British power against the day when national strategy could abandon the defensive for the offensive. Behind its strength must come the vast imports of oil, steel, guns, tanks, aircraft, and food, without which there was no future but defeat. Behind it must come the men, from the Dominions and Colonies and later from the United States, who would add their strength to the armies that, one day, would have to fight again in Europe. And behind it, too, must sail the troops and the stores to strengthen those other theatres of war, in Africa and later in the Far East, where it was vital to hold the enemy.

In those summer months of 1940 the task appeared stupendous. It is not easy now, writing so many years after the event, to recapture the spirit that so vividly animated the nation at war. It is to be read, perhaps, in the speeches at that time of the Prime Minister; it is to be glimpsed in a study of the statistics and the reports of the battle for Britain; it is to be sensed in the courage of fighter pilots who won their fight against tremendous odds, in the doggedness of an Army that, tired, defeated, and snatched at the last moment from annihilation, turned again without weapons to defend their country from invasion, to the tenacity of a Navy that had faced savage losses to bring the Army home but had still found the ships and the men to stand between the enemy and his ultimate victory, and to a civilian population that volunteered in its millions to fight, in the Home Guard and with makeshift weapons, the superbly trained armies of the would-be invaders. It was the spirit of a nation under arms, its courage and determination fortified by adversity and danger.

And in this spirit the Navy could not fail. The Royal Air Force had won their battle in the skies and the nation, watching in breathless admiration, could breathe again. It was for the Navy now to win the greater battle of the seas, to give to Britain the chance, behind its shield, to rebuild her shattered strength.

# Chapter 4

## ATLANTIC, MEDITERRANEAN, AND MATAPAN

THE preoccupation, during the summer and autumn of 1940, of British naval forces with the threat of seaborne invasion across the Channel inevitably reduced the number of ships available for anti-submarine operations in the Atlantic. What was equally inevitable was that, released from their duties in the Norwegian and French campaigns, the U-boats would return to the Atlantic in the greatest force that they could muster. And to supplement the depredations of the U-boats, a "wave" of six armed merchant raiders was sent out, partly to add to the expected harvest of merchant shipping, and partly to draw away the defence in order to ease the task of the U-boats.

Such hopes as the enemy had pinned on the threat of invasion as a knock-out blow against Britain faded as the summer and autumn passed without any sign of faltering in British resolution. In its place, other means of obtaining the victory came up for consideration. To Admiral Raeder, Commander-in-Chief of the German Navy, these means were already apparent. The vulnerability of Great Britain to a sustained attack on her trade was as well appreciated by the German naval leaders as it was by those of Britain, for it was the traditional chink in any island nation's armour. It was, perhaps, fortunate that other war leaders in Germany were less versed in the profound effect that sea power could exercise in any campaign against a maritime nation. Both Keitel and Goering, commanding the Army and Air Force respectively, had their own theories to pursue and their own priorities to nurse, and between them they succeeded in diverting from the Navy, and thus from the U-boat arm, a reasonably large proportion of the available manufacturing potential. This competition in priorities was referred to Hitler who, though paying frequent lip-service to Raeder's demands,[1] was by this time already too much involved with more grandiose schemes to concern himself with these inter-Service squabbles. He was engaged in working out details of Operation "Felix", which was the capture of Gibraltar, and of the possibility of acquiring one of the Canary Islands from Spain in exchange for French Morocco.[2] As a result Germany had no more U-boats in September 1940 than she had in September 1939, and by that much the attack against the weakest link in the British chain was eased. Italian U-boats, operating in the Atlantic from Bordeaux, were not in sufficient strength greatly to affect the issue.

The U-boat attack was still further eased by two more decisions of that autumn, one American, one British. Towards the end of August 1940 an offer was received from the United States of fifty obsolete destroyers in exchange for facilities for the construction of American naval bases, to be held on long leases, in Newfoundland, Bermuda, the Bahamas and certain West Indian Islands, and British Guiana. It came at a time of increasingly heavy losses in the Atlantic when the need for more escorts, of any sort, was urgent in the extreme. The offer was accepted gratefully, and the first of the American "four-stackers", to be absorbed into the Royal Navy as "Town" class destroyers, began to arrive at the end of September. They were committed to the Atlantic battle almost immediately.

The second decision was an internal one. On 3rd October the Admiralty put forward a memorandum to the Chiefs of Staff advocating the acceptance of a "period of relief" in the event of ports on the south or east coast being occupied by German invasion forces. This might mean, in certain cases, a period of as much as three days before adequate naval forces could arrive on the scene, but it would free immediately twelve destroyers and thirty anti-submarine trawlers for more vital work on the trade routes. The memorandum was accepted by the Chiefs of Staff and, on their recommendation, confirmed by the War Cabinet, who were no doubt fortified in their decision by messages, received the same day from the British Ambassadors in Ankara and Sofia, that they had received information to the effect that the German Government did not now expect to succeed in invading England.

The capture by the enemy of northern France and the Biscay coast not unexpectedly made the use of the south-western approaches to Britain too precarious a route for ocean convoys. The area was far too close to the new U-boat and air bases of the enemy to be used with any measure of security from attack. So, from June 1940 onwards, both incoming and outgoing convoys were routed to the north of Ireland, and plans were made to establish the main naval and air headquarters for the battle of the Atlantic at Liverpool instead of Plymouth. This new headquarters, under Admiral Sir Percy Noble, was set up early in 1941.

Until this time the general pattern of convoy had entailed anti-submarine escort for outgoing convoys to a point about 200 miles west of Ireland. From there the merchant ships sailed unescorted in company for a further twenty-four hours before the convoys dispersed and ships proceeded independently to their destinations. The anti-submarine escort which had taken them out then met an incoming convoy, which had been brought over by an ocean escort consisting normally of an armed merchant cruiser, and returned with it through the U-boat areas to its British destination.

The new U-boat bases in France, of course, made it essential to extend the distance of close anti-submarine escort farther out into the Atlantic. Ideally, and as a measure to be adopted at the earliest possible moment, anti-submarine escort for the whole of a convoy's passage was recognised as the ultimate necessity, but neither in June 1940, nor, indeed, for some months to come, did the necessary long-endurance escorts exist. In July the limit of close escort was extended another hundred or so miles westward, with a further extension again in October, but it was not until June of the following year that total anti-submarine escort across the Atlantic was established, and still another month was to pass before convoys bound to the southward could be given continuous anti-submarine escort as far as Freetown, in Sierra Leone.

With these physical limitations in the extent of convoy protection, limitations caused by the shortage of escort vessels and their lack of long endurance, the U-boats and raiders made hay while the sun shone for them. July, August, September, and October of 1940 all saw heavy merchant ship losses in the Atlantic, the U-boats alone sinking 217 ships of more than 1,100,000 tons during those 123 days. It was a period which the U-boat commanders themselves called "the happy time", for they achieved these gigantic figures with a loss to themselves of no more than six of their own craft. Among the U-boat commanders operating during these months were many of their best-known "aces", men like Prien—who had penetrated the defences of Scapa Flow in October 1939 to sink the battleship *Royal Oak*—Schepke and Kretschmer—both of whom were decorated for sinking over 100,000 tons of shipping—Endrass, Frauenheim, and two or three others. Between them, these few captains were responsible for the major part of the sinkings, though the others were not far behind them.

Their task was immensely facilitated by the inadequacy of the escort, both in numbers and range. Operating from their new Biscay bases, even the smaller 500-ton U-boats could establish patrol areas as much as 600 miles to the westward, far beyond the point where the anti-submarine escort could meet the incoming convoys. There was little opposition to them out there and their targets were virtually defenceless. In closer waters the great majority of their sinkings were of ships proceeding independently or of stragglers from existing convoys, and the lesson from this fact was not difficult to learn. Only through adequate end-to-end convoy and exemplary convoy discipline could the losses be lowered. The straggler took her life in her own hands.

During September the U-boats in the Atlantic began to pose a new problem to the defence. Anti-submarine warfare was based on the dual combination of asdic and depth charge, the first to locate, the second to destroy. To the U-boat making a conventional submerged attack it was a formidable foe. But the asdic could not locate

U-boats on the surface, and it was from the surface, in order to escape the asdic's probing beam, that the U-boats now began to attack. They came in at night, using the darkness to shroud themselves from visual detection.

With the surface attack at night came the birth of the "wolf-pack" tactics. In its essentials this was no more than the concentration of U-boats in the path of an oncoming convoy. A first convoy sighting was no longer followed by an individual attack, but by long-range shadowing and reporting until the pack had been assembled. Only then was the mass attack unleashed, to swamp the inadequate escort by sheer weight of numbers and to take a savage toll of the unfortunate merchant ships. In September two successive convoys[3] were attacked by a pack of ten U-boats north-west of Ireland, and sixteen ships were sunk out of them. And in October the toll was heavier still. Again it was two North Atlantic convoys[4] that suffered, a pack of eight U-boats attacking them on four successive nights. They were aided by bright moonlight and they sank no fewer than thirty-two ships.

There was at first little answer to this method of attack. The asdic was useless; the U-boat, with its tiny silhouette, almost invisible in the darkness. What was needed was, first, a method of surface location in the dark, and then of turning night into day in the area of location in order to illuminate the attack. Ship-borne radar was the answer to the first requirement, and "snowflake", an artificial illuminant more efficient than searchlight or starshell, the answer to the second. Both these, however, still lay in the future so far as the anti-submarine escort was concerned.

Another answer, and one which was to develop into a truly powerful deterrent to the U-boats, was air escort of the convoys. In combination with ship escort, virtually complete protection was assured, for the aircraft, ranging over the convoy area, forced the shadowing U-boat to submerge and thus to lose touch. When fitted with ASV (airborne radar), escorting aircraft had an even wider range of effectiveness, for their sets could detect surfaced U-boats in thick weather where the human eye would fail. But in this early period of the battle the necessary numbers of long-range aircraft did not exist in Coastal Command, and there were insufficient carriers to remedy the lack by the provision of ship-borne aircraft over the convoys.

For the time being, therefore, there was little more to be done than to try, through evasive routing, to divert the convoys clear of the estimated positions of the U-boats. This, at best, was a hazardous answer, for although some of the best brains in the Navy were concentrated in the U-boat Tracking Room at the Admiralty, they were at this period but groping in the dark for the key. Later, as the raw material of Naval Intelligence improved, the Tracking Room was to achieve some spectacular successes.

Yet, for all the inadequate weapons and the shortage of escorts, both surface and air, the convoys came through. Some, of course, were never found by the U-boats and reached their destinations unscathed, others suffered the full force of the enemy's onslaught. Those were grim months in the Atlantic, months when death stalked across the waters, to strike suddenly and savagely in the dark and the cold of a North Atlantic night. The fate of Britain hung in the balance, poised precariously on the maintenance of her merchant shipping routes with the outer world. Only courage and endurance were left to sustain the savage battle that was being waged across the oceans, both to bring in the vital imports on which the whole life of the nation depended and to take out those reinforcements to the Middle East on which the whole structure of British strategy now rested.

These months, indeed, exemplified the "finest hour" of the seamen of Britain and her maritime Allies. Men, taken from the sea and still suffering from exposure after their ships had been sunk, would use the occasion of their first stepping ashore again to ask for another ship. Captains and crews, in port after a hazardous crossing, would speed the turn-about of their ships to make them the more quickly available for the next convoy. The officers and men of the escort vessels drove themselves to the very edge of endurance, and beyond. Of all the weapons that were arrayed against the U-boats in this tremendous battle, there were only courage and endurance that were never in short supply.

U-boats, however, were not the only cause of maritime loss. The first squadron of long-range reconnaissance Focke-Wulf "Kondor" aircraft, based near Bordeaux, began to operate out into the Atlantic in August with a dual role, reporting the positions of convoys and attacking stragglers or ships routed independently. During the four months from July to October 1940 they added another 290,000 tons of shipping to the total loss, quite apart from the indirect damage they caused through locating convoys for the U-boats.

Farther afield, in the wastes of the South Atlantic, Pacific, and Indian Oceans, the armed raiders too were reaping their harvest. Six had set out from German ports between the end of March and the beginning of July, and all were still at large. With the virtual closing of the Mediterranean to through traffic by the entry of Italy into the war, almost all reinforcements to the Middle East theatre were forced to take the long sea route around the Cape of Good Hope. These troop convoys all required an ocean escort, absorbing the whole of the cruiser strength of the stations through which they passed. There were none left from which to provide raider-hunting groups such as had been formed to search out the *Graf Spee* in 1939.

Nor, indeed, were raider-hunting groups the correct answer to the problem. The raiders picked their victims from the large numbers of Allied ships which still crossed the oceans unescorted. Nothing was easier for them than to pounce upon some single ship, capture or sink her, and then disappear again into the vast open spaces of the oceans. To try to track them down was a naval undertaking of a magnitude far beyond the resources of the local Commanders-in-Chief, a task greater indeed than that of searching for the proverbial needle in the haystack. In terms of normal visibility from a masthead look-out it was, in absolute fact, the equivalent of trying to find the needle in a hayfield of just over sixty acres in area.

In the light of after-knowledge we know now that the raider-hunting groups were a most uneconomical use of ships. The real answer to the raiders was to remove their prey from the open seas and to force them to seek out convoys for their victims. Only thus could they be tracked down, by making them reveal themselves in those places where the British naval strength already lay. It is a point of some interest in this connection that all these enemy raiders had instructions never to approach a convoy while on their cruises of destruction.

During the four months ending in October 1940, these six raiders added to our merchant ship losses to the extent of over 225,000 tons, all of it without exception from unescorted merchant ships. In the light of the heavy losses suffered, the slight delay in shipping which full convoy would impose might well have been a small price to pay for immunity from the raiders' grasp.

While this vital battle for the sea communications of the world was being waged in the oceans, another, no less vital, was being fought in the Mediterranean. After an initial hesitation at the time of the Italian declaration of war, when a tentative proposal by the First Sea Lord to withdraw the Mediterranean Fleet from the eastern basin had produced both a strong protest from Admiral Cunningham and a prompt veto from the Prime Minister,[5] the Chiefs of Staff had been firm in their resolve to hold the Middle East at all costs.[6] The troop and supply convoys ran steadily and successfully from Britain, and the safe arrival of each at Suez added perceptibly to the build-up in strength in this important theatre.

German eyes, too, were beginning to look in this direction. Expansion to the eastward was barred by Russia, where the Non-Aggression Pact, signed in 1939, was still in force, although now beginning to wear a little thin. To the west stood the sea power of Britain, hard pressed by the U-boats but still forming a massive barrier to any German intrusion in that direction. But in the south there seemed to be a door that was opening, with an Italian foot already thrust across the step. A big heave there might well fling it open, to shatter the ring which British sea power had thrown around the German menace. The more that Hitler studied it, the more glittering did the prize appear, giving an ultimate promise of a break-through into the Indian Ocean and the possibility of a junction with the naval and military power of Japan.

Three possible courses of action presented themselves to the eager eye of the German ruler. Perhaps Spain could be persuaded, with the promise of Gibraltar and French Morocco, to permit the passage of German troops to attack Gibraltar and Portugal. Such a move would bring Germany right into the Atlantic, through the use of the Azores and the Canary Islands, and would also open the road to Dakar in French West Africa. It would bring, too, control of the entire western Mediterranean basin by the elimination of Gibraltar as a British base. Occupation of the Azores would give vastly improved opportunities for attacking the Atlantic shipping, while Dakar as a naval base would make almost impossible the continuance by Britain of her reinforcement convoys to the Middle East. Admiral Raeder, in his reports to Hitler, stressed continually the great advantages which possession of Dakar would bring to Germany,[7] and the vital role it could play in breaking the stranglehold of British maritime supremacy.

Spain, however, was not yet ready to play the German game. The British attack on the French ships at Oran had made a profound impression in Madrid, proving to the Spaniards that there was still plenty of fight left in the British lion. Moreover, Spain herself was a maritime power and knew from her own historical experience how effective the imponderable weapon of sea power could be in war. In reply to Hitler's requests for Spanish acquiescence in these German moves, Franco demanded to see a German invasion of England actually launched before he committed himself. Further expostulations by Hitler had the result of Franco raising his demands still higher, now to include the cession to Spain of Gibraltar, French Morocco, Oran, and additional territory in West Africa. Finally, the two dictators met each other at Hendaye in October, to thrash the matter out between them. What transpired at this meeting is not known, but Hitler returned from it infuriated and wrote to Ciano, the Italian Foreign Minister, that sooner than go through such an experience again he would rather have three or four teeth out.[8]

A second line of action to bring Germany into the Mediterranean theatre was the direct stiffening of the Italian Army in Libya by German contingents, a combination of the two to drive back the British forces in Egypt and eliminate the naval base at Alexandria on which Admiral Cunningham's fleet depended. In this case it was Italian pride that proved the initial stumbling-block, for Mussolini was in no mood in those early days to welcome German intervention in what was essentially an Italian sphere of influence. Less than six months later, smarting from the effect of General Wavell's great offensive, Mussolini was to sing a very different tune.

The third means of German intervention into the Mediterranean theatre was an advance through the Balkans, to bring Hitler's forces to the Mediterranean coastline of Greece, to safeguard the Rumanian oil wells from air attack, and at the same time to weaken Russia strategically by turning her southern flank. In the longer term view it would also bring the possibility, through exploitation of the new positions held on that coast, of so threatening the British position in the eastern Mediterranean as eventually to make it untenable. This plan was known as Operation "Marita", and Hitler gave orders for detailed planning to begin on 12th November.[9] One month later he combined it with another operation, to which he gave the code-name "Barbarossa". This was the invasion of Russia, planned to follow the march to the Mediterranean coast.

This German intervention in the Mediterranean, to which Admiral Raeder paid so much importance, was rudely upset by the Italian invasion of Greece on 28th October. Among the Nazi war leaders only Raeder fully appreciated the tremendous importance which the Mediterranean theatre could play in the German war plans, the equally tremendous danger that defeat there could have on the whole German strategic concept. But his constant warnings to Hitler passed unheeded, or at best received but lip-service from the Nazi leader, who was now pinning his faith on a lightning land campaign against the Russian colossus in the East. Operation "Marita" was placed temporarily on the shelf, leaving Mussolini to pull his own chestnuts out of the fire he had kindled in Greece, and Operation "Barbarossa" occupied all Hitler's thoughts.

Italy's invasion of Greece was no surprise to the British Chiefs of Staff. They had discussed the possibility at a meeting on 23rd August and had then come to the conclusion that any material assistance to Greece could not be made available until the British Middle East bases were secure from an Italian attack on Egypt.[10] In the following month British-Greek conversations for a co-ordinated defence of Crete were held, and it had been agreed then that naval assistance in the event of invasion could be expected within thirty hours, but that military and air assistance would inevitably be limited.[11] When the actual Italian invasion of Greece took place, Crete was hurriedly occupied in accordance with the pledge to Greece and a forward naval base established at Suda Bay, though with considerable limitations in the matter of defence, not only through the lack of suitably placed airfields but also because of great shortages of most other types of defence material. The spirited resistance by the Greek Army and its remarkable success in driving the Italian invaders back into Albania shelved for the moment, though only for the moment, any question of substantial military reinforcement on the Greek mainland. A small number of Royal Air Force aircraft, and some Fleet Air Arm torpedo bombers to act against Italian supply shipping, proceeded to Greece where they gave most valuable assistance.

It is against this background that the next phase of the Mediterranean sea war must be studied. The military reinforcement of the Middle East had been accompanied by a naval reinforcement of Admiral Cunningham's fleet, while the successful Fleet Air Arm attack on Taranto had still further redressed the adverse balance. Yet, in spite of all, the Italian Navy still had, ship for ship, a good margin of superiority both in speed and in gun-range over the ships to which they were opposed. What they appeared to lack, in the evidence of the two surface ship brushes that had already taken place off Calabria and Cape Spartivento, was the aggressive leadership which could turn these material advantages to effect in the Mediterranean battle.

Early in December 1940, General Wavell launched his attack on the Italian Army in Libya, and within four days had scored his first remarkable success at the battle of Sidi Barrani. From then on the Italian Army was subjected to a series of shattering assaults which drove it ever back with fantastic losses. This advance on shore required a corresponding support from the Mediterranean Fleet, and Admiral Cunningham's ships were called upon to assist to the utmost in maintaining the Army's momentum.

Early in the campaign an Inshore Squadron was formed whose duty was to follow the advance, to keep it adequately supplied by sea, and to assist generally by bombardment of shore positions and by clearing and bringing into operational use the North African ports as they were captured by General Wavell's forces. Tobruk fell on 22nd January, Derna on the 30th, Benghazi on 6th February, and both Tobruk and Derna were quickly cleared by the Navy and used for the passage of supplies for the advancing troops. Benghazi, however, presented a more difficult problem, for added to extensive damage in the harbour area was the fact that it was within air striking range from the Sicilian airfields. Several small ships were sunk there while trying to bring the port into operation and finally, in the absence of adequate anti-aircraft defence, the hope of using Benghazi as an advanced supply base had to be abandoned.

This outstandingly successful campaign on land owed much to the flexibility of British sea power in the sea areas around those coasts. Because of the extreme shortage of mechanical transport ashore, seaborne supplies played a vital part in keeping up the momentum of the British advance. Indeed, the whole of this remarkable campaign stands out as a shining example of that close co-operation of sea, land, and air power which alone can bring victory in an operation of such a nature. Fundamentally, this was a victory which sea power alone had made possible, for in its essentials it had depended on the integrity of British sea communications for the transport of the Army and its weapons to this theatre of operations. That was the naval commitment, the cornerstone of all strategic planning.

Here, then, was the rosy side of the picture. In Egypt and Greece the enemy was on the retreat, in the Mediterranean sea areas the Italian Navy still remained subdued after its rough handling at Taranto and appeared completely to have lost the initiative. But even as the sun shone upon these Allied efforts, the storm clouds were gathering over the horizon. To stiffen the Italian Air Force came the well-trained, anti-shipping German *Fliegerkorps X*, which included two dive-bomber units with fifty-four *Stukas* among its 120 aircraft. It was based in Sicily. Also preparing to intervene in the

North African fighting was a German armoured corps, placed under the command of General Rommel. And up in the Balkans, with its eyes on the Greek Mediterranean coastline and the advantages to be gained from an occupation of it, lay in wait another armoured corps, with an infantry division and airborne troops to accompany it. Hitler was setting the Middle Eastern stage with all the ingredients of high drama.

It was the *Luftwaffe*, from its Sicilian airfields, which struck first. The apparently favourable naval situation in the Mediterranean was seized by the Admiralty to stage a complicated operation which embraced the passage of military supplies from Gibraltar to Malta and Greece, more supplies and troops from Alexandria to Malta, and eight empty ships from Malta to Alexandria. The entire Mediterranean Fleet and the whole of Force H were engaged to cover these movements and the whole operation was given the code name "Excess". The ships from Gibraltar and Alexandria left harbour on 6th January, 1941.

The general pattern of the operation followed the normal plan which had been evolved for the passage of convoys to Malta. As the merchant ships entered the Mediterranean from Gibraltar they were given close escort by cruisers and destroyers as far as the Sicilian Narrows, with the big ships of Force H providing distant cover in case the Italian Fleet should venture out. The Mediterranean Fleet from Alexandria met the convoy in the Sicilian Narrows, where the junction enabled it to exchange guardians for its onward passage to its destination. In Operation "Excess" the first part went entirely according to plan, and the few attempts by the Italian Air Force to interfere were easily beaten back by naval fighters from the *Ark Royal*, the carrier with Force H.

During the morning of 10th January, Admiral Cunningham joined the convoy, with the battleships *Warspite* and *Valiant* and the carrier *Illustrious*. Force H was now on its way back to Gibraltar, its part in the operation having been successfully accomplished. The Mediterranean Fleet, however, had been shadowed and reported almost since leaving Alexandria, and it was virtually certain that there was trouble in store, if only of the Italian variety. But in the afternoon of the 10th a new enemy appeared in the sky. No longer was it only Italian aircraft to threaten the passage of the ships; now the menacing forms of Junkers 87 dive-bombers brought a far more vivid portent of danger. They chose the *Illustrious* as their target and dived down on her in concentrated attacks. In the space of four or five minutes she was hit six times by heavy bombs, while three more very near misses added considerably to the damage. Sorely struck, she reached Malta that night, only to become the victim of more furious attacks when enemy reconnaissance planes spotted her there. Again she was hit but, by tremendous efforts on the part of her company and the dockyard, she was patched up sufficiently to slip away thirteen days later and reach Alexandria in safety.

The success of the dive-bombers in hitting the *Illustrious* was not the end of the story of Operation "Excess". On the 11th the Mediterranean Fleet was still within range of their devastating attacks and two cruisers, the *Gloucester* and *Southampton*, fell victim to their bombs, the *Southampton* being damaged so severely that she had later to be sunk by our own forces. Fourteen ships in four convoys had reached their destinations in safety, but the cost to the Mediterranean Fleet had been a heavy one.

The disablement of the *Illustrious* and the loss of the *Southampton* pointed only too clearly to the new enemy in the Mediterranean picture. No longer was the Italian Navy and Air Force the only threat to be considered, the intrusion of the *Luftwaffe* into this new sphere posed a new and more menacing problem. It seemed a reasonable assumption that the air attack on Malta was certain to be stepped up and that the central Mediterranean waters were to be subjected to an air dominance as effective as that which had already been experienced by the Navy off Norway and in the English Channel. Both these assumptions were fulfilled within a very few days of the arrival of *Fliegerkorps X*.

This new threat from the air, however, was not the only factor to cloud the Mediterranean sky. In view of the disastrous reverses sustained by the Italians, both in Albania and in North Africa, Hitler had been forced to modify his own plans and to intervene in both theatres as the only means of preventing a complete collapse. On

11th January[12] he issued the directive which set these new plans in motion, and what at first had been viewed as precautionary movements now took on the force of reality. Operation "Marita", the advance into Greece, became a firm commitment and the move of *Fliegerkorps X* to Sicily, originally a temporary measure, was now made permanent, with orders not only to cover troop and supply convoys from Italy to North Africa but also to hold up the British advance in Cyrenaica until the Afrika Korps could intervene in the fighting.

The Greeks, too, in their campaign in Albania, were beginning to meet stiffer resistance from the air, presaging the forthcoming German intervention in this Italian-instigated campaign. Their supplies were already falling below the danger-point. This matter was under urgent discussion in London, mainly with a view to the desirability of large-scale British intervention in Greece when the expected German invasion took place.

It was fully recognised by the War Cabinet that any decision to reinforce Greece in the event of German invasion through the Balkans must inevitably bring to a stop General Wavell's advance in North Africa. But the political advantages of such a move, particularly in Turkish, Russian, and United States eyes, were stressed[13] both by the Chiefs of Staff and by the War Cabinet, and were held fully to justify the drawbacks they would impose in North Africa. The general conclusion of the Defence Committee of the War Cabinet was that, after the capture of Tobruk, operations in Libya should be limited to what could be done without great loss and that substantial assistance to Greece should be given the first priority. So the die was cast and the curtain raised on another tremendous Mediterranean drama, in which the British Fleet was to be stretched to new and almost unbelievable limits of endurance and fortitude.

It was at this crucial moment, with the promise of additional entanglements in Greek waters hanging over the ships of the Mediterranean Fleet, that the Prime Minister, in his capacity as Minister of Defence, put forward new proposals for more aggressive action in that theatre. An earlier project to seize the small island of Pantellaria in the Sicilian Narrows, proposed by Admiral of the

Fleet Sir Roger Keyes, had rightly been condemned by Admiral Cunningham as adding one more commitment to his already overburdened fleet. He considered, moreover, that Pantellaria could serve no useful purpose in view of the proximity of the Sicilian airfields. This proposal was now revived again, only to be turned down once more by the Chiefs of Staff. So instead of the attack on Pantellaria, the Prime Minister now asked for plans to be prepared for attacking the principal islands in the Dodecanese, with a date for attack not later than 1st March.

This requirement was submitted to the two Commanders-in-Chief concerned, Admiral Cunningham and General Wavell, and the gist of their reply was that, with the forces at their disposal, they could not possibly undertake more than one operation at a time. They also pointed out that a new enemy was appearing in the Mediterranean, and that what might well have been possible against Italian opposition was a very different proposition when the opposition was German. And there the matter lay until, in the course of the next few weeks, events at sea overtook the plans and rendered them nugatory.

Indeed, during those weeks, the fleet was faced with so many commitments in the eastern Mediterranean that there were insufficient ships and aircraft to carry out, in the central area, the many essential duties that fall to the proper exercise of sea power. With the military reinforcement of Greece established as the first priority by the War Cabinet, and with the need to escort those convoys to their destination, the Italian convoys bringing succour to their demoralised army in Tripolitania were of necessity allowed to pass almost unscathed. The few British submarines available put up a gallant fight and worked tirelessly in most difficult conditions, but they alone could not bar a sea route so short that the danger area could be crossed under cover of darkness. To do that effectively required surface forces and ample aircraft, and neither of those was available. The Italian convoys continued to sail and to arrive in comparative safety, and the succour they brought was potent in the extreme. During this month of March they ferried across the Mediterranean General Rommel and his Afrika Korps.

Farther eastward the troop convoys were running from Alexandria to the Piræus carrying much of the Army in North Africa and its supplies to a new theatre of war. The first convoy had left Alexandria on 5th March, and during the next two months over 66,000 troops were carried to Greece and Crete under the protection of the Royal Navy without the loss of a single man or item of equipment at sea. There was, at first, virtually no interference from the enemy against this tempting target, even though, in comparison with the Italian troop convoys to Tripoli, these British ones to Greece had a far longer and more exposed route to cover. It was reasonably certain, however, that this immunity from attack could not last, and that sooner or later they would prove sufficient of an attraction to sting the Italian Fleet into activity. Admiral Cunningham was well aware of this danger and was on the look-out for any signs of Italian naval movements which might presage an attack.

Signs of movement came, through Naval Intelligence reports, on 25th March. On the strength of these reports Admiral Cunningham, as a first move, diverted all shipping from the sea area south and west of Crete, so that the enemy blow, should it fall, would find no target at which to strike.

The Italian Navy had, in fact, been prodded into activity by the German Naval Staff.[14] A substantial squadron, consisting of the new battleship *Vittorio Veneto*, eight cruisers, and a screening force of destroyers, all under the command of Admiral Iachino, sailed from their various bases on the 26th to rendezvous off Syracuse and to strike a blow at the British convoys on their way to Greece. In point of fact, they put to sea under a misapprehension, relying on claims by the German *Fliegerkorps X* that they had damaged the *Barham* and *Warspite* in bombing attacks on Alexandria and that both ships were out of action.[15]

In the meantime Admiral Cunningham was making his own dispositions. Vice-Admiral H. D. Pridham-Wippell (Vice-Admiral Light Forces) was ordered to be in a position south of the western end of Crete at dawn on 28th March with the cruisers *Orion*, *Ajax*, *Gloucester*, and *Perth*, and four destroyers. The Commander-in-Chief himself sailed from Alexandria at dusk on the 27th, with the

*Warspite*, *Barham*, *Valiant*, and *Formidable* (which had replaced the damaged *Illustrious*), screened by nine destroyers.

At first light on the 28th, air searches were flown off from the *Formidable* and the first enemy report soon reached the flagship. This was of a force of Italian cruisers and destroyers in the same general area as the Vice-Admiral Light Forces. Admiral Cunningham altered the course of the fleet to close the enemy and increased to full speed. While this was happening, Admiral Pridham-Wippell's ships were themselves sighted by an aircraft catapulted from the *Vittorio Veneto*, and Admiral Iachino, who was on the point of abandoning his sweep into Ægean waters, turned to close the British cruisers. And at almost the same moment, over the northern horizon, a squadron of three Italian *Zara* class cruisers was sighted from the *Orion*. They closed rapidly and opened fire with their 8-inch guns shortly after 8.0 a.m.

To the Commander-in-Chief, on the bridge of H.M.S. *Warspite*, the situation appeared confused. There were some inaccuracies in the enemy positions as reported by the *Formidable*'s aircraft, and it was difficult for him to determine accurately either the composition or the positions of the various enemy squadrons. But as further reports came in, and especially the visual sighting report of the three *Zaras* from the *Orion*, the situation became clearer and Admiral Cunningham realised that he had to deal with two distinct groups of enemy cruisers, each with destroyers in company. As yet, neither side was aware that anything more than light forces of the other were at sea.

The action began in the traditional way, with Admiral Pridham-Wippell attempting to lead the enemy cruisers down towards his advancing Commander-in-Chief, still some ninety miles distant to the south-east. For nearly an hour there was a running fight at extreme range between the cruisers, with no ships on either side being hit. Finally, at 9.0 a.m., the Italian cruisers broke off the action and, reversing their course, steered to the westward. They had received orders from Admiral Iachino to do so as he considered that they were being drawn into waters where they were in danger of attack from British shore-based aircraft.[16]

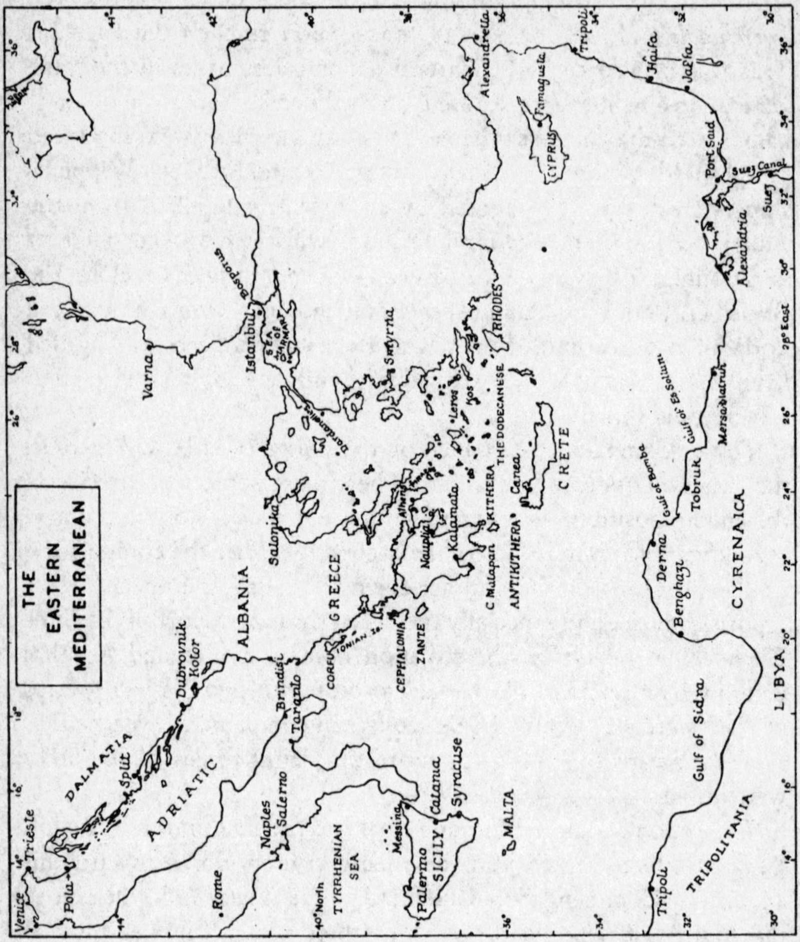
THE EASTERN MEDITERRANEAN
DALMATIA
ADRIATIC
Trieste
Venice
Pola
Split
Dubrovnik
Kotor
ALBANIA
GREECE
Salonika
Varna
Istanbul
Bosporus
SEA OF MARMARA
Dardanelles
Smyrna
Rome
Naples
Salerno
Brindisi
Taranto
TYRRHENIAN SEA
40° North
CORFU
IONIAN SE.
CEPHALONIA
ZANTE
Messina
Palermo
SICILY
Catania
Syracuse
MALTA
Kalamata
Nauplia
Athens
C Malapan
KITHERA
ANTIKITHERA
Canea
CRETE
THE DODECANESE
Leros
Kos
RHODES
CYPRUS
Famagusta
Alexandretta
Tripoli
Haifa
Jaffa
Port Said
Suez Canal
Suez
Alexandria
Mersa Matruh
Gulf of Es Sollum
Gulf of Bomba
Tobruk
Derna
Benghazi
CYRENAICA
LIBYA
Gulf of Sidra
TRIPOLITANIA
Tripoli
28° East

Admiral Pridham-Wippell, having reported the alteration of course to his Commander-in-Chief, himself steered a parallel course in order to keep in touch. In the *Warspite* it appeared to Admiral Cunningham that his cruisers might be heading for some trouble, for the second force of enemy cruisers should by now, if their original reported position had been correct, be approaching the area. As a result he ordered the *Formidable*, shortly after 9.30 a.m., to fly off a torpedo striking force to relieve the pressure on the *Orion* and her consorts.

A little over one hour later the whole situation in the battle was dramatically transformed. Just before 11.0 a.m. the look-out in the *Orion*'s foretop sighted, away up to the north, the unmistakable outline of a battleship. This was the *Vittorio Veneto* which, ever since her aircraft's sighting of Admiral Pridham-Wippell's cruisers, had been making her best speed towards the battle. And she was a formidable opponent indeed, having a substantial margin in range and a fractional margin in speed over the *Orion* and her three companions. Within a minute or two she had opened an extremely accurate fire with her 15-inch guns, though fortunately doing no more than very minor damage from shell splinters. Admiral Pridham-Wippell at once altered course to the southward and made smoke to shroud his movements from this new and dangerous enemy.

The situation in which the Vice-Admiral Light Forces now found himself was one of potential danger. On his port quarter was the *Vittorio Veneto*, firing at him with her 15-inch guns and shooting, moreover, with remarkable accuracy. Away on his starboard quarter the Italian cruisers, emboldened by this new turn of events, were altering course south-westward again to join the action. They, too, had a good margin of superiority, both in speed and gun-range. But such danger as existed was quickly removed by the arrival of the *Formidable*'s strike aircraft. Sent out by Admiral Cunningham to attack the cruisers, they sighted instead the *Vittorio Veneto* and gratefully accepted this new and far more valuable target. Though all their torpedoes missed, the effect was to discourage the enemy from continuing the chase. Both enemy forces altered course to the north-west and set a course for home. By the time the *Orion* emerged from her smoke-screen the Italian ships were over the horizon and the sea was clear. Admiral Pridham-Wippell decided to rejoin his Commander-in-Chief, and made contact with the battle-fleet about an hour later.

There remained to Admiral Cunningham but one hope now of stopping the flying enemy, a hope bound up in the torpedoes of the Albacores and Swordfish of the *Formidable* and a few similar aircraft based in Crete and Greece. Only if they could hit the *Vittorio Veneto* and slow her down could the British battle-fleet reach her and bring her to action. A second strike from the *Formidable* was flown off and reached the enemy at 3.15 p.m. It produced the result for which Admiral Cunningham was praying. Lieutenant-Commander J. Dalyell-Stead, leading the squadron, hit the *Vittorio Veneto* on her port quarter and fractured the port outer shaft, though he lost his own life through superb gallantry in pressing home his attack to point-blank range. The *Vittorio Veneto*'s speed was temporarily reduced to sixteen knots, and hopes of catching the enemy during the night began to rise.

The *Vittorio Veneto*, now but forty-five miles ahead and steaming at reduced speed, placed herself in the centre of a compact group of cruisers and destroyers, forming a most difficult target to hit. From the air her speed was estimated at fifteen knots; she had in fact, been able later to increase to nineteen, and those extra four knots were to make a big difference in the final stages of the battle.

During the afternoon Admiral Cunningham detached the Vice-Admiral Light Forces with his cruisers to regain touch with the enemy. Steaming at thirty knots they narrowed the distance between the opposing forces, but not sufficiently fast to catch up before dark. The battle-fleet, at its full speed of twenty-four knots, was also in hot pursuit, but now with little hope of reaching the enemy battle-ship and forcing an action unless she could once again be slowed down. Accordingly, the Commander-in-Chief ordered the *Formidable* to fly off a third striking force, timed to reach the enemy at dusk. At half-past seven that evening, from the bridge of the *Orion*, Admiral Pridham-Wippell saw the enemy's reaction to the air attack some fifteen miles ahead of him. The searchlights were plainly visible and the air was filled with a tremendous barrage of "flaming onions" and tracer shell of various colours. "They must have been very gallant men who went through it", wrote the Vice-Admiral in his report.

One hit was scored, but unfortunately it was not the battleship which suffered. The ship that was hit was the cruiser *Pola*, in position abeam of the *Vittorio Veneto*. The aircraft's torpedo hit her on her starboard side and brought her to a complete stop. She remained alone, completely disabled and in the path of the advancing British battle-fleet while the rest of the Italian ships steamed off to the westward. Her crew, demoralised by this adverse turn of the wheel of fortune, broached the wine casks.

"Probable hits" on the battleship were reported to the Commander-in-Chief, but this, though encouraging, was not sufficiently precise for Admiral Cunningham to be certain of catching the *Vittorio Veneto*. Through a signal from the *Orion* the Commander-in-Chief knew that Admiral Pridham-Wippell's cruisers had regained touch with the distant enemy, and as a result he now ordered a destroyer force to forge ahead and attack. This would commit the British battle-fleet to a night action, but the risks always inherent in a fleet action during the hours of darkness were well worth accepting with so great a prize almost within grasp. It seemed as though the desired result could hardly fail of achievement, for the cruisers already in touch with the enemy should be able to direct the destroyers on to their target.

The sun had set just before 7.0 p.m. and the twilight had faded into darkness as the destroyers, steaming at twenty-eight knots, drew ahead of the fleet. The sea was calm and there was no moon. The last reported course and speed of the enemy was approximately north-west and thirteen knots, and Captain Mack, leading the destroyers, expected to come up with them in about two and a half hours' time. What he could not know was that, almost at the moment of his leaving the battle-fleet, the Italian force altered course to the northward and increased speed to nineteen knots.

An unfortunate chain of events deprived Admiral Cunningham

of the results he had worked so hard to achieve. Captain Mack, in his chase after the enemy, decided to steer to the northward of the *Vittorio Veneto* and then, when his reckoning put him ahead of her, to turn to the southward to search. This choice, instead of the alternative of passing south of the *Vittorio Veneto* and searching northward, had the disadvantage of making him pass between our own cruisers and the enemy they were shadowing, forcing Admiral Pridham-Wippell to turn away to the northward and to lose touch. An added complication was a radar contact of three ships reported from the *Ajax*, one of Admiral Pridham-Wippell's cruisers, which in the *Orion* was thought to be Captain Mack's destroyers coming up to the attack. They were, in fact, the Italian cruisers *Zara* and *Fiume*, and probably a destroyer, making a belated return to help the crippled *Pola*. They had the effect of making Admiral Pridham-Wippell alter course still farther to the northward in order to open the way for what he assumed to be the advancing destroyers.

Thus it was that the *Vittorio Veneto* was missed. At 11.15 that night, after a devastating action with the Italian cruisers, Admiral Cunningham sent a signal ordering all forces not actually engaged in sinking the enemy to retire to the north-east. To the best of his knowledge at that time the cruisers and also the destroyers were in contact with the main enemy force, as both forces had recently made the Night Alarm signal which had been received in the flagship. But in fact neither force was in touch, both Night Alarms having been made on the sighting of a red rocket fired into the night sky. Admiral Pridham-Wippell withdrew his cruisers on receipt of the signal, but Captain Mack, on inquiring whether the signal referred to him, was informed "after your attack".[17] At midnight, estimating that he was far enough ahead of the enemy, Captain Mack turned his destroyers to the southward on a searching course. But by now the enemy's earlier alteration of course and his increase in speed had taken him clear of the pursuit and there were no ships left for the destroyers to find. The red rocket was subsequently revealed as a visual signal from the *Vittorio Veneto* to indicate an alteration of course to her accompanying ships. By so narrow a margin was the great prize missed.

In the meantime the stationary *Pola* lay in the path of the advancing battle-fleet. A minute or two after 10 p.m. the *Valiant*'s radar picked up the enemy ship at a range of nine miles and Admiral Cunningham at once altered the course of the fleet to close. The three battleships and the *Formidable* bore down on the unsuspecting *Pola*, all of them in tense readiness for the inevitable action that loomed so close ahead. The range was closing rapidly when the *Stuart*, one of the screening destroyers on the starboard beam, made the Night Alarm. But even before it was reported in the flagship Admiral Cunningham himself had seen the cause of it as he stood on the *Warspite*'s bridge, straining for a first sight of the enemy.

Crossing the path of the fleet from north to south he saw the heavy outlines of darkened ships steaming through the night. They were no more than two miles ahead, point-blank range for a 15-inch gun. The next three or four minutes were decisive, the whole fate of the night battle depending on the battleships being able to alter course to bring their guns to bear without being sighted by the unsuspecting Italians.

At once the Commander-in-Chief ordered the fleet to alter course together to starboard and the 15-inch turrets of the battleships were trained round on to the new targets. The *Formidable*, unable as a carrier to take part in the forthcoming gun battle, drew out of the line to starboard to leave the arena free for the *Warspite*, *Valiant*, and *Barham*. And as the firing arcs of the turrets were opened, allowing all turrets to bear, the destroyer *Greyhound* opened her searchlight.

Its beam, piercing the night's darkness, lit up in vivid relief the unmistakable outline of an Italian 10,000-ton cruiser. It was the *Fiume*, and the range was 2,900 yards. For a second or two more all was silence, then the night was shattered by a full broadside from the *Warspite*, followed almost immediately by one from the *Valiant*. Over six tons of high-explosive shell ripped into the unhappy *Fiume*. In the tremendous explosion that followed, her after-turret was lifted high into the air and blown overboard, and she drifted away out of the line, a sea of flame. Half an hour later, still burning furiously, she blew up and sank.

The *Barham*, last ship in the British line, had in the meantime sighted the damaged *Pola* and her turrets were already trained on to her. But as the *Greyhound*'s searchlight lit up the new enemy she shifted her aim to the leading ship in the Italian line and fired a broadside. This was the destroyer *Alfieri*, and the *Barham* hit her along the whole length of the ship. She then shifted her fire to the next astern, the 10,000-ton cruiser *Zara*, which by now was the target for all three battleships. She was hit at least twenty times in rapid succession by 15-inch shells and, like the *Fiume*, one of her turrets was blown bodily overboard by the force of the explosions. She, too, drifted out of the line, wrecked and burning.

Barely five minutes after the first gun was fired the action was over. The battleships withdrew, leaving it to the destroyers to finish off the hapless enemy. This they did to perfection, their torpedoes sending to the bottom not only the *Zara* and the *Pola*—the *Fiume* had already blown up and sunk—but also the destroyers *Alfieri* and *Carducci*. At the end of their night action they withdrew to the north-east to rejoin the fleet, bringing with them as prisoners-of-war most of the crew of the *Pola* and as many from the other ships as they had been able to pick up out of the water. As soon as he was out of range of enemy aircraft, Admiral Cunningham wirelessed to the Italian Admiralty the position in which the action had been fought so that they could send out a hospital ship to rescue those who were still afloat in boats and on rafts.

So the battle ended. The cost to the Mediterranean Fleet was one Swordfish aircraft, flown by the gallant Dalyell-Stead who had hit the *Vittorio Veneto* with his torpedo. There were no other casualties and no damage. But to the enemy the cost had been heavy, with three fine modern cruisers and two destroyers sunk, and the fleet flagship damaged by a torpedo hit.

Matapan, however, was more than a resounding naval victory won on the night of 28th March, 1941. It was a milestone along the path to British naval supremacy in the eastern Mediterranean, a supremacy on the maintenance of which the whole future course of the war was to depend. It is true, as Admiral Cunningham pointed out in his despatch, that the result could not be viewed with complete satisfaction since the damaged *Vittorio Veneto* had been allowed to escape,[18] but in the final analysis, viewed now through the perspective of the years, its result was sufficiently shattering to remove a challenge to our sea communications in that area that would otherwise have proved embarrassing in the extreme. At a moment when the whole of the Greek coastline was shortly to fall into the hands of the enemy, when the whole British position in the Middle East depended on retaining control of the sea routes in that area in order to prevent the enemy from breaking out of the ring that enclosed him, the Italian Fleet was so roughly handled that it never again ventured into those waters to challenge British naval might.

The victory of Matapan rang round the world. From far and wide came messages of appreciation, from the War Cabinet, the House of Commons, and the naval staffs of many nations. To Admiral Cunningham H.M. The King telegraphed, "My heartiest congratulations to all ranks and ratings under your command on your great victory."[19]

# Chapter 5

## THE DARKENING SCENE

ALTHOUGH the victory at Matapan eased the situation in the eastern Mediterranean by discouraging any further Italian naval adventures in these waters, it did nothing to minimise the new problems which were arising farther west. Almost as the echoes of that notable battle died away in the darkness of a Mediterranean night, others shattered the stillness of a desert dawn. Rommel, moving forward cautiously on the Tripolitanian front with the object of seizing a local feature to improve his defensive position, suddenly found the road to Egypt opened in front of him. A mistaken report of an enemy approach had caused the premature destruction of the principal petrol dump for the British armour, and for that calamity there was no redress. Shorn of their motive power, the British tanks fell an easy prey to the advancing Germans and, seizing his opportunity, Rommel swept across the desert up to the Egyptian border. Tobruk alone remained in British hands, cut off by land and open only to supply by sea.

So swift a reversal of fortune brought with it new and imperative duties to Admiral Cunningham's ships. On the Navy alone now rested the burden not only of maintaining those essential communications on which the whole security of the Middle East theatre of war rested, but also of disrupting those on which the enemy relied to maintain his new effort in North Africa. The strategical picture which faced Admiral Cunningham at this bleak moment in the campaign was to tax both his skill and his resolution to the utmost.

There was already in operation the passage of troops to Greece and the reinforcement of Crete, both absorbing large numbers of ships. There was, at this time too, an urgent requirement to pass an essential convoy of fast merchant ships loaded with tanks and aircraft through the Mediterranean to Alexandria in order to allow General Wavell to return to the offensive. There was also an obvious need to bring as much disruption as possible to Rommel's supply line across the Mediterranean, a disruption which could be performed to any significant degree only by surface ships acting in conjunction with aircraft. This in its turn entailed the use of Malta as a base, and thus called for additional naval effort to supply and reinforce it.

So, almost in snowball fashion, the naval duties in the Mediterranean grew, to be augmented almost daily as the pattern of German intervention in this Italian sphere unfolded itself. With Rommel's advance to the east the flow of British and Dominion soldiers to Greece came to an abrupt halt. At the same time the Greeks failed to redeploy their Army as agreed, and the line they chose to defend could not be held. Retreat was inevitable, followed a few days later by a forced withdrawal from Greece as the German divisions swung down into the Balkan cockpit.

The situation in the Mediterranean, which now called for new exertions on the part of the fleet almost to the limit of endurance, was eased slightly by the elimination of the Italian threat in the Red Sea. Mussolini's East African empire was crumbling rapidly as a result of the land campaign conducted by General Cunningham and the sea campaign by Vice-Admiral R. Leatham, Commander-in-Chief East Indies. One by one the Italian ports along the Eritrean coast were being put out of action and their complement of enemy ships sunk or destroyed. The finishing touches to the sea campaign were contributed in the main by a squadron of the *Eagle*'s Swordfish, working from Port Sudan. They accounted for eight Italian destroyers based at Massawa, thus finally freeing those important waters, through which ran the main Middle Eastern supply line, from enemy seaborne interference.

Although this East African campaign was somewhat overshadowed by the more dramatic events which were taking place farther north, it does present an interesting little example of the influence which sea power can play on an essentially military operation. The ability to carry large numbers of troops by sea, to put them ashore in the required place, and to supply them with the means of carrying out their task had in this case proved decisive and had completely eliminated what might have developed, in the larger North African campaign, into an uncomfortable threat to a main artery of sea communication.

One immediate result of the Red Sea campaign was to free three destroyers—the *Kimberley*, *Kandahar*, and *Kingston*—for work in the Mediterranean. This welcome reinforcement allowed Admiral Cunningham to release a striking force of four destroyers—the *Jervis*, *Janus*, *Mohawk*, and *Nubian*—to operate from Malta against the Axis lines of communication to North Africa. In conjunction with air reconnaissance by Malta-based aircraft they quickly justified their new role by annihilating a Tripoli-bound convoy of five merchant ships escorted by three destroyers. In a brilliantly fought little action which accounted for the whole of the enemy, the loss to the attacking force was but one destroyer, H.M.S. *Mohawk*.

Yet, welcome as was the news of this interruption in supplies to the enemy in North Africa, with its implied promise of more to come, it was little more than a drop in the ocean. Completely to stop this enemy traffic called not only for a far heavier scale of surface attack than could be mounted from Malta, but also for extensive air reconnaissance and for command of the air above the narrow waters between Sicily and the North African shore. Without those, success in attack on this supply shipping could hardly become much more than spasmodic.

The importance of cutting off these supplies to the enemy was as fully appreciated in London as it was in Alexandria, but the geographical and physical difficulties in carrying it out were less vividly apparent. In directives sent to Admiral Cunningham and General Wavell on 14th and 18th April,[1] the Prime Minister stressed the importance of this task. It was, he said, the prime duty of the Mediterranean Fleet to stop all seaborne traffic between Italy and

Africa by the full use of surface craft, aided by aircraft and submarines. Heavy losses in ships of all kinds were to be accepted. The port of Tripoli was to be rendered inaccessible by bombardment and/or blocking, if necessary with a battleship on the active list. "The reputation of the Royal Navy", he wrote, "is engaged in stopping this traffic."

The First Sea Lord, following up the Prime Minister's directive, signalled to Admiral Cunningham that Tripoli should be subjected to a combination of a fleet bombardment and a blocking operation, using H.M.S. *Barham* and a "C"-class cruiser as blockships.[2] In his reply, the Commander-in-Chief protested vigorously against this proposed use of H.M.S. *Barham*, "a first-class fighting unit whose passing is liable to give an inestimable fillip to failing Italian naval morale".[3] In the face of Admiral Cunningham's objections, the Admiralty agreed to defer for the time being the blocking operation, but ordered the bombardment to be carried out.[4]

At dawn on 21st April the first naval shells began to fall in the harbour area of Tripoli. All the major units of the Mediterranean Fleet took part in this operation, which achieved complete surprise, though the dust caused by a simultaneous attack from the air to some extent hampered the naval guns. Only one ship in the harbour was sunk and the amount of damage done to the port installations was insufficient to cause more than a temporary delay to the enemy build-up of essential supplies. An hour and a half later the fleet was on its way back to Alexandria, having suffered neither casualty nor damage. Nor was it molested on its way back to its base.

Although at the time it was thought that Tripoli had been extensively damaged, the venture was hardly one which could be repeated with impunity. German dive-bombers were based within easy striking distance, and there was inadequate fighter protection for the fleet due to the lack of suitable aircraft in the Middle East theatre. It was unlikely that the Commander-in-Chief could count on equally good fortune a second time. Admiral Cunningham lost no time in giving the Admiralty his views on operations of this nature.[5]

The question of a repetition of the operation did not, however, arise at this moment, for by now the fleet was engaged in other, and more vital, activities. During March the Navy had carried some 58,000 soldiers and their equipment to Greece; now, in April, it was to carry them back, though partly to Crete as well as to Egypt.

Hitler, infuriated by the defiance of Yugoslavia to his demands for a free passage for his troops, had on 27th March ordered the "crushing" of that country simultaneously with an attack on Greece.[6] On 6th April, after a savage air bombardment of Belgrade, an overwhelmingly strong German force thrust its way southward, swamping Yugoslavia and outflanking the gallant Greek Army which had been engaged so valiantly and successfully against the Italians in Albania. It was all over very quickly. The Yugoslav Army was forced to lay down its arms on 17th April, and that of Greece, outflanked, hampered by lack of air support, and exhausted by its five months' struggle against Mussolini's soldiers, surrendered to the Germans on 20th April in order to avoid the humiliation of submission to the Italians.

The course of these Balkan events was not entirely unforeseen in London, though the speed of the collapse came as a surprise. The evacuation of Greece had been a topic of discussion in the War Cabinet as early as 17th April, and the final decision was taken on the 21st.[7] The operation, which was begun on the 29th, was given the code-name "Demon", and from the start had to face a severe handicap. This was the virtual destruction of the Piræus, the port of Athens and the only harbour with facilities for carrying out a large-scale evacuation, by the earlier blowing-up of an ammunition ship, hit during the first German raid on the port.

The task called for as many cruisers and destroyers as could be collected together and Admiral Cunningham denuded his battle-fleet of its destroyer screen in order to make available the maximum number possible. The conduct of the operation at sea was placed in the hands of Vice-Admiral Pridham-Wippell, with his flag flying in the *Orion*. Ashore in Greece Rear-Admiral Baillie-Grohman was in charge.

In many ways Operation "Demon" was a repetition of the withdrawal from Dunkirk, though without the same advantages. Here the distances were far greater, the embarkation ports more widely separated and far less highly organised, base facilities virtually non-existent, and there was also no friendly fighter cover to hold back the onslaught from the air, as there had been over Dunkirk. In this way it was an operation even more hazardous than "Dynamo", but in its execution it was as triumphantly successful. The final total of men brought back from Greece was just over 50,000. But, like its predecessor at Dunkirk, the losses in ships were grievous. The effect of these losses was, in fact, doubly severe, for they were occurring not only in an area that was becoming increasingly difficult to reinforce in face of the still growing enemy air power in the Mediterranean, but also in an area whose strategical importance was growing ever more apparent as the course of the war unfolded itself. A third reason, the forthcoming evacuation from Crete which was to call for yet greater efforts from the Mediterranean Fleet, was as yet not even dimly foreshadowed.

For six days Operation "Demon" continued, and for the skill and coolness of the officers and men of the Royal and Merchant Navies it possibly surpassed even the Dunkirk evacuation. The navigational hazards, with ships having to work at night in inshore, unlighted, and sometimes inadequately charted waters, were extreme, but only one ship, the *Ulster Prince*, was lost through stranding and subsequent bombing. The work of the Navy was vastly assisted by the wonderful discipline of the tired, hungry, and footsore soldiers, who for three weeks had been retreating under the scourge of a merciless air attack. The despatch from Admiral Baillie-Grohman, commanding inshore, described this military discipline as "magnificent".[8]

But withdrawals, no matter how gallant or how successful, do not win wars. The decision to go to the aid of Greece had been, and still is, a subject of controversy. It was, rightly and inevitably, a political decision, and there is no doubt that it produced a most favourable impression on the United States at a time when President Roosevelt was pushing through Congress his "Lease-Lend" measures, on which British hopes of victory largely depended. Nor was the intervention in Greece an entire loss militarily. It delayed Hitler's attack on Russia from 15th May, the date originally planned, until 22nd June, and it is at least arguable that those five weeks of delay, during good campaigning weather, may well have made all the difference between German success and German failure in Russia. On moral grounds, too, there can be no doubt that the decision was correct. A pledge to Greece had been given, and military expediency is ever a lame excuse for dishonouring an obligation.

There are therefore some reasons for believing that this Greek campaign, in spite of its losses and its disastrous ending, yet played a not inconsiderable part in the course of the war as a whole. Its strains and stresses, especially on the hard-pressed Mediterranean Fleet, were severe, but that was only to be expected in any operation of this kind conducted under the hazards of enemy control in the air. The inevitable losses at sea were borne with the traditional naval fortitude, and Admiral Cunningham could content himself with the reflection that his ships had upheld the high traditions of their Service in particularly difficult and hazardous circumstances.

Many of the troops brought back from Greece were put ashore in Crete, where it was hoped sufficiently to strengthen the island to be able to resist attack. Yet even here, in the three weeks of respite granted while the Germans prepared their attack, these hopes were dashed to destruction mainly by the chronic shortage of aircraft in the Middle Eastern theatre. The eighteen serviceable Royal Air Force fighters in the island on 1st May had been reduced by enemy action to seven by the 19th, and these, with no replacements available, were then withdrawn to Egypt. The island was thus left bare of all fighter cover apart from a tiny contribution which the Fleet Arm made from its own meagre resources and which in any case appeared late on the scene because of damage to the *Formidable*. It was hardly surprising, in these conditions, that the Navy's task of sustaining the defenders with reinforcements and supplies was performed with heavy loss. Nearly half the engineer field stores and field guns despatched to Crete were sunk *en route*, and of the fifteen supply ships which successfully reached Suda Bay, eight were sunk or seriously damaged in harbour by air attack.

As the sultry, summer days passed, the indications of an enemy attack became more apparent. Aircraft were known to be congregating in large numbers on the newly-occupied airfields on the Greek mainland, and the scale of bombing attack on the island grew daily and nightly. Although the fight ahead was obviously destined to be a grim one, the strategical importance of Crete as an advanced base in the Ægean from which to defend the sea communications of the eastern Mediterranean was so great that the War Cabinet ordered the island to be held at all costs.[9] General Wavell, the Commander-in-Chief, was hopeful. "I feel at least", he wrote, "that we will give an excellent account of ourselves. With the help of the Royal Navy I trust that Crete will be held."[10]

The German attack came at dawn on 20th May. As expected, it was completely airborne, the first time such a method had been used in war on a scale of this size. The first objectives were the airfields at Maleme and Heraklion, and the airstrip at Retimo. In the light of all existing knowledge at that time it appeared most unlikely that an airborne invasion by itself could succeed without seaborne support, and it was on the Mediterranean Fleet's capacity to destroy the expected reinforcing troop convoys that the hopes of the defenders lay. In spite of the total lack of air cover over Cretan waters, Admiral Cunningham was reasonably confident that this part of the Navy's task could be virtually guaranteed.

The first naval forces, comprising nearly half the Mediterranean Fleet, sailed for the defence of Crete on 14th May. Though they carried out many sweeps in the surrounding waters there were no signs of enemy seaborne activity and the ships returned to Alexandria on the 19th, being relieved in Cretan waters by the other half of the fleet. These preliminary operations were no more than precautionary moves in the battle and were unimportant, though it was during these operations that Petty Officer A. A. Sephton won the first Victoria Cross to be awarded in the Mediterranean Fleet since the start of the war. As director gunlayer of H.M.S. *Coventry*, he was mortally wounded during a dive-bombing attack on a hospital ship but continued to work his director with conspicuous fortitude and success until the attack was over. He died the following day.

As the first enemy troop-carrying planes unloaded their living cargoes of parachutists over the Maleme airfield on the morning of 20th May, British forces of cruisers and destroyers were to the east and west of the island, withdrawing to the southward after their normal night sweeps into the Ægean in search of troop convoys. The main force, comprising the *Warspite* and *Valiant*, with one cruiser and eight destroyers in company, was in support to the south-east. Patrols carried out along the northern coast of Crete on the following night of the 20th/21st also sighted no shipping, and by dawn of the 21st the various forces concerned were again withdrawing, satisfied that no seaborne reinforcements were making for Crete. During that night the enemy airfield on the island of Scarpanto, east of Crete, was bombarded by the destroyers *Jervis*, *Nizam*, and *Ilex*, but without effecting much damage.

So far, all was going reasonably well. Ashore the German losses were very heavy; they would have been immeasurably heavier had there been even one British fighter to take advantage of the easy targets provided by the slow-moving, troop-carrying aircraft. Possession of the airfield at Maleme was still in dispute, and elsewhere pockets of enemy troops were being held and mopped up. There seemed still to be a good chance of defeating the air assault provided that the Navy could guarantee that no enemy reinforcements should come by sea.

The day of the 21st gave a foretaste of what was in store when the *Juno*, one of the destroyers of a force commanded by Rear-Admiral King whose task was to carry out the night patrol north of Crete in search of troop convoys, was sunk in a dive-bombing attack. At the time this force was cruising to the southward of the Kaso Strait, awaiting the hours of darkness before proceeding once more through the Strait for the night sweep from the eastward of Crete. Farther to the west, where a second force, under Rear-Admiral Glennie, was off the Antikithera Channel waiting to make a similar night sweep from the westward, the cruisers *Ajax* and *Orion* were damaged by near-misses, but not so badly as to be unable to take part in further fighting. Though these setbacks were not severe in view of the overwhelming and unchallenged strength of the German air force in the Cretan skies, they were in fact but the start of a stream of losses which was seriously to weaken the Mediterranean Fleet in a critical phase of the Middle Eastern campaign.

On the night of 21st May Rear-Admiral King's force proceeded through the Kaso Strait for their normal sweep into the Ægean from the eastward and that of Rear-Admiral Glennie through the Antikithera Channel for a similar sweep from the westward. Both forces were ordered to patrol the northern coast of Crete during the hours of darkness and then carry out a daylight sweep up to the northward before withdrawing again to the south.

Rear-Admiral Glennie's force was soon in action. Just before midnight the ships encountered a troop convoy composed mainly of Greek caïques, crowded with German soldiers. The destroyers created havoc in the convoy, sinking at least a dozen caïques and two or three small steamers. No enemy soldier reached Crete alive. Rear-Admiral Glennie, because of shortage of anti-aircraft ammunition, cancelled his daylight sweep to the north and withdrew his ships to the westward.

Rear-Admiral King's force made no sightings during the night and at dawn set out on their sweep up into the Ægean. The ships were sighted from the air and the inevitable attacks by dive-bombers followed. They were largely unsuccessful, though the cruiser *Carlisle* had her speed reduced to twenty-one knots through damage from a near-miss.

As the ships proceeded northward a single caïque, crowded with German troops, was sighted. It was at once sunk by the Australian cruiser *Perth*. Continuing their sweep up to the north, the ships sighted an enemy destroyer about an hour and a half later, and then a second. While the *Perth* and *Naiad* were engaging the first, the destroyer *Kingston* closed the second, claiming two hits. Behind her the *Kingston* sighted, and reported to Rear-Admiral King, a large number of caïques, obviously a second troop convoy.

But by now, because of the continuous air attacks, anti-aircraft ammunition in the squadron was running short and each minute was drawing the ships nearer to the German airfields on the mainland. Rather than jeopardise his whole force, Rear-Admiral King decided to withdraw to the westward, satisfied in his own mind that the enemy convoy was turning back. It did, in fact, turn back and its troops failed to reach Crete, but nevertheless it was a good opportunity missed of inflicting a very severe loss on the enemy, and one which Admiral Cunningham later deplored, for the convoy was of considerable size.

In their withdrawal towards the Kithera Channel, where they were to join forces with the main support squadron, under Rear-Admiral Rawlings, the cruisers and destroyers of Rear-Admiral King's squadron attracted the attention of more and more enemy aircraft. The ominous black shapes of the dive-bombers seemed to hang poised in the sky, awaiting the chance to attack and almost entirely undeterred by the curtains of anti-aircraft fire thrown up by the ships. This was understandable, for so close were the German airfields in Greece that even seriously damaged planes had a good chance of reaching safety. Although the air attacks were incessant, only the *Carlisle* was hit, fortunately with little damage, and the *Naiad*'s speed reduced to nineteen knots by near-misses.

Shortly after noon, with the *Naiad* falling astern, Rear-Admiral King asked Rear-Admiral Rawlings for support as his own supply of anti-aircraft ammunition was almost exhausted. Although his own ships had had their trials and tribulations at the hands of the enemy's air attack, Rear-Admiral Rawlings brought his ships back at their best speed to bring aid to a hard-pressed comrade.

As the two forces met in the Kithera Channel, Rear-Admiral Rawling's flagship, H.M.S. *Warspite*, was hit by a bomb which caused a good deal of damage and reduced her speed to eighteen knots, and the destroyer *Greyhound*, detached from the screen to sink a caïque, was hit and sunk while returning. But there was still worse in store. The cruisers *Gloucester* and *Fiji* and the destroyers *Kandahar* and *Kingston* were sent to pick up survivors of the *Greyhound*, a task made more difficult by the enemy's machine-gunning of the life-boats lowered by the rescuing ships. While returning at high speed on completion of their task, the *Gloucester* was overwhelmed in a mass attack, set on fire, and her upper deck battered into a shambles. To stop to pick up survivors under a sky thick with enemy aircraft was to court disaster, and all that could be done by the other ships was to drop all available boats and floats in the hope of returning later, when darkness would shroud the scene from the enemy's pilots, to complete the work of rescue. The *Gloucester* sank at 4.0 p.m. with a loss of 49 officers and 673 ratings.

Still the tale of disaster was not complete. As the *Fiji*, *Kandahar*, and *Kingston* made their way southward they were hotly pursued by enemy aircraft. Attack after attack was made on the ships, but by fine seamanship and accurate gunfire the enemy was held at bay. Over twenty separate bombing attacks were thus survived, and hopes of a respite rose as the daylight began to fade. Then, from the cover of low cloud, flew one Messerschmidt fighter. It swept down in a shallow dive and dropped its single bomb close amidships on the port side of the *Fiji*. The cruiser took up a heavy list, but though severely damaged was still able to steam at seventeen knots. Half an hour later another single aircraft swept down out of the clouds. The *Fiji* was hit again, her list increased considerably, and a little later she rolled over and sank. The *Kandahar* and *Kingston*, dropping boats and floats for the *Fiji*'s men, continued to the southward to avoid a similar fate, and returned to the rescue when darkness had fallen, picking up 523 officers and men. On completion of that duty they shaped course to rendezvous with Rear-Admiral King to the southward of Crete.

It had been a bad day at sea, so bad indeed that the naval forces were, by order of the Commander-in-Chief, withdrawing to the main base at Alexandria. The day had only reinforced the painful lessons learned in Norway and at Dunkirk, that it is not enough to command the seas unless there is command of the air above the sea as well. The air battle had been lost by default before it had begun, through the withdrawal of the fighters on 19th May to a base in Egypt beyond flying range to Crete. Now, because the air battle had been lost, the sea battle and the land battle too were lost and the fate of Crete was sealed.

It had been a bad day ashore in Crete as well. Gallantly as the soldiers there had fought—and their actions had indeed been most gallant—they could no more stand up to unopposed attack from the air than could the ships afloat. At dawn on the 22nd the vital Maleme airfield was still disputed territory, and the New Zealanders mounted a counter-attack to try to break the still tenuous German hold upon it. It failed, and the enemy, quite oblivious to serious losses, began to operate a "taxi" service of the big Junkers 52 troop-carrying planes, each carrying a complement of up to forty fully equipped men. It was the turning of the tide; from that moment the Cretan battle became a rearguard action. And looming large through the cloud of battle there rose an uneasy question mark in the mind of Admiral Cunningham. It was the spectre of another evacuation, an operation that would call from the remaining ships and crews of the Mediterranean Fleet yet further demands on their endurance and fortitude.

There was, however, one more drama to be enacted at sea before the curtain was dropped on this first phase of the battle. Steaming up from Malta to reinforce Rear-Admiral King was the 5th Destroyer Flotilla, the *Kelly*, *Kashmir*, *Kipling*, *Kelvin*, and *Jackal*. They joined at 4.0 p.m. and, with the coming of darkness, were detached with orders to patrol the waters off the north-western end of Crete. On the way the *Kipling* had trouble with her steering engine and turned back, but the defect was later rectified and Commander St. Clair Ford, her captain, decided to wait in the area south-west of Crete for the return in the morning of the rest of the flotilla. As events turned out, it was a most fortunate decision.

The *Kelvin* and *Jackal*, after a search of Kissamo Bay, returned independently to Alexandria. The *Kelly* and *Kashmir* carried out a short bombardment of Maleme, heavily damaged two caïques, and at dawn retired at high speed round the western end of the island, also bound for Alexandria. And there the German bombers found them. The ships survived two attacks, but a third, consisting of twenty-four dive-bombers, swamped the defence and gave them no chance. The *Kashmir* was hit and sank in two minutes, while the *Kelly*, struck while under full helm at thirty knots, turned turtle, floated upside-down for a few minutes, and then went to the bottom.

Seven miles to the southward lay the *Kipling*, awaiting the return of her flotilla mates. Commander St. Clair Ford had watched the

German attack and was now closing at full speed to the rescue. In spite of six bombing attacks made on the *Kipling* she succeeded in picking up 279 officers and men, including the Captain (D), Lord Louis Mountbatten. With them safely on board she set a course for Alexandria, pursued by enemy aircraft. She beat off every attack and reached her base in safety, though for the last fifty miles she had to be towed in by the *Protector*, having run completely out of fuel.

In London, remote from the overwhelming stress of unopposed air mastery, it was difficult both for the War Cabinet and for the Chiefs of Staff fully to appreciate the wellnigh impossible situation being faced in and around Crete. On 25th May Admiral Cunningham was told by the First Sea Lord that the Mediterranean Fleet "must accept whatever risk is entailed in preventing any considerable reinforcement reaching the island by sea, either by night or day".[11] Admiral Cunningham had, in fact, done just that, but it had already cost him two cruisers and four destroyers sunk, and one battleship, two cruisers, and four destroyers considerably damaged. And even as he was reporting that fact to the Admiralty he learned of further casualties. The aircraft carrier *Formidable* was hit twice and severely damaged after a Fleet Air Arm attack on Scarpanto airfield, and the destroyer *Nubian* had her stern blown off.

Two days later, on 27th May, the Prime Minister, in a signal to the sea, land, and air Commanders-in-Chief in the Mediterranean, said, "Victory in Crete is essential in this turning-point in the war. Keep on hurling in all you can."[12] Again, just this had been done, with ships taking every advantage of the hours of darkness to land troops and supplies, but it had all been in vain in face of the German air power. "Such continuous and unopposed air attack", wrote General Wavell, "must drive the stoutest troops from their positions sooner or later."[13]

But already it was far too late even to attempt to retrieve this lost battle in Crete. Even as the Prime Minister's signal was being deciphered in Cairo on the morning of 27th May, the inevitable decision to evacuate Crete was taken. It was confirmed later in the day by the Chiefs of Staff,[14] "saving as many men as possible without regard to material", and adding a directive to Admiral Cunningham "to take any steps possible to prevent seaborne landings which would interfere with the evacuation".

There were, on that 27th May, some 22,000 soldiers still in Crete. They were 360 miles from Alexandria, and an attempt to evacuate that number in the face of overwhelming air attack at such a distance from the nearest Allied base was to present the Navy with new problems of incalculable difficulty. Worn, weary, and subjected as they had been to prolonged strain, the ships of the Mediterranean Fleet once more set sail for Cretan waters to bring back as many as possible of their military comrades. "I have never", wrote Sir Andrew Cunningham later of this interval between the first battle and the evacuation, "felt prouder of the Mediterranean Fleet than at the close of these operations, except perhaps at the fashion in which it faced up to the even greater strain which was so soon to be imposed upon it."

It was originally planned for the embarkation to take place from four points in the island; Heraklion, on the northern coast, and Sphakia, Plaka, and Tymbaki, in the south-western corner. As it turned out, only Heraklion and Sphakia were used, and from these two ports nearly 16,000 troops were lifted, though unhappily not all of them were to reach Alexandria in safety. The German dive-bombers were still there in tremendous force to dispute with their attacks the sea routes around Crete.

The Heraklion garrison, consisting of nearly 4,000 men, was taken off in the small hours of 29th May. At 6.0 a.m. on the 28th the cruisers *Orion*, *Dido*, and *Ajax*, and the destroyers *Decoy*, *Jackal*, *Imperial*, *Hotspur*, *Hereward*, and *Kimberley*, under the command of Rear-Admiral Rawlings, sailed from Alexandria, bound for Heraklion via the narrow Kaso Strait at the eastern end of the island. They were sighted and attacked from the air during the northward passage, and the *Ajax* was damaged by a near-miss. She was ordered to return to Alexandria, but the rest of the ships succeeded in passing through the Kaso Strait during the dark hours undetected by the enemy's dive-bombers. They reached Heraklion just before midnight on the 28th and the destroyers immediately entered harbour to bring the troops out. In order to make the southward passage of the Kaso Strait in darkness, the latest time for leaving Heraklion was 3.0 a.m. Shortly before this hour the evacuation was complete and the ships sailed for Alexandria with all the soldiers on board. Their troubles were just about to begin.

The first casualty was the *Imperial.* She had been slightly damaged by a near-miss during the air attack of the previous evening and it was at this crucial moment, while the force was steaming at full speed to be clear of Cretan inshore waters before daybreak, that her helm became jammed. Rear-Admiral Rawlings was faced with a difficult decision, whether to stand by her in the hope of repairs being effected or whether to take off the men on board and sink her. He chose the latter and ordered the *Hotspur* to carry out the operation. As a result the *Hotspur* was dangerously crowded with over 900 men on board, though the sinking of the *Imperial* did mean that the squadron could maintain its full speed and would not be impeded by a "lame duck".

This setback, however, had caused some delay and the ships were now an hour and a half late on their timetable. Instead of being through the Kaso Strait and well on the direct route back to Alexandria by dawn, they were only just about to enter it from the northward as the sun began to rise. And there, silhouetted against the dawn and hanging in the sky like buzzards in search of prey, were the ominous black shapes of the dive-bombers.

One after the other the attacks came in. The first ship to be hit was the *Hereward*, and she was so badly damaged that her speed dropped from thirty knots to less than fifteen. Again Rear-Admiral Rawlings was faced with a heart-rending decision, whether to leave her to her fate or to imperil all his ships by standing by her. His choice was the only one possible in the circumstances and when last seen the *Hereward* was making for the coast of Crete, only five miles away, her guns still blazing at the attacking enemy aircraft. She did, in fact, reach the island and succeeded in beaching herself, and most of her complement, with the soldiers she was carrying, survived.

But the squadron's tribulations were not yet over. The bombers were following them down towards Alexandria, and ten more attacks were made before at last they reached the comparative sanctuary provided by friendly Fulmar fighters of the Fleet Air Arm. In those attacks the *Decoy* and *Dido* were both damaged, and the *Orion* hit on three separate occasions, the last time causing severe casualties among her crew and the soldiers on board.

This was hardly an encouraging start to the evacuation, for of the 4,000 men embarked some 800 had been killed, wounded, or re-landed in Crete from the wrecked *Hereward*. Yet a decision to continue the evacuation was inevitable, if only because, as Admiral Cunningham pointed out to the Admiralty,[15] "to leave men deliberately in enemy hands was against all our traditions". Yet so serious were the losses in this first evacuation attempt that even the Admiralty was daunted. Admiral Cunningham, at this time, had much in mind the danger in which the Army stood. He also had in mind the centuries of tradition that lay behind the Navy and remarked to his staff that although it took the Navy three years to build a new ship it would take 300 years to build a new tradition. The Navy had always gone to the Army's help in similar circumstances, and Admiral Cunningham decided that the evacuation would continue so long as he had a ship in which to bring off soldiers. Such argument was unanswerable and the decision was taken to accept the risk of continued losses in ships in carrying through the operation, no matter how hazardous it should prove.

That it was a bold decision in the circumstances none can deny, for further heavy losses could well reduce the fleet to a state where it could no longer hold the sea communications on which the entire campaign in the Middle East depended. That it was also the right decision was proved not alone by its success but also by the many solid and strangely touching expressions of gratitude from soldier to sailor which this operation produced and which do so much to cement the Forces in resolution and fortitude.[16] With a signal to the fleet, "Stick it out, we must never let the Army down", Admiral Cunningham sent his ships back to Crete to bring back as many more men as they could carry.

For the next four nights Sphakia was the scene of embarkation. Surprisingly enough the enemy forbore to attack the area by night, and the scale of air attack in daylight on the ships while on passage was much reduced, partly due to the fact that the Royal Air Force had fitted a few fighters with extra fuel tanks which enabled them to operate farther out to sea. H.M.A.S. *Perth* was hit and damaged on the morning of 30th May, and the destroyers *Kandahar*, *Kelvin*, *Napier*, and *Nizam* suffered minor damage in air attacks, but no ship was sunk and no soldier lost. Close on 16,500 men were brought back in safety, and the only naval loss was that of the anti-aircraft cruiser *Calcutta*, sunk on the morning of 1st June when she was sent out from Alexandria to provide additional protection to the last force returning from Sphakia.

Of the 32,000 British and Dominion soldiers landed in Crete, nearly 16,000 were thus left behind in killed, wounded, and prisoners-of-war. Nearly 12,000 of them were prisoners. The total German casualties were about 12,000, the majority of them valuable, highly trained airborne personnel.

Of those left behind in the final night's evacuation from Sphakia some made their own perilous way back to the British lines. Perhaps typical of these is the exploit of Major Garrett, of the Royal Marines. He had originally gone to Crete with the units of a Mobile Naval Base Defence Organisation, a very highly trained Royal Marine body of soldier-technicians, to provide the defence of Suda Bay. Only a part of the organisation had arrived in the island, and on its invasion by the Germans the Marines had dropped their specialist duties to fight in the field. They formed part of the rearguard behind which the troops retired on Sphakia, and to their magnificent courage and stubborn fighting against great odds during the retreat many thousands of men owed their escape. They were the last troops in the list for embarkation, and none was able to reach the ships on the last night of evacuation.

Major Garrett, finding a damaged landing-craft which had been abandoned and had drifted ashore, collected 4 officers and 134 other ranks all prepared to make a bid for freedom. They got their landing-craft afloat and on the first day reached the tiny uninhabited island of Gaudhopoula, twelve miles from the coast of Crete. That night, with the aid of only a small-scale map of North Africa, they left their island, bound for Tobruk 200 miles away. Their available petrol was exhausted the following evening, but hoisting a square sail made from blankets sewn together on a mast constructed with oars, they sailed on in the general direction of Africa. The unwieldy craft was held on a vague, southerly course by parties of men diving overboard and pushing her bows round to the required direction.

Seven days later, with the men now enduring the last extremities of hunger and thirst, their landing-craft grounded gently on the coast of Africa, a few miles east of Sidi Barrani and well within the British forward positions. In spite of their privations Major Garrett fell his men in and they marched, ragged but triumphant, to the nearest British unit, still with that military precision which is so justly the pride of the Royal Marines.

The cost of the battle of Crete had been heavy indeed. Admiral Cunningham has recorded[17] that it was with a heavy heart that he took stock of his remaining resources after the battle. It had cost the Mediterranean Fleet, in killed alone, nearly 2,000 officers and seamen. Including those ships which had to leave the station for major repairs, the Fleet had lost two of its four battleships, its only carrier, four cruisers, one anti-aircraft cruiser, and eight destroyers. Other ships were out of action for various periods for less extensive repairs. "It is not easy", wrote Admiral Cunningham in his official report, "to convey how heavy was the strain that men and ships sustained. Apart from the cumulative effect of prolonged seagoing over extended periods it has to be remembered in this last instance that ships' companies had none of the inspiration of battle with the enemy to bear them up. Instead they had the unceasing anxiety of the task of trying to bring away in safety thousands of their own countrymen, many of whom were in an exhausted and dispirited condition, in ships necessarily so overcrowded that even when there was opportunity to relax, conditions made this impossible. They had started the evacuation already overtired, and they had to carry it through under conditions of savage air attack, such as had only recently caused grievous losses in the Fleet. It is perhaps even now not realised how nearly the breaking-point was reached, but that these men struggled through is the measure of their achievement, and I trust that it will not lightly be forgotten."

Yet the German victory was a hollow one. The 7th Airborne Division, the pride of Goering's *Luftwaffe*, and the only one that Germany possessed, was destroyed in Crete. Certainly it won that island for Germany, but its destruction there lost to Germany the chance of gaining Cyprus, Syria, and Iraq, and of outflanking the whole of the Middle East theatre of war, which were the further objectives for this division, listed by Hitler in his Directive (No. 31) issued on 9th June. The cost of victory in Crete was indeed heavy in men; it was heavier still in the lost opportunities which followed the annihilation of the German 7th Airborne Division.

The loss of Crete, with all that it meant in the strategical picture in the eastern Mediterranean, was a sad blow to British hopes. It brought the main fleet base of Alexandria, and indeed the whole of the Canal Zone, within much easier flying distance of enemy aircraft, and in German hands it threatened the whole security of that vitally important area.

But Crete, though it had loomed large in Admiral Cunningham's commitments, was by no means his only concern in the developing pattern of the war in that area. There was still Malta to be maintained and sustained; there was Tobruk, cut off by land, to be provisioned and supplied from the sea; there were ships to be provided to support the operations in Syria against the Vichy French; there was the Axis line of reinforcement and replenishment across the Sicilian narrows to be watched and attacked; and there was our own continued build-up of strength in Egypt to be maintained. It was this last preoccupation which was of the most immediate importance, for an advance on land from Egypt into Cyrenaica would have the double effect of relieving the beleaguered fortress of Tobruk, with its consequent easing of pressure on Admiral Cunningham's hard-run ships, and also of driving back the enemy from the Egyptian border and reducing the land threat to the Canal Zone.

This land operation, known as "Battleaxe", was a failure. It was launched on 13th June, but the new British tanks, ferried out through the Mediterranean with so much difficulty and dislocation of naval forces, failed to stand up to the mechanical demands which desert fighting made upon them. Two days after the initial advance, General Wavell's forces were back "practically to our starting positions with heavy loss of tanks".[18] The hoped-for relief of Tobruk had failed, and the fortress continued to depend on the "Tobruk run" for its daily supplies and sustenance. This arduous duty fell partly on the Inshore Squadron, made up of four destroyers, three sloops, two gunboats, and a number of smaller, auxiliary vessels, and partly on the remaining destroyers in the fleet, all of which took a turn at this "Tobruk run". Fighter protection during daylight hours was provided by the Royal Air Force and the Fleet Air Arm, and for some months yet the sustenance of Tobruk was to call for extended efforts on the part of the ships of the Inshore Squadron.

Malta, too, presented yet another problem of acute difficulty. With the fall of Crete there were fears, natural enough, that the airborne experiment so successful there might well be repeated at the expense of that vital link in the defence chain. On 5th June the Governor of Malta, General Dobbie, sent a long appreciation of the position to the War Cabinet,[19] asking for substantial reinforcements, especially of fighter aircraft. At that date there were but twenty-eight Hurricanes in Malta and a few naval Swordfish aircraft, and on them was falling the heavy brunt of the continuous and savage air battle. And since it was from Malta that the main attack on the German-Italian supply route to North Africa must needs be based, its retention on that score alone was of tremendous importance. The Chiefs of Staff fully agreed to the need for reinforcement[20] and this, of course, meant yet one more important commitment for the Mediterranean Fleet and for Force H.

The experiment, made after the battle of Matapan, of using destroyers from Malta to attack this route had been dropped because of the impossibility of operating surface ships from a base so systematically bombarded from the air. It was therefore left to the Swordfish aircraft of the Fleet Air Arm, to the bomber squadrons of the Royal Air Force, and to submarines of the 10th Flotilla based there to make this route as hazardous as possible for the enemy. And nobly they did so. The losses of submarines in the clear waters of the Mediterranean were severe, but the price was not unwillingly paid. A heavy toll was taken of the enemy supply ships as they ventured out to run the gauntlet across this narrow strip of sea, and Malta's contribution to Rommel's loss of supplies during these months amounted to seventy-six ships of 350,000 tons.

The two ends of this short enemy supply route were under constant patrol by submarine flotillas based on Malta and Alexandria, while a third flotilla, operating from Gibraltar, sought for victims off Naples, Genoa, and the Sardinian coasts. Still others found worthwhile targets in the Ægean Sea, where they did much to dislocate the enemy's seaborne traffic between his newly-won outposts in Greece and Crete and the Black Sea. But of all these operations, those directed against Rommel's direct supply line were of far the most importance, and the names of such submarines as *Upholder*, *Upright*, *Urge*, *Unbeaten*, *Unique*, and *Ursula* began to figure more and more in the official despatches as they took their toll of enemy supplies and reinforcements. The Victoria Cross awarded to Lieutenant-Commander M. D. Wanklyn of the *Upholder* after a particularly hazardous attack in which he sank the 18,000-ton *Conte Rosso* out of a strongly protected convoy, was a measure of the daring and skill of the intrepid young men who manned the submarines. It was their successes, more than any other cause, that prevented Rommel from exploiting the favourable position he had reached after his startling victories on land in North Africa.

In spite of the defeat in Crete, in spite, too, of the severe losses in ships which that operation had entailed, the waters of the eastern Mediterranean were still being held by Admiral Cunningham's attenuated fleet. His few ships barred the way to a German descent on North Africa from their new Grecian bases, and prevented, too, the establishment of a second line of supply to Rommel's armies still poised on the Egyptian border. It was in the main hard, unspectacular work, but it preserved the tenuous line of sea power which still stood between Hitler and his ultimate goal.

Germany, her frontal attack across the eastern Mediterranean hamstrung through the loss of her 7th Airborne Division in

Crete, engaged instead in "back-door" efforts to escape beyond the net cast by British sea power in this important area. Nazi instigation and promises of armed support had encouraged the Iraq Government, under the leadership of Rashid Ali, to attack British bases at Habbaniyah and Basra, and to establish a block on the oil pipeline to the Mediterranean at Rutbah Wells. German agents were known to be entering Iraq from Turkey and Persia, presumably to prepare for the arrival of airborne troops, and German aircraft were engaged by R.A.F. fighters over Mosul and Damascus. Swift action by the Middle East forces, however, forestalled this threatened German move, and by the end of May the danger was finally liquidated when the discredited Rashid Ali fled from Iraq.

A second, and similar, threat existed in Syria, where strong French forces, loyal to the Vichy regime, were beginning to co-operate with the Germans. Reports from several sources showed that the French airfields at Aleppo and Palmyra had been handed over to German control[21] and that French troops, led by officers with anti-British leanings, were massing on the Palestine border. A German occupation of Syria was obviously contemplated, and any firm establishment of the enemy there would both outflank all our Middle East positions and threaten the important oil pipeline from the Kirkuk fields. There was but one course of action, and British troops, with a large contingent of Free French under General Catroux, advanced into Syria on 8th June. At the same time ships of the Mediterranean Fleet bombarded transport and tanks on the coast road and engaged the enemy's gun positions, causing "considerable deterioration in morale among the troops exposed . . . to this gruelling flank fire from the sea".[22] They also contained the Vichy French naval forces still at Beirut. It proved a longer operation than had been expected, for the French defenders fought stoutly, but in the final outcome, as in Iraq, the German threat was forestalled. Both these "back doors" were closed in time, and the Mediterranean link in the sea ring could still be firmly held.

In their strategic review after the fall of Crete, the Chiefs of Staff had predicted that both Alexandria and the Mediterranean

Fleet would be increasingly threatened by enemy air power. It was strange that the German command did not immediately seize so golden an opportunity of delivering a death-blow to Admiral Cunningham's ships. But the reason was soon to become apparent with electrifying force. For months Hitler's brain had been full of Operation "Barbarossa", and his way now was clear. Immediately after the Cretan campaign he had given orders for the Mediterranean air forces to be pruned severely in order to build up the necessary numbers to support his new venture. This build-up was watched by British Intelligence with something like amazement and almost disbelief, but as day followed day and the movement to the East continued, there came the moment when there could be no further room for doubt.

On 22nd June the blow fell. At dawn that day German armoured divisions rolled out across the Russian frontier, and German aircraft flew deep into Soviet territory, blasting the Russian lines of communication with their bombs. The threat to Egypt from Greece and Crete receded under the physical demands of this new campaign, with which Hitler had now burdened the Axis war machine, and the lessened menace of the dive-bombers, though still not fully removed, enabled Admiral Cunningham to contemplate his still gigantic task with a more hopeful eye. As Hitler marched his troops into the deep unknown of the Russian wilderness, the Mediterranean Fleet, licking its wounds after the recent battles, returned to its task of holding the ring with a new determination and fortitude.

# Chapter 6

## THE ATLANTIC MENACE

"THE U-boat", wrote Admiral Doenitz on 1st September, 1939, "will always be the backbone of warfare against England, and of political pressure on her." Admiral Raeder, the naval Commander-in-Chief, agreed with his colleague. "It is imperative", he noted at the end of 1940, "to concentrate all the forces of the Navy and the Air Force for the purpose of interrupting all supply shipments to Britain. This must be our chief operational objective in the war against Britain."[1]

British and American experts also agreed. When the staff conversations between Great Britain and the United States, referred to in an earlier chapter, were held in Washington in February and March 1941, the joint delegations emphasised in their final report the cardinal and fundamental importance to the whole structure of strategic policy of the ability to use the seas for merchant shipping. In their view the only hope of Great Britain, and of the United States if she were drawn in, of continuing the struggle depended entirely upon retaining the command of the sea and the consequent flexibility which it brings in the ability to move men and munitions quickly and efficiently where they are most needed. The British Chiefs of Staff found no difficulty in endorsing that profound truth when they reported to the War Cabinet on the Anglo-U.S. Staff conversations.[2]

The United States had, by the end of 1940, already passed beyond the stage of neutrality into that of non-belligerency. In a nation-wide broadcast on the eve of 1941 President Roosevelt had gone even further, stating: "We must produce arms and ships with every energy and resource we can command. We must be the great arsenal of democracy." The implication of that declaration was obvious, for an arsenal could be of little value unless it delivered its weapons to the seat of war. As American production grew, bringing an increasing flow of war material to hard-pressed Britain, the importance of the transatlantic shipping routes grew with it.

To Admiral Raeder his course was clear. Doenitz, commanding the U-boats, was perhaps too much wrapped up in his beloved charges to consider deeply the wider application of the attack on trade, but Raeder's view was more embracing. To supplement the U-boats he was prepared to send out, in addition, his major fleet units to prowl the ocean highways. Towards the end of the year he had four of these warships preparing for raider operations—the *Scheer*, *Hipper*, *Gneisenau*, and *Scharnhorst*. Two more, the giant *Bismarck*, and the cruiser *Prinz Eugen*, were approaching completion. From all these he expected a notable addition to the mounting total of tonnage sunk.

The first out was the pocket battleship *Scheer*. She left Germany at the end of October 1940, and as she emerged into the Atlantic out of the Denmark Straits she ran straight into a convoy of thirty-seven ships homeward bound from Halifax. The sole escort was the armed merchant cruiser *Jervis Bay*, commanded by Captain E. S. F. Fegen. With reasonably good fortune the *Scheer* could well have expected to annihilate the entire convoy, but she met instead so dogged and spirited a defence by the *Jervis Bay* that she was baulked of her full prey. Ordering the convoy to scatter behind a smoke-screen, Captain Fegen steamed out to challenge, and to delay as much as possible, this powerful adversary. The fight could, of course, have but one conclusion, but the time gained by the *Jervis Bay* was invaluable. The short November day was already drawing to its close when the *Scheer* at last finished off her weakly-armed adversary, and the swift fall of darkness saved most of the convoy. Thanks to Captain Fegen's gallantry and self-sacrifice, thirty-two of the thirty-seven ships lived to sail again another day, and the posthumous Victoria Cross awarded to him nine days later was swift recognition of a supremely gallant act.

The next warship to leave Germany was the cruiser *Hipper*. She failed to discover the Halifax convoy route, but on shifting her area of operations farther south made contact on Christmas Eve with a troop convoy bound for the Middle East. She shadowed the convoy at long range throughout the night and, at dawn on Christmas Day, closed in to reap her reward.

She had, however, caught a "tartar". Troop convoys were invariably strongly escorted and this one was no exception. Three cruisers and a carrier were in attendance, and the *Hipper* was easily driven off, escaping in the low visibility of the Christmas dawn. But she had been hit and that, combined with machinery defects, decided her captain to return to Brest for repairs. She was the first major German warship to enter a French Biscay port.

Next to erupt upon the North Atlantic scene were the battle-cruisers *Scharnhorst* and *Gneisenau*. They sailed from Kiel on 23rd January, 1941, but were sighted by British agents as they steamed out of the Baltic. Within a few hours the information was in the Admiralty. It was at once signalled to the Commander-in-Chief, now Admiral Sir John Tovey, who had relieved Admiral Forbes during the previous month. The Home Fleet sailed from Scapa and took up a position south of Iceland to cover both exits into the Atlantic. In the early morning of 28th January the cruiser *Naiad* reported a radar contact of the two enemy battle-cruisers, and later caught a fleeting glimpse of them, only to lose sight a moment or two later in the heavy snow showers. Alarmed, the *Scharnhorst* and *Gneisenau* doubled back at their maximum speed into Arctic waters, where they refuelled from a waiting tanker before making a second attempt to break out. This time they were more fortunate, and on 4th February reached the North Atlantic unobserved, with designs upon the convoy traffic.

Four days later they sighted the smoke of an east-bound convoy and closed for the kill. But, like the *Hipper* before them, they were to have an equally rude awakening from any dreams they may have had of a quick success. Among the ships of the convoy they recognised the unmistakable shape of a battleship. She was the *Ramillies*, acting as ocean escort for the homecoming merchant vessels. The two enemy ships turned away and made off at full speed before the *Ramillies* could identify them. In fact, she only sighted one of the two and reported her as a *Hipper*-class cruiser.

Admiral Lütjens, in command of the German ships, lay low for a few days and then reappeared on the convoy route farther to the westward. Here, on the 22nd, he fell in with a number of ships recently dispersed from an outward-bound convoy. Five were sunk and then, worried by the raider distress signals which they had sent out, the *Scharnhorst* and *Gneisenau* again disappeared into the blue.

The two battle-cruisers next looked for victims on the Sierra Leone route, but once again were foiled. They found a convoy but it was being escorted by the battleship *Malaya*, whose aircraft, and later the *Malaya* herself, sighted and reported them. Making use of their superior speed both the enemy ships got away. But their presence in the area was now known and they could remain there only at their peril.

Admiral Lütjens took them back to the North Atlantic, and it was there that they achieved the greatest success of their cruise. On 15th and 16th March they sank or captured sixteen ships in quick succession from recently dispersed convoys. But once again the broadcasting of raider distress signals from the ships attacked alarmed Lütjens, for he knew that they would not remain unanswered for long. They broke away from this profitable hunting-ground on the 16th and made for Brest. They were only just in time, for the *Rodney*, attracted by the distress signals, reached the area no more than three or four hours after their departure.

In the meantime, the *Hipper* had sailed from Brest on a second sortie into the South Atlantic. This time she was more fortunate, meeting a group of nineteen unescorted ships bound from Freetown for home. There was no fear of opposition here, and she sank seven of them before returning to Brest. There she was heavily attacked by British bombers, but escaped damage. She finally returned safely to Germany, making the passage of the Denmark Straits in safety under cover of thick weather that hampered all our patrols.

None of these excursions by surface warships went unchallenged, and both the Home Fleet and Force H were out in force in the hope of bringing the enemy to battle. But in the immensity of the two Atlantic oceans in which they operated, the chances of encounter were relatively minute. All the advantages lay with the enemy, both through their reluctance to fight and through their superior speed which enabled them to escape when challenged. It was hardly surprising that none of them was brought to battle, though many thousands of miles were steamed in the search for them.

Although these forays by the German fleet units had caused much concern and a serious dislocation of the normal convoy cycle, and although they accounted for more than a quarter of a million tons of shipping, they did not constitute the main threat to the essential supply shipping. It was the U-boats which presented the greater and more intractable problem. Already, in those early months of 1941, the correct answer to the U-boat threat was evolving, and was indeed recognised, though bedevilled to some extent by differing theories of interested authorities and to a much greater extent by desperate shortages of air and surface escorts. In its bare essentials the conduct of anti-submarine warfare was recognised as being very similar to that of anti-raider warfare; to avoid if possible the main concentrations of U-boats and, for the rest, to force the U-boats to come to those areas where the anti-submarine forces were at their strongest. And those areas were in the vicinity of convoys adequately protected by both air and surface escort, where the battle could be joined at odds most favourable to the defence.

But in those early months of 1941, and indeed for many more months yet to come, the necessary surface escorts existed only on the slipways in the building-yards or as designs still on the drawing-boards. By herculean efforts, and by pressing every possible vessel into the pool, surface anti-submarine escort all the way across the Atlantic, and also all the way down to Freetown, was achieved by the summer of 1941. This, however, was done largely at the expense of a suitable reserve of ships for emergencies and also of adequate and intensive training in anti-submarine measures. Periods of rest, of refresher courses in tactical anti-submarine exercises, even of periodical ship maintenance and refit, had to go by the board at this difficult period, and one sees a picture of escort crews, their eyes red-rimmed with fatigue, haggard and unshaven, driving themselves to the very edge of endurance in their ceaseless task of shepherding their charges across the danger-studded oceans. It was a case of throwing everything into the immediate battle, and of looking to future production both to provide the required numbers of escort ships and enough spares to carry out the necessary specialist training.

Of equal importance was air escort of the convoys. It was the combination of the two, around and above the convoy, that alone could sound the death-knell of the U-boats. As yet the full acceptance of this doctrine, with all that it implied in concentration of effort, was open to some strongly expressed doubts by theorists who favoured a more "attacking" policy, as exemplified by bombing attacks on U-boat bases, by offensive air patrols over the U-boat transit areas, and by "hunter-killer" groups roaming the main trade routes in search of U-boats. As the battle developed, all these methods, with the exception of the first, had their successes, but they were all costly in terms of human and material effort in comparison with the rate of U-boat killing around the convoys.

It is difficult, over so vast a stage as the seas which both divide and join the Empire, to visualise the immensity of this battle of the Atlantic. The term is in itself a misnomer, for it really embraced more than the two Atlantic oceans alone. The Indian Ocean, across which run the main sea routes to Australia, New Zealand, India, the East Indies, the Middle East, and the naval base at Singapore, was as important to global strategy as was the Atlantic, through which flowed supplies to the European and African theatres of war. The Arctic Ocean was the only highway by which supplies could be taken to hard-pressed Russia at the start of her great campaign, though later a second supply route was opened through the Persian Gulf. All of them demanded protection from the assault of the enemy, and although we have come to look upon this battle of the defence of shipping as "the battle of the Atlantic", a more accurate description might well be "the battle of the oceans".

In terms of miles this vast battle ran into hundreds of thousands each week, in terms of ships it meant as many as a thousand at sea on any one day, all of them to be guarded against the danger of swift, unseen attack. That was the yardstick against which it must be measured, a vast and ceaseless conflict conducted over millions of square miles of ocean.

In this great battle, during these early months of 1941, the problems of air escort were, perhaps, even more pressing than those of surface escort, which itself was still far from solution. The new anti-submarine corvettes[3] were by now beginning to come forward in encouraging numbers, but they possessed neither the speed nor the endurance to perform the task as it needed to be done. It was not until the new frigates[4]—larger, faster, and more seaworthy than the corvettes—appeared on the scene that we had at last a ship which answered all the requirements of anti-submarine warfare. The first batch of them did not enter the battle until 1942.

Progress in the provision of suitable air escort was slower. So far as aircraft were concerned Coastal Command was the Cinderella of the Royal Air Force, lacking at this time both a suitable weapon with which to attack a U-boat and also a suitable aircraft to undertake the task of convoy escort and support. The first lack was rectified by the modification of the naval depth-charge as an attack weapon from the air, but the second was a far more intractable problem. Range and endurance were the key necessities here, but the priorities of Bomber Command bore heavily on the fulfilment of Coastal Command's requirements.

The provision of air cover over the convoys had, it was soon discovered, a profound effect on the U-boats. A convoy which had both air and surface escort was virtually immune from attack, and the regularity with which they escaped the fate of less adequately protected convoys could not fail to tell its story. What, in effect, air cover over the convoys achieved at this period of the war was to drive the U-boats farther to the westward, beyond the range of the shore-based air escort. It was in that area alone that they could cruise with any reasonable chances of success.

By operating from airfields in Northern Ireland and on the west coast of Scotland, Coastal Command aircraft could cover threatened convoys to a distance of 600 miles out into the Atlantic, though such cover was limited to daylight hours. With the use of bases in Iceland, a distance of 400 miles from that island could be covered. A little later in the year, following a conference of British and Canadian air authorities, nine very long-range Catalinas were transferred to the Canadian Air Force and escort could be given to a distance of 600 miles from the Canadian coast. This, however, was the limit of shore-based escort, and another two years were to elapse before these distances could be improved. Even within these limits, shortages in actual aircraft numbers made air escort, at best, no more than spasmodic, depending on variations in the number actually operational at any one period.

These limiting aircraft ranges from the various shore bases produced a gap in mid-Atlantic of some 400 miles, over which no shore-based aircraft could operate. This gap, of course, did not appear until the Catalinas began their operation from Canada later in 1941, but even before its appearance the reaction of the U-boats was significant. Almost without exception they established their patrol areas beyond the reach of the escorting aircraft, where they had only the surface escort to contend with. It was even more marked when, at last, the Canadian air operations began. They then left the Canadian coastal areas and crowded into the centre gap. The inference was obvious, and such measures as were possible were put in hand to close the gap with ship-borne aircraft. But in the natural exigencies of war, and in the pressure of conflicting operational claims, the provision of escort carriers was a lengthy project and the time-lag before their appearance was to prove immensely costly in the tale of sunken ships.

On 10th December, 1940, the Prime Minister announced in the House of Commons[5] a decision of the Defence Committee of the War Cabinet to place Coastal Command under the operational control of the Admiralty. This move reflected Admiralty fears that maritime aircraft might be switched, without reference to naval requirements, to other tasks in the air war. The decision took effect as from 15th April, 1941, and from the first worked happily and smoothly. What could, in other circumstances, have so easily

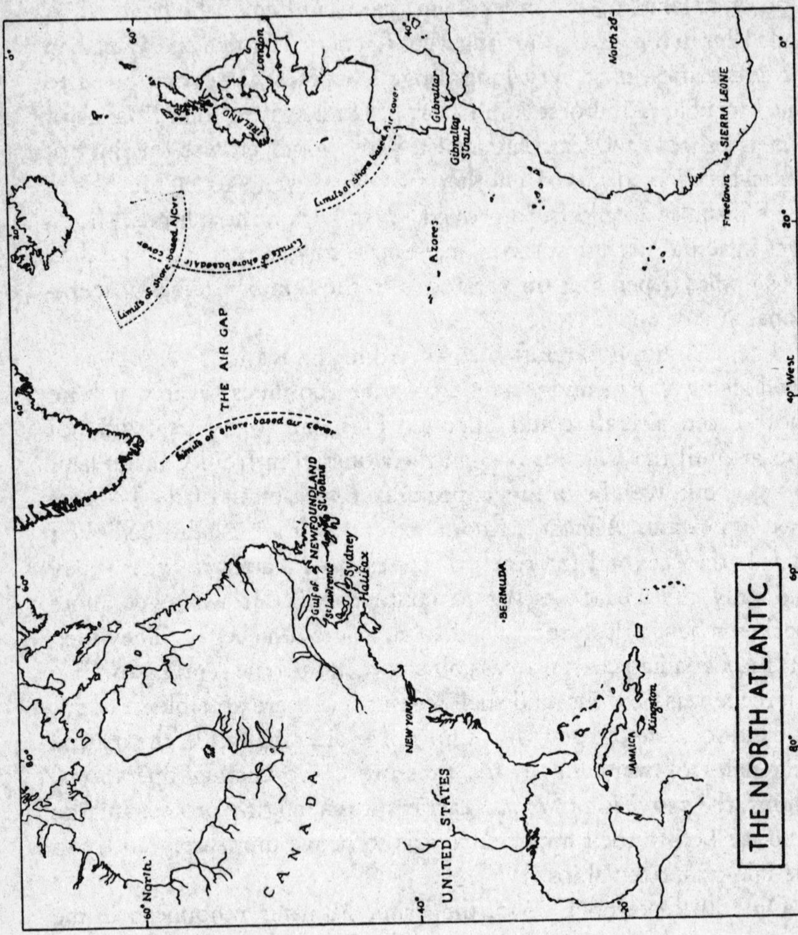
THE NORTH ATLANTIC
CANADA
UNITED STATES
NEW YORK
BERMUDA
JAMAICA
Kingston
Gulf of St Lawrence
NEWFOUNDLAND
St Johns
Sydney
Halifax
THE AIR GAP
Limits of shore-based air cover
Azores
IRELAND
London
Gibraltar
Gibraltar Strait
SIERRA LEONE
Freetown
60° North
40° West
North 20

developed into an inter-Service squabble was implemented in a spirit of co-operation and singleness of purpose that was to bring a high reward in the struggle that still lay ahead.[6]

Although, by April 1941, the Navy could thus appreciate the true answer to the U-boat threat, there was still a long road to travel before that answer could become fully operational. There were other schools of thought still to be convinced, other priorities clamouring for the limited supplies of very long-range aircraft needed to provide the all-essential air escort. As 1941 progressed, the shortages of surface escorts eased as the war emergency building programme began to take effect,[7] but the numbers of suitable aircraft lagged alarmingly behind. Much of their air effort, too, was dissipated in the less productive forms of U-boat hunting, mainly in the shape of offensive patrols flown over the U-boat transit areas. The blame for this, of course, lay at least in part at the doors of the Admiralty, for although there was considerable pressure from the Air Staff for Coastal Command aircraft to be thus used "offensively", the Admiralty at this stage had the necessary powers to enforce their own requirements in the operational use of Coastal Command. It is but fair to add that there were still many authorities in the Admiralty itself who agreed with the Air Staff's thesis.

It is interesting to record a recommendation of the Committee, set up to study the air aspect of the U-boat war, issued at this period. This set out: "The old principles of employing aircraft to give close escort to convoys, whether threatened or not, should be replaced by a new conception of the use of air power in the war at sea. Henceforth, the principal role of the aircraft should be offensive, to seek out and destroy the U-boats wherever they were to be found rather than to wait for them to come to us." It was an attractive theory, but was not borne out by results. And, moreover, in the true exercise of air power, who were the Admiralty to challenge the opinions of the chiefs of this new and rapidly growing Service? The new set-up with Coastal Command demanded infinite tact and a large measure of autonomy if friction were to be avoided.

There were other pitfalls, too, for some too hasty travellers along this hard and uphill road which led towards Atlantic security. The long-term solution, recognisable even in 1941, was bedevilled by the intense urgency of the supply problem at this particular stage of the war. Time was an essential factor, and the trade convoy, if more sure of arrival than the independent ship, took on the average more than twice as long to reach Britain.

It was to achieve the best practicable shipping delivery rate that the Admiralty had agreed, at the start of the war, to permit ships with a speed of fifteen knots and above to sail independently of convoys, relying on their speed to avoid attacks by wandering U-boats. These independents had suffered a higher percentage of loss than the slower convoys, but the increased speed of shipping turn-round provided by their swifter arrival was held to justify the losses. But at the end of 1940, when so much was still needed to sustain and supplement the national war effort, the War Cabinet, at the instigation of the Import Executive and against the advice of the Admiralty, decided to reduce the minimum speed of independently sailed ships from fifteen knots to thirteen. The desire, of course, was to speed imports by cutting down the inevitable delays that convoy brought in its train, and in its intention was a laudable effort to prosecute the receipt in Britain of those supplies on which the nation depended for its very life.

The result was disastrous. As compared with ships in convoy, the loss rate of the independents of between thirteen and fifteen knots was three times as great. Admiral Sir Percy Noble, Commander-in-Chief Western Approaches and as such responsible for the operational conduct of the Atlantic U-boat war, pressed strongly for a resumption of the upper limit in speed. In the face of the loss figures there could be no argument, and the fifteen-knot minimum was reintroduced in May 1941. In terms of ships and of lives lost it had been a tragic mistake.

Looking back across the intervening years one can discern, in the light of after-knowledge, the first gleams of light penetrating the darkness of this savage battle. The correct tactical procedure was emerging from the angry flow of conflicting theories and the oppressive gloom of opposing priorities. But to those engaged in this stern struggle at that time all was darkness and these initial gleams were not yet apparent. The monthly totals of tonnage sunk continued to rise to figures that in their immensity carried forebodings of ultimate defeat, and although U-boats were being sunk out in the Atlantic, still more were taking their place to swell the numbers lurking in the hidden depths of the oceans. No sign of the coming dawn was discernible in the darkness of the Atlantic night.

The desperate need called for desperate measures. On 6th March the Prime Minister issued a directive on the battle of the Atlantic which has since become famous. "We must take the offensive against the U-boat and the Focke-Wulf wherever we can and whenever we can. The U-boat at sea must be hunted, the U-boat in the building yards or in dock must be bombed. The Focke-Wulf and other bombers employed against our shipping must be attacked in the air and in their nests. Extreme priority will be given to fitting out ships to catapult or otherwise launch fighter aircraft against bombers attacking our shipping. Proposals should be made within a week."[8]

It was a clarion call, and it came in a month dark with menace when merchant ship sinkings, by raider, by U-boat, and by bomber, totalled over one hundred ships of more than half a million tons.

But not all was loss. In this same month of March the destroyer *Wolverine* and the corvettes *Camellia* and *Arbutus*, escorting an outward-bound convoy, attacked and sank two U-boats, one of which was later identified as *U.47*. This was Gunther Prien's boat, and Prien was on board. He was one of the greatest of the U-boat "aces", a man from whom many of the U-boat commanders drew their inspiration. Ten days later another resounding success was achieved by the escorting destroyers of a homeward-bound Halifax convoy, during a wolf-pack attack, when they sank two out of five attacking U-boats. Those that were sunk were *U.99*, by H.M.S. *Walker*, and *U.100*, by H.M.S. *Vanoc*. The two U-boat commanders were Otto Kretschmer and Joachim Schepke, after Prien the two most outstanding U-boat commanders in the German Navy and both of them decorated by Hitler with the Knight's Cross and Oakleaf for having each sunk more than 200,000 tons of shipping.

The loss of Prien, Kretschmer, and Schepke, all within a space of ten days, and all at the hands of convoy escorts, was a tremendous blow to the U-boat Command. Just how tremendous, however, was not yet apparent in the British Admiralty, for it had been impossible to gauge there the personal influence which these three men exercised on the morale and audacity of their fellow U-boat commanders. For perhaps the first time since the start of the war there was a feeling among them that the U-boat might not be entirely invincible, that the "happy time" had ended, that the defence was catching up, and that attacking convoys accompanied by battle-trained escorts was very different from attacking independent ships. There was, perhaps, a suspicion of a crack in the imposing edifice of U-boat mastery, so carefully nurtured by Admiral Doenitz.

In London, however, no sign of this could yet be appreciated. The elimination of these three "aces" was greeted with relief, though not with any thoughts that the burden of U-boat warfare would be materially lightened. The road ahead still stretched away into the future, long, black, and forbidding, and its end seemed very far away. The deaths of Prien and Schepke, and the capture of Kretschmer, may not have meant the turning of a corner, but at least it was a bend in the road, and a bend in the right direction.

# Chapter 7

## THE *BISMARCK* OPERATION

THE successes of the *Scheer*, *Hipper*, *Scharnhorst*, and *Gneisenau* in their cruises against the Allied seaborne trade so encouraged Admiral Raeder that he began to plan an even bigger and better operation on similar lines, to take place in April 1941. He had the *Scharnhorst* and *Gneisenau* sheltering in Brest harbour; at Gdynia lay the 42,500-ton battleship *Bismarck* and the 10,000-ton cruiser *Prinz Eugen*, their trials completed and both now ready for their first operational appearance upon the stage of war.

This new operation was to be the most important of all the German naval efforts and was given the code name "Rheinübung" As originally planned it was to last three months, with the two battle-cruisers from Brest joining the *Bismarck* and *Prinz Eugen* as soon as they reached the open Atlantic. So powerful a squadron at large in the oceans was confidently expected completely to paralyse British shipping in the Atlantic and to bring it almost to a standstill. Indeed, had all four ships succeeded in concentrating in the Atlantic they might well have achieved almost exactly that.

Intensive planning went into Operation "Rheinübung". Before the warships sailed, tankers were despatched to strategic positions from which the raiders could refuel. Independent merchant ships, disguised as neutrals, were placed in areas in which they might pick up useful information about convoy routes and times of sailing. Supply ships and weather-reporting trawlers were sent out to support and aid the venture. An extensive wireless intelligence network was set up to try to plot the positions and courses of convoys and independent ships as they traversed the oceans. As little as possible was being left to chance, and Admiral Lütjens, so successful with the *Scharnhorst* and *Gneisenau*, was again placed in overall command, flying his flag in the *Bismarck*.

Yet chance so often disrupts the best laid of schemes. The *Scharnhorst*, refitting at Brest, was found to require more extensive repair than had been expected and was now not expected to be ready until the first week in June. During April the *Gneisenau* was hit by a torpedo from a Coastal Command aircraft and severely damaged. She moved into dry dock, and five nights later was hit four times during a raid by Bomber Command on the port. She, too, would not now be ready for "Rheinübung". Yet so eager was the German Naval Staff to act as early as possible that it was decided to send out the *Bismarck* and *Prinz Eugen* on their own, to be joined later by the *Scharnhorst* when her refit was completed.

Admiral Tovey, in the *King George V* in Scapa, was acutely aware of the possibility of a further German break-out. He knew, of course, that the *Bismarck* and *Prinz Eugen* were now operational, and his experience with the previous warship raiders had shown him the general pattern of their break-out routes. His anxieties over the *Scharnhorst* and *Gneisenau*, which had for some weeks tied up most of the Home Fleet in a long, grinding patrol to the west of Brest, were temporarily allayed by the damage they had received from the air, and as a result he was able to strengthen his watch on the two northern exits into the Atlantic, the Iceland-Faeroes gap and the Denmark Straits. Both were constantly patrolled by cruisers while the Home Fleet lay at Scapa, admirably placed to cover the watching cruisers on the first signs of an enemy break-out.

Almost from the start the German plans went awry. The long refit of the *Scharnhorst* ruled that ship out of the reckoning, leaving only the *Gneisenau* to join the other two. Then came the damage to the *Gneisenau* during the April air attacks, bringing to a full stop the intention to send out the Brest reinforcement for the enterprise. To cap this tale of misfortune, the *Prinz Eugen* developed an engine-room defect which delayed the date of sailing from the full moon period of April until the third week in May. This was a serious postponement, for by May there is little darkness in the Denmark Straits, through which the break-out was to be made. It may well be that this particular delay gave birth to a sense of urgency which, in the end, clouded Admiral Lütjens's judgment when things began to go wrong.

Just before the two warships sailed from Gdynia they were visited by Hitler, who addressed the two crews. He gave them both a "pep" talk, in the course of which he prophesied that the United States would never enter the war. "You are the pride of the Navy," he told the men of the *Bismarck*, just before they sailed with high hopes of success.

As the two ships steamed up the Great Belt and the Kattegat, fortune frowned on them once more. The German Admiralty, in an excess of security-consciousness, had cleared the area of all merchant shipping to prevent any leakage of information about the sortie. But at dawn on 20th May, to their chagrin, the *Bismarck* and *Prinz Eugen* sighted the Swedish cruiser *Gottland* steaming parallel with them in her own territorial waters. The secret was now out and on the following morning they were photographed in Kors Fjord, near Bergen, by a reconnaissance aircraft of Coastal Command, which had been sent out to search for them. The intelligence was signalled at once to the Home Fleet.

Admiral Tovey ordered the *Hood*, *Prince of Wales*, and six destroyers to proceed to the south of Iceland to give cover to the two cruisers, *Norfolk* and *Suffolk*, which were patrolling the Denmark Straits. That left only the flagship, the *King George V*, four cruisers, and three destroyers at Scapa, and they were brought to short notice to proceed to sea. Two other capital ships, the battle-cruiser *Repulse* and the aircraft carrier *Victorious*, had been allocated to the escort of a troop convoy, but the Admiralty cancelled this arrangement and placed these two additional ships at the disposal of the Commander-in-Chief. They too were brought to short notice.

The next essential step was to discover the day of departure of the enemy ships from Bergen. Air patrols were flown across the North Sea throughout the 22nd, but cloud was down to 200 feet and the

Norwegian coast was wrapped in fog. All was uncertainty, and the one vital piece of information that would provide the signal for the start of the operation was missing. As the negative reports from the air patrols came in throughout the day, the Commanding Officer of the Royal Naval Air Station at Hatston, in the Orkneys, took matters into his own hands. He despatched a naval aircraft with a most experienced observer[1] across the North Sea with instructions to comb the Bergen fjords. All depended on the success of its mission. The aircraft was heavily engaged as it crossed the Norwegian coast, but the pilot flew low up and down the Bergen fjords, searching for the quarry. The fjords were empty. As the aircraft flew homewards it signalled the vital information back to base and at 8.0 p.m. it was in the hands of the Commander-in-Chief. Two and three-quarter hours later the Home Fleet was at sea and the operation had begun.

Throughout the night and all next day the Home Fleet steamed to the west-north-westward into a steep, rising sea. The weather was closing in and the gusty wind threatened a westerly gale later. As the ships made their way out into the Atlantic their bows were flinging the spray high over their forecastles.

Far away to the north of Iceland the weather was calmer, though with patches of thick mist hanging over the water. Snow clouds threatened to reduce visibility to a matter of a few yards. This was just the sort of weather for which Admiral Lütjens was hoping to aid him in his break-out. As he rounded the north coast of Iceland his meteorological experts forecasted that it would be thick in the Denmark Straits, with visibility less than 400 yards. He decided to take the plunge.

His weather experts were wrong in their forecast. The centre of the Straits was, indeed, shrouded in dense mist, but close to the ice edge, the track that Admiral Lütjens had selected, was clear with visibility up to eight or ten miles. Yet the German Admiral held on to his chosen course, confident that there were no British ships in the vicinity.[2] It was therefore with considerable chagrin that, at 8.15 p.m., he received a report from the *Prinz Eugen*'s look-out that a three-funnelled cruiser was in sight at a range of just over six miles.

This was H.M.S. *Norfolk*. In point of fact, the *Bismarck* and *Prinz Eugen* had been sighted an hour earlier by H.M.S. *Suffolk*. Her enemy report had not got through to the Commander-in-Chief, but it had reached the *Norfolk* and she had closed to make contact. As she came in sight of the German ships she was greeted with a few salvoes.

By 8.30 p.m. the *Norfolk*'s enemy report was being decoded in the *King George V*. It showed the enemy to be about 600 miles to the north-westward of the Commander-in-Chief, and he altered the course of the fleet to that bearing and increased speed to twenty-seven knots. H.M.S. *Hood*, which with the *Prince of Wales* had been earlier despatched to the Iceland area, had already received the information, for she had taken in the *Suffolk*'s sighting report. She too turned to the north-west and increased speed. She was 300 miles from the enemy and the respective courses were converging. The two forces should meet in the morning.

Admiral Lütjens was confident that he could shake off the pursuit by bursts of high speed, sharp alterations of course, and the use of smoke. But in spite of all he could do, the *Norfolk* and *Suffolk* hung on to him, reporting his movements with what appeared to the Germans to be uncanny accuracy. This, of course, was ship radar, and it came as a complete and shattering surprise to the German Admiral. All the German intelligence reports had until then indicated that it was not yet fitted in British ships; in their own it was used only for gunnery ranging.

Admiral Lütjens was now faced with a difficult decision, whether to turn back in the face of this unexpected threat or whether to continue on his course and chance an encounter with the British Fleet. He decided to go on under the erroneous belief that the Home Fleet was still at anchor in Scapa Flow.[3]

The *Norfolk* and *Suffolk* hung on grimly throughout the night, shadowing just beyond extreme gun range and reporting every alteration of course. Throughout the night, too, the *Hood* and the *Prince of Wales* made ground steadily to the north-west, closing the enemy. Farther away still the Commander-in-Chief, with the *King George V*, *Repulse*, and *Victorious*, was steering a course which, he hoped, would bring him into contact with the *Bismarck* and *Prinz Eugen* later in the day.

As the two enemy ships emerged into the Atlantic they met the force of the wind and the heavy swell that was running. The *Norfolk* and *Suffolk* were still in contact, sometimes losing sight of their gigantic quarry in the rain and falling snow, but always picking her up again by radar. The Arctic twilight was beginning to grow into day, and as a result the shadowing becoming easier. At 3.30 a.m. on the 24th they had a clear sight of her, twelve miles ahead, still steaming at twenty-eight knots. The sighting signal went out, and an hour and a quarter later the *Suffolk* intercepted a signal from the destroyer *Icarus*, escorting the *Hood*. It gave her position as some distance astern of the *Norfolk*, and was the first intimation to Rear-Admiral Wake-Walker, commanding the cruisers in the Denmark Straits, that the *Hood* and the *Prince of Wales* were in his vicinity.

In the *Hood* and the *Prince of Wales* the ships' companies were already at action stations. Vice-Admiral Holland, flying his flag in the *Hood*, intended first to make contact with the *Norfolk* and *Suffolk* and then engage the enemy, concentrating the fire of the two capital ships on the *Bismarck* and that of the two cruisers on the *Prinz Eugen*. The northern day dawned with a leaden sky and a strong, freshening wind that whipped the tops of the waves into foam. At 5.15 a.m. smoke was sighted on the starboard quarter. It was quickly identified as the *Norfolk*. The daylight of the northern morning increased rapidly, and twenty minutes later, at 5.35 a.m., the loom of a large ship could be seen on the north-western horizon. A few moments later it was recognised as the *Bismarck*, with the *Prinz Eugen* ahead of her. Although the *Norfolk* and *Suffolk* were still too far away to join action with the enemy, Vice-Admiral Holland's reaction was immediate. Two minutes after sighting the *Bismarck* the flag signal "Blue pendant four"[4] was flying from the *Hood*'s yardarm, and she and the *Prince of Wales* turned 40 degrees together to starboard towards the enemy.

At 5.52 a.m. the *Hood* fired her first salvo at a range of 25,000 yards. Thirty seconds later the *Prince of Wales* also opened fire.

The enemy replied two minutes later. Almost at once both sides were hitting each other.

The *Hood*, laid down during the first war with Germany and launched in 1919, was an old ship. Being a battle-cruiser she was lightly armoured, and her magazines were but scantily protected. A fire was started by a hit near her mainmast, which spread until the whole of the midship section seemed to be in flames. She was still firing and had, in fact, a signal flying ordering a turn of 20 degrees to port when suddenly, exactly at 6 a.m., she was hit again by plunging fire from the *Bismarck*. A shell exploded in "X" magazine and she was torn asunder by a tremendous explosion. Her bows reared up into the air and then sank vertically. For a minute or two her stern remained afloat, hidden in a vast pillar of smoke, then it, too, sank. Three minutes after the explosion nothing remained of the great battle-cruiser but a huge pall of smoke that drifted away across the waters of an angry sea.

The *Prince of Wales*, following astern of the *Hood*, was forced to alter course to starboard to avoid the wreckage of Vice-Admiral Holland's flagship. This brought her nearer to the enemy ships, and both of them concentrated on her at a range that closed to 14,500 yards. She was hit by the *Bismarck* and her bridge wrecked. Unlike the *Hood* she was a new ship, so new indeed that she had not yet had time to "work up" into full operational efficiency. She was also subject to "teething" troubles with her turret machinery, and as she turned away behind a smoke-screen her after turret jammed, putting four of her big guns out of action for two hours.[5]

But the *Bismarck* had been hit three times by the *Prince of Wales* during the action, and one of the hits was to play a vital part in the later stages of the operation. The shell passed right through the ship, holing two oil tanks. The loss of this oil was not unduly important, but what was far more serious was that the oil in the tanks forward of the damage, a thousand tons of it, could not be used as the suction valves were inaccessible in a flooded compartment.[6] It was this fact that caused Admiral Lütjens to signal home at 8 a.m. that he was going to abandon the operation and make for the Biscay port of St. Nazaire.

Even as she made her signal the forces that were to encompass her destruction were gathering. The Commander-in-Chief, still 360 miles away to the south-east, was steaming at high speed on a converging course. The battleship *Rodney*, escorting the liner *Britannic*, was ordered to leave her charge and steer west to close the *Bismarck*. The *Ramillies*, with a homeward-bound convoy, was told to place herself to the westward of the *Bismarck* to guard against a break in that direction, and the *Revenge* was sailed from Halifax for a similar purpose. The cruiser *Edinburgh*, patrolling in mid-Atlantic in search of German shipping, was ordered to close and assist in the task of shadowing. Admiral Somerville, commanding Force H, was summoned from Gibraltar with the battle-cruiser *Renown* and the carrier *Ark Royal*. He sailed within an hour of receiving the signal from the First Sea Lord, and in his hands he carried the ultimate fate of the *Bismarck*. The net was closing.

After the sinking of the *Hood*, the *Prince of Wales* came under command of Rear-Admiral Wake-Walker in the *Norfolk*, and they and the *Suffolk* settled down to shadow the enemy. Throughout the whole of this day of the 24th they kept in touch, and nothing that the *Bismarck* could do could shake them off. There was a brief flurry of action shortly before 7.0 p.m., when the German battleship apparently tried to waylay the *Suffolk* in the mist, but there were no hits on either side and the ships settled down again into their long, stern task of shadowing.

It was just before this incident that Admiral Lütjens tried to use the *Prinz Eugen* as a lure to draw off the shadowers. By signal to her captain he proposed the *Bismarck* turning away to the westward in a rain squall while the *Prinz Eugen* carried straight on. Captain Brinckmann, of the *Prinz Eugen*, composed a long signal of protest against this decision,[7] but before he could transmit it a suitable rain squall gave the *Bismarck* the opportunity she required. She disappeared from the *Prinz Eugen*'s view, leaving the unhappy Brinckmann alone in a hostile ocean.

The ruse did not work out as Admiral Lütjens had hoped. The faithful *Suffolk*, still in touch, followed the *Bismarck* and continued accurately to report her every movement. It was at this juncture that the *Prinz Eugen* disappeared from the story. She continued to the southward, just managed to reach an oiler in time, and then, deciding that discretion was the better part of valour, shaped a course for the Bay of Biscay and Brest.

At 3.0 p.m. on the 24th the Commander-in-Chief was still some 270 miles from the flying *Bismarck*, steering a converging south-westerly course that would bring him in contact with the enemy, provided that both his and the *Bismarck*'s courses were held, at about 9 a.m. the following day. Yet, in spite of the distance that still separated them, he had in his hand a weapon with which he could strike a blow. He detached the carrier *Victorious* to a position from which she could launch a torpedo bombing attack and at 10 p.m. that night the *Victorious* turned into the wind and flew off nine Swordfish, led by Lieutenant-Commander E. Esmonde. The weather was as bad as it could be, with a dark, foaming sea sweeping down from the north-westward. The Swordfish with their heavy loads climbed slowly into the darkness, obscured by clouds and rain squalls.

At about 11.30 p.m. the leading aircraft picked up two ships on her radar. They were the *Prince of Wales* and *Norfolk*, still in contact. The *Norfolk* directed them on to the *Bismarck*, and just before midnight they broke through the cloud to deliver their attack. Unfortunately, the ship below them when they broke through was not the *Bismarck*, but an American coastguard cutter. This lost for them the element of surprise, for they were sighted by the *Bismarck*. Nevertheless, their attack was pressed home with great gallantry. One torpedo hit the enemy on the starboard side abreast the bridge, but did no damage beyond shaking the ship violently.

All now seemed set fair for battle, with the Home Fleet closing in steadily on the enemy. There was, however, trouble in store. The *Suffolk*, still holding the *Bismarck* with her radar, was zigzagging to avoid possible attack by U-boats. At 3.6 a.m. on the 25th she obtained a contact and began an outward zig of 30 degrees to port. Ten minutes later she turned back, expecting to regain contact on reaching radar range again. But on her return there was no answering echo in her searching beam. The *Bismarck* had disappeared into the darkness.

It was thought that she had most probably broken away to the westward, and it was in that quarter that the search was now directed. It was led by the *Suffolk*, to the south-westward, the *Norfolk* following in the same direction an hour or two later. As soon as it was daylight the *Victorious* flew an air search to the north-westward on instructions from the Commander-in-Chief, but the wind-swept sea in that quarter was empty.

The *Bismarck* had, in fact, turned to the westward, but she had continued her turn right round, slipped unseen under the sterns of her shadowers, and was now on a direct south-easterly course for St. Nazaire. The closing course steered by the Home Fleet had thus become an opening course, and each hour that passed made the distance between the opposing forces greater instead of less.

Admiral Tovey was thus faced that morning with a decision of great perplexity. He knew that the *Bismarck* had been hit, first by the *Prince of Wales* and then by a torpedo from one of the Swordfish from the *Victorious*, but he had no indication as to the extent of the damage. He himself thought it likely that she would try to make for harbour, but he rightly felt that it was the greater danger against which he had to guard. And that greater danger was the peril in which the Atlantic convoys would stand should the *Bismarck* contact one of her oilers and, thus replenished, continue her cruise against the all-essential trade. So it was to the westward that he concentrated his attention, for it was so obviously in that quarter that the greater danger lay.

It was a little later that morning that Admiral Lütjens made his great mistake. If he had kept quiet he might possibly have succeeded in reaching St. Nazaire unscathed; instead, he transmitted a long wireless message to Germany giving an account of his action with the *Hood* on the previous morning. In the British Admiralty, of course, as soon as it was known that the *Bismarck* was at sea, every wireless direction-finding station in the Empire had been instructed to keep watch on her frequency, and this was their great chance to play a part in the chase.

As the bearings came in by signal they were plotted in the Admiralty and then signalled out individually to the Commander-in-Chief under the erroneous belief that some of the ships in the fleet were fitted with direction-finding receivers and would themselves have taken bearings. As soon as they were received in the flagship they were plotted on the chart. Unfortunately it was a navigational chart, not the special kind for wireless bearings, and it gave a position too far to the north, making it appear that the *Bismarck* was breaking-back towards the North Sea.

On that assumption the Commander-in-Chief redisposed his forces, altering course to the north-eastward. He broadcast to all his ships the estimated position[8] of the enemy, and the fleet settled down to the chase again in that quarter.

The bearings plotted in the Admiralty, however, gave a clear indication that it was a Biscay port to which the *Bismarck* was making. The First Sea Lord signalled to Force H, which was not under the direct command of Admiral Tovey, to act on that assumption. H.M.S. *Rodney*, which as yet had not joined the Commander-in-Chief, received similar instructions. Finally, after much anxious thought in the Admiralty, Admiral Tovey was informed that the appreciation there was that *Bismarck* was making for the west coast of France.[9] The Home Fleet at last turned towards the Bay of Biscay, but the precious hours gained by the *Bismarck* had given her a flying start. The British ships were now about 100 miles astern of their quarry and, moreover, were getting low in oil. Only Force H, coming up from Gibraltar, was well placed to intercept, though the old battle-cruiser *Renown*, in which Admiral Somerville was flying his flag, was no match for the brand-new *Bismarck* with her heavy armour and her powerful guns. Admiral Somerville, however, also had the carrier *Ark Royal* under his command, and her Swordfish squadrons were well trained and old hands at the game.

The day of 26th May was the day of the airmen. Just before 10.30 a.m. a Coastal Command Catalina, searching from Lough Erne, broke suddenly through low cloud to sight the massive battleship below her. She was badly shot up by extremely accurate gunfire but, although too damaged to shadow, she survived the attack.

Within a matter of minutes her sighting report was bringing a new flame of hope into a situation that was, through lack of positive news, beginning to grow ever more hopeless.

The *Bismarck* had been found and the hunt was on again.

Twelve minutes later the *Ark Royal*'s Swordfish found her, independently of the Catalina's sighting report which, of course, they could not receive on their sets. They were flying searches ahead of Force H, and once they had the *Bismarck* in view they never let her go. Throughout the day they kept in contact, and as the afternoon wore on the *Ark Royal* at last reached the position from which she could fly off a striking force of torpedo bombers. She ranged her Swordfish on deck, armed with torpedoes, and just before 3.0 p.m., in a heavy sea and under a lowering, overcast sky, they flew off the heavily pitching and spray-swept deck in search of the enemy.

In the meantime other steps had been taken to keep the *Bismarck* in sight. The cruiser *Sheffield*, of Force H, was detached to make contact and shadow. The 4th Destroyer Flotilla, detached from a convoy and ordered to join the Home Fleet to replace Admiral Tovey's own screen which had been forced to leave him through lack of fuel, were also steering for the *Bismarck*. Captain Vian had intercepted the Catalina's sighting report in the morning and had decided to take his destroyers direct to the scene, "knowing that the Commander-in-Chief would wish me to steer to intercept the enemy".[10] It was a bold decision that was to prove of great worth that night and the following morning.

Neither the *Sheffield* nor Captain Vian's destroyers were yet in touch with the enemy when the first striking force of Swordfish arrived overhead. The pilots had not been informed that the *Sheffield* was in the vicinity, and when they picked up a ship in their radar sets it was natural for them to assume that it was the *Bismarck*. They dived down through the low cloud and launched their torpedoes at the wrong ship. The *Sheffield*, realising what had happened, increased to full speed and took violent avoiding action, fortunately with complete success, and was perhaps slightly mollified by a signal from the last of the Swordfish, "Sorry for the kipper."

The disappointment in the *Ark Royal* was intense. So much had been hoped for from this attack from the air, so much had depended upon its success. Unless the *Bismarck* could somehow be stopped she would get clear away and the *Hood* would go unavenged.

The weather was deteriorating rapidly. The threatened gale had at last unleashed its full force over the eastern Atlantic, and towering seas were making the *Ark Royal* pitch through a height of from fifty to sixty feet. It was from this heaving flight deck that the Swordfish, hastily refuelled and rearmed, took to the air for a second shot at the flying enemy. The ultimate result now lay in their hands. This time the pilots were told to contact the *Sheffield* first, which would then direct them on to the true target.

The *Bismarck*, steaming steadily south-eastward, was now passing through historic waters. Down the years they had echoed to the guns of British fleets, led by Hawke and Anson and Keppel. They had seen the ships of Boscawen, Cornwallis, and Nelson. Many French and Spanish warships had succumbed in these waters to British naval guns; now a German man-of-war was shortly to experience the same dismal fate.

The *Ark Royal*'s Swordfish made contact with the *Sheffield* at about 8.30 p.m. and were directed by her on to the *Bismarck*, twelve miles distant. The enemy was steaming under a cold front, with thick cloud down to 700 feet. A co-ordinated attack was impossible under such conditions and each sub-flight went in independently. In spite of the appalling weather the attacks were pressed home most gallantly and two torpedoes hit the ship. One of them sealed her fate, hitting her right aft, damaging her propellers, jamming her two rudders, and putting the steering engine out of action. The *Bismarck* slowed down to eight knots and, unable now to steer, swung up bows to wind.

It was at this moment that the unhappy *Bismarck* sighted five destroyers approaching in line abreast. They were Captain Vian's 4th Flotilla—*Cossack*, *Maori*, *Sikh*, and *Zulu*—and the Polish *Piorun*. On board the German ship the situation must have appeared ominous indeed, for even the darkness of the coming night could not help her now with these new enemies to keep her in view. An immediate award of the Iron Cross was offered to anyone who would go down to the flooded steering compartment and free the rudders, but the task was beyond anyone on board.

All through the night she was harried by the destroyers. Both the *Cossack* and the *Maori* hit her with torpedoes, and the *Sikh*, too, claimed a hit on her. And thus they held her through the hours of darkness, waiting to hand her over to the avenging guns of the *King George V* and the *Rodney* in the morning.

That the *Rodney* was there at all was a triumph on the part of her engineering department. She was long overdue for a refit, and in the state of her machinery her maximum speed was seventeen knots. By almost incredible exertions her engineers had worked her up to twenty-one knots during the chase to the south-eastward and held her at that speed for over twenty-four hours. Now her reward was waiting for her just over the horizon.

The day dawned out of a leaden sky. The sea was still rising and the two Home Fleet battleships were shipping it green over their bows. They had had to reduce speed because of the serious oil fuel situation, but the Commander-in-Chief was no longer worrying. His fears had been set at rest by the *Ark Royal*'s Swordfish and by Captain Vian's gallant destroyers which, he knew, would never let go their grip. And although the *Sheffield* had been forced to give up shadowing when her radar had been damaged by a near-miss, the *Norfolk* was there now to mark the victim. She had seen the start of the operation far away in the Denmark Straits; she was to see the end of it in waters not far from those in which Hawke had shattered a French enemy nearly two hundred years earlier.

At 8.20 a.m. on the 27th, the look-out in H.M.S. *Rodney* reported a ship on the port bow. It was the *Norfolk*, and she flashed a welcoming signal, "Enemy bears 130 degrees, 16 miles." The gale was still blowing out of the north-west, bringing with it heavy and blinding rain squalls. Through them, the eyes of the Commander-in-Chief peered hopefully down the bearing for a first sight of the elusive enemy. Twenty-three minutes later, looming on the starboard bow, the indistinct outline of a large ship emerged out of a rain squall. A flutter of flags crept to the yardarm of the fleet flagship, the signal for which every man in the Home Fleet had been praying for three long days and nights. "Enemy in sight."

The scene on board the *Bismarck* on the fateful morning has been described for us by survivors of the action. An exchange of heroics between Admiral Lütjens and the German Fuehrer did nothing to allay the sickening fears that began to assail the men of the trapped ship. Frequent announcements over the ship's loudspeaker system of help on the way, of scores of U-boats in the vicinity, and of hundreds of planes to give immunity from attack were belied by their patent absence on the scene. All that was visible to the men on board was concrete evidence of the long arm of British naval might in the harrying attacks of the destroyers. They knew that the net was around them and that already it was drawn tight.[11]

Four minutes after sighting, the *Rodney* opened fire with her 16-inch guns. Her first salvo sent a column of water towering 150 feet into the air close alongside the doomed ship. Her third hit the *Bismarck*, pierced the side armour, and burst inboard. The *King George V*, opening fire one minute after the *Rodney*, also began to hit the enemy. For a few minutes the *Bismarck*'s return fire was accurate enough to cause the *Rodney* to manœuvre to avoid being hit, but it soon became so ragged that the two ships could hardly realise that they were under fire.

One by one the *Bismarck*'s big guns were knocked out. A great fire was raging on her upper deck and she lay wallowing in the Atlantic swell, a black, ragged ruin of a once-proud ship. Admiral Tovey, to put her out of her misery, ordered any ship still with torpedoes to close and sink her. At 10.25 a.m. the cruiser *Dorsetshire* fired two into her starboard side, steamed round her bow, and fired another into her port side. It was the final blow; the great ship heeled over to port and began to sink by the stern. A minute or two later she turned turtle and slid below the angry sea. The *Dorsetshire* and the *Maori* picked up 110 survivors.

The *Dorsetshire*, indeed, should not have been there. On 26th May she was bringing home a convoy from Freetown when she picked up on her wireless the Catalina's sighting report. Leaving the convoy in the care of an armed merchant cruiser, she steamed away towards the battle. A heavy sea slowed her down a little, but just after 8.30 a.m. on the 27th she sighted a destroyer ahead. It was the *Cossack*, which directed her on towards the enemy. Twenty minutes later she sighted the flash of the *Bismarck*'s guns. It was thus that she arrived to deliver the *coup de grâce*, having steamed 600 miles to do so.

There was an echo of her achievement in the First Lord's room at the Admiralty a few days later when, with the First Sea Lord, Mr. A. V. Alexander was discussing the question of awards for individual gallantry. The case of Captain Martin, of the *Dorsetshire*, came up, whether to reward him or to try him by court-martial for leaving his convoy without orders. "I think we can afford to be lenient," said Sir Dudley Pound with a twinkle in his eye, and Captain Martin was awarded a well-deserved D.S.O.

The sinking of the *Bismarck*, an operation of exceptional naval interest, was a triumph of skill and co-operation on the part of all the forces concerned, air as well as sea. It demonstrated once again the innate facility of sea power to concentrate on the objective over vast distances and to bring to bear overwhelming might at the crucial point of impact. It shows, too, a smooth and happy co-operation between the Admiralty, which could assess and signal out to all ships and squadrons the immediate value of Intelligence reports as they came in, and the Commander-in-Chief afloat, who was thus able to maintain wireless silence at a critical juncture of the operation. In his official despatch Admiral Tovey paid handsome tribute to the part played by the Admiralty in this victory, as well as to the skill and understanding of all the forces engaged during the prolonged chase.[12]

The loss of the *Bismarck* had serious repercussions in Germany. The star of Raeder began to wane, that of Doenitz to rise rapidly towards its zenith. It was to be another year and a half before Raeder, goaded into exasperation by the continual bickering of Keitel and Goering over the Navy's share of men and materials and by arbitrary limitations on big ship construction imposed by Hitler, finally hauled down his flag in resignation. But his conception of German naval strategy came to an end with the sinking of the *Bismarck*.

Never again, throughout the course of the war, did major German warships put to sea to cruise against the Allied trade. Apart from the disguised merchant raiders, that aspect of the war at sea was left to Doenitz and his U-boats.

Within a month of the end of the *Bismarck*, the German military onslaught was biting deep into Russian soil. Both in London and in Washington the necessity of sustaining Russia with plentiful supplies, if she were to play any considerable part in the war, was fully appreciated. The need to meet Russian demands fell upon the Home Fleet, for through its power alone could the sea route to Russia around the north of Norway be opened. On 21st August the first consignment of Hurricane aircraft were carried from Reykjavik, in Iceland, to Archangel; on 28th September the first full convoy sailed, to inaugurate a service that was to last to the end of the war. The first few convoys went through without difficulty, but it did not take long for the Germans to appreciate the immense value of the supplies which were traversing the northern routes to assist their new enemy. By the end of the year strong German naval and air forces were concentrating in new bases in the far north of Norway, a forewarning of the fury which was so shortly to fall upon the ships using this exposed sea route of supply. An epic story of valour and endurance was later to be written in these bitter Arctic waters, but at this early stage of the northern supply route it was only the weather that was to prove an implacable foe.

Before the convoy cycle to Russia had started there had occurred, during the second week in August, the spectacular meeting between Mr. Churchill and President Roosevelt in Placentia Bay, Newfoundland. The Prime Minister crossed the Atlantic in H.M.S. *Prince of Wales* and on 9th August met the President on board the American cruiser *Augusta*. It was at this meeting that they produced their famous Atlantic Charter, that message from the two great democracies which was to bring a new hope to the submerged people of Europe and Asia and the promise of a new singleness of purpose in the actions of the two main protagonists in the battle for freedom. But perhaps of more importance in the purely naval sphere was the agreed adoption of "Naval Plan No. 4", under which the United

States Navy was to take over immediate responsibility for that stretch of the Atlantic which lay between America and Iceland. This plan, in addition to giving to U.S. warships the power to destroy German surface raiders which might venture to attack any convoy between Iceland and America, also allowed the U.S. Navy to escort convoys as far as Iceland, even those comprising ships not of American registry.

This arrangement, at one step, eased the heavy pressure in the Atlantic caused by the shortage of British and Canadian escorts. With this American help, the British escort ships need now proceed no farther west than south of Iceland, there to meet and bring home the convoys escorted across the western half of the ocean by the vessels of our transatlantic partners. To the ships themselves, however, and to their crews, it meant no easing of the task, no chance of relaxation from the ceaseless burden of convoy. The economy in force in the Atlantic which Naval Plan No. 4 introduced merely meant that three British escort groups could now be switched to other, equally arduous, duties with the Gibraltar and Sierra Leone convoys.

But Naval Plan No. 4 meant even more in its political impact on a world torn by war. Here, indeed, was tangible proof of the community of interest of the English-speaking nations, of a virtual alliance between the great American power in the West, with its huge industrial potential, and Great Britain, both implacably opposed to the Nazi and Fascist creeds. There could be little comfort for Germany or Italy in the announcement, made by President Roosevelt on 11th September, of the coming into force of the plan.

As a result of it Hitler was presented with demands from Raeder and Doenitz for permission to operate against American shipping. The Fuehrer, however, heavily engaged in the Russian adventure and confident that the end of September would bring him the success there which he so ardently desired,[13] delayed until mid-October the retaliations which Raeder and Doenitz demanded, in the hope that, by so doing, he could yet pull some of his chestnuts out of the fire.

The easing of the surface escort situation in the Atlantic by the adoption of the American "Plan No. 4" did nothing, however, to solve the problems of air escort. There still remained those ominous gaps, beyond the reach of shore-based aircraft, across which the convoys had to pass. In the case of the convoys to Gibraltar, this gap carried an additional danger in the shape of the German long-range Focke-Wulf Kondors, which combined the role of bomber with that of reconnaissance aircraft for the U-boats. The Kondors did, in fact, also operate on the Atlantic convoy routes, but to a much lesser extent than the Gibraltar route which lay so much closer to their French bases.

The Admiralty, in grappling with this problem, had wasted little time. By the end of 1940 catapult equipment had been ordered suitable for fitting in ships, and the first four so fitted, flying the White Ensign and known as fighter catapult ships, came into service in April 1941. These ships sailed in the convoys, and their equipment enabled them to launch a Hurricane fighter as soon as one of the German Kondors was sighted. Their first success came in August, when a Hurricane from the *Maplin* shot down a Focke-Wulf 400 miles out to sea.

At the same time as these catapult merchant ships were being fitted with their equipment, the Admiralty was also engaged on a more ambitious experiment which had the same general object in view. They took in hand a captured enemy merchant ship, the *Hannover*, and fitted her with a full flight deck. She became the first of a long line of escort carriers, and although her own career was regrettably brief, she carried in her conception the final and irrevocable defeat of the U-boat menace.

This fact was so obvious that it did not require the operational experience of H.M.S. *Audacity*, as the *Hannover* was renamed on entering the Royal Navy, to point the way ahead. The Battle of the Atlantic Committee, studying the impact that the escort carrier was likely to bring to the U-boat battle, recorded that it was "deeply impressed" and pointed out also that such ships could be used "to provide a convoy with its own anti-submarine air patrols". This was in May 1941, and that month saw orders being placed for the conversion of five similar ships in this country, while six more were

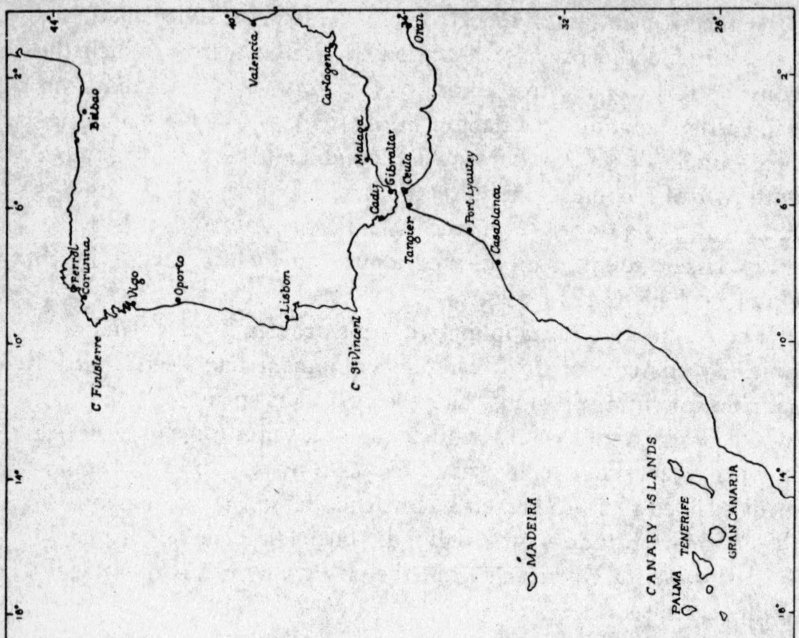
GIBRALTAR APPROACHES
Scale of Nautical Miles
approx
0 100 200 300
THE AZORES
FLORES
FAIAL
SAO MIGUEL
MADEIRA
CANARY ISLANDS
PALMA
TENERIFE
GRAN CANARIA
C Finisterre
Ferrol
Corunna
Vigo
Oporto
Lisbon
C St Vincent
Cadiz
Gibraltar
Malaga
Cartagena
Valencia
Bilbao
Tangier
Ceuta
Oran
Port Lyautey
Casablanca
44°
40°
36° North
32°
28°
30°
26°
22°
18°
14°
10°
6°
2°
23° West

requested from the United States under Lend-Lease terms. Their conversion, however, was of necessity a long-term project, and for another year and more the U-boats were to be free to roam the oceans without having to meet this devastating threat to their operational capacity.

H.M.S. *Audacity*, carrying six Martlet fighters on her flight deck —she had no hangar—became operational in September 1941. She was sent to join the Gibraltar convoy escorts and almost at once her extreme value became apparent. On 21st September she scored her first success by shooting down a Focke-Wulf Kondor during a fierce U-boat attack on an outward-bound convoy. Her presence in the convoy came not only as a surprise to the attacking U-boats but as so great a menace to their success that Admiral Doenitz, commanding the U-boat arm, gave orders for her destruction. She was designated as the primary target in any future operation.

It was in December that she met her end. She was part of the escort of a homeward-bound convoy from Gibraltar which was singled out for particularly heavy attack by wolf-pack methods. The battle was continuous, day and night, and the *Audacity*'s Martlets did sterling work, shooting down two Focke-Wulfs. They acted also as an anti-submarine patrol although, as fighters, they were not particularly fitted for this role.

The surface escort was led by Commander F. J. Walker in the *Stork*. He was already one of the most experienced of escort group leaders; later his uncanny skill was to stamp him as the most famous and successful of them all. This particular battle was his first outstanding success and, indeed, the first really heavy defeat that the U-boats had experienced since the start of the war. Of the nine U-boats which Doenitz had concentrated for this attack, four were sunk for the loss of two merchant ships and one escorting destroyer. Towards the end of the battle Doenitz threw in three more U-boats under experienced captains and it was one of these which torpedoed and sank the *Audacity*. At the time she was operating unprotected ten miles away from the convoy, well outside the defensive screen of escorts, and her loss was not therefore due to any direct failure of the surface escorts in their protective duties.

Doenitz himself, in his official report on the operation, had this to say on the presence of the *Audacity*: "The worst feature was the presence of the aircraft carrier. Small, fast, manœuvrable aircraft circled the convoy continuously, so that when it was sighted the boats were repeatedly forced to submerge or withdraw. The presence of enemy aircraft also prevented any protracted shadowing or homing procedure by German aircraft. The sinking of the aircraft carrier is therefore of particular importance, not only in this case but also in every future convoy action."[14]

To Doenitz the appearance of an escort carrier with a convoy was the writing on the wall. That it should make its appearance on the Gibraltar convoy route first and not in the Atlantic was a direct result of the German Navy shifting their main emphasis of U-boat warfare to the Mediterranean at the expense of the Atlantic. Raeder, who always had a far greater strategical grasp of the general war situation than any other German leader, had managed to persuade Hitler as early as June 1941 of the vital consequences to Germany of a defeat in the Mediterranean area,[15] and during September six U-boats passed through the Straits of Gibraltar to operate in the Western Mediterranean. Others followed rapidly. The inadequacy of the Italian Navy in transporting sufficient supplies to Rommel's Afrika Korps was the main reason for this influx, and the second British offensive in the western desert proved an added spur. In Raeder's view, "the British North African offensive and the reports of intended Anglo-French landings in French North Africa constitute a grave threat to the Mediterranean and to Italy. In so far as our Navy can influence the situation, the area round Gibraltar now becomes vitally important. The strategic importance of holding our position in the Mediterranean compels us to concentrate the main operational strength of the U-boats in the Gibraltar area until the situation improves."[16]

This concentration, amounting in all to twenty-seven U-boats, brought the Atlantic operations almost to a standstill. The breathing space against attack there, however, brought little rest to the escort-ship crews. The majority of them followed the U-boats, to augment the escort force on the heavily threatened Gibraltar run. There the same arduous convoy duties kept them at the fullest stretch. This additional escort strength, combined with the fact that the sea round Gibraltar made the task of the U-boats more difficult because of its clarity, earned that area the name of "the Gibraltar mousetrap" by the U-boat commanders. They suffered several losses.

The collapse of the British offensive in North Africa, which came to a halt with the turn of the year, allowed the U-boats west of Gibraltar to return once more to their hunting-ground in the Atlantic. But even as they took up their patrol positions in this great and profitable area, shattering events were taking place on the other side of the world. They were to transform the whole war situation almost in the twinkling of an eye, and to confront British sea power with a sterner test than it had ever faced before throughout the whole of its long history.

The enigma of Japanese intentions in the Far East dated back to the French surrender in the summer of 1940. That collapse had opened a door to Japanese infiltration into south-east Asia through the occupation of French Indo-China, on which it was well known that Japanese eyes were cast in eager anticipation. In itself such an aggression would not be immediately threatening, even though it would bring to Japan the effective control of the South China Sea by means of the well-placed naval base at Kamranh Bay. Indo-China, however, provided an open door into Siam, and if the Japanese stepped through that the consequences to Malaya might be disastrous.

This was a situation fraught with danger, although on the credit side there were some heartening features. Japan was still engaged in her endless struggle with China, and might well wish to bring that adventure to a successful conclusion before embarking on a new one. In the central Pacific, based on Pearl Harbour, in Oahu Island, lay a strong American fleet, and the United States was not likely to sit passively on the sidelines and watch Japan extend her Pacific Empire at the expense of the many American interests in that area. To the south, in the Dutch East Indies, there was a useful squadron of cruisers, destroyers, and submarines of the Dutch Navy which could be counted upon to fight any Japanese inroads on Dutch territory. There was also Great Britain, heavily engaged elsewhere, it is true, but even then no negligible opponent. It seemed unlikely at the time that Japan would willingly throw down the gauntlet to such powerful adversaries and invite them simultaneously into the lists against her.

As one looks back through the years towards those dramatic moments in Far Eastern waters at the close of 1941, it appears amazing how gravely Japanese capabilities were underrated by the Allies. It is difficult now not to feel surprise at the faulty appreciation made by the Chiefs of Staff. It sprang mainly, of course, from lack of good Intelligence, but one cannot help catching a glimpse, too, of wishful thinking. Old beliefs die hard, and to Mr. Menzies, Prime Minister of Australia, who was showing an understandable nervousness at the lack of naval, military, and air strength at Singapore, went an appreciation of Japanese air capabilities obviously based on reports of air encounters in the occasional Russian-Japanese brushes during the Manchurian campaign between the wars. These reports it is true referred to military aircraft, but the lack of up-to-date intelligence undoubtedly caused a false impression to gain ground. How far this was from the truth, and how rude and painful was to be the awakening, could perhaps best be described by the survivors of the *Prince of Wales* and *Repulse* no more than three days after the outbreak of war in the Far East.

At the end of July 1941 Japan took the first step towards the abyss. Her troops occupied Saigon, capital of Indo-China, and she demanded from Vichy the right to join in the "defence" of the country. The sky over Malaya and the vast archipelago of islands stretching down towards Australia grew dark with menace. The occupation of Indo-China was followed by Allied economic action in the immediate freezing of Japanese assets in Britain, the United States, and the Dutch East Indies, bringing all trade to an immediate standstill. In this concerted action lay the warning to Japan that any further advance towards war was likely to meet united opposition.

Opposition, however, needs force to make it effective. The main strength of the United States Pacific Fleet was concentrated at Pearl Harbour; in the Dutch East Indies Admiral Doorman's ships stood in the path of a Japanese drive to the south. Great Britain was represented in Singapore by three cruisers and four destroyers, with the elderly battle-cruiser *Repulse* and the small obsolete carrier *Hermes* on the adjacent East Indies station, based on Ceylon. A rapid reinforcement of Malaya, military and air as well as naval, was an imperative necessity if the implied threat to resist further Japanese aggression were not to be purely a hollow one.

Admiral Pound, the First Sea Lord, was fully aware of this need, and had indeed made plans to send out sizable reinforcements to the East, based on Trincomalee. A total eastern fleet of seven capital ships, including the *Rodney* and *Nelson*, and a second carrier, the *Ark Royal*, was planned. But many of the ships earmarked for this duty were not immediately available, and it was hoped that the United States Pacific Fleet would prove a sufficient shield for these vital waters until the British concentration could be completed.

The Prime Minister, however, had other views. He was looking for the immediate deterrent, the force that, by its presence in those waters, might yet give Japan cause to delay her final step into war. After much discussion, it was finally decided to send the *Prince of Wales* to join the *Repulse* in the Indian Ocean, and to base them both on Singapore. The carrier *Indomitable* was to have accompanied the *Prince of Wales*, but she had been damaged in an accidental grounding at Kingston, Jamaica, and so was not available. The *Prince of Wales* sailed alone on 25th October, flying the flag of Admiral Sir Tom Phillips as the new Commander-in-Chief, Eastern Fleet. She joined the *Repulse* at Colombo on 28th November and the two ships reached Singapore on 2nd December.

Even as they arrived the die had long been cast by Japan, though as yet in secret. Twenty-two days earlier the first ships of a gigantic striking force had left their Japanese bases to rendezvous in a bare, windswept bay in the Kurile Islands, north of Japan. There they took on board provisions collected in advance. And from there, on 26th November, six aircraft carriers, two battleships, two cruisers, and eleven destroyers, accompanied by a fleet train of eight tankers and supply ships, sailed on their secret mission into the central Pacific. At 6.0 a.m. on 7th December the striking force reached its destination, a point about 275 miles north of Pearl Harbour. Complete wireless silence at sea had afforded no clue to the American intelligence officers that Japanese ships had left their bases; heavy weather in the Pacific had shrouded the ships from aerial reconnaissance.

Yet even then complete surprise should not have been achieved. There was, in the United States, knowledge through a deciphered Japanese signal that an attack on Pearl Harbour was imminent, and the authorities there had been warned. In the entrance to Pearl Harbour, four full hours before the aircraft appeared overhead, the destroyer *Ward* had a sighting report of a periscope and sank a Japanese midget submarine two hours later. No notice was taken. A military radar operator, manning his set beyond the appointed hour because his breakfast was late, plotted the course of the approaching bombers and reported them to the officer of the watch and still no notice was taken.

"Pearl Harbour was still asleep in the morning mist," wrote Commander Nakaya, who was leader of the first strike of aircraft. "It was calm and serene inside the harbour, not even a trace of smoke from the ships at Oahu. The orderly groups of barracks, the wriggling white line of the automobile road climbing up to the mountain-top; fine objectives of attack in all directions. In line with these, inside the harbour, were important ships of the Pacific Fleet, strung out and anchored two ships side by side in an orderly manner."[17] At 7.50 a.m. the first bombs rained down out of a peaceful sky on the unsuspecting ships. The attack was completely successful, and the United States Pacific Fleet was reduced from a powerful fighting force to a shambles. All that escaped the attack were three carriers which were at sea that morning on exercises. The way was open now to the Japanese to push their empire down into the rich lands of the south-west Pacific, for the only force capable of stopping them had been annihilated in this savage, unforeseen blow from the skies.

The Japanese succeeded in doing for Britain in one aggressive move what Mr. Churchill had failed to achieve in months of patient diplomacy. They had brought the United States fully into the war, with all her vast wealth and genius now deployed in the fight against the dictators. Faced with the inevitable, Hitler and Mussolini declared war on the United States on 11th December. And out of the tragedy of Pearl Harbour was forged a new and infinitely powerful brotherhood of arms that was to hold in its grasp the doom of all the Axis powers.

# Chapter 8

## THE EDGE OF DISASTER

THE late summer and autumn of 1941 had brought some encouraging turns of fortune to the Allied cause as a whole. After the heavy merchant shipping losses in the Atlantic of March, April, May, and June, with an average of more than half a million tons each month, those of the next five months dropped to less than one-third of this massive total. The *Bismarck* had been sunk and there were no more surface warships out on the trade routes to threaten the convoys.

There had been successes in the Mediterranean and Middle East too. The steady reinforcement of the Egyptian front with troops and supplies continued without interruption by the enemy, with an average of one full convoy each month making the long voyage round the Cape. Three substantial convoys had been taken through to Malta without undue difficulty or loss, the third of them at the end of September. At one moment during this operation there had seemed to develop a chance of a major action when the Italian Fleet put to sea to intercept. They turned for home, however, long before contact was established, and the hope of a victory died with the now familiar sense of frustration. As the convoy entered the Grand Harbour at Malta the escorting cruisers led it in with guards paraded and bands playing, while most of the population of Valletta clustered in a serried mass on the bomb-scarred battlements and the ancient harbour echoed to the roar of their frenzied cheering. It was a touch of peacetime pageantry amid the grim reality of war, a tiny jewel of naval defiance that lifted up the hearts of the much-enduring Maltese people.

Malta also had other reasons to cheer. In an attempt to revive the success of 16th April, when four destroyers operating from Malta had annihilated a convoy carrying supplies to Rommel, a force of cruisers and destroyers, known as Force K and under the command of Captain W. G. Agnew, was based there, arriving on 21st October. On the night of 8th/9th November it struck its first blow in a brief and overwhelming action in which it sank the whole of a convoy escorted by a force more powerful than itself. By noon on the 9th it was back in Malta without loss or damage to ship or man. Ten days later it repeated the exploit, again destroying an entire convoy. As a result of these two operations, "brilliant examples of leadership and forethought" in the words of the Commander-in-Chief, Rommel's movements in North Africa were brought almost to a complete stop through lack of reinforcements and of fuel—and that at a moment when he was heavily engaged with the Eighth Army as it advanced through Libya.

Force K made its presence felt yet again when, on 1st December, it sank another supply ship and a tanker, together with its destroyer escort. The loss of supplies for the German-Italian army in North Africa caused by these operations was now becoming so serious that Hitler, in order to bolster up Rommel's resistance, was forced to reinforce the German air strength in the Mediterranean by one *Fliegerkorps* of about 200 aircraft. It had to be withdrawn from the Russian front, and by that much eased the burden on our hard-pressed Allies in their struggle.

But already the goddess of fortune was showing her fickleness. If there were many who, during the summer and autumn months of 1941, had discerned her smiles directed towards the Allied cause, there were few who could fail to recognise her frowns as the year drew to its close. There was one last flicker of a smile in the early hours of 13th December when the destroyers *Sikh*, *Legion*, and *Maori*, together with the Dutch destroyer *Isaac Sweers*, encountered the Italian cruisers *Alberto di Giussano* and *Alberico da Barbiano* off Cape Bon in Tunisia. Commander G. H. Stokes, leading the force, took his ships close inshore in order to gain the advantage of virtual invisibility against the background of the land and succeeded in sinking both the enemy cruisers by torpedo attack. Each was carrying a deck cargo of cased petrol for Rommel, and this loss, grievous as it was to the Italian Navy, was no less depressing to the Afrika Korps. This, however, was but a fleeting smile, for already the storm clouds were gathering.

It has been mentioned in the previous chapter that, in order to give support to Rommel's supply route, the U-boats had been ordered to concentrate in the Mediterranean and in the Gibraltar approaches. They scored their first really big success on 13th November when *U.81* torpedoed H.M.S. *Ark Royal* as she was returning from the second of two sorties towards Malta to fly off reinforcing aircraft. The carrier, listing heavily, was taken in tow by two tugs, but sank some fourteen hours later when within twenty-five miles of safety at Gibraltar. Of her entire ship's company only one man was lost.

This was, indeed, a bitter blow, for she was the only carrier in the Mediterranean. Moreover, there was at the time no other with which to replace her, for the *Formidable* and *Illustrious* were both under repair for damage sustained in action, and the *Indomitable* was in dock after her grounding in the West Indies.

In the eastern Mediterranean an equally serious blow was struck at Admiral Cunningham's fleet when the battleship *Barham* was torpedoed and sunk with heavy loss of life by *U.331*. This was on 25th November, when the fleet was out in search of a reported convoy of tankers bound for North Africa. But there was worse still to follow. The cruiser *Galatea* was torpedoed and sunk by *U.557* on 14th December, and five days later a gallant attack by Italian "human torpedoes" on the main fleet base at Alexandria successfully crippled Admiral Cunningham's two remaining battleships, the *Queen Elizabeth* and *Valiant*. Both were extensively flooded by the explosion of the charges attached to their underwater hulls by these Italian "charioteers", and it was to be many months before the two ships were again in service.

Nor was this the full tale of disaster in the Mediterranean. Force

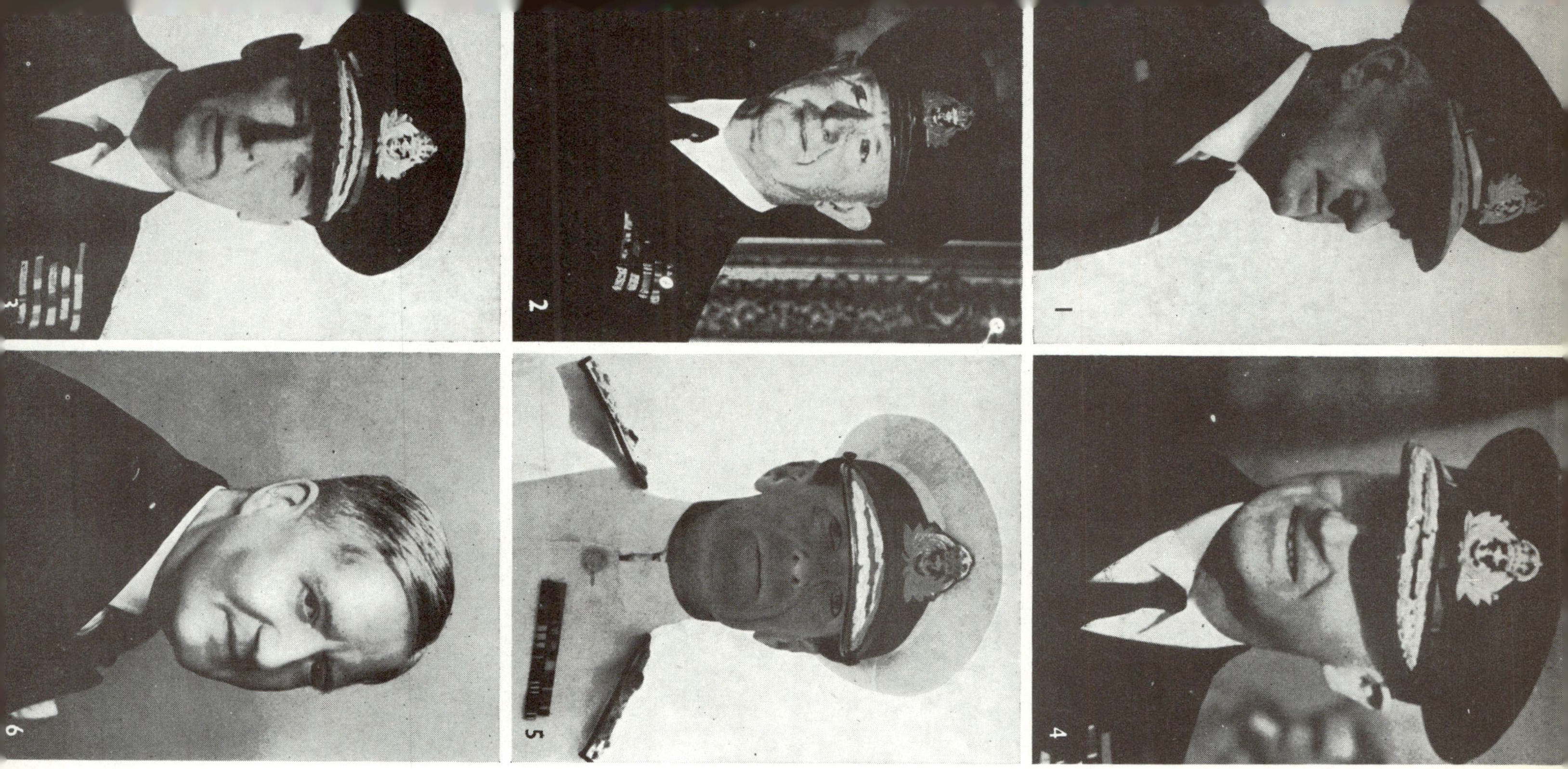

*(Admiralty Official Photographs)*

(1) Admiral of the Fleet Sir Dudley Pound, First Sea Lord 1939-43. (2) Admiral of the Fleet Sir Andrew Cunningham, Commander-in-Chief Mediterranean 1939-43, First Sea Lord 1943-46. (3) Admiral of the Fleet Sir John Tovey, Commander-in-Chief Home Fleet 1940-43. (4) Admiral Sir Bertram Ramsay, Flag Officer Dover 1939-42, Naval Commander-in-Chief, Expeditionary Force, 1943-45. (5) Admiral Sir Philip Vian. (6) Admiral Sir Bruce Fraser, Commander-in-Chief Home Fleet 1943-44, Commander-in-Chief British Eastern Fleet 1944-45.

(*Photo: Imperial War Museum*)

(*Above*) The pocket battleship *Graf Spee* burning off Montevideo after being scuttled.

(*Below*) H.M.S. *Glowworm* ramming the *Hipper* off the Norwegian coast in April, 1940. An artist's impression.

(*By permission of John Thornycroft & Co. Ltd.*)

(*Above*) The German battle-cruiser *Gneisenau* at full speed.

(*Below*) Dunkirk, May 1940. A destroyer is about to enter the harbour.

*(Photographs: Imperial War Museum.)*

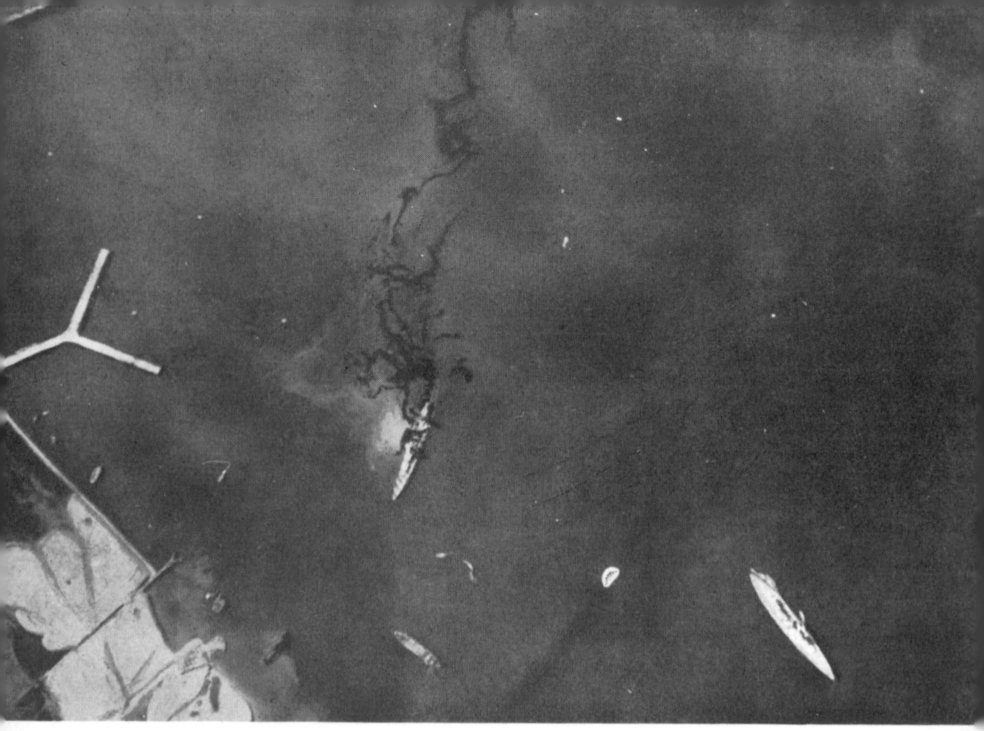

(*Above*) After the Fleet Air Arm raid on Taranto. The Italian battleship *Cavour* beached and partially submerged.

(*Below*) A Fairey Swordfish torpedo bomber, the main naval strike aircraft for the first three years of the war.

(*Photographs: Imperial War Museum*)

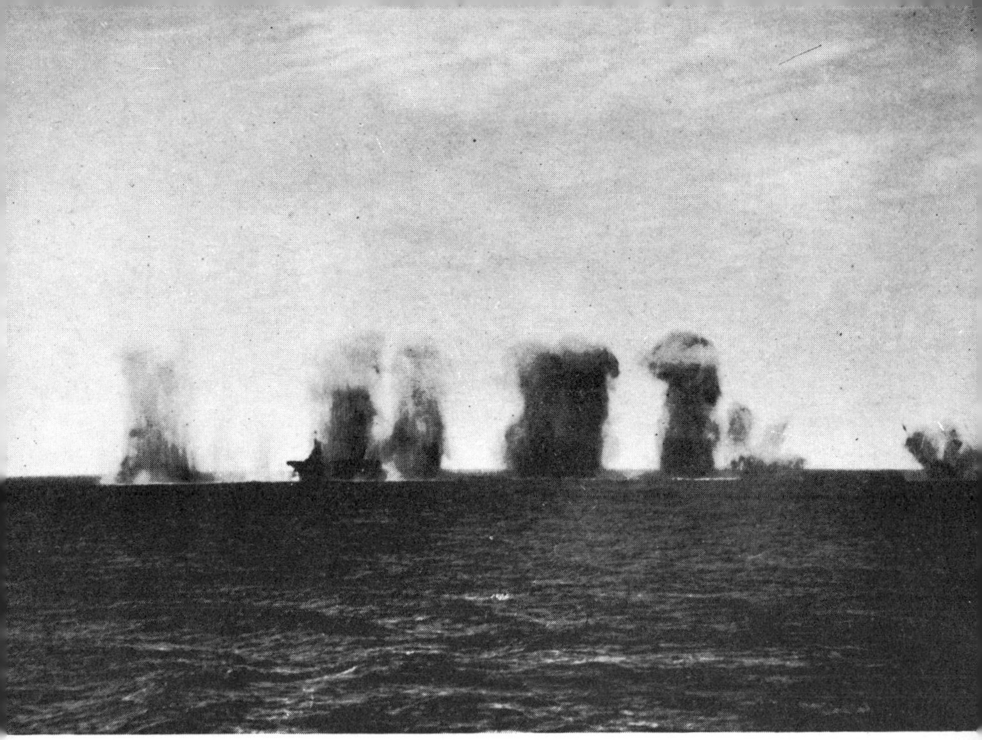

(*Above*) The Battle of Cape Spartivento. Italian bombs dropping round the aircraft carrier *Ark Royal*.

(*Below*) German dive-bombers reach the Mediterranean. The *Illustrious* is hit and set on fire. Six hours later she reached Malta under her own steam.

(*Photographs: Imperial War Museum.*)

(*Above*) The Battle of Sirte. A British destroyer emerging from the smoke screen to attack the Italian fleet.

(*Below*) Out in the open. A destroyer about to attack with torpedoes during the Sirte battle. The smoke screen can be seen in the background.

(*Photographs: Imperial War Museum.*)

(*Above*) H.M.S. *Ark Royal* torpedoed. She sank later when almost within reach of Gibraltar.

(*Below*) *U.660* sinking after being attacked by the corvettes *Starwort* and *Lotus*. Her crew is swimming over to be picked up.

(*Photographs: Imperial War Museum.*)

(*Above*) An Atlantic convoy zig-zagging at sea. This photograph was taken from the Coastal Command escorting aircraft.

(*Below*) The German battleship *Bismarck* firing at the *Hood*, a photograph taken from the German cruiser *Prinz Eugen*.

(*Photographs: Imperial War Museum.*)

(*Above*) The magazines of the battleship *Barham* exploding after she had been torpedoed by a U-boat in the Mediterranean. The ship can be seen lying right over on her side in the water.
(*Below*) Convoy to Malta. Wounded men of the cruiser *Manchester* torpedoed by an enemy M.T.B., are brought up on deck before the ship is abandoned.

(*Photographs: Imperial War Museum.*)

(*Above*) The tanker *Ohio*, deep in the water, reaches Grand Harbour after her ordeal in a Malta convoy.

(*Below*) The invasion of North Africa. One of the troop transports off Oran is protected by a smoke-screen.

(*Photographs: Imperial War Museum.*)

(*Above*) North Russian convoys. A tanker is set on fire by a German aircraft, and another ship is burning. An incident during the passage of Convoy PQ 18.

(*Below*) H.M.S. *Nairana*, an escort carrier, pitching in a heavy sea off northern Norway.

(*Photographs: Imperial War Museum.*)

(*Above*) Naval landing craft passing the cruiser *Mauritius* on the way in to the beaches at Salerno.

(*Below*) The Mediterranean victory. The surrendered Italian battleships *Italia* and *Vittorio Veneto* at anchor "under the guns of the fortress of Malta".

(*Photographs: Imperial War Museum.*)

ght) The German battleship
pitz in her Norwegian hide-
. Her gun turrets are disguised
l the lines of anti-torpedo nets
, be seen behind her.

low) The Fleet Air Arm
ack on the *Tirpitz* in Alten
rd. A photograph taken from
attacking Barracuda.

otographs:
*Imperial War Museum.*)

(*Above*) Invasion of North-West Europe. Admiral Ramsay, General Eisenhower, and Field Marshal Montgomery on board the cruiser *Apollo* off the Normandy beaches.
(*Below*) German beach defences in Normandy. Submerged at high water, they caused much damage to the landing craft until they were cleared. Each was armed with an explosive mine.

(*Photographs: Imperial War Museum.*)

(*Above*) Mulberry Harbour. A "Phoenix", designed to form the outer breakwater, being towed across Channel shortly after D-day.

(*Below*) One of the supporting gun vessels during the victorious attack across the Schelde on Walcheren. She has been hit and is sinking, and her crew can be seen about to abandon ship.

(*Photographs: Imperial War Museum.*)

(*Above*) The Atlantic victory. A German U-boat, *U.541*, with the White Ensign flying above the Nazi naval flag, comes in to surrender.

(*Below*) A Japanese suicide aircraft attacks H.M.S. *Formidable*. Aircraft in the after deck park are burning furiously. The carrier was operational again within four hours.

(*Photographs: Imperial War Museum*

K, which had been doing such sterling work from Malta in the disruption of supplies to Rommel, came sadly to grief. Early in the morning of 19th December, while out in search of a supply convoy, the cruisers *Neptune*, *Aurora*, and *Penelope*, all of Force K, ran into a minefield and were damaged. The *Aurora* and *Penelope* succeeded in reaching Malta in safety, but the *Neptune*, her steering gear shattered in the explosion, drifted on to a second mine, and later still on to a third. She capsized, and all but one of her ship's company perished with her. The destroyer *Kandahar*, proceeding to the rescue of the stricken *Neptune*, was herself mined and had her stern blown off. She was later sunk by the *Jaguar* after her crew, by a feat of superb seamanship, had been taken off.

These disasters in the Mediterranean could hardly have come at a more inopportune moment. The long, patient build-up of the Eighth Army in Egypt had at last reached a stage which justified another trial of strength with the enemy land forces in North Africa, and on 18th November the assault had begun. For sixteen dramatic days the issue swung precariously in the balance while the great armoured battle of Sidi Rezegh swayed backwards and forwards. It ended in a victory which swept the enemy out of Libya. The garrison of Tobruk, maintained by the Navy for ten months of siege, was at last liberated by the advancing British forces, and on Christmas Eve Benghazi was once again in the hands of the Eighth Army.

It was at this stage of the advance on land that the losses at sea began to tell their inevitable tale. With the forward airfields in Cyrenaica in British hands, the Royal Air Force was able to some extent to play the part of the non-existent aircraft carrier and give cover to the Inshore Squadron as it established by sea a supply route for the Army through the ports of Tobruk, Derna, and Benghazi. This, however, was only a part of the essential task of sea power. Of equal importance was the stopping of the enemy convoys which carried to Rommel the supplies he needed from the European mainland. This task was now beyond the capacity of the attenuated Force K, especially as these convoys were now sailing with escorts of battleships and cruisers which made them virtually immune from surface attack. Submarines and aircraft based in Malta did what they could to hold up these convoys, so vital to Rommel, but they alone could not fill the gap caused by the absence of sufficiently powerful surface forces in the central Mediterranean.

The vicious circle was thus complete. The lack of sea power in this area allowed Rommel to receive the reinforcements and supplies that he needed, and with these he was able once more to contemplate the offensive. On 21st January he struck at the Eighth Army's outposts and a week later was back in Benghazi. It was the first step of a long advance eastward which was not only to drive the Eighth Army steadily back but was also to deprive the Royal Air Force of their Cyrenaican airfields. That in its turn deprived the Navy of its only source of air cover and inevitably curtailed its operations on the Eighth Army's flank. Without that assistance the Army was forced to retire to shorten its lines of supply. Thus was the loss of power at sea quickly reflected in the land battle.

Although Rommel was unable to reach the full extent of his advance in one bound, the regular arrival of his supplies enabled him in the end to build up stocks sufficient to take him across the Egyptian border. By 1st July he was within fifty miles of Cairo and Alexandria, and it seemed as though, after two years of patient war, the whole of the Allied Middle East policy was in ruins. But Rommel, too, was outrunning his supplies. He was finally held on the El Alamein line, as much by his own supply problems as by the tenacity of the Eighth Army.

The inability to reinforce Admiral Cunningham at this critical juncture was dictated by the need to build up a new fleet in the Far East, where the precipitous assault by Japan had not only added two new oceans to the Navy's commitments but also had resulted in overwhelming disaster to the British forces in that theatre. These two facts, exacerbated by the severe losses in the Mediterranean, were now thrusting the Navy almost to the verge of defeat, and not in the Mediterranean alone.

In the desperate need to find ships with which to try to hold the Japanese advance, the First Sea Lord had earlier warned Admiral Cunningham, and also Admiral Somerville of Force H, that it might be necessary to withdraw all capital ships from the eastern and western Mediterranean, leaving the task of guarding the convoys and of striking the enemy at sea to light surface forces, submarines, and aircraft. While expressing his anxiety to assist in the new crisis by all means in his power, even to that of releasing his capital ships, Admiral Cunningham pointed out that the proposal would at best be a gamble which could only be justified by the retention in strength of the Cyrenaican airfields, coupled with a considerable reinforcement of the air strength in Malta.

In the end, this doctrine was forced upon Admiral Cunningham, and without the Cyrenaican airfields on which he depended for adequate offensive power in the central Mediterranean. As mentioned above, they were lost in Rommel's advance of 21st January, and Admiral Cunningham's two remaining capital ships were effectively removed by the Italian assault. Control of the waters around Malta had to be left to the island's own resources in aircraft and submarines, and the naval task in the eastern Mediterranean had to be borne by cruisers, destroyers, and submarines, supported by the Fleet Air Arm and the Royal Air Force. On them now fell the whole brunt of the sea war in those matters. Tankers from Haifa, bringing the oil fuel on which the whole Middle East position depended, had to be escorted; reinforcement convoys delivered to the Middle East bases; and all enemy movements at sea restricted to the utmost. At times it appeared a superhuman task.

For a time, indeed, control of the eastern Mediterranean seaways was tenuous, even spasmodic, and so far as Malta was concerned every attempt to supply from Alexandria ended in failure. Yet the Haifa supply route was successfully defended, aircraft and submarines continued to harass Rommel's supplies, and the few ships left to Admiral Cunningham, hard pressed though they were, succeeded in holding the enemy out of the eastern Mediterranean throughout those anxious months when all our affairs seemed to be going awry. Hitler's greatest chance of victory, by overrunning the whole of the Middle East, was held at sea, on land, and in the air, though the defence throughout was desperately thin.

Events in home waters permitted no rosier view. During February 1942 the *Scharnhorst*, *Gneisenau*, and *Prinz Eugen* had broken out from Brest and had returned to their home ports by way of the English Channel. The shock to the public at their dramatic escape through waters traditionally held by the Royal Navy was extreme. The German success appeared to expose weaknesses in the Navy which in fact were not really there, though their passage did expose a lamentable state of operational deficiency in the performance of the obsolescent Swordfish aircraft when opposed by modern fighters.

For nearly eleven months the *Scharnhorst* and *Gneisenau*, and for nearly nine months the *Prinz Eugen*, had lain at Brest after their Atlantic cruises, the objects of repeated and costly bomber attacks. All of them had been damaged at one time or another by bombs, and the *Gneisenau* by a torpedo as well, but by the beginning of 1942 it was known at the Admiralty that all three were fully repaired and ready for sea. There were also very strong indications that they were preparing to make a break for their home ports. There was no doubt in the Admiralty mind that, if they did so, they would make it through the English Channel, where they could count on strong fighter cover all the way, rather than by the longer route north of Scotland.

For some little time Hitler had convinced himself that an Allied attack on Norway was impending. He expressed this opinion at a meeting with Raeder on 12th January, 1942, where the problem of the ships at Brest was discussed.[1] Hitler was determined to withdraw them and station them in Norway, in spite of all the dangers of bringing them through the Channel. "The situation at Brest," he said, "is like that of a patient with cancer who was doomed unless he submitted to an operation. An operation on the other hand, even though it might have to be a drastic one, would offer at least some hope that the patient's life might be saved. The passage of the German ships through the Channel will be such an operation and has therefore to be attempted."[2] Planning started at once.

Responsibility for the British side of the operation was in the hands of the Vice-Admiral, Dover, Sir Bertram Ramsay. By 3rd February his preliminary dispositions were made, the Admiralty having placed at his disposal a small force of one minelayer, six destroyers, and six motor torpedo boats.[3] At Admiral Ramsay's request they were augmented by six Swordfish of No. 825 Squadron, under the command of Lieutenant-Commander E. Esmonde, stationed at Manston, Kent.

It seemed to the Vice-Admiral, Dover, and to the Admiralty and Air Ministry as well, that the enemy would almost certainly use the hours of darkness in which to pass through the narrow waters of the Dover Straits. He would also almost certainly need high water for the passage in order to give him the maximum protection from minefields. The night of 11th/12th February provided these conditions, with fourteen hours of darkness and high water at Dover one hour after sunrise. Allowing two hours either side of high water to provide sufficient depth for the ships to pass safely, Admiral Ramsay expected to find them off Dover about an hour before dawn on the 12th.

In order to provide the maximum warning of an enemy movement, the submarine *Sealion* was sent to patrol off Brest Roads and Coastal Command were ordered to fly nightly searches by Hudson aircraft fitted with radar. It was hoped by these means to get at least six hours' warning, and with luck considerably more, before the German ships approached the Dover narrows.

On the night of the 11th, so certain was he that his appreciation was correct, Admiral Ramsay sat late in his Operations Room at Dover. The aircraft patrols were out and the Admiral waited confidently for their sighting reports. The hours passed and all was silence from the Channel. Arriving reluctantly at the conclusion that he must have been mistaken, Admiral Ramsay finally retired to bed in the small hours of 12th February.

Yet the three German ships, in fact, were out and were even then steaming steadily up the Channel. By one of those unfortunate coincidences which so often seem to happen on great occasions, the ASV (radar) gear of the most westerly search aircraft broke down at the critical moment. For three hours the waters off Brest were left uncovered, and during those three hours the enemy ships sailed. What, perhaps, was even worse was the failure of the R.A.F. headquarters concerned to inform Admiral Ramsay of the breakdown. The second reconnaissance aircraft, patrolling between Ushant and

Ile de Brehat, also reported a failure of its ASV. The aircraft was recalled, but unfortunately no relief machine was despatched to cover this area in its place and the German ships passed through it unlocated. Once again Admiral Ramsay was not informed of the failure to search these waters. The third aircraft, between Havre and Boulogne, was too far to the west and it was not until it had returned to base that the ships reached that part of the Channel.

This particular failure was, of course, due to the belief that the enemy would try to pass through the Dover Straits during dark hours. Basically it was that assumption which caused the enemy ships to be missed, through flying the third patrol too early in the morning. Nevertheless, had the ASV been working in either of the two more westerly patrol aircraft, the report for which Admiral Ramsay had been waiting would certainly have come through, and he would have been able to mount his attack at the time and place most favourable for success. Had even the failures in the other two aircraft been reported to him he could probably have taken naval measures to search for and report the German ships. It might well have made all the difference in the final result.

At 10.45 a.m., by which time the naval forces allocated to Admiral Ramsay had reverted to the normal daylight notice of four hours from the fifteen minutes maintained during the night, a radar plot of surface ships off Cape Gris Nez was received. It was at too great a range to determine either the number or the size of the ships concerned, and Admiral Ramsay's Headquarters asked for an additional "Jim Crow" reconnaissance to be flown. These "Jim Crows" were flights by fighters between Fécamp and Ostend every two hours during daylight in order to observe movements of enemy ships. Twenty minutes later the "Jim Crow" report was being studied at Dover. It stated that the radar plot consisted of from twenty-five to thirty vessels, consisting of small destroyers or sloops, accompanied by E- or R-boats.

In fact, it was the *Scharnhorst*, *Gneisenau*, and *Prinz Eugen*, screened by six destroyers and escorted by fifteen torpedo boats and twenty-four E-boats (motor torpedo boats). By good fortune the

Group Captain at No. 11 Group, which supplied the "Jim Crows", himself took up a fighter to verify the report. Twenty minutes later he was back, and the truth reached Dover via No. 11 Group, Fighter Command, and the Admiralty.

It was a most unpleasant surprise. The basis of Admiral Ramsay's plan had been first to attack the enemy in the Dover Straits with Swordfish torpedo bombers and motor torpedo boats, where the maximum advantage could have been derived from our numerical and tactical air superiority, and then to finish off the ships by bombers, coupled with an attack by Beaufort torpedo bombers of Coastal Command. Now it was too late for the first attack, for the enemy ships were already in the Straits and would be through them long before any ship or aircraft could reach them.

Nevertheless, the striking forces of motor torpedo boats and Swordfish were immediately ordered into action and the Royal Air Force was asked for maximum fighter cover. A total of eighty-four fighters was promised. But once again things went wrong. By the time the six Swordfish were in the air only ten of the eighty-four had materialised, and it was with this meagre escort that the gallant Esmonde set out to lead his half-squadron against an immensely powerful force of surface ships protected by the greatest strength of fighter cover that the enemy could muster. He must have known that he was flying to his death, for without a strong fighter cover he had no chance.

First to reach the enemy were the motor torpedo boats from Dover. The promised British fighters had not arrived and without their help it was impossible to penetrate the German outer screen of E-boats. Torpedoes were fired through the screen at the battle-cruisers, but none reached their mark.

As the last of the motor torpedo boats was attacking, the Swordfish arrived. That they had arrived at all was a wonderful tribute to the determination of their pilots, for enemy fighters had intercepted them off Ramsgate and had subjected them to savage attack all the way. All were damaged, but somehow their pilots kept them in the air. Esmonde, in the leading Swordfish, had his lower port main plane completely shot away yet still retained control. Finally, when only 3,000 yards from his target, he was heavily hit again and crashed into the sea.

The other Swordfish continued to close the enemy. Subjected to incessant attacks by the enemy fighters, they yet remained in the air long enough to drop their torpedoes. But by then it was all over for them. The fantastic odds that they had faced, both from anti-aircraft fire from the German ships and from the enemy's fighter cover, were too great for survival. Not one Swordfish returned from this gallant sortie, and no more than five of the eighteen men who flew them were picked up. Of these five, only two were un-wounded.

This epic attack of the Swordfish was described by Admiral Ramsay as "one of the finest exhibitions of self-sacrifice and devotion to duty that this war has yet witnessed".[4] To Lieutenant-Commander Esmonde went a posthumous award of the Victoria Cross for his amazing gallantry, the five survivors were awarded four D.S.O.s and a C.G.M. between them, and the remaining twelve airmen were each posthumously mentioned in Despatches.[5]

But in spite of all this gallantry no German ship had yet been hit. They steamed steadily on and by now were out in the more open waters of the southern North Sea, with their goal almost in sight. The bold gamble in forcing the Channel in daylight looked like succeeding.

There remained the six destroyers, based on Harwich, which had been placed under Admiral Ramsay's control for this operation. Like the other ships concerned, they had reverted to four hours' notice on the morning of the 12th when no report of the German ships had come through. Fortunately, when the alarm was received shortly before noon, they were still at sea carrying out firing practice.

Immediately on receipt of Vice-Admiral, Dover's, signal, they set course for the enemy. To reach them in time meant that the destroyers would have to cross a known German minefield. There was no hesitation. This was the last chance of stopping the enemy, and to Captain Pizey, leading the destroyers, the risk was one which, in the particular circumstances, had to be accepted. Five of the six destroyers got across safely, the sixth ran her main bearings before reaching the mine barrier and was forced to turn back.

By four o'clock in the afternoon the destroyers were in contact, but their attacks were as unfruitful as had been the earlier ones of the motor torpedo boats and the Swordfish. They had to face an additional difficulty as they strove to reach a good attacking position, for as the short February day approached its end the wind, which had been moderate in the morning, freshened into a gale which knocked up a heavy and confused sea over the shallows off the Dutch coast. The visibility, too, was closing down rapidly and the destroyer captains had great difficulty in finding their massive opponents. Seas were breaking green over the small ships fore and aft, there were continuous sheets of spray over the bridges, and at times the guns' crews were working knee deep in water.[6]

While the destroyers were making their attacks, the Royal Air Force was also playing its part in the battle. Two hundred and forty-two aircraft of Bomber Command, 398 fighters, and 28 torpedo-dropping Beauforts of Coastal Command were engaged. But they were all too late, the atrocious weather making it almost impossible even to find the enemy, let alone to do him any damage. Their attacks were as unsuccessful as were those of the Navy.

Yet the two German battle-cruisers were not to reach their home ports unscathed. Both of them hit mines laid earlier in the waters off the German coast. The damage to the *Gneisenau* proved to be slight, but the *Scharnhorst*, which hit two mines, had one of her engines put out of action and shipped over a thousand tons of sea water. She finally limped slowly into Wilhelmshaven, where she had to dock for major repairs which lasted many months.

The failure to bring the enemy to decisive action sent a wave of dismay throughout the country. In the eyes of the public it seemed as though the Navy had let them down, and that the shield of sea power, for so long the nation's safeguard, had perished. "Vice-Admiral Ciliax [the German admiral in command] has succeeded where the Duke of Medina Sidonia failed", wrote *The Times* in a leading article. "Nothing more mortifying to the pride of sea power has happened in Home waters since the 17th Century."[7]

It was not quite as bad as that. There must always be the occasional ships which get through, no matter how strong the opposition posed against them. In this case the opposition was relatively minute, for it was not possible to tie up strong forces within reach of the Channel for a problematical operation of which even the date was in doubt. The failure to stop the ships was lamentable, though understandable in the light of the failure to warn Admiral Ramsay of the radar breakdown in the two western search aircraft. But it bore some fruit by the attention it focused on the plight of the Navy in respect of its air striking power. In the competition for modern aircraft the Fleet Air Arm had been sadly overlooked. The public dismay at the events of 12th February in the English Channel now led to a "new deal" in the matter of naval aircraft, bringing at last to the Navy a flow of powerful American types capable of holding their own in the stresses of modern naval warfare.

The unhappy events in the Mediterranean and in Home waters, however, paled almost into insignificance compared with the magnitude of the defeat in the Far East. In the previous chapter the events leading up to the despatch of the *Prince of Wales* and *Repulse* to Singapore were described. The two ships reached their destination on 2nd December, 1941. Eight days later both had been sunk by the Japanese and the Allied Far Eastern strategy lay in ruins.

With the sinking of the *Prince of Wales* had perished the new Commander-in-Chief, Admiral Sir Tom Phillips. It is therefore impossible to know what thoughts lay in his mind as he took his two ships up towards the northward from Singapore on 8th December. It was his intention to attack Japanese transports and warships which had been reported off Singora, on the coast of Siam, and off Khota Baru, in the north of Malaya.[8] Before sailing he had asked for air reconnaissance and for fighter cover while in these northern waters, but within six hours of leaving Singapore he was told by signal that the fighter cover for which he had asked would not be forthcoming because of the loss of the northern Malayan airfields.

Admiral Phillips had been Vice-Chief of Naval Staff before his appointment to command the Eastern Fleet. He knew, therefore, the risks to which ships are subjected while operating under skies dominated by enemy air power, and the lessons of the Norwegian and Cretan campaigns must have been still fresh in his mind. But it seems that events were moving too quickly for Admiral Phillips, for the Japanese assault on Malaya came within an hour and a half of the attack on the American Fleet at Pearl Harbour. From the very outset the British army and air forces in northern Malaya were being driven back, and it was unthinkable to Admiral Phillips to let that situation go by default while he had powerful ships available. Hoping to gain by surprise what he was losing through lack of air cover, he set out on the venture which was to lose him his fleet and his life.

The Japanese plan was a massive one.[9] Several simultaneous landings were planned in Malaya and Siam, the troops being embarked in twenty-eight transports. A total of two battleships, seven 8-inch cruisers, three 6-inch cruisers, twenty-four destroyers, and twelve submarines were disposed as close escort and covering forces for the operation. In addition, ninety-nine bombers, thirty-nine fighters, and six reconnaissance aircraft were based within reach at Saigon and Soktran, in southern Indo-China. All this, of course, was unknown to Admiral Phillips, but it made his chances of success slender in the extreme, even if he had achieved the surprise at which he aimed at the moment of arrival.

The British squadron, known as Force Z and comprising the *Prince of Wales*, *Repulse*, and the destroyers *Electra*, *Express*, *Vampire*, and *Tenedos*, sailed from Singapore in the evening of 8th December. During the early afternoon of the 9th, Force Z was sighted and reported by the Japanese submarine *I.65*, and during the same evening three Japanese aircraft were sighted from the *Prince of Wales*. It was obvious that all chance of surprise had already been lost. Admiral Phillips continued on his northerly course for another hour and then altered westwards towards Singora. It was not until another hour and a quarter later, at 8.15 p.m., that he finally abandoned the operation and turned for home.

How near he was to action on this evening only became apparent when the Japanese records became available for study after the war. Warned by the submarine sighting report, four heavy cruisers under Admiral Kurita were steering south-eastward to rejoin the battle-fleet. At the moment when Admiral Phillips altered course towards Singora they were but fifteen miles to the northward of him and a continuation of his course for only five minutes more would have led to contact, possibly even to a repetition of the battle of Matapan, in which the Italian heavy cruisers had suffered so severely at the hands of British capital ships.

Equally possible, of course, was a foretaste of what in fact was to occur on the following day. The Japanese 22nd Air Flotilla, highly trained and based at Saigon, received the signal from *I.65* at about 4.0 p.m. They were then about to take off for Singapore, loaded with bombs. Hurriedly they changed their bombs for torpedoes, and by 6.0 p.m. were airborne in search of Force Z. In the rapidly gathering darkness they failed to find the ships and returned to base to await another chance on the morrow.

While Force Z was steaming homewards through the night a signal was received from Singapore reporting a Japanese landing at Kuantan, half-way down the Malayan coast. The Commander-in-Chief decided to investigate, and at dawn on the 10th was approaching the land at twenty-five knots. The *Repulse* sighted and reported an enemy reconnaissance aircraft, but Admiral Phillips was not to be deterred. Shortly before nine o'clock in the morning the *Express* which had been detached to investigate Kuantan, rejoined the fleet with the report of "complete peace" there, and the Commander-in-Chief then altered course to the northward to investigate a tug which had been sighted towing a string of barges. The time was then a little after 10.0 a.m.

In the meantime the enemy had not been inactive. The Japanese Commander-in-Chief, Admiral Kondo, was well aware of the movements of Force Z from the various shadowing reports he had received on the afternoon and evening of the 9th. His plan was to attack at dawn with all available naval aircraft and to complete the destruction with the battle-fleet, which he was bringing south at its best speed.

The shadowing aircraft lost touch during the night, but another Japanese submarine, *I.58*, sighted Force Z shortly before 2.30 a.m. on the morning of the 10th. She attacked with five torpedoes, all of which missed and none of which was sighted by the British Fleet. She lost touch soon after 3.0 a.m., but aircraft from Saigon were ready to take up the task. A small reconnaissance group of twelve aircraft took off at 5.0 a.m., followed an hour later by the whole striking force of eighty-four aircraft, fifty armed with torpedoes and thirty-four with bombs.

It was only as they were returning from a deep and fruitless search to the south that they first sighted, and bombed, the *Tenedos*, which had been detached earlier and was about 140 miles to the southward of the *Prince of Wales*. It was then a minute or two after 10.0 a.m. Twenty-five minutes later a shadowing aircraft was seen from the *Prince of Wales*. It reported her to the striking force, and from that moment on until the end, a couple of hours later, the British ships were never out of sight of Japanese aircraft. Their ordeal was upon them.

The action can perhaps best be visualised during its eighty minutes of conflict by the signals which were received in the War Room at Singapore during the early afternoon of 10th December.[10] They tell the tragic story in a shattering crescendo of disaster.

| *Time of Receipt* | *From* | *To* | *Message* |
|---|---|---|---|
| 1204 | *Repulse* | Any British man-of-war | Enemy aircraft bombing. |
| 1240 | *Prince of Wales* | " | *EMERGENCY*. Have been struck by a torpedo on port side. *Repulse* hit by 1 torpedo. Send destroyers. |
| 1304 | S.O. Force Z | " | *EMERGENCY*. Send all available tugs. |
| 1310 | *Electra* | " | *MOST IMMEDIATE*. H.M.S. *Prince of Wales* hit by 4 torpedoes. *Repulse* sunk. Send destroyers. |
| 1310 | S.O. Force Z | " | *MOST IMMEDIATE*. H.M.S. *Prince of Wales* disabled and out of control. |
| 1311 | *Prince of Wales* | " | *EMERGENCY*. Send all available tugs. |

| | | | |
|---|---|---|---|
| 1317 | C.-in-C. Eastern Fleet | „ | *MOST IMMEDIATE.* Am disembarking men not required for fighting ships. Send ? ? fast as possible. |
| 1317 | *Electra* | „ | *MOST IMMEDIATE.* Send tugs. |
| 1321 | *Electra* | „ | *MOST IMMEDIATE.* H.M.S. *Prince of Wales* sunk. |

As the first message from the *Repulse* was received in Singapore, fighters were ordered to the scene. Five of them took off from Sembawang within seven minutes of the receipt of the signal in Air Headquarters, but already they were too late. They arrived on the scene as the *Prince of Wales* rolled over and sank, and flew over the destroyers during their work of rescue. From the *Repulse* 42 officers and 754 men out of a total complement of 1,309 were picked up; from the *Prince of Wales* 90 officers and 1,195 ratings were rescued out of 1,612.

There remains one last glimpse of this sad disaster. It is from the report of one of the fighter pilots, made to Admiral Sir Geoffrey Layton, who assumed command of the Far East Fleet on the death of Admiral Phillips. "I had the privilege to be the first aircraft to reach the crews of the *Prince of Wales* and the *Repulse* after they had been sunk. I say the privilege, for, during the next hour while I flew low over them, I witnessed a show of that indomitable spirit for which the Royal Navy is so famous. I have seen shows of spirit in this war over Dunkirk, during the 'Battle of Britain', and in the London night raids, but never before have I seen anything comparable with what I saw yesterday. I passed over thousands who had been through an ordeal the greatness of which they alone can understand, for it is impossible to pass on one's feelings in disaster to others. . . . After an hour lack of petrol forced me to leave, but during that hour I had seen many men in dire danger waving, cheering, and joking as if they were holiday-makers at Brighton waving at a low flying aircraft. It shook me, for here was something above human nature. I take off my hat to them, for in them I saw the spirit which wins wars."[11]

Such doubts as may have still existed as to the Japanese efficiency in the air had now received their answer. Within three days of the outbreak of war they had not only smashed the United States Pacific Fleet as it lay at anchor in Pearl Harbour, but had also accomplished a feat at sea which no other belligerent nation had achieved in more than two years of war. Operating over 400 miles

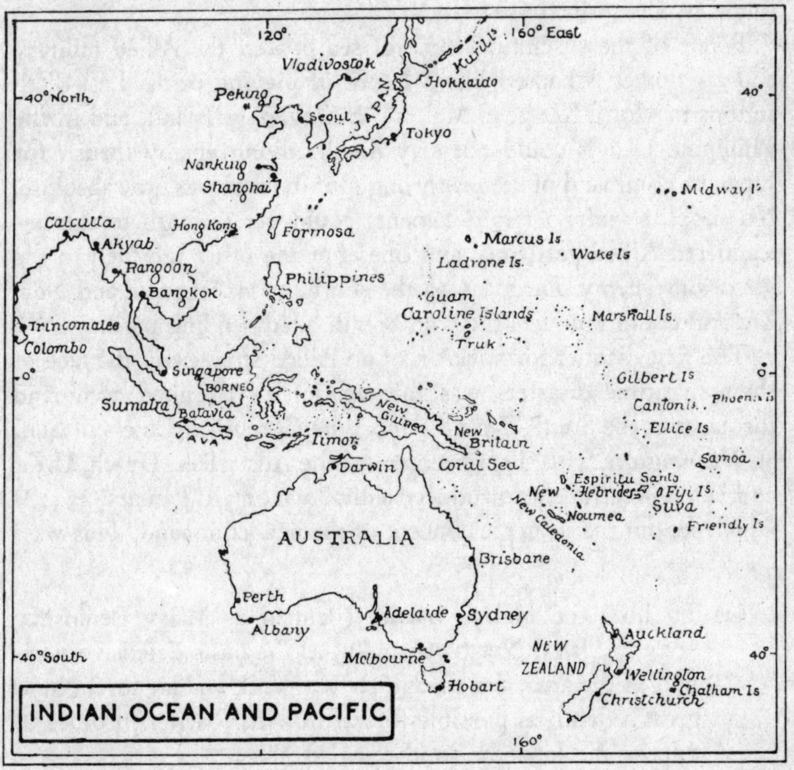


from their base, they had sunk two capital ships at sea, one of them a fine, modern battleship but recently completed and commissioned. The whole attack lasted less than two hours, and as the Japanese aircraft flew homewards, having lost no more than three of their number, they could feel well pleased at their forenoon's work.

But they had done more than sink battleships. They had removed, in two devastating strokes, almost the entire Allied sea power in the

Far Eastern theatre. And with that gone, all was gone. There was little left now beyond the three American carriers which had escaped the holocaust at Pearl Harbour and a few cruisers, destroyers, and submarines to dispute the Japanese advance through the rich chain of islands which lay to the southward. Rice, oil, rubber, tin—almost all the raw materials of which they stood in need were to be found in plenty in those islands.

Bereft of the sustaining force of sea power, the Allied military and air power collapsed like a house of playing-cards. Last-ditch actions in Hong Kong, in Malaya, in Singapore Island, and in the Phillipine Islands could not stay the headlong enemy thrust, for Japanese command of the sea throughout the area was now absolute. No supplies and no reinforcements could get through to the beleaguered Allied garrisons, and one after the other they fell to the victorious enemy. Far away to the south, even Australia and New Zealand could now feel the cold breath of impending peril.

The first distinct formulation of an Allied strategy in the face of these maritime disasters was the creation of a united command throughout the South-West Pacific. The Combined Chiefs of Staff at Washington, with the agreement of the Australian, Dutch, U.K., and U.S. Governments, produced a directive on 3rd January, 1942,[12] which set out the strategic concept of the new command. This was:

(*a*) To hold the Malaya barrier (defined as Malay Peninsula, Sumatra, Java, North Australia) as the basic defensive position of the area, and to operate sea, land, and air forces in as great a depth as possible forward of that barrier in order to oppose the Japanese southward advance.

(*b*) To hold Burma and Australia as essential support positions for the area, with Burma as additionally essential for the defence of India and the support of China.

(*c*) To re-establish communications through the Dutch East Indies with Luzon, in order to support General MacArthur in the Phillipines.

(*d*) To maintain essential communications within the area.

General Sir Archibald Wavell was appointed supreme commander and took over his duties on 15th January, but he was fighting a losing battle from the first. Before arriving in the area he telegraphed to the Chiefs of Staff in London asking what resources he could expect with which to carry out his task. The reply he received was to the effect that the Chiefs of Staff themselves did not know.[13] It was hardly an encouraging start, for the forces in the area were already fully committed and still desperately thin.

The pattern of Japanese strategy, as revealed in their advance through the islands, was based on a close co-ordination of sea, air, and land power. Almost all their operations followed this pattern, a period of long-range bombing of the main objective, limited amphibious or airborne operations to seize nearby airfields in order to cover the main landings, and then the arrival of the troop convoys with heavy naval escort and support. The little that now remained of Allied naval force in the theatre was powerless to interfere effectively against this methodical and ordered advance, while the aircraft which General Wavell disposed were far too few and too dispersed to stem the Japanese tide. Day by day the tale of disaster grew.

By the end of January the enemy were in possession of the oil centres of Balikpapan and Tarakan in Borneo, they were ashore in the Celebes, they had captured Rabaul in New Britain, Kavieng in New Ireland, and Kieta in Bougainville Island, in the Solomons. At the beginning of February Surabaya and Madang, in Java, were heavily bombed, the traditional sign of forthcoming assault. By the 14th Palembang and its great oil refinery was in their hands, and the subsequent occupation of Sumatra was but a matter of time. By that move the island of Java was outflanked, and the four main straits which linked the Java Sea with the outer oceans came under Japanese control.

All the conditions for the attack on Java were completed by 25th February, for on that day the Dutch island of Bali fell. Its airfield was within 150 miles of the naval base at Surabaya, and from it the Japanese could provide air cover for their invasion forces. The next move, according to the Japanese pattern, should be the sailing of the assault troops. And on that same day a report was received at

Surabaya from General MacArthur, still holding out in the Philippines, that a large convoy of over a hundred ships had been sighted near the entrance to the Makassar Strait.[14] It was but a comparatively short run down from there into the Java Sea.

It was with the intention of attacking this convoy that the Dutch Rear-Admiral Doorman sailed from Surabaya in command of a mixed force of cruisers and destroyers. They were almost all that were left now. British, Australian, Dutch, and American ships comprised the squadron of five cruisers and nine destroyers, and they put to sea without time to develop even a common signals plan. Their complete lack of integration as a fighting force was a handicap under any conditions; pitted against an enemy as efficient and as well-trained as the Japanese Navy, their chances of success were negligible from the outset.

A sweep through the southern part of the Java Sea on the 27th revealed no trace of the enemy convoy and on the afternoon of that day Admiral Doorman decided to return to Surabaya to refuel. As he was about to enter harbour, new reports of two convoys came in and he at once reversed his course in search of the enemy. The British destroyer *Electra*, leading the line, sighted smoke at about 4.0 p.m., and within a few minutes action was joined with a strong enemy force of four cruisers and twelve destroyers.

The action was begun at long range and remained inconclusive until the British cruiser *Exeter* was hit in a boiler room and her speed severely reduced. Admiral Doorman led his other cruisers between her and the enemy, making smoke, and ordered the three British destroyers to counter-attack. As they came out of the smoke, the *Electra* was hit in her boiler room and all steam lost. She came to a standstill, a sitting target for the Japanese destroyers. She fought back to the end, but one by one her guns were silenced and finally, riddled by enemy shellfire, she turned slowly over and sank.

Darkness was falling as the damaged *Exeter* was ordered back to Surabaya, but the remainder of the force altered course to the northward to try to work round the Japanese escort and get at the convoy. The Japanese admiral, however, not only had his convoy well clear of the scene of action, but had also received reinforcements. He was, moreover, excellently served by his air reconnaissance; and while Admiral Doorman had little idea of the whereabouts of his enemy in the gathering darkness, his opponent, Admiral Nishimura, knew exactly the position of the Allied forces. The end was a foregone conclusion. Two Dutch cruisers, the *de Ruyter* and *Java*, and the British destroyer *Jupiter* were sunk. The remainder managed to break away successfully to find a temporary refuge in Batavia and Surabaya.

But the end had not yet been reached. The Japanese, controlling all the exits of the Java Sea, held these remaining ships in a trap whose jaws had to be forced if they were to escape. The four American destroyers of Admiral Doorman's force succeeded in slipping unobserved through the narrow channel between Bali and Java and reached Australia in safety. The remainder were not so fortunate. The Australian cruiser *Perth*, accompanied by the U.S. cruiser *Houston*, attempted to escape by the Sunda Strait and ran straight into the Japanese invasion fleet. They succumbed after a most gallant fight against tremendous odds. The *Exeter*, the destroyer *Encounter*, and the U.S. destroyer *Pope* also tried the Sunda Strait, sailing from Surabaya at dusk on the 28th. At dawn on 1st March the sea was clear and hopes began to rise that the way might be open. They were doomed to disappointment. At 8.0 a.m. smoke was sighted on the horizon, and very soon its source was revealed as a strong force of Japanese cruisers and destroyers. The last battle of the *Exeter* and her two destroyers was as bitter and as gallantly fought as was that of the *Perth* and the *Houston* in the same waters during the previous night.

The road to Java was now completely open. Japanese forces landed at each end of the long island on 1st March, virtually unopposed. There were no Allied ships to dispute the landings, none to stop the build-up of men and supplies with which to nourish the assault. Within a week Java had fallen, and its immense riches were firmly in the grasp of greedy Japanese fingers. The last link in the Malaya Barrier, on which it had been hoped to hold the enemy, had gone, and the threat to the Australian mainland was patent.

Nothing like this had ever been seen in war before. In three short months, in battle against two of the world's great powers, the Japanese had staged an advance of more than 3,000 miles and had shattered all opposition at infinitesimal cost to themselves. Wherever their troops had landed they were in firm and complete control, wherever their ships had fought they had gained annihilating victories. The Japanese had won an empire by whirlwind conquest and they were still hungry for more.

But the bitter cup of defeat had not even yet been drained to its dregs by the Allies. The Japanese plan of conquest included Burma as a western bastion to their new empire, and already an army was on the march. The capture of Rangoon on 8th March and of Akyab on the 31st guaranteed its southern flank from interference by the British Eastern Fleet, now re-forming in the Indian Ocean, and the occupation of the Andaman Islands on 23rd March gave Japan the entry into those waters. An obvious corollary was a naval attack into the Indian Ocean to serve the new British Fleet there with the same medicine that had been administered to the American ships at Pearl Harbour.

With the sinking of the *Prince of Wales* and *Repulse* off Malaya, the Admiralty had turned with new vigour to the task of building up a fleet in the East. It was a matter of immediate necessity. The Indian Ocean had sprung suddenly into vital prominence with the Japanese entry into the war, for on the safe passage of the supply ships and troop transport across it would depend the ability to assemble the forces which would one day be needed to drive the Japanese back.

It was desperately hard to find the ships. The U-boats were back in the Atlantic in force, and there was no hope of finding ships there which could be spared for the new campaigns in the East. The convoys to North Russia across the Arctic were a new commitment which could not be abandoned, and with the passage of each convoy the opposition was growing. In the Mediterranean the pressure was equally severe and already the fleet there was cut to the bone. Yet somehow the ships had to be found, for too much now was at stake. To lose the shipping routes of the Indian Ocean by default was quite unthinkable.

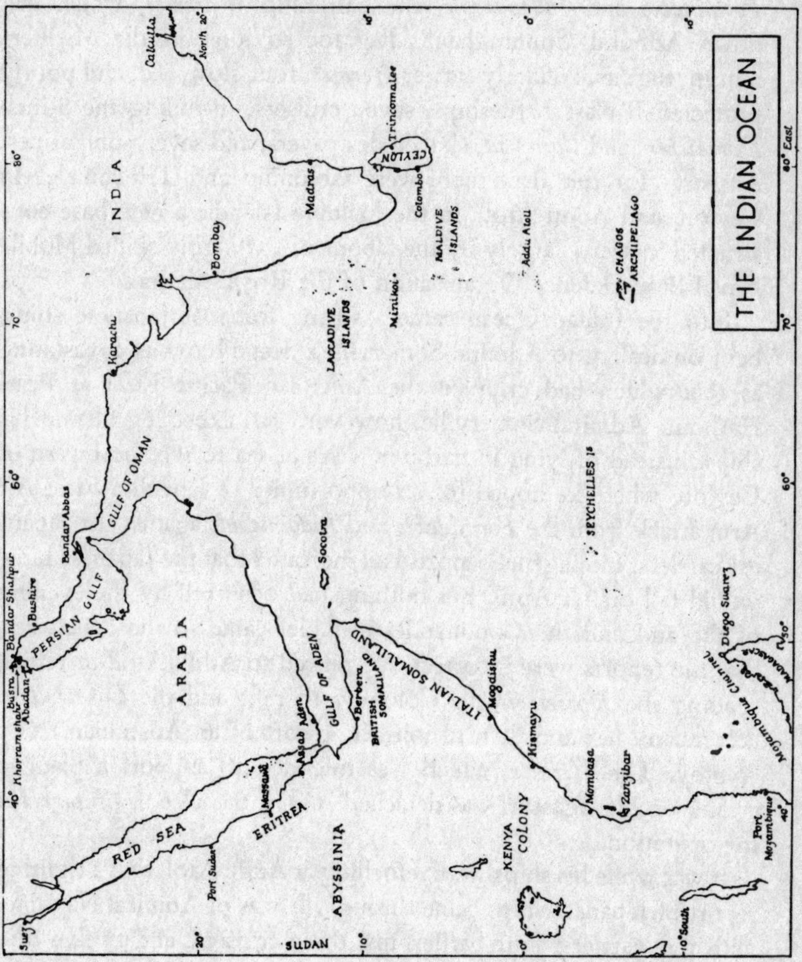
THE INDIAN OCEAN
INDIA
ARABIA
PERSIAN GULF
GULF OF OMAN
RED SEA
ERITREA
ABYSSINIA
SUDAN
KENYA COLONY
ITALIAN SOMALILAND
BRITISH SOMALILAND
GULF OF ADEN
Socotra
LACCADIVE ISLANDS
MALDIVE ISLANDS
Minikoi
Addu Atoll
CHAGOS ARCHIPELAGO
SEYCHELLES Is
CEYLON
Colombo
Trincomalee
Madras
Bombay
Karachi
Calcutta
Bandar Abbas
Bushire
Bandar Shahpur
Busra
Abadan
Khorramshahr
Suez
Port Sudan
Massawa
Assab
Aden
Berbera
Mogadishu
Kismayu
Mombasa
Zanzibar
Port Mozambique
Mozambique Channel
Diego Suarez
MADAGASCAR
40°
50°
60°
70°
80°
80° East
North 20°
20°
10°
0°
10° South

Towards the end of March Admiral Sir James Somerville arrived in Colombo to hoist his flag as the new Commander-in-Chief of the Eastern Fleet. It comprised the two new aircraft carriers *Formidable* and *Indomitable*, the battleship *Warspite*, which had flown Admiral Cunningham's flag for so long in the Mediterranean, the small, elderly carrier *Hermes*, four slow, old, and poorly protected R-class battleships, seven cruisers, including the 8-inch *Dorsetshire* and *Cornwall*, sixteen destroyers, and seven submarines. As bases for this fleet there were Colombo and Trincomalee in Ceylon, and Addu Atoll, in the Maldive Islands, a new base constructed in secret largely by the labour of the highly skilled Mobile Naval Base Defence Organisation of the Royal Marines.

Into the Indian Ocean came a strong force of Japanese ships, bent on dealing to Admiral Somerville's fleet a blow as devastating as that which had crippled the American Pacific Fleet at Pearl Harbour. Admiral Somerville, however, was expecting it, and his ships, instead of lying in harbour, were at sea to the southward of Ceylon, where he hoped for an opportunity to launch a Fleet Air Arm attack from the *Formidable* and *Indomitable* against the Japanese carriers. Intelligence reports had indicated that the Japanese blow would fall on 1st April, but nothing had occurred by the evening of the 2nd and the Commander-in-Chief came to the conclusion that the reports were incorrect. He retired to Addu Atoll to refuel, sending the *Dorsetshire* to Colombo to refit and the *Cornwall* to accompany her and then to join the escort of an Australian troop convoy. The *Hermes*, which was intended to support a planned assault on Madagascar, was detached to Trincomalee to prepare for the operation.

It was while his ships were refuelling at Addu Atoll that a sighting report of Japanese ships came through. It was of Admiral Nagumo, with five carriers, four battleships, three cruisers, and twelve destroyers approaching Ceylon, though the report reaching the Commander-in-Chief was not sufficiently definite to indicate its full composition. Admiral Somerville at once sailed from Addu Atoll, but it was now too late to intercept. Colombo, in which Nagumo had hoped to find the British Fleet, was empty of the big prize, and though a fair amount of damage was done to the port by the Japanese carrier aircraft, the enemy were made to pay heavily for it by the exertions of defending fighters.

Admiral Nagumo, having missed the British Fleet, sent his reconnaissance planes far and wide in search of it. It was, perhaps, fortunate that they failed to find it, for Nagumo's five carriers carried a devastating punch and Britain could not now afford any repetition of the disaster which had befallen the *Prince of Wales* and *Repulse*. The ships so recently sent to the Indian Ocean had only been collected by cutting other requirements to the bone. If they were lost now, there were no others with which to replace them.

The *Cornwall* and *Dorsetshire* had sailed from Colombo as soon as news of the sighting of the Japanese ships had been received, and were on their way to join the Commander-in-Chief as he steamed up from Addu Atoll. They were sighted by the Japanese aircraft searching for the main fleet. Within an hour or two some fifty bombers were overhead. The two ships were overwhelmed by the weight of the attack and both of them, very heavily hit, were sunk.

Four days later the Japanese returned. Their target this time was Trincomalee, and they caused serious damage in the port. Again the reconnaissance aircraft searched for Admiral Somerville's fleet and again failed to find it. History, however, was once more to repeat itself. Though they missed the fleet they found the *Hermes*, and they sank her almost as easily as they had sunk the *Cornwall* and *Dorsetshire* four days previously.

Over the whole wide area of conflict, in the Mediterranean and the Atlantic as well as in the south-west Pacific, the Allied skies were black indeed. For the time the tide was running strongly for the enemies, European as well as Asiatic. As the British Prime Minister surveyed the dismal scene in all the various theatres of war, it must have been with a heavy heart that he wrote to President Roosevelt, "When I reflect how I have longed and prayed for the entry of the United States into the war, I find it difficult to realise how gravely our British affairs have deteriorated since December 7th".[15]

The U.S. President could, with almost equal truth, have written similar words back to Mr. Churchill.

# Chapter 9

## MEDITERRANEAN AND ARCTIC CONVOYS

FROM the state of quasi-war, which can perhaps best be dated by President Roosevelt's nation-wide "Emergency" broadcast of 27th May, 1941,[1] the United States, with the declaration of war against Germany and Italy by Congress on 11th December, emerged as a fully-fledged combatant in the Atlantic. The declaration presented to Raeder and Doenitz the chance for which they had long been waiting. Hitler, in the expectation of a favourable decision in Russia by the end of the year, had forbidden operations in American waters during the quasi-war period, but no such ban could hold good now. On the day following the U.S. declaration of war Hitler and Raeder met together in Berlin and reached speedy agreement on the desirability of sending U-boats to attack the shipping along the U.S. coast.[2] Only six were immediately available, but many more were expected to become operational very shortly as the massive building programmes, started at the end of 1940, began to bear fruit.

What Doenitz, commanding the U-boats, lacked in quantity for the start of this new offensive he made up for in quality. He chose his six most experienced commanders for the task, and their immediate success was, from the U.S. point of view, "both unprecedented and humiliating".[3] The first of the U-boats arrived in January 1942, and others followed quickly. They wasted no time. The sinking of the British passenger ship *Cyclops* by *U.123* on 12th January heralded the great assault, and no day passed without a heavy toll exacted from the virtually defenceless ships as they made their coastwise passage.

It was for the U-boat captains what they called their "second happy time". In spite of British experience, made fully available through Rear-Admiral Ghormley, the President's special naval observer in Britain, the United States had made no plans for the institution of convoy for the great volume of shipping that flowed up and down between the Gulf and Caribbean ports and the main harbours of the U.S. eastern seaboard. Instead, they relied on air and surface patrol of the shipping lanes and, later, the employment of hunter-killer groups in special areas. Neither was effective, and the terrible toll mounted alarmingly. What was particularly galling was the very high proportion of tankers, perhaps the most precious of all ships in time of war, included in the losses. Well might Doenitz, with perfect truth, exclaim: "Our submarines are operating close inshore along the coast of the United States of America, so that bathers and sometimes entire coastal cities are witnesses to that drama of war, whose visual climaxes are constituted by the red glorioles of blazing tankers."[4]

From her own meagre resources Great Britain offered help. Ten corvettes and twenty-four anti-submarine trawlers were turned over to bring some relief to the problem, but in the absence of convoy there was little material benefit from this transference. The reluctance of the American Navy to institute convoy, even when provided with, as Admiral Ghormley expressed it, "information fresh from the laboratory of war, and of priceless value to national defence"[5], was difficult to understand. It was also particularly galling to Britain, who depended for her very existence on all those imports which were being sunk with such impunity. Admiral Sir Percy Noble, responsible as Commander-in-Chief Western Approaches for the Atlantic battle, wrote to the First Sea Lord on 8th March: "The Western Approaches Command finds itself in the position to-day of escorting convoys safely over to the American eastern seaboard and then finding that many of the ships thus escorted are easy prey to the U-boats off the American coast or in the Caribbean."[6] It was a situation which, though extremely delicate as reflecting on the conduct of maritime war by an Ally in her own waters, had somehow to be brought to an end. Both Admiral Pound, the First Sea Lord, and Mr. Churchill, the Prime Minister, brought what pressure they could to bear on their opposite numbers in the United States, and early in May a partial convoy system was introduced. The result was electrifying. In those areas where convoy was instituted the sinkings declined almost to vanishing-point, with the exception of independently routed ships and stragglers from the convoys. This partial introduction of convoy along the American coast was made possible only by the diversion of two complete British escort groups from the Atlantic, which in fact reduced the Atlantic convoy cycle from six to seven days. That, however, was a price well worth paying if it brought to a stop the holocaust in American waters. It was to be another three months before convoy was fully to cover the whole area, including the Gulf of Mexico and the Caribbean, but by the end of July the U-boats were withdrawing. It was convoy, and convoy alone, that had beaten them.

Admiral Doenitz had calculated that an average of 800,000 tons of Allied ships sunk each month was more than sufficient to produce an Axis victory.[7] During the first seven months of 1942 the total sinkings by Axis U-boats were 681 ships of over three and a half million tons, a monthly average of just over half a million tons. The Germans, relying on the optimistic reports of their U-boat captains, thought the figure much higher and, indeed, above their monthly target. Yet even the actual rate of sinkings was well above the replacement tonnage that could be provided by new merchant ship building, and a continuance at that rate would inevitably have gravely impaired the Allied capacity to continue the struggle.

By the summer of 1942 Britain had made great strides along the road of efficient merchant ship protection. Many costly lessons had been learned, some more were still to be learned, but in general the correct pattern of anti-submarine warfare had emerged. In March 1942 the Naval Staff at the Admiralty prepared for the Americans a review of all British experience in the Atlantic battle so far, which was summarised under four main headings.

(*a*) The comparative failure of hunting forces.

(*b*) The great value of aircraft in convoy protection.

(*c*) The supreme importance of adequate training and practice.

(*d*) The value of efficient radar.

It was in these four headings, which might well have been elevated to the status of cardinal principles, that the ultimate safety of the Merchant Navy depended.

The limitations of the hunting forces were, perhaps, the hardest cross of all for the Navy to bear. "To go to sea," wrote the Naval Staff, "to hunt down and destroy the enemy makes a strong appeal to every naval officer. It gives a sense of initiative and of the offensive that is lacking in the humdrum business of convoy protection. But the difficulties of locating a U-boat intent on evasion are apt to be forgotten; the odds are all in favour of the U-boat, and the anti-submarine hunting force is impotent."[8]

Yet, although the correct doctrine was thus early recognised, there were still many intractables to hinder and delay the full performance of the task. While the United States were wrestling with their own shipping problems during the U-boat onslaught along their coasts, they were also actively engaged in bringing across the Atlantic an army to Britain. The many troop convoys, together with the weapons and supplies needed in modern military war, were adding a heavy burden to the essential Atlantic traffic, already hard enough pressed as it was to keep Great Britain supplied. The British belt had to be tightened another notch or two as the great building-up of force proceeded.

This was, however, but one of the intractables. Others were the shortage of "long-legged" escorts, of trained crews, and above all of very long-range aircraft. The new frigates, admirably designed for the Atlantic battle, began to come forward during 1942, though more slowly than had been hoped. Anti-submarine training of the escort groups was still being hampered by the constant operational need to commit every available ship and man to the battle as soon as possible, though in this respect there was a considerable improvement on earlier years. The very long-range Liberators, so urgently needed to provide air cover for the convoys in the distant wastes of the Atlantic, were irritatingly slow in arrival and added to the perplexities and difficulties of the battle at this crucial stage.

Brooding over the whole Atlantic scene, and dark with menace, was the constant increase in the number of operational U-boats available to the enemy. During the first six months of 1942 the operational strength rose from 91 to 140, while the U-boat sinkings by Allied forces totalled no more than thirty. It was not a happy picture to contemplate from a short-term viewpoint.

Over the longer view, however, there were gleams of light to point towards a rosier dawn. The "hedgehog", an ahead-throwing mortar, removed one of the great drawbacks of the depth-charge dropping method by enabling the attacking ship to hold a U-boat in its asdic beam right up to the moment of attack. In all earlier attacks there had been an appreciable time-gap between the final asdic contact and the dropping of the charges while the ship herself passed over the U-boat and steamed clear of the area of explosion. The increase in accuracy of attack which the "hedgehog" brought was to some extent minimised by the fact that it fired contact charges which required a direct hit to produce a kill, but the "hedgehog" itself paved the way to the "squid", which combined the killing power of the full-depth charge with the ahead-firing method. Asdic and "squid", with radar and aircraft as partners, were to prove a deadly combination.

There were other advances, too, which were to play their part in the battle. High-frequency wireless direction-finders were fitted in some of the escort vessels, enabling them to take the bearing of a U-boat's signals. It made the location of attacking U-boats far more rapid and effective than the previous reliance on the shore direction-finding stations only. At the same time there were three equally devastating advances in Coastal Command aircraft. The first was the fitting of radar sets which could pick up a surfaced U-boat at a considerable range; the second was the equipping of the first squadron of "Leigh Light" aircraft, which would automatically illuminate the target at night a few moments before the attack; the third was the development of the shallow-setting depth charge for aircraft which enabled them to add U-boat killing as well as U-boat spotting and anti-U-boat reconnaissance to their accomplishments.

As yet, however, the full harvest of these scientific advances was still for future gathering. At this particular moment in the war—the first half of 1942—the balance in the Atlantic was still tipping towards the U-boats, and at times tipping much too heavily for comfort. The sombre battle under, on, and over the Atlantic waters was being fought with a cold fury and a savagery that knew no quarter; a battle of swift, unseen attack, of murderous thrust and counter-thrust. Through it all ran the merchant ships in ceaseless convoy, bringing to Britain the men, the arms, the oil, the raw materials, and the food on which depended, in the long run, the launching of the counter-offensive. Once before in the world's history had Europe lain beneath the heel of a conqueror, and it was then, in 1810, that the American Senator Timothy Pickering, at a dinner given to the British Minister, had drunk a toast to "the world's last hope—Britain's fast-anchored isle". Now, in 1942, the same toast was being drunk, for Britain was to be the spring-board of re-entry into tortured Europe. That her anchors held fast at this crux of the war, that the forces of liberation could gather and train for the great day to come, was due to the devotion and fortitude of the Merchant Navies of the Allies and to the anti-submarine escorts of all the free nations that shepherded them through these death-strewn waters.

The preoccupation of the British and Canadian escort forces with the passage of supplies to Britain was matched farther south by an equal preoccupation of the Mediterranean Fleet and Force H in keeping Malta supplied. That gallant island, sore beset during the reverses which had befallen our land forces in North Africa, was still proving a most irritating thorn in the Axis flank. In February 1942, as Rommel's advance overran our Cyrenaican airfields, the scale of enemy bombing attacks on Malta was stepped up considerably, reaching a climax of ferocity in April and May. In the eyes of the War Cabinet and the Chiefs of Staff so violent an attack could mean but one thing, a softening-up process for its eventual capture by the enemy. Such an assault was indeed planned under the code name of

Operation "Herkules", but the calls of Rommel for reinforcements and supplies in Cyrenaica and Egypt made its achievement impossible. Nor was the importance of its capture fully realised by the German Army leaders. "As we now have Tobruk", wrote Jodl, Chief of the Army High Command, on 22nd June, 1942, "we no longer require Malta." The German and Italian troops intended for "Herkules" were sent to Rommel, and on 21st July all orders for "Herkules" were cancelled.

This, however, was not known in Britain and it was in the light of an expected Axis attempt at capture, and in consequence of the vast destruction being caused by the heavy air raids, that the passage of essential supplies to Malta reached a new urgency during 1942. Too much was at stake to allow the island to be lost without a desperate fight. In enemy hands it would give him a virtually impregnable bridge for the running of supplies to his North African armies; in British hands it could still shelter naval and air forces with which to harass the Axis ships that carried them. The supply route from Italy to the North African ports was ever a nightmare to the enemy, and Malta was the "bogy" which so often troubled the Axis dream of a North African victory.

Valiantly as the defenders of Malta fought against this Axis onslaught, the problem of running in supplies in sufficient bulk to sustain them was beset with tremendous difficulties. Command of the sea and of the air above it in the central Mediterranean were both firmly held in Axis hands, and it was certain that every attempt to run a convoy to the beleaguered island would need to be conducted as a major fleet operation. During 1942 four convoys reached Malta, two from Alexandria and two from Gibraltar, but all of them suffered very severe losses in transit, both in merchant ships and escorts. Two others were forced to turn back by the severity of the attack upon them.

Apart from these convoys, supplies were brought in by submarines and by the two fast minelayers *Manxman* and *Welshman*, which relied on their great speed of thirty-six knots to get them through. Twenty small cargoes arrived by submarine and six by the minelayers during the first eight months of 1942, but welcome as they were, they did little more than touch the fringe of the major problem of supply. The provision of fighter aircraft for Malta's defence was less difficult, for these could be taken by carrier to within flying reach of the island and then flown off to complete the journey by air. H.M. ships *Argus*, *Eagle*, and *Furious*, and the U.S.S. *Wasp* despatched some 350 Spitfires and Hurricanes between them. But in spite of all this, the problem of supplying Malta with all that it needed could be solved only by the arrival of merchant ships carrying the island's necessities in bulk.

A convoy from Alexandria to Malta had got through in January, a second in February had been forced to turn back. In March, Admiral Cunningham planned to send a third. It was his last big operation before being relieved as Commander-in-Chief by Admiral Sir Henry Harwood, and he enrolled the support of the Army and the Royal Air Force to give it every chance of success in its mission. Feint attacks in the desert to threaten the enemy's forward airfields were the Army's contribution; bombing attacks on airfields in Crete and Cyrenaica, and the provision of fighter cover over the convoy to the limit of endurance, were the Royal Air Force's. Both were nobly performed. The convoy itself—three merchant ships and the naval auxiliary *Breconshire*—sailed from Alexandria on 20th March, with a small escort. It was joined the following morning by the main strength of the Mediterranean Fleet—three cruisers, one anti-aircraft ship, ten large and six Hunt-class destroyers. On the next day the cruiser *Penelope* and the destroyer *Legion* joined the convoy from Malta to help to right it through the dangerous waters of the central Mediterranean. So far all had gone well, and the few air attacks made by Italian torpedo-carrying planes had been half-hearted and easily avoided.

During the morning of this same day, 22nd March, Rear-Admiral Vian, in command of the escort, received a signal from a British submarine on patrol reporting the sailing of an Italian squadron. Judging from its position it should reach the convoy during the afternoon in the Gulf of Sirte, and Admiral Vian disposed his forces for action. A freshening south-easterly wind was beginning to knock up a heavy sea.

Just after 1.30 p.m. a shadowing aircraft dropped a line of four red flares ahead of the convoy, obviously to signal its position to approaching ships. Half an hour later the look-out in the cruiser *Euryalus* sighted smoke to the northward. Over the horizon came the enemy, the cruisers *Gorizia* and *Trento* (8-inch) and *Giovanni Della Bande Nera* (6-inch), together with four destroyers, and Admiral Vian led his striking force out to engage them, at the same time making smoke to shield the convoy from view. In his determination to get the convoy through to Malta he had already practised his squadron in the tactics to be employed and the ships took up their battle formation without a hitch. This bold front seemed temporarily to dissuade the Italian force and they turned away after about ten minutes of firing at extreme range.

Meantime the convoy was being subjected to a heavy and sustained bombing attack, this time by German aircraft. But the steady shooting of the anti-aircraft ship *Carlisle* and of the close escort of Hunt-class destroyers broke up the German formations and saved the merchant ships from damage. In the heavy sea then running the guns' crews on the destroyers' forecastles were drenched by the spray thrown up, and in spite of the slippery foothold played a noble part in holding the enemy at bay.

As Rear-Admiral Vian led his striking force back to the convoy after driving off the Italian squadron, a new threat developed to the north-east. To join the cruisers of the first attack came the battleship *Littorio* with two more destroyers, to make a formidable squadron which could, if led with determination, annihilate both Rear-Admiral Vian's escorting force and the convoy.

Once more extensive smoke-screens were laid to shroud the convoy from view, and the south-easterly wind drifted it up towards the enemy. It soon covered the whole area of battle, presenting to the slender defensive forces the inestimable advantages of surprise attacks on the enemy and at the same time a cloak of partial invisibility from the enemy's gunlayers.

Rear-Admiral Vian, aware at once of his weakest point of defence, stood away to the eastward with his cruisers to head off a probable enemy attack from that quarter. It was the weather position, so much beloved in battle during the days of sail, and on this day it was the position from which the defensive smoke-screen would be of no avail. Maybe the Italian admiral was impatient to reach the convoy, maybe the importance of the weather gauge was not so apparent to him as it was to Rear-Admiral Vian, but he decided to attack from the west. Thus, as he stood in towards the vital convoy, there were only British destroyers to bar his way.

By this time the sea had risen appreciably and the *Sikh*, *Lively*, and *Hero*, as they closed to engage the enemy, were rolling and pitching violently and their decks were swept with solid water as the waves broke over them. They attacked their overwhelming adversaries with guns and torpedoes—three destroyers pitted against a battleship, three cruisers, and six destroyers—and at the same time extended the smoke-screen westward to cover the now threatened merchantmen. But hard as they fought they could not prevent the Italian squadron from working round to the west and thus opening up a direct route to the convoy down to the south.

It was at this moment, when it seemed that the enemy must achieve his object, that out of the smoke-screen steamed Rear-Admiral Vian in the *Cleopatra*, accompanied by the *Euryalus*. He had returned from his search to the eastward, to make a dramatic appearance at the crucial moment. The two cruisers attacked the *Littorio* with torpedoes and forced her to turn away. Satisfied that the danger from the west was temporarily averted, the admiral turned back to the east once more to guard against attack from the most vulnerable quarter.

Meanwhile, five more destroyers, attracted by the *Sikh*'s report, were coming up to join the battle in the west. They were the *Jervis*, *Kelvin*, *Kingston*, *Kipling*, and *Legion*, and they sighted the *Littorio* just after 6.30 p.m. at a range of 12,000 yards. Approaching through the smoke at full speed in line abreast, and under heavy fire from the enemy battleship and cruisers, they closed to a range of 6,000 yards and swung round to fire a "broadside" of torpedoes. The enemy squadron turned away to avoid them, and once again, at the critical moment, the *Cleopatra* and *Euryalus* emerged from the smoke. Rear-Admiral Vian, finding the eastern sector still clear of the enemy, had returned to the battle in the west. For ten minutes the two cruisers fought a gun duel with the Italians, forcing them always away from the vital merchant ships. Finally, the enemy settled down resolutely on to a north-westerly course which took them away from the convoy and home to the security of their Italian bases. The Battle of Sirte was over and the convoy was saved.[9]

Yet, in spite of the victory, there was sadness in store. During the battle the convoy had been steering to the south, away from the threat of the enemy. This diversion inevitably delayed its time of arrival and, instead of reaching Malta in the dark hours before dawn, the sun was up while the merchant ships were still a few miles short of Grand Harbour. There the German bombers found them. One was hit and sunk twenty miles from the island. The naval auxiliary *Breconshire* was hit and disabled only eight miles off and was beached. The remaining two steamed triumphantly into Valletta, to the echoing cheers of the people of Malta, only to be both sunk later at their moorings before they could be fully unloaded.

This loss of supplies raised serious problems. If Malta was to be retained—and its retention was of cardinal importance in the whole concept of Middle East strategy—the supply crisis had somehow to be overcome. During April the enemy's air attacks reached a new pitch of violence, and the island's fighter defence was whittled away by serious losses. Another ferry trip by the *Wasp* and the *Eagle* early in May provided a reinforcement of sixty-two Spitfires, and these arrived just in time to turn the scale in the air battle. They flew in on the morning of 9th May, were armed and refuelled on arrival, and were airborne again later that same morning to meet the German bombers, of which they destroyed and damaged thirty. They followed it up on the 10th by shooting down another sixty. Thereafter the scale of enemy air attack began to dwindle perceptibly.

But Spitfires alone were not enough. Food and fuel and ammunition were also needed, and they could only be brought in sufficient quantities in ships. In May the call of the Russian convoys for escorts was so insistent that Malta had to tighten her belt in patience, but by June it was now or never. A convoy *had* to get through to the island if it were to remain in British hands.

A double operation was planned, a convoy of six ships from Gibraltar and one of eleven from Egypt, timed to reach Malta on consecutive days. It was hoped that this simultaneous operation would tempt the enemy to divide his forces so that at least one of the convoys might succeed. In the end two merchant ships of the Gibraltar convoy reached Malta, while the eastern convoy was forced to give up and return after serious losses. The pitifully small result from a very considerable naval effort was the measure of the opposition ranged against it by the enemy.

For the eastern convoy the Mediterranean Fleet was strengthened by units of the Eastern Fleet, and the eleven merchant ships had an escort force of seven cruisers and twenty-six destroyers, with several smaller warships and the old, unarmed battleship *Centurion* masquerading as a capital ship. In addition, nine submarines were in patrol areas to the north of the convoy route in order to intercept and to attack the Italian Fleet if it came out, while the maximum air striking force, both from Egypt and Malta, was to harass the Italian ships before they made contact.

It was the lack of capital ships in the Mediterranean that was at heart the cause of failure in the passage of this convoy. Cruisers and destroyers could not possibly hold off Italian battleships, and in the hot days of a Mediterranean summer there was no hope of a repetition of the stormy weather which had helped the March convoy to reach Malta. If the air striking force and the submarines failed to stop the Italian Fleet, then the convoy could not go through.

Neither the airmen nor the submarines succeeded. Even though one Italian cruiser was crippled in the air attack and was later sunk by the submarine *P.35*, the main body of the Italian Fleet came on undeterred. The convoy had to be turned, at least temporarily, and by the time the way was once again clear because of the return of the Italian ships to their bases, the escort had not enough ammunition left to meet the inevitable air attacks which it would still encounter in the approach to Malta. Throughout two long days the convoy had been subjected to vicious and continuous attack by German bombers, and almost every ship had fired nearly three-quarters of its entire outfit of anti-aircraft ammunition.

The Italian Fleet never made contact with the convoy, never, in fact, approached within a hundred miles of it. But its presence in those waters, coupled with the fact that Rear-Admiral Vian, commanding the escort, no longer had the advantage of exceptional weather conditions, as in March, with which to tackle battleships with his cruisers, made it suicidal to attempt to go on. The whole effort cost us one cruiser, three destroyers, and two merchant ships lost, and three cruisers, the *Centurion*, a corvette, and three merchant ships damaged. It had cost the enemy one cruiser sunk and the battleship *Littorio* damaged by an aircraft torpedo, but the cost to him was well worth the achievement of his main object in denying to Malta the supplies so desperately needed here.

The western convoy had better fortune. Its main escort consisted of the battleship *Malaya*, the carriers *Eagle* and *Argus*, three cruisers, and seventeen destroyers. It encountered no opposition until it reached the narrow waters between Sardinia and Tunisia. There the first of the air attacks came in, and from then on there was no peace, though with little damage beyond one merchant ship sunk and one cruiser, the *Liverpool*, damaged by an aerial torpedo. At the entrance to the Sicilian narrows the main covering force turned back. Its part in the operation was completed, for battleships and carriers could not operate in narrow waters under the threat of nearby land-based aircraft. Beaufighters from Malta took over the air escort from the carriers, and the convoy, reduced by its single loss to five merchant ships, went on under a close escort of nine destroyers and the anti-aircraft cruiser *Cairo*.

Early next morning, with the convoy now about 150 miles from Malta, a force of two Italian cruisers and five destroyers was sighted hull down to the eastward. Five of the escorting destroyers—the *Bedouin*, *Ithuriel*, *Partridge*, *Matchless*, and *Marne*—steamed out to do battle whilst the remainder made smoke to shroud the convoy. With the merchant ships thus protected, the rest of the escort then came out to engage the enemy.

In the running fight that followed, at times at almost point-blank

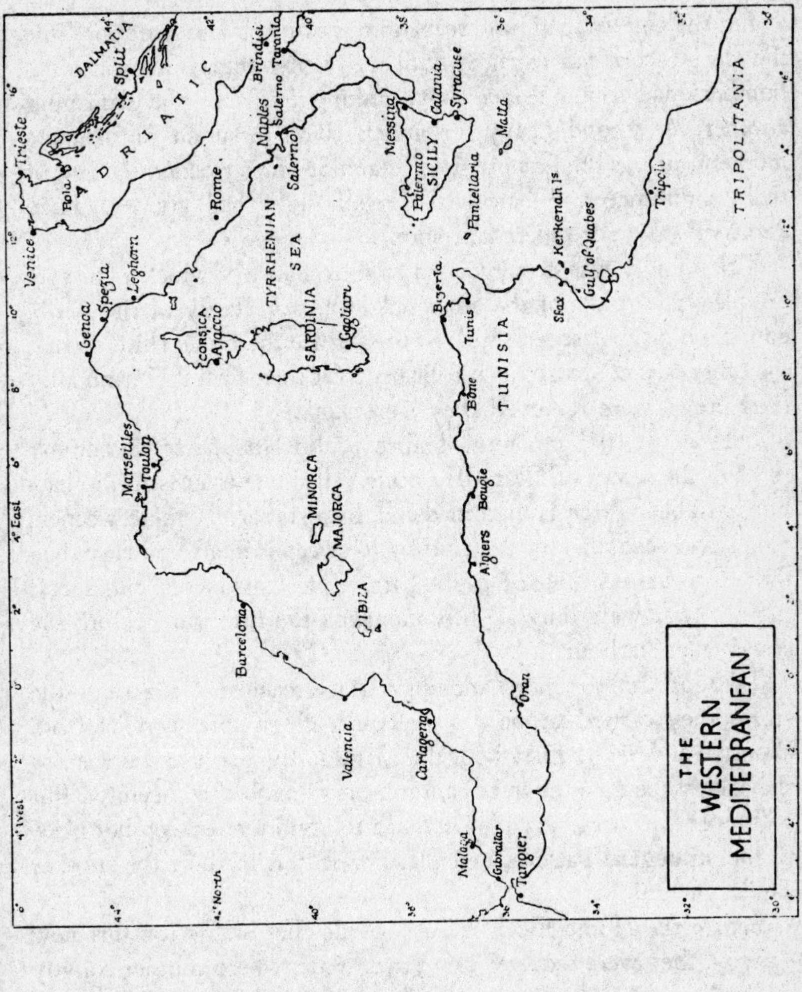
THE WESTERN MEDITERRANEAN
ADRIATIC
DALMATIA
Trieste
Pola
Split
Venice
Genoa
Spezia
Leghorn
Rome
Naples
Salerno
Brindisi
Taranto
TYRRHENIAN SEA
CORSICA
Ajaccio
SARDINIA
Cagliari
SICILY
Palermo
Messina
Catania
Syracuse
Pantellaria
Malta
Marseilles
Toulon
MINORCA
MAJORCA
IBIZA
Barcelona
Valencia
Cartagena
Malaga
Gibraltar
Tangier
Oran
Algiers
Bougie
Bône
Tunis
Bizerta
TUNISIA
Sfax
Kerkenah Is
Gulf of Quabes
Tripoli
TRIPOLITANIA
4° East
4° West
4° North

range, the *Bedouin* and *Partridge* were both hit, as also were one Italian cruiser and one destroyer. In the end the enemy squadron was driven off, though later it returned to re-engage the damaged *Bedouin*.

But the convoy had not escaped attack during this action. While the close escort was engaged with the enemy ships, German dive-bombers had found the convoy, sinking one ship and damaging another. A second heavy air attack came in at an unfortunate moment, just as the first escort of Malta Spitfires reached the end of their endurance and before the relief flight had arrived. They damaged one more merchant ship.

The convoy was now reduced to four ships, of which two were cripples as a result of the air attack. Captain Hardy of the *Cairo*, commanding the escort, resolved to sacrifice these two ships so that the other two could go on at full speed for their final dash, and after their crews were removed they were sunk.

One more trial remained before at last the harassed convoy reached the safety of Grand Harbour. All the entrances to the harbour had been extensively mined and, by an error, the minesweepers which had accompanied the convoy to sweep it in arrived later than the other ships. Five of the escorting destroyers hit mines and though four were only slightly damaged the fifth sank before she could reach harbour.[10]

Two of the six merchant ships thus reached Malta, and the stores they carried brought a welcome, if temporary, relief from shortage and want. They kept the island in the battle and denied to the enemy the great prize of capture, on which he had been set. But still more was necessary if Malta was to continue to keep her place in the strategical pattern, and plans were put in train for another similar operation.

Before the Home Fleet could provide the escorts for this new convoy, they were required up in the Arctic, where another convoy to Russia needed their presence. With the conclusion of that operation, back they came to Gibraltar, in August, in greater force than ever before. The full escort for the fourteen merchant ships of this new convoy consisted of two battleships, three carriers, six cruisers, one anti-aircraft cruiser, and twenty-four destroyers, to make of this the biggest of all the Mediterranean convoy operations. The enemy, aware from the unusual concentration of ships that such an operation was planned, greatly increased the strength of the German and Italian air forces in Sardinia and Sicily.

The convoy followed the same pattern as the June one, with the capital ships and carriers turning back in the Narrows as soon as the convoy arrived within reach of fighter cover from Malta. As in the previous operation, this first part went reasonably well, except for the sinking of the elderly carrier *Eagle* by a torpedo from *U.73*.

Apart from one merchant ship damaged and detached to take the inshore route round Cape Bon, the convoy reached the Sicilian Narrows intact. The main escort then turned back and the merchant ships continued their course with the close escort of three cruisers, the anti-aircraft cruiser, and thirteen destroyers. They had enjoyed good fortune so far, but now their luck was to desert them.

In an attack by a U-boat the cruiser *Nigeria* was damaged and had to turn back to Gibraltar, the *Cairo* had her stern blown off and had to be sunk, and the tanker *Ohio*, of the convoy, was hit. As the convoy was turning to the southward away from the direction of the attack, German dive- and torpedo-bombers arrived overhead. Dusk had already fallen and the long-range fighters from Malta were at the end of their endurance. There was little defence against these aircraft, and they sank two and damaged one from out of the convoy.

These losses themselves were not unduly severe, but what was unfortunate was the wide separation of the merchant ships which ensued as a result of the attacks. They were now no longer a convoy, but strung out at wide intervals along the route to Malta. The cruisers and destroyers did their best to round up and protect the stragglers but, scattered over so large an area, they remained wide open to attack. And when the attack came, during the middle watch, it was disastrous. It was made by Italian motor torpedo boats, and they sank the cruiser *Manchester* and four merchantmen and damaged a fifth, all in the space of three hours.

The convoy was now reduced to seven merchant ships, two of them damaged, and there was still a day's steaming ahead of them before they could reach Malta. A day's steaming meant a day's air attacks, and the enemy lost no time. By 8 a.m. the first raid was overhead, and one of the remaining seven merchant ships was hit several times and blown up. Two hours later the second raid came in, further damaging the *Ohio*, whose oil was vital to Malta, and disabling one other. Yet the ships struggled on, and that evening the leading three, one damaged and very low in the water, steamed slowly into the Grand Harbour.

There remained three merchantmen at sea, all disabled. One of them was the *Ohio* with her vital cargo. At 7 p.m. German bombers found one of the damaged ships and sank her; a second steamed safely into Grand Harbour on the following afternoon. That left only the *Ohio*. She was getting near now, in tow of a destroyer and a minesweeper. Another attack by bombers missed the tanker but parted the tow. It was passed again and the slow procession continued. Finally, during the morning of the next day, the *Ohio* passed between the breakwaters of Grand Harbour, and the oil that she carried, on which Malta depended for her continued defiance of the enemy, had arrived.[11] Her master, Captain D. W. Mason, was awarded the George Cross for his magnificent determination and skill in bringing his ship through.

Such was the August convoy. Five ships out of fourteen had reached the island, and the price paid to get them there was an aircraft carrier, a cruiser, an anti-aircraft cruiser, and a destroyer. It had been a heavy cost in terms of ships and men lost, but it saved Malta from starvation and surrender. And in the light of the plans that were already afoot for new operations in this Mediterranean theatre of war, the arrival of those five successful merchant ships marked a turning-point.

As one looks back at those years of battle and endeavour in the Middle Eastern campaign, two episodes stand out as the essential foundations on which were based the successes that were later to crown all the bitter fighting.

The first was the capture of Massawa, the Italian naval base in the Red Sea. It opened the route by which merchant convoys could reach the Egyptian battle front, bringing the men and the weapons which later gave us our victory in the desert. The second was the denial of Malta to the enemy. While it still stood in British hands it remained an ever-present threat to the troop and supply convoys on which Rommel depended for his victory. To the fact that it stood firm throughout those anxious months, and that from its airfields and harbours issued the aircraft, the surface ships, and the submarines which continually attacked his convoys, Rommel owed his eventual defeat. Against the cost in lives and in ships must be set the inestimable part which Malta played in the final Mediterranean victory.

The Malta convoys, fought through against such bitter and overwhelming opposition, can perhaps be said to have been even more a victory of the Merchant Navy than of the Royal Navy. Vice-Admiral Syfret, commanding the August convoy, summed them all up when he wrote in his report: "Tribute has been paid to the personnel of His Majesty's ships; but both officers and men will desire to give first place to the conduct, courage, and determination of the masters, officers, and men of the merchant ships. The steadfast manner in which these ships pressed on their way to Malta through all attacks, answering every manœuvring order like a well-trained fleet unit, was a most inspiring sight. Many of these fine men and their ships were lost. But the memory of their conduct will remain an inspiration to all who were privileged to sail with them."[12]

As with Malta, so also with Russia, though in her case the need was probably not quite so urgent. But she was still in the battle, still engaging the greater part of the German Army and nearly half the German Air Force, and such supplies as she could obtain from the West undoubtedly helped to keep her going.

The carrying of supplies round the North Cape, which had begun in the autumn of 1941 as a trickle, had by mid-1942 grown into a flood, and was inevitably attracting more and more enemy attention. During January the battleship *Tirpitz* moved up to Trondheim, being joined there a month later by the pocket-battleship *Scheer*. The *Prinz Eugen*, home from Brest, also reached Trondheim with the *Scheer*, but she limped in badly damaged by a torpedo from the

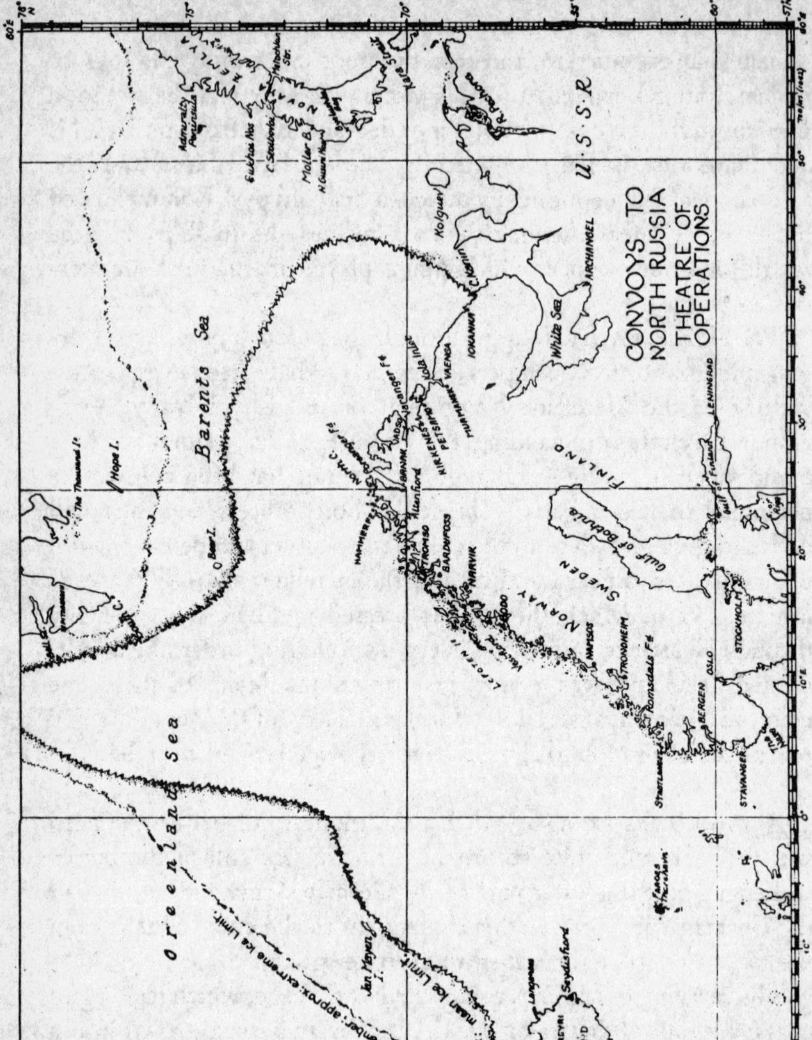
CONVOYS TO
NORTH RUSSIA
THEATRE OF
OPERATIONS
Greenland Sea
Barents Sea
U.S.S.R.
FINLAND
SWEDEN
NORWAY
ICELAND
Jan Mayen I.
Bear I.
Hope I.
Kolguev
White Sea
ARCHANGEL
Kola Inlet
MURMANSK
PETSAMO
KIRKENES
VARDO
TROMSO
NARVIK
BODO
TRONDHEIM
BERGEN
OSLO
STOCKHOLM
STAVANGER
LENINGRAD
Gulf of Bothnia
Gulf of Finland
Lofoten Is.
Romsdals Fd.
REYKJAVIK
AKUREYRI
Seydisfiord
Faroes
Admiralty Peninsula
Moller B.
Mean Ice Limit
April; approx:
September: approx: extreme ice limit

*Trident*, one of four British submarines sent to patrol off that Norwegian port.

The arrival of the *Tirpitz* and the *Scheer* in these Norwegian waters could mean only one thing, and Admiral Tovey, Commander-in-Chief of the Home Fleet, expected a surface attack by them at any moment on the convoys to North Russia as they made their precarious passages across the roof of the world.[13] As the days began to lengthen the merchant ships were deprived of their cloak of winter darkness, while it would be still another two or three months before the ice barrier began to melt and thus allow the convoys to be routed farther north, away from the enemy-held coast.

The Chiefs of Staff were as fully aware as Admiral Tovey of the danger presented by the presence of the *Tirpitz* in these Norwegian waters.[14] They realised also the restricting effect she had on the Home Fleet, whose main strength had now to be engaged in guarding against her possible forays aimed at the Russian convoys at a time when battleships were urgently needed elsewhere. The only way to reach her, as she lay at anchor in the fastnesses of the Trondheim Fjord, was by air, and the Chiefs of Staff gave instructions for such attacks to be carried out. But the narrow waters of the fjord made attack by the torpedo bombers of the Fleet Air Arm impossible, and Trondheim lay at the extreme range of the Royal Air Force's heaviest bombers. Sixteen of them had a shot at her on the night of 29th January, but their bombs failed to hit.

On the evening of 6th March a signal was received from the *Seawolf*, one of the submarines patrolling off Trondheim, reporting that she had sighted a large enemy warship. It was the *Tirpitz*, screened by three destroyers, and she was in search of Convoy PQ 12, which had sailed from Iceland on the 1st. As always with the passage of these Russian convoys, the Home Fleet was at sea to provide distant cover. On this occasion it comprised the battleships *King George V* and *Duke of York*, the battle-cruiser *Renown*, the aircraft carrier *Victorious*, the cruiser *Berwick*, and twelve destroyers. By midnight of the 6th Admiral Tovey was in possession of the *Seawolf*'s sighting report, and the prospect was opening before him of treating the *Tirpitz* as he had treated her sister ship, the *Bismarck*, ten months earlier.

But it was not to be. The day of 7th March dawned to disclose a tempestuous sea, a full gale, snow squalls, and "sea smoke," a condition in Arctic waters which gives the impression of thick white fog at sea level. This, combined with severe icing conditions, made it impossible to launch aircraft from the *Victorious*. Had it been possible to fly a search, the *Tirpitz* would almost certainly have been located[15] and brought to action. As it was, she, the Home Fleet, and two Russian convoys (one outward, the other homeward bound) passed through the same waters without sighting each other. So thick was the "sea smoke," indeed, that the two convoys actually passed through each other without realising the fact. Admiral Ciliax, in the *Tirpitz*, had no knowledge of the presence of the Home Fleet in these waters, or even that it was at sea.[16] He also had tried to fly off search aircraft from the *Tirpitz* and had been similarly prevented by the weather. It was not until two days later that he realised the narrowness of his escape.

The occasion of this realisation was an attack on the *Tirpitz* by Albacores from the *Victorious* on the morning of the 9th. By then Ciliax had abandoned his fruitless search and was returning to Narvik. A search flown from the *Victorious* found the enemy ship as she was steaming south, and twelve torpedo-carrying Albacores were directed on to her. "It is a wonderful chance," signalled Admiral Tovey to them as they flew off, "God be with you." But in spite of an attack, carried out according to the Germans themselves with "determination and dash",[17] all the torpedoes missed. By British naval standards, however, it was a bad attack, made by aircrews who had not had adequate opportunities of training and who failed to seize the tactical advantages which might have been theirs had they been more experienced.

The escape of the *Tirpitz* brought home to Admiral Raeder the extreme danger in which she stood during operations of this kind without the protection of air cover. Fortune had smiled on Admiral Ciliax on the 7th, 8th, and 9th March, but she might not smile so benignly on a future occasion. Admiral Raeder decided to move up less important ships to the Norwegian bases and to use the *Tirpitz* only under the most favourable conditions. The *Hipper* reached Trondheim on the 21st March, and two months later a second pocket-battleship, the *Lützow*, joined the squadron in northern waters. For the rest, a strong force of U-boats and of aircraft, assisted by destroyers, were expected to bring the sinkings of ships up to a number that would make the convoys impossibly expensive.

The next four convoys to Russia, PQ 13 to 16, passed through with varying success. PQ 13 was unfortunate in meeting a gale so severe that the merchant ships were scattered far and wide. In this defenceless state enemy destroyers, U-boats, and aircraft reaped a rich reward, sinking five out of the twenty ships which sailed from Iceland. The escorting destroyer *Eclipse* was badly damaged by enemy destroyers, while the cruiser *Trinidad* had the cruel misfortune of hitting herself with one of her own torpedoes when its steering mechanism failed to function in the extreme cold. On the other side of the balance was the loss to the enemy of one of his destroyers, the Z.26.

PQ 15, sailing at the same time as the return convoy QP 11, also ran into trouble. An air attack sank three ships, while one ship of the returning convoy was sunk by a German destroyer. But more critical, in the existing state of escort forces, was the loss and damage to naval ships. The cruiser *Edinburgh*, escorting QP 11, had her stern blown off by two torpedoes from a U-boat and had to turn back towards Murmansk, escorted by two destroyers, the *Foresight* and *Forester*. They were found by three German destroyers, and all were hit. The *Edinburgh* was now so badly damaged that she had to be sunk by our own destroyers after her crew had been taken off; the *Foresight* and *Forester* managed to reach the haven of their Russian base after a slow and painful passage. But once again there was some consolation for this mishap in the sinking of the German destroyer *Hermann Schoemann*.

This, however, was not the end of the naval losses. The destroyer *Punjabi* was accidentally rammed and sunk in very thick weather by the fleet flagship, the *King George V*, and the damaged *Trinidad*, patched up and on her way home for permanent repairs, fell a victim to a dive-bomber which started a fire and did so much damage that the ship had to be abandoned and sunk three hours later.

In the face of losses such as these, all of them incurred through this commitment of supplying Russia, the continuation of the convoys to North Russia came under serious consideration. The strategic situation, as was pointed out by Admiral Tovey, was wholly favourable to the enemy. His ships would be working close to their own coast, supported by shore-based air reconnaissance and striking forces, and protected by a screen of U-boats between Spitzbergen and Norway. The British ships were without shore-based air support, were operating 1,000 miles from their base, and with their destroyers, in the event of mishap, carrying insufficient fuel to escort a damaged ship to harbour. These difficulties were fully appreciated in the Admiralties in both London and Washington. "The whole thing is a most unsound operation with the dice loaded against us in every direction",[18] wrote the First Sea Lord to his opposite number in the United States, Admiral King, and the American agreed. Yet all suggestions to defer the convoys until once more the winter darkness of the far north should provide a cloak against heavy attack were doomed to failure in face of the political need of keeping Russia supplied. Since navies are, in every respect, the instruments through which policies are translated into action, the pleas of the First Sea Lord were turned down. A new, and still larger, convoy was assembled, and sailed from Iceland on 27th June for its normal twelve-day passage across the enemy's northern doorstep.

Admiral Pound was full of forebodings as the convoy sailed. The latest reconnaissance reports placed the *Scheer* and *Lützow* at Narvik, the *Tirpitz* and *Hipper* at Trondheim. In addition, of course, were the very strong forces of U-boats and aircraft which the enemy kept based in northern Norway for the express purpose of attacking these convoys. Admiral Raeder, although his influence with Hitler had been on the wane for some time, was still at the helm of the German Navy, and the First Sea Lord knew well enough that he would want to justify the existence of his big ships by a successful action. Admiral Pound conveyed some of these forebodings to Admiral Tovey in a telephone conversation before the Home Fleet sailed and remarked that, if serious trouble threatened, they could always order the convoy to scatter.

To Admiral Tovey the suggestion that the convoy might be told to scatter appeared contrary to the lessons which were being learned in all convoy operations. The whole experience of the anti-submarine battle to date proved that it was the independent ship and the straggler which suffered, and that ships in convoy, even with a weak escort, stood a far better chance of coming through in safety against attack both by aircraft and U-boats. And so far as surface-ship action went, there were precedents from which solid comfort could be drawn. Commodore Harwood's action off the River Plate in December 1939 had shown that cruisers, handled imaginatively, need not unduly fear the larger guns of a more powerful adversary. Captain Fegen's supreme gallantry in the *Jervis Bay* in November 1940 had saved a convoy from annihilation in the face of tremendous surface odds. And only four months previously Admiral Vian had shown, in the Battle of Sirte, that with four small cruisers and eleven destroyers he could save a convoy in the face of one battleship, two large and one small cruisers, and six destroyers.

In the Arctic the odds were, perhaps, rather more formidable than those which had faced Admiral Vian, though it is open to doubt whether the enemy would have used the *Tirpitz* as anything more than a rallying-point for the other ships of the force, leaving the actual convoy battle to the pocket-battleships and the *Hipper*. But be that as it may, PQ 17 was by no means defenceless, even against so heavy an attack as that feared. Admiral Hamilton, commanding the close support force, had four 8-inch cruisers and three destroyers, and could call on six more destroyers in the escort force. Certainly it was a force greatly inferior to the expected enemy, yet, had it gone into action, it would in all probability have been able to inflict serious damage before being sunk.

There was, too, the Home Fleet. Its task was to provide distant cover for the convoy in the event of an enemy threat by surface ships. Admiral Tovey had proposed, should there be strong evidence of the *Tirpitz* and *Scheer* leaving their bases, that the convoy should be turned back towards his advancing ships in the hope of reaching their protection in time. The First Sea Lord, however, had decided that the convoy must go on.

Convoy PQ 17, consisting of thirty-five merchant ships, made good progress for the first seven days, passing north of Bear Island (between Spitzbergen and North Cape) on the early morning of 3rd July. So far all had gone well, but it was now about to enter the crucial waters in which attack could be expected. In the conditions of Arctic summer, with the sun above the horizon by day and night, it could not hope to get past without being sighted and reported by the German air reconnaissance.

By 3rd July the German surface ships were all on the move. The *Scheer* and *Lützow* had left Narvik for a temporary base farther north in Altenfjord. The *Scheer* alone arrived there, the *Lützow* running aground when leaving Narvik and becoming too badly damaged to play any further part. The *Tirpitz* and *Hipper* had also sailed from Trondheim, bound for Narvik. These departures, which brought the German ships considerably nearer to the convoy route, were all quickly discovered by reconnaissance aircraft of Coastal Command and duly reported to the Admiralty.

On the following day the first attacks on the convoy began, all by aircraft. They were beaten off, with the loss of three merchant ships to aircraft torpedoes.

On the same day Admiral Raeder ordered the *Tirpitz* to join the *Scheer* in Altenfjord, a fact quickly noted by the Operational Intelligence Centre in the Admiralty. This gathering of surface ships could have but one object, the destruction of the convoy by overwhelming surface strength. A moment's calculation revealed that the enemy ships could reach the convoy during the night of the 4th. So far as the Admiralty could visualise the situation in the light of the latest available intelligence, when it was discussed by the First Sea Lord at a specially called meeting in the evening of the 4th, the enemy squadron was already on its way.

Thus had arisen, in the Admiralty picture, the very state of affairs in which Admiral Pound had warned Admiral Tovey that he might scatter the convoy. The Home Fleet, in its role of distant cover, was too far to the west to intervene; the close support of four cruisers and nine destroyers was held to be no match for the powerful guns of the *Tirpitz* and the pocket-battleships. It was in this situation that the First Sea Lord, with the assent of his colleagues, came to the decision to order the cruisers to withdraw to the westward at high speed and the convoy to scatter.[19]

In fact, neither the *Tirpitz* nor the *Scheer* had yet left Altenfjord. The post-war studies of the German naval archives reveal that Hitler had laid down stringent orders that the German capital ships were not to sail until and unless the British carriers had been sighted and attacked.[20] As the First Sea Lord's meeting in the Admiralty broke up, with its decision to scatter the convoy already taken and the signals being ciphered, a further gleam of information reached the Operational Intelligence Centre. It was, unhappily, not decisive, but gave an indication that the *Tirpitz* and *Scheer* were still at anchor in Altenfjord. It was at once taken to Admiral Pound by Rear-Admiral Clayton, in charge of the Operational Intelligence Centre. The First Sea Lord decided, probably because of the lack of positive information, that the Admiralty signals should stand.

In the light of what followed we know now that the decision to scatter the convoy was an error of judgment on the part of the Admiralty. It may be that the shortage of cruisers—both the *Edinburgh* and the *Trinidad* had already been lost in these waters—may have influenced Admiral Pound not to risk the four with Admiral Hamilton in what he no doubt expected to be a hopeless action. But to this error of judgment in the Admiralty was added another in the vicinity of the convoy itself, when the destroyers of the close escort withdrew with Admiral Hamilton. It is difficult to understand why he did not order them back. He thought, not unnaturally from the urgency of the Admiralty's signals, that the enemy ships were close at hand and his idea was to lead them away from the convoy and towards the Home Fleet, where six additional destroyers might prove of inestimable use in a fleet action. The enemy's objective was almost certainly the merchant ships and it seems unlikely that he would be deflected from it by an unprofitable chase to the westward in which the British ships had a useful margin of superiority in speed. Unfortunately, Admiral Hamilton retained the destroyers with him even when it became apparent that no enemy ships were present. As a result the merchant ships, no longer a convoy for they had obeyed the order to scatter, had no defence apart from four corvettes and two anti-aircraft ships which were all that now remained of the original escort. These, in fact, did collect small groups of ships and shepherd them through. Had the six destroyers been available they too could have shared this valuable work.

The *Tirpitz*, *Scheer*, and *Hipper* finally left harbour about noon on 5th July, being promptly sighted and reported by British and Russian submarines on patrol. There was now, however, no task left for them to carry out. As information of the havoc being caused to the erstwhile convoy by above- and under-water attack came through to them by signal, they reversed their course and returned to Narvik.

Of the original convoy of thirty-five merchant ships, no more than eleven reached their destination. The remainder met their death in the icy waters of the Barents Sea, victims of the U-boats and the bombers. The loss in valuable war cargo destined as aid to the hard-pressed Russian armies was serious, the loss of the ships and their gallant crews was tragic.

But there was more to the disaster than that. One American battleship, two cruisers, and several destroyers were included in the distant cover and in the close support force for the first time in these Arctic convoy operations. There were American and Russian merchant ships in the convoy. Unfortunately these events caused doubts, most difficult to disprove, to arise as to the determination of the Navy when threatened by superior forces. Such doubts of course were unfounded and everything done by the Royal Navy during the passage of PQ 17 was unquestionably done in all good faith.

It is, perhaps, to be wise after the event to remark that the direct control of operations at sea by the Admiralty, always permissible in emergency, was not really applicable in these particular circumstances. All that was required was a signal from the Admiralty to the Commander-in-Chief and to the Flag Officer Detached Squadron (Admiral Hamilton) of the possibility (or probability) of meeting strong enemy forces. Had that been done the convoy would have been escorted all through the danger zone and the risk of meeting superior forces willingly faced.

The episode of PQ 17 was a sad one of error upon error, and its consequences were tragic. Out of the whole sorry story there was but the courage and endurance of the men of the ships which went on alone to kindle a redeeming flame of maritime endeavour and fortitude.

The disaster of PQ 17, however, could not be allowed to deflect the major strategical requirement of aid to Russia. As the year of 1942 grew slowly older the ultimate pattern of victory was beginning to emerge out of the kaleidoscopic activities of a war fought over a world-wide battlefield. Three eventful years had passed since Hitler had first pressed the trigger, and through the ups and downs of fortune, through the actions won and lost, the Allied grip was now visibly beginning to tighten. North, south, east, and west the Axis threat had been contained, and the ring of force that held it in check was not only growing stronger both in men and the weapons of war, but was also slowly beginning to contract. The inexorable power of sea command, with its flexibility of attack, its defensive depth, its ability to carry men and weapons to any and every theatre of conflict, its power of denying to the enemy the raw materials of war, was beginning to exercise its inevitable pressure. To those who could discern, even though faintly, the shape of things to come, the frenzied propaganda of the Axis powers seemed to assume a shriller tone.

In this broad pattern of Allied strategy, now beginning to turn slowly from the long defence towards a more forward policy, the resistance of Russia was playing a vital, even a decisive, part. The whole of the free world had applauded her gallant stand against the first terrific onslaughts of the summer of 1941, had watched enthralled her great recovery of the following winter, and now suffered with her in her agony as the second German offensive bit deeply into the Caucasus. There could be no question of allowing the tragedy of PQ 17 to bring to a halt the flow of war material to so gallant an ally. The convoys continued.

Painful lessons often bring in their train a remedial action, and the operation of passing convoy PQ 18 to Russia was no exception. The convoy sailed in September with a close support force consisting of the anti-aircraft cruiser *Scylla* and no fewer than sixteen destroyers, in addition to its normal close escort. In order to provide these additional destroyers, Admiral Tovey had obtained the First Sea Lord's approval to dispense with its battleship cover for this convoy. This support force remained with the convoy throughout the whole of the danger period, and then brought home the empty ships of the returning convoy. But now, for the first time, an escort carrier, H.M.S. *Avenger*, sailed with the convoy. She carried twelve Sea Hurricane fighters and three anti-submarine Swordfish. In addition, two squadrons of torpedo-carrying Hampdens of the Royal Air Force were based in north Russia for operations against German surface ships, should they come out.

The first air attacks on the convoy were made on 13th September and, due partly to a tactical error in handling the Sea Hurricanes from the *Avenger* and partly to the refusal of the captains of the United States merchant ships which formed the starboard wing column of the convoy to obey the order to turn towards their attackers, eight merchant ships were sunk, all of them American. Already U-boats had accounted for two more, so that ten in all out of the thirty-nine ships in the convoy had gone to the bottom. It was hardly an encouraging start. There was, however, a different story on the following day, for by then a more satisfactory technique of handling the fighters from the carrier had been evolved. As the heavy enemy air attacks came in, they were largely broken up by the Sea Hurricanes before they could reach torpedo range, and the ships' anti-aircraft guns did the rest. The day ended with a very heavy loss to the enemy and with only one more ship in the convoy sunk.

Finally, after further air and U-boat attacks on the next two days,

Convoy PQ 18 reached north Russia with only two more losses. Twelve merchant ships and an oiler had been sunk, but it had cost the enemy thirty-three torpedo planes, six bombers, and two reconnaissance aircraft.[21] Three U-boats out of the twelve sent to operate against the convoy had also been sent to the bottom, one of them largely due to good work by the *Avenger*'s Swordfish.

The use of an escort carrier on this north Russian convoy route provided the main answer to the problem of defence against U-boats and aircraft. It was an application of one of the chief lessons learned on the great convoy routes of the Atlantic; that air cover was an essential part of convoy protection. What the *Audacity* had achieved in closing the "air gap" on the Gibraltar route, the *Avenger* repeated above the Arctic circle.

Although it was not apparent at the time, the passage of PQ 18 marked the high-water level of German air attack against the northern convoys. Events which were shortly to take place some thousands of miles to the south on the coasts of North Africa forced the withdrawal of much of the German air strength deployed in Russia, and their departure made easier the future supply to Russia of the tanks, guns, and aircraft which were to deal the enemy such savage blows as the Russian counter-attacks in the East gathered force. It was but one more example of the profound influence which the ubiquity of sea power could exercise on campaigns fought thousands of miles apart.

It was also these events in North Africa, with their overriding demand for ships of war of every class, that delayed the next Russian convoy for three months. In the face of insistent Russian demands for help, a few ships were sailed independently during the next three months. This, however, was hardly an operation of war that could commend itself to the Naval Staff, for it ran counter to all that had been learned so painfully throughout the three years of modern war. Five of the thirteen ships that sailed in this fashion reached their destination, a proportion that was held to be satisfactorily high. As a political gesture it may have been justified; as a naval operation it was condemned by one and all.

When the Home Fleet at last received its ships back from the

North African operations, Admiral Tovey decided to sail the next convoy in two groups. The first, of fifteen merchant ships, reached Russia without mishap or enemy attack. A covering force of two cruisers, the *Sheffield* and *Jamaica*, and two destroyers, under the command of Rear-Admiral Burnett, accompanied it all the way to the Kola Inlet, and then turned back to meet the second half of the convoy which had sailed from Iceland a week after the first. Their task was to cover this second convoy as it traversed the dangerous Barents Sea.

This second half, consisting of fourteen ships escorted by six destroyers and five smaller vessels, met with no trouble until it was well beyond Bear Island, but it had been delayed by a gale which resulted in Admiral Burnett's two cruisers being some thirty miles to the northward instead of to the westward of the convoy as he had intended. Neither he nor Captain Sherbrooke, commanding the close escort, knew each other's position.

In the early morning of 21st December one of the escorting destroyers, H.M.S. *Obdurate*, sighted two strange destroyers to the northwards of the convoy in the semi-darkness of the Arctic winter. She closed to investigate, thinking that they might be Russian, only to be greeted when she came within range by a salvo of shells. Captain Sherbrooke in the *Onslow* at once turned towards the flash of the guns, signalling to the *Orwell*, *Obedient*, and *Obdurate* to join him.

A few minutes later Captain Sherbrooke sighted a far more formidable adversary in the shape of the German 10,000-ton cruiser *Hipper*. Together with the *Orwell*, the *Onslow* steered towards the new enemy, engaging her fitfully through gaps in the smoke-screen with which the convoy was now shrouded. Her return fire was inaccurate and desultory, and she was hit three times before she suddenly "pulled herself together"[22] and hit the *Onslow* savagely with a few well-directed salvoes, wrecking her bridge, putting half her guns and torpedo tubes out of action, and severely wounding Captain Sherbrooke. Although in great pain, and with one eye shot through, Sherbrooke refused to leave his shattered bridge until he was satisfied that the *Hipper* had been driven off and that the next senior officer of the escort, Lieutenant-Commander Kinloch of the *Obedient*, had a clear understanding of the situation. In recognition of his gallantry and determination in driving off a far stronger enemy and safeguarding the merchant ships of the convoy, Captain Sherbrooke was later awarded the Victoria Cross.

An hour later the *Hipper* returned to the attack. The *Obedient*, *Orwell*, and *Obdurate*, after laying smoke to screen the convoy, steamed out once more to do battle. They drove the *Hipper* off again, but not before she had concentrated her fire on the destroyer *Achates*, which was laying more smoke astern of the convoy. The little *Achates* was quickly crippled, with heavy casualties on board, but she continued with her task of laying smoke for another two hours, getting lower and lower in the water until finally she was unmanageable. Only then did she signal for assistance. It was too late, and she sank before she could be taken in tow after having carried out most valuable work in shrouding the convoy from observation. It was a superb example of devotion to her duty.

In the meantime, however, the two cruisers of the support force, the *Sheffield* and the *Jamaica*, still some thirty miles farther north, had received Captain Sherbrooke's enemy report. At the time Admiral Burnett was investigating a radar contact, which delayed him in answering the call of the destroyers. Nine minutes later, with the contact satisfactorily accounted for as a straggler from the convoy, Admiral Burnett was hastening southwards at thirty knots and before long, over the horizon ahead, the cruisers sighted the flash of gunfire. A second radar contact led them to the *Hipper*. She was just hauling off from the threat of torpedo attack from the *Obedient* and her fellow destroyers, and suddenly found herself under accurate fire from the *Sheffield* and *Jamaica*. Before she could realise what was happening she was heavily hit, and then hit twice more before she could get clear. This was enough for the German Admiral, who immediately ordered all his forces to break off action and retire to the west. But before that order could be carried out the two British cruisers sighted two German destroyers, part of the *Hipper*'s force. The *Sheffield* and *Jamaica* turned towards them and sank one, the *Friedrich Eckholdt*, in a hurricane of fire.

While all this fighting was taking place to the north, the convoy had in fact narrowly escaped disaster, all unsuspected either by the destroyer escort or by the cruisers. The German plan had been for the *Hipper* and her three destroyers to draw off the escort to the north, thereby laying the convoy open to attack by the pocket-battleship *Lützow* and three other destroyers from the south. Tactically, the plan worked to perfection. While Commander Kinloch, who had just taken over from Captain Sherbrooke, was collecting his destroyers some miles to the north, the *Lützow* had made a sudden appearance within two miles of the merchant ships, approaching from the unguarded south. The danger was extreme, with the whole convoy open to attack at point-blank range. But the *Lützow* hesitated, and a minute or two later a providential snow squall blotted out the sight of the ships from her menacing guns: nor did she send her destroyers in to attack. By the time it cleared, the gallant *Obedient* and her sisters were there to guard against this new threat, and soon afterwards the *Lützow* received the German Admiral's signal to withdraw. She fired a few ineffective rounds at long range at the convoy on her way to join him, and the fighting ended with a brief exchange of fire between the German ships and Admiral Burnett's cruisers before full darkness closed down. The convoy, saved by the stubborn defence of its destroyers carried out with inspired and traditional gallantry, proceeded on its way to reach its destination without further trouble.

It was a remarkable result. "That an enemy force of at least one pocket-battleship, one heavy cruiser, and six destroyers, with all the advantages of surprise and concentration, should be held off for four hours by five destroyers, and driven from the area by two 6-inch cruisers, is most creditable and satisfactory", wrote Admiral Tovey in his report.[23] But it was more than that. It showed up the German Navy at its most timid and least enterprising, and seemed to point to a crack in morale that boded no good for the enemy's future at sea.

In Germany itself it had shattering results. The unfortunate Raeder was summoned to the "Wolf's Lair" where Hitler had his headquarters and was forced to listen to a ninety-minute tirade from his Fuehrer. He condemned the German Navy for its refusal to fight to a finish—conveniently forgetting for the moment that he himself had given orders that capital ships were not to run risks—and sketched German naval history from its earliest beginnings in scathing terms. Capital ships, he raged, were nothing but a waste of men and material and served no purpose except to tie up aircraft and smaller vessels for their defence during their inactivity. Goering added fuel to the Fuehrer's flaming anger by complaining bitterly of the "waste" of *Luftwaffe* squadrons in guarding big ships while they swung idly round their anchors. Finally Hitler ordered Raeder to prepare a memorandum on paying off all the capital ships and heavy cruisers.[24]

In this order from the Fuehrer Raeder foresaw the sentence of death on the Navy he had striven so hard to create. In a last despairing effort he presented to Hitler, on 15th January, a child's guide on the correct use of sea power, but even this, fortified with all the arguments he could produce, was of no avail. His influence with Hitler, which had been on the wane since the *Bismarck* had been sunk over eighteen months earlier, had by now reached vanishing-point, and at the end of the month he resigned and hauled down his flag as Commander-in-Chief.

Thus Hitler deprived himself of the services of the one man in Germany who might conceivably have won him the war. Raeder was a brilliant strategist who from the start had seen clearly the need for a balanced Navy. He had emphasised, in 1941, the great strategic possibilities in the Mediterranean theatre, following the Nazi successes in Greece, Crete, and North Africa, and had his advice been taken then it could well have produced a situation to which the Allies had no answer. Quite how near Germany came to winning at that moment it is difficult to say, but it is at least arguable that Raeder's suggestions, if carried through, might have brought her to the threshold of victory. But the chance had been missed, largely because Hitler saw in himself alone the architect of a literal *Deutschland über Alles*. No lesser mortal could be permitted to usurp that destiny.

In Raeder's place Hitler promoted Doenitz to the rank of Grand

Admiral and appointed him Commander-in-Chief. Doenitz had been a submarine commander in the First World War and was still devoted to his beloved U-boats. To the growing difficulties which were now facing the German Navy in every theatre of war he had at first but one solution—more and yet more U-boats—though later he came to realise the need and the value of capital ships in the conduct of sea affairs. But at this period, himself out of temper with the big ships, he had little difficulty in convincing Hitler of the soundness of his views. The building programme was ordered to be stepped up in stages from eighteen to forty-five completed U-boats per month, and in addition there was to be a monthly output of three of the new Type XXI prefabricated U-boats with a much higher submerged speed. In the view of the Grand Admiral, this accelerated U-boat programme would prove the complete answer to all Germany's naval woes.

# Chapter 10

## THE TURNING OF THE TIDE

FOR three years now Britain and her Allies had been necessarily committed to the defensive, a long period of stubborn fighting designed to hold each of the enemies within the limits of their main campaign areas. The chief weapon of this defence was sea power, exercised in the widest application of its meaning, with the Royal Navy and Royal Air Force acting in conjunction to deny the enemy the use of the sea as a means of transport while retaining it for our own use, and with the Army holding the essential bases from which such sea power could be exercised. In some cases, as at Hong Kong and Singapore, there had been failure; in others, such as Alexandria, Malta, and Gibraltar, the defence had stood firm.

Around the European enemy, to the north, west, and south, the barrier of sea power was still securely held. Three times in those first three years had it been tested to the uttermost: in 1940 when Hitler stood on the Channel coast gazing across the narrow strip of water which still makes Britain an island; in 1941 when an attenuated Mediterranean Fleet held the seas of the Levant after the German capture of Crete; in 1942 when a savagely battered Malta defiantly barred the path to an Axis conquest of North Africa. In each case it was the resilience of sea power which had enabled Britain to hold the enemy back.

In 1941, barred from expanding westward or southward by this ring of British sea power, Hitler had struck eastwards into the great Russian plains. And even in that great land campaign, fought out hundreds of miles from the oceans, the long fingers of sea power stretched out to fasten their grip around him. Across the oceans to the north, along the sea lanes to the south, flowed a steady stream of weapons and supplies to the Russian armies, to help to slow down, to stop, and finally to drive back the eastward rush of armed German might.

In the Far East the same tremendous drama was being enacted. In the Indian Ocean, far back from the fighting front, a tenuous line of British sea power was in being. To the south of the Japanese campaign area the seas around Australia were being held, to the east the rapid resurgence of American sea power was forging a weapon with which to break into and demolish the Japanese sea barrier.

The first tests of this new American naval might came in May and June of 1942. The ease and speed with which the Japanese had made their vast conquests bred a desire to establish and consolidate a defensive perimeter behind which to digest their gargantuan meal. A snap American bomber raid on Tokyo, on 18th April, 1942, launched from the carriers *Hornet* and *Enterprise*, proved that there was a gap in the defensive ring and reinforced this desire. Over-estimating their own industrial capacity for sustaining war, and under-estimating the huge Allied potential, the Japanese decided to thrust their perimeter outwards and to consolidate on a line including the Aleutian Islands, Midway, Samoa, Fiji, New Caledonia, and Port Moresby in New Guinea.[1]

This was a blunder of the first magnitude, and one from which all their future woes were to stem. Already their strategic area, so easily gained, was too large to be defended successfully against the inevitable growth of Allied strength; to add to its area by nearly one-third, and that third, moreover, based on far-flung outposts separated by thousands of miles of ocean, was to court irretrievable disaster. Japan consumed the major part of her naval and air power in the attempt, and in the losses she suffered she opened wide the door to her eventual staggering defeat.

Her first thrust in this new expansion programme was to the southward, where her goal was Port Moresby. Here, as the assault and support forces were moving down through the Coral Sea, the Japanese Navy, for the first time since the outbreak of the Eastern war, met really determined opposition. It had been a stroke of fortune that, during the attack on Pearl Harbour, the three carriers of the U.S. Pacific Fleet had been at sea exercising. Thus they had escaped destruction and were ready now to fight their first battle. At a range which rarely narrowed to less than 160 miles the carrier-borne air forces of the United States and Japan fought out their action in the early days of May. Each side lost a carrier, but the Japanese invasion force was turned back and their attempt to occupy Port Moresby ended in failure. A second attempt was planned for July,[2] but by then, however, it was to be too late.

The failure in the Coral Sea was followed a month later by the attempt to add Midway Island to the Japanese sphere. This was planned on a far more ambitious scale, calling for the use of the main fleet of Japan, yet its result was disastrous. Although the United States was still suffering from the losses at Pearl Harbour, Admiral Nimitz, the U.S. Commander-in-Chief, succeeded in scraping together three carriers and a handful of cruisers and destroyers. Aided by good Intelligence and the failure of the Japanese to scout ahead of their fleet, the carrier-borne aircraft of the *Hornet*, *Enterprise*, and *Yorktown* swept down on the main Japanese carrier force and overwhelmed it with bombs and torpedoes. Four Japanese carriers went down, and this crippling loss changed, in one action, the whole face of the Pacific campaign. In this one blow Japan lost the strategic initiative and was never able again to regain it.

In the midst of those resounding and far-reaching battles in the Pacific, fought so gallantly and successfully by the United States Navy against heavily superior forces, the British, too, delivered their blow against possible Japanese expansion, in the Indian Ocean. Their rapid advance down the islands to Java, the possibility that Port Moresby would fall to them, and their foothold in the Indian Ocean from their occupation of the Andaman Islands and capture of Rangoon, all emphasised the strategic importance of Madagascar, lying off the south-east coast of Africa. It was held in some strength by the forces of Vichy France, on the whole hostile to Great Britain, but of far greater strategic import was the fact that it could well form the meeting-place of Japanese and German U-boats. The island contained a magnificent harbour at Diego Suarez and two smaller ones at Tamatave and Majunga. As an enemy U-boat base it would provide a grave threat to the convoys which, coming round the Cape of Good Hope, supplied both the Middle East and Far East fronts in Egypt and India. Vichy had once before yielded to Japanese demands without a struggle in Indo-China; it could so easily happen again.

Detailed planning for Operation "Ironclad", as the capture of Diego Suarez was called, began in March 1942, when an American agreement to reinforce the Home Fleet temporarily with U.S. ships made it possible to allocate our own ships for the enterprise. The nucleus of the naval force engaged was Force H, guarding the western Mediterranean from Gibraltar, and its place was taken temporarily by a squadron from the Home Fleet. Force F, as the Madagascar squadron was called, was reinforced for the operation with the carrier *Indomitable* from the Eastern Fleet, and she joined the rest of the force on 3rd May as it was steaming up from Durban. The assault on Diego Suarez was fixed for 4.30 a.m. on the 5th.

The plan was a simple one. The great harbour of Diego Suarez, lying in the north-eastern corner of the island, was strongly defended with gun batteries. In the north-western corner of the island lies the great William Pitt Bay, cutting deeply into the land and separated from Diego Suarez Bay by a neck of land about four miles wide. Although the entrance to William Pitt Bay was studded with rocks and reefs, making the approach a very difficult one, it was decided to make the assault landings there and thus to take the Diego Suarez defences in the rear.

As the assault forces, under the command of Major-General Sturges, R.M., approached the island, the destroyers *Laforey*, *Lightning*, and *Anthony* were sent on ahead to mark out the approach channel with buoys. This was done without interference from the French defenders. They had considered that the channel was impossible of navigation during dark hours and that in consequence the defending guns need not be manned.

Through the unlit and tortuous channels the assault ships moved up into the inner bay. They were preceded by two minesweepers, the *Romney* and *Cromarty*, themselves led by the corvette *Freesia*. About seventeen moored mines were cut, and at three o'clock in the morning one detonated in the *Romney*'s sweep. The explosion echoed round the vast harbour, but it awoke no sign from the French garrison. A quarter of an hour later a second mine was detonated, and once again the stillness of the night was shattered. The garrison ashore slumbered on, secure in their belief that the passage of the bay could not be attempted at night.

By 3.30 a.m. all was ready. The ships were in and had anchored silently, the commandos and assault troops were in their landing-craft and moving in to the beaches. The navigation of the assault craft was as faultless as that of the ships which had carried them in, and the men went ashore exactly as planned.

As they landed, naval aircraft from the carriers provided fighter protection over the beaches and attacked French shipping in Diego Suarez harbour. The submarine *Béveziers* was sunk by depth charges dropped by Swordfish aircraft, and other ships and anti-aircraft batteries damaged by torpedoes and bombs. The airport at the town of Antsirane was bombed by Albacores from the *Indomitable* and the hangars, full of French fighter aircraft, were left burning fiercely as the *Indomitable*'s planes turned for home.

Shortly before 6.0 a.m. the first "success" signal from ashore was seen by the watching ships, telling of the capture of one of the main batteries. Others followed, and by 6.30 a.m. some two thousand troops were ashore and advancing rapidly across the neck of land towards the main objective. A few enemy posts, which were defended stoutly and were holding up the defence, were silenced by shore bombardment from the guns of the destroyers.

In the meantime a strong naval force patrolled outside William Pitt Bay to prevent any enemy interference from seaward. It included the battleship *Ramillies*, the two carriers *Illustrious* and *Indomitable*, and seven destroyers. The cruiser *Hermione*, at first with this force, was detached to proceed round the north of the island and make a diversion off the entrance to Diego Suarez Bay.

During the morning hopes for a speedy capitulation of the French garrison were dashed by a wireless broadcast from the military commander at Diego Suarez stating that he would defend the place to the last man. As the day wore on it became apparent that this was no empty boast, for the defence stiffened and the assaulting troops were held up.

By noon of the following day, 6th May, Vice-Admiral Syfret, in command afloat, was informed that the assault had failed. "At about 14.00", he wrote, "the General (Sturges) arrived on board. He was hot, begrimed, and unhappy. Things were not going well, he said."[3] In fact, they were going much better than he thought and were on the brink of success, but the difficulties of communication ashore had made it impossible to report all the advances of the troops, some of whom had by now penetrated the main French defence line.

Vice-Admiral Syfret offered "any and all assistance"[4] which the Fleet could give and General Sturges asked if from twenty to thirty seamen could be put ashore in the town of Antsirane to attack the defence line from the rear. The Vice-Admiral did better. He called the destroyer *Anthony* alongside his flagship and in her embarked fifty Royal Marines from the *Ramillies* under Captain Price. Within an hour they were on their way.

A heavy sea outside the harbour caused a good deal of seasickness among the marines, hardly the ideal preparation for the stern task that was awaiting them later that night. As the *Anthony* rounded the northern point of the island she ran into more sheltered waters and the pangs of seasickness subsided.

Just after 8.0 p.m. she reached the entrance to Diego Suarez Bay and threaded her way in under a heavy fire from the shore batteries guarding the port. A strong offshore wind made it impossible to hold the ship alongside the deep water quay, but Lieutenant-Commander Hodges, the *Anthony*'s captain, backed her stern to the jetty and held it there long enough for the marines to scramble ashore. It was a task which, in the strong wind and darkness, called for fine judgment and seamanship. With the marines ashore, he took the *Anthony* out to sea again, once more running the gauntlet of the shore batteries.

The Royal Marines, left now to their own devices and with no means of retreat, groped their way south through the dockyard. They managed to find a route into the town and, with a few hand grenades, forced the surrender of the naval depot, taking into custody the commandant of the naval barracks. As they fired their "success" signal, the troops outside the town pressed home their attack on the main French defence line. Within a few hours it was all over; the town of Antsirane and the whole of Diego Suarez Bay was firmly in British hands; a result largely due to the success of that hazardous enterprise launched suddenly and unexpectedly by the *Anthony* and a handful of marines at the enemy's back door.

With the capture of Diego Suarez the threat to the Middle East convoys was greatly minimised. Marauding U-boats, intent on attacking those important reinforcement convoys, would now have to operate far from their normal bases and with no convenient harbour in which to seek shelter almost alongside the route. Yet at the end of May the base at Diego Suarez was to have a taste of the might-have-been. By this time, because of urgent calls elsewhere, Vice-Admiral Syfret's anti-submarine forces had been reduced to two corvettes, and in the bright moonlight of the night of the 30th, the *Ramillies* and a tanker, the *British Loyalty*, were both hit by torpedoes. A few days later two Japanese were rounded up in the country north of Diego Suarez and killed by a Commando patrol. Papers found on them revealed that they were the crew of a midget submarine, launched from the Japanese submarine *I.20*.

In Home waters, during the first three months of 1942, good news was mingling with the bad. If the escape of the three German ships from Brest during February had provided a grave shock to public opinion, the small combined operations raid on Bruneval in the same month and the larger operation at St. Nazaire at the end of March gave proof enough that a swing from the defensive towards a more offensive policy was in the air. These were both more than the general "nuisance" raids, which had so characterised British strategy nearly two hundred years previously during the Seven Years' War, in that they were also undertaken with definite tactical objectives; yet they had the same effect in forcing the enemy to keep troops stationed along the whole length of the north-west European coastline to guard against possible blows. They also served to keep the enemy guessing where the next assault should fall.

The raid on Bruneval took place on the night of 27th/28th February; its object the capture of what was hoped would be a new type of enemy radar set. A small naval force of motor gunboats and assault landing-craft left Portsmouth in the evening and reached the coast of France shortly after midnight. At the same time airborne troops were dropped in the vicinity of the radar station, overpowered the defence, and rushed the post. Tearing out the radar set they fought their way down to the beach, covered by a small military force landed from the assault craft and by fire from the motor gunboats. By 3.0 a.m. they were embarked and on their way back to Portsmouth.

A much more ambitious operation was the raid on St. Nazaire on 28th March. Here the principal tactical objective was the immobilisation of the large "Normandie" lock, capable of being used as a dry dock, and the only one outside Germany large enough to take the battleship *Tirpitz*. The immobilisation of the lock was to be performed by the destruction of the lock gate by the old ex-American destroyer *Campbeltown*, which was to ram the gate and scuttle herself there. She had on board three tons of high explosive, timed to blow up about two and a half hours after the ramming. Subsidiary tactical objectives were the destruction of as much dock machinery as possible, for which purpose a force of Commandos was embarked. Commander R. E. D. Ryder was in charge of the naval side of the operation; Lieutenant-Colonel A. C. Newman was the military commander.

Inevitably a comparison falls to be made between the blocking of Zeebrugge, on St. George's Day, 1918, and the destruction of the lock gates at St. Nazaire on 28th March, 1942, for operations were very similar both in conception and execution. Both involved frontal attacks on defended ports, both had as objectives a denial of the ports to specific enemy ships, U-boats in the case of Zeebrugge and the *Tirpitz* in the case of St. Nazaire. Success in both cases too, depended on surprise. Differences between the two operations were those of degree. Zeebrugge lay eighty miles from Dover with an entrance open to the sea; St. Nazaire was 400 miles from Plymouth and lies five miles up the River Loire. In 1918 there were no close-range, quick-firing weapons and no radar to constitute a threat to the assaulting force. Admiral of the Fleet Sir Charles Forbes, the Commander-in-Chief at Plymouth, remarked that he regarded the St. Nazaire operation as much more difficult than that on Zeebrugge.[5] And while Zeebrugge was a failure in that it did not stop the passage of U-boats for more than twenty-four hours, St. Nazaire was a resounding success.

The force, trained in secrecy at Falmouth, sailed in the early afternoon of 26th March. It comprised one motor gunboat, carrying the naval and military force commanders, sixteen motor-launches taking the Commandos, H.M.S. *Campbeltown*, one of the old ex-American "four-stackers" turned over in 1940 in the "destroyers for bases" deal, as blockship, also carrying Commandos, one motor torpedo boat, and two escorting destroyers which, however, did not enter the river.

All went well until dawn on the 27th, when a U-boat was sighted on the surface. She was attacked by the two escorting destroyers, the *Tynedale* and *Atherstone*, was hit by gunfire and hunted with depth charges, and thought to have been sunk. In fact, she survived and surfaced in the afternoon to report by wireless the presence of the British force. Fortunately she signalled the course of the British ships as west instead of east, a fact which caused the German authorities at St. Nazaire to consider that the motor-launches were withdrawing after a minelaying operation.

As the two destroyers returned after the attack on the U-boat the sky became overcast with low cloud, which considerably lessened the risks of detection from the air. Throughout the day no ships more dangerous than French fishing-trawlers were sighted and, as darkness fell, the little force took up a special cruising order designed for the attack. At 10 p.m. it made contact with the submarine *Sturgeon*, acting as a beacon at a point forty miles from St. Nazaire, and left her astern as the ships continued in towards their objective.

So far all had gone well, and surprise, thanks to the westerly course reported by the U-boat, was complete. But as St. Nazaire drew nearer the danger of discovery grew, for the port was very strongly defended with searchlights, shore batteries, and radar. Yet all remained quiet ashore and the flotilla of small vessels, with the *Campbeltown* in their midst, pressed steadily on towards their goal. They reached a position no more than two miles from the lock gate still unchallenged; then the first searchlight from the northern shore was switched on. It was followed by all the others along both sides of the river, lighting up the assaulting force in full clarity. The time for surprise was over, and further immunity from attack could be gained only by subterfuge.

Commander Ryder made a bogus identity signal and flashed, in German, that the ships were "proceeding up harbour in accordance with instructions". Most of the searchlights were switched off. A little later one of the shore batteries opened fire and Commander Ryder made the signal for "a vessel considering herself to be fired on by friendly forces". The firing ceased.

Four precious minutes—the equivalent of one mile—were gained by this stratagem. But obviously it could not last. With about half a mile to go, the force was recognised as obviously hostile and a furious fire was opened from both banks of the river.

Lieutenant-Commander S. H. Beattie, commanding the *Campbeltown*, increased to full speed and drove his ship straight for the lock gates. She was hit repeatedly down her whole length, but no vital damage was done to check her way. At 1.34 a.m., only four minutes after her scheduled time, she struck the centre of the lock gate, her forecastle ablaze and her guns firing fiercely. So deeply did she penetrate that the explosive charge, stowed thirty-six feet from her stem, was brought level with the edge of the lock gate, the perfect position for maximum damage. The charge she carried was due to explode two and a half hours later, and the doom of the lock gate appeared inevitable.

That was the main objective secured; it was for the subsidiary ones now to be achieved. In a hail of fire from both banks of the river the motor-launches had been attempting to reach their allotted landing-places. Some were successful, their Commandos getting ashore and setting about their tasks of destruction; others were less fortunate, being driven off by the heavy gunfire or being set ablaze before reaching their landing-points.

Approximately 40 per cent. of the Commandos got ashore under their leader, Colonel Newman, and soon the sound of explosions in the surrounding buildings told the story of demolitions being carried on among the pumping stations and other dock machinery. Very considerable damage was done, and in places made even more effective by the Germans adding to the destruction as they fired wildly at the largely unseen attackers. In one case enemy forces on both banks were shooting at each other with a heavy cross-fire.[6]

At this stage, as Commander Ryder looked round the harbour, he counted "seven or eight blazing motor-launches and was forced to realise that we (motor gunboat) were the only craft left in sight".[7] There had been no withdrawal signal from the Commandos ashore, and no contact by wireless with the shore. With his motor gunboat's deck piled with seriously wounded men, and with the fire from the guns ashore growing ever more intense, it was very quickly apparent that the men in the town could not be taken off because of the damage to the motor-launches. At the same moment that Commander Ryder reached this difficult decision to withdraw without the Commandos, Colonel Newman had come to the same conclusion ashore and was already organising his troops for an attempt to escape inland.

Seven of the eighteen small craft engaged in the operation reached the open sea, all of them damaged and all with a large number of wounded men on board. There they were met by the destroyers *Fernie* and *Brocklesby*, which had to leave them almost immediately, however, to drive off a flotilla of five German torpedo boats. By the time they had completed this task, the small craft were widely separated, three of the motor-launches having proceeded far to the westward. From the badly damaged remainder the crews and wounded were removed and they were sunk by our own destroyers, but the three to the westward could not be found although a search was made for them.

They were having their own adventures. During the afternoon they were discovered by an enemy Heinkel aircraft which, after circling them, came in to attack. It was promptly shot down. Two hours later a Bloehm and Voss seaplane shadowed them and dropped a bomb. It was hit and driven off to the westward. As darkness fell, the three small craft altered course for home, hoping to reach the Scilly Islands. During the following morning they sighted the Lizard and made their own way safely into Falmouth, a very gallant remnant of the two flotillas which had sailed three days previously.

The sequel to this inspired raid occurred at about noon on the following day. Neither the explosive charge in the *Campbeltown*, nor two torpedoes with delayed action warheads fired into the lock gate, had exploded when expected, because the fuses used were of improvised design. During the morning of the 28th a large number of German senior officers had gone on board the *Campbeltown* to consider how best to remove her. They were standing on the forecastle when the ship blew up beneath them. A little later the two torpedoes followed suit, adding to the carnage. In their bewilderment and dismay the German troops gave way to panic and opened fire, killing some hundreds of their own men and, unhappily, many innocent French workmen.

Five awards of the Victoria Cross were made to mark the extreme courage and fortitude of the men who fought this remarkable action. Commander Ryder, the senior naval officer of the force, and Lieutenant-Commander S. H. Beattie, commanding H.M.S. *Campbeltown*, each received the award for their extreme gallantry and determination in pressing home the attack in the face of intense fire at point-blank range. Colonel Newman received it for his brilliant leadership and great personal courage ashore. Able-Seaman W. A. Savage and Sergeant T. R. Durrant, of the Commandos, both fought their guns to the end in spite of severe wounds and both received the award in recognition of their extreme devotion to duty and gallantry.

Behind what might be called the "façade" of these raids, with their evidence of growing Allied power, there was a very real foundation of solid build-up in operational strength. In spite of still serious losses of merchant ships—the monthly average throughout the whole of 1942 was some 650,000 tons—there was arriving a steady stream of men and munitions both in Britain and in the other campaign areas. To the output of British and Dominion shipyards and factories was now added the vast industrial potential of the United States, reorganised with true American "hustle" on a war basis of maximum output, and even the heavy sinkings at sea could not prevent enough reinforcements getting through to add materially to the force stationed in Britain.

With this growth of power came American pressure to launch out into new adventures. Basic agreement for a major military operation against Germany in 1942 had existed between the British Prime Minister and the American President since their meeting in Washington at Christmas, 1941, but the decision of where, when, and how was left open for future decision. The problem was discussed by the Combined Chiefs of Staff at a series of meetings in Washington, with Admiral Sir Andrew Cunningham and Field-Marshal Sir John Dill as the British representatives, and every possible target for an amphibious attack was canvassed. Those mentioned included Norway, Denmark, Holland, Belgium, the Pas-de-Calais, the Cotentin Peninsula, Brest, the Gironde, Tunisia, Algeria, and French Morocco. A proposal to land in French North Africa was finally turned down by the Combined Chiefs of Staff on 7th March, 1942, and by the following month agreement was reached, though with considerable reluctance on the part of Mr. Churchill and the British Chiefs of Staff, to mount a cross-Channel invasion in February, 1943. General Dwight Eisenhower was appointed as Commander, U.S. Military Forces, Europe, and arrived in London on 24th June to initiate the detailed planning.

Almost as he set foot in Britain two shattering events were to reopen the whole problem. The Soviet Foreign Minister, Mr.

Molotov, visited Washington and painted so gloomy a picture of Russian ability to hold out against the German summer offensive that the diversion of a substantial proportion of enemy troops elsewhere became an essential strategical necessity. And at precisely the same moment came news of the fall of Tobruk and Rommel's advance into Egypt. The threat to the Suez Canal became very real and urgent, and the fate of the Middle East—and with it so much of British hopes and plans—trembled precariously in the balance.

The whole question of a "second front" in 1942 was once again thrashed out by the Combined Chiefs of Staff, this time meeting in London. The Americans still favoured a cross-Channel operation, even if it only entailed the occupation of a beachhead in France in 1942, to be held throughout the winter for future exploitation in the spring of 1943. The British Chiefs of Staff pointed out the difficulties involved in such an operation, the incessant attack by the *Luftwaffe* for months on end, the hazards of seaborne supply across the Channel in winter, and also the fact that such a beachhead would not draw more than a very limited number of German troops away from the Russian front. The American Chiefs of Staff remained unconvinced.

It was to the Prime Minister, more than to anyone else, that the final decision to land in North Africa was due. Mr. Churchill had never forgotten that tragic battle of the Somme fought in 1916, a battle fought for a political, rather than a strategical, reason. He remembered that terrible 1st July when thirteen British divisions, volunteers all and the fittest and finest of the English race, rose out of their trenches to attempt a useless and purposeless advance. On that 1st July—the first of 140 days of senseless slaughter—the British Army, imbued with a dedicated faith, lost 57,000 casualties, of whom 20,000 were dead at the end of the day. Mr. Churchill could never forget that squandering of a nation's richness for the purpose of making a gesture, and was determined that it should never happen again. He knew well enough that it is victories, not gestures, which win wars. He knew, too, that America had known no Sommes and had no such tragic experience to guide her counsels.

In the end, faced by Mr. Churchill's indomitable refusal to substitute emotion for thought and worn down by argument, the Americans agreed to a joint landing in French North Africa. The decision was taken on 25th July, 1942, and that evening Mr. Harry Hopkins, President Roosevelt's personal representative in Britain, cabled the single word "Africa" across the Atlantic. "Thank God!" replied Mr. Roosevelt in a laconic reply to Mr. Churchill.[8] And on the same day the British Prime Minister gave to this great operation, which was to shape the whole future course of the war, the code-name "Torch".[9]

While the planning for Operation "Torch" was beginning, the policy of continued raids against objectives on the German-held coasts of Europe was continued. They culminated in a large-scale Anglo-Canadian raid against Dieppe, originally planned for 4th July but postponed on account of bad weather and finally abandoned. Partly because of widespread public agitation for a "second front now", partly to give Canadian troops in Britain a chance to assuage their burning desire to fight somewhere, and partly to try to relieve the pressure on Russia by keeping the Germans guessing where they were to be hit next, the decision was taken to remount Operation "Jubilee", as the raid on Dieppe was called. It was finally fixed for 4.50 a.m. on the morning of 19th August.

Once more the lessons of a former war were forgotten. A not dissimilar operation was the landing on the Gallipoli beaches in 1915, where the absence of supporting gunfire from the sea resulted in an appalling slaughter. The same story was repeated on the Dieppe beaches in 1942, where only the 4-inch guns of eight destroyers were provided to give covering bombardment. "At no time was the support which the ships were able to give sufficient for the purpose", wrote the Chief of Combined Operations in his report after the assault, "and this was one of the main reasons why the landing at the . . . beaches was unsuccessful."[10] The Naval Force Commander, in his report, considered that the presence of a battleship "would probably have turned the tide in our favour".[11]

It may well be that the achievement of surprise, so successful in the raid on St. Nazaire, was considered a sufficient substitute for a heavy covering bombardment, but on this occasion surprise was not achieved. During the approach one of the assault groups encountered a German coastal convoy and the resulting action gave away to the enemy ashore the secret of the assault. It also fatally disorganised one of the flank landings at Dieppe, whose objective was the capture of an enemy shore battery. The few men who did get ashore on this flank met overwhelming opposition and the entire force was either killed or captured.

The other flank assault was a complete success, destroying its shore battery quickly and efficiently, and re-embarking with comparatively few casualties. The success there, however, was not sufficient to swing the scale of disaster elsewhere.

The main landings were on the sea-front of Dieppe itself, and it was here that the issue was decided. An essential preliminary to success was the capture of various gun positions which commanded the length of the beach. Covering fire by the destroyers enabled the landing-craft to get in with little delay and very few casualties, but once the troops were ashore they were met by a murderous fire. The tank landing-craft, following astern of the assault craft, were all severely hit and got their tanks ashore only with very great difficulty and some five or ten minutes later than was planned. This delay had most unfortunate results, for by then the German cross-fire on the beach had built up to so great an intensity that the demolition parties, who were to blow exits in the sea wall, were unable to carry out their task owing to very heavy casualties.

It was at this critical moment that the guns of a battleship, had one been present, might have turned the failure into success. The effect of a naval shore bombardment by guns of the heaviest size is devastating, and often decisive. Within the ring of their protective blast the assaulting force might well have been able to reorganise on the beach after the initial landing and even to get the tanks into the town, where their presence would probably have been decisive. As it was, they never got off the beach, and there they had to be left when the raid was abandoned.

If the raid on Dieppe has to be written off as a tactical failure, it was yet redeemed in two important aspects. One of them was the exhibition of a standard of gallantry, both by the assaulting troops and by the crews of the landing-craft, that was hardly excelled throughout the entire war. The other was that lessons were learned, in some cases re-learned after an interval of years, which were to prove of incalculable value in the big amphibious operations which still lay ahead. The successes which attended them were very largely based on lessons learned in the failure at Dieppe.

In the meantime there were irritating delays in the planning for Operation "Torch", which in Mr. Churchill's mind was to be only part of an even larger concept of attack upon the enemy. The United States Chiefs of Staff conceived a dislike of the proposed landings inside the Mediterranean and put forward new plans at the end of August. These called for the abandonment of the easternmost landing at Algiers, leaving only two assaults, those at Casablanca and Oran, to mark the start of the operation. This curtailment was vigorously opposed by Mr. Churchill[12] and after considerable argument the original plan for three landings was finally restored.[13] But the altercation had caused delay and "Torch", at first envisaged for October, was as a result put back to November.

In Mr. Churchill's plans the Anglo-United States attack in the West was to coincide in timing with a British attack from Egypt. Here again there were difficulties and delays. The planned battle to break out of the constricting limitations of the Alamein Line depended largely on the build-up of armour, all of which had to come by sea and most of it from the United States. Three hundred Sherman tanks were shipped out from the United States to the Middle East, their crated engines all stowed in a single ship. Out of the convoy that carried the tanks and engines, that one vital ship with the engines was sunk by a U-boat. The American barrel was scraped and 300 more Sherman engines sent out in a special fast ship. They reached the Egyptian front in safety, and just in time to contribute a decisive blow when the great battle opened.

In this great two-pronged attack on the Axis forces in North Africa can perhaps be seen the earliest example of the true interplay of sea, land, and air forces in the execution of a tremendous offensive.

Behind the shield of the British and United States Navies the military forces gathered for the attack, men and munitions and the weapons of war. Across the oceans they came, guarded by the ships of the two fleets, to concentrate for the assault from east and west. And inside the main area of conflict, from bases at Alexandria, Malta, and Gibraltar, other sea and air forces were engaged at their fullest stretch in stopping the supplies on which the enemy depended for the coming battle. The true expression of maritime power, exercised in its widest sense, was making as certain as possible that success should crown the great adventure.

Some measure of the success in stopping the enemy's supplies to North Africa can be gained by the study of enemy documents captured at the end of the war. Out of 96,500 tons of shipping which put to sea from Italy in October 1942, only 58,000 tons reached North Africa. The rest was sent to the bottom by our naval and air forces. The figures for fuel were even more devastating, for of 10,000 tons shipped less than 4,000 tons reached Libya. On 15th October the German Naval Command in Italy reported that "the supply position and the naval war in the Mediterranean will shortly be faced with a catastrophe", while Rommel himself, reporting to Berlin three days after the opening stage of the Alamein battle, stated that the Panzer Army had only enough fuel for three more days of fighting. It is in the light of figures such as these that the maritime contribution to the land campaign must be judged.

In overall command at sea in the western Mediterranean was Admiral Sir Andrew Cunningham, thus making a welcome return to the Mediterranean, where he had won his greatest triumphs, from Washington, where he had been head of the British Admiralty Delegation and, as such, one of the chief planners of Operation "Torch". On 1st November he hoisted his flag in H.M.S. *Nelson* as Naval Commander Expeditionary Force. His Deputy Naval Commander was Admiral Sir Bertram Ramsay, whose organising genius had been so apparent in the dark days of 1940. Then it had been a case of lifting a British army from an enemy-controlled shore and bringing it back to England. Now the wheel was turning, and a British army was going back to strike a first blow in a series of assaults that were eventually to shatter the whole structure of the Axis war strategy.

As the day of decision approached, two related incidents provided a touch of the macabre to the great operation. On 20th September a Catalina crashed into the sea near Cadiz. A body drifted ashore and was handed over to the British by the Spanish authorities. On it was found a letter addressed to the Governor of Gibraltar giving the target date of the assault. The letter had been opened, possibly by the action of sea-water, possibly by an enemy agent.[14] There existed the chance of compromise, and as a result the target date was altered from 4th to 8th November.

The other incident was very much more hopeful. At midnight on 21st October the darkened British submarine *P.219*, later named *Seraph*, lay off the coast of North Africa. From her, four small canvas boats put off and pulled in towards the landing-beach, carrying a special mission of senior United States officers headed by General Mark Clark.[15] Ashore they met General Mast, commander of the French military forces in the Algiers area, and between them they reached a happy agreement on the general French reaction to the plan. During the dark hours of the morning of the 23rd the American party struggled through a choppy sea in their tiny boats to re-embark in *P.219*, not without an involuntary ducking when two of the boats capsized. Even as they were wringing the water out of their clothes on board the submarine, the first "Torch" assault convoy sailed from the United Kingdom.

An immense naval force was collected to escort and cover the convoys during their passage to Gibraltar and onwards to their respective goals. Force H, under Vice-Admiral Sir Neville Syfret, was augmented to a strength of three battleships, three aircraft carriers, three cruisers, and seventeen destroyers, and was to act as covering force to the two landings inside the Mediterranean, with a main duty of holding at bay the Italian Fleet should it venture out. As cover for the landing outside the Mediterranean, at Casablanca, two cruisers and three destroyers were sent to cruise in the area of the Azores.

Three naval task forces were assembled to cover the landings, the westernmost one at Casablanca being provided by the United States. Those for Oran and Algiers came from the Royal Navy and between them consisted of 137 warships, including one battleship, five carriers, six cruisers, and twenty-six destroyers. The United States force supporting the Casablanca landing amounted to ninety-one ships, including three battleships, four carriers, four cruisers, and thirty-four destroyers.

By 1st November the last of the four assault convoys from Britain was on the high seas and that from the United States was well on the way. It remained now to steer them safely through the U-boats, of which some forty were at sea in the Atlantic. As fortune would have it, a homeward-bound convoy from Sierra Leone was sighted by enemy aircraft and a "wolf-pack" of U-boats gathered to harry it as it steamed northwards. Ten ships were sunk out of it, but the U-boats were thus drawn away from the route of the "Torch" convoys, so much more rewarding a prize. All the assault convoys reached the Gibraltar area without being attacked, though in some cases they were reported by stray U-boats and aircraft. The enemy, strangely enough, failed to connect these movements to the southward with any offensive thrust in North Africa.

As the various support forces and convoys—an armada of some 340 ships—were moving into position for the great assault, stirring events were already in train in Egypt. General Alexander and General Montgomery had opened their campaign against Rommel on 23rd October and for nine days the battle swayed fiercely without any definite decision either way. A valiant attack by 9th Australian Division on 30th October towards the coast drew off the main enemy strength and at 1.0 a.m. on the morning of 2nd November General Montgomery launched his spearhead. For two more days there was fierce fighting as Rommel committed his last reserves of armour in a desperate rearguard action, but by the 4th the hole in the Alamein Line had been successfully punched and the British pursuit force was beginning to stream through after a fleeing enemy. As they swept forward into the desert on 6th November the "Torch" convoys reached Gibraltar.

For 240 years the narrow waters of the Gibraltar Straits had seen the might of British ships of war. Time and again they had echoed to the sound of British naval guns and throughout the years had welcomed all the heroes of the British Navy. Rooke, Leake, and Shovell, Torrington and Wager, Hawke, Boscawen, and Saunders, Rodney and Howe, Hood, St. Vincent, and Nelson—all these and many more had fought in those historic waters. Now they were to see another great British fleet and to welcome another great British admiral.

By 7th November the central and eastern Task forces, whose objectives were Oran and Algiers respectively, were well inside the Mediterranean. Before dawn on the 8th the ships were in position and the assaulting troops, who were to land on beaches east and west of the two towns, were on their way in. For the first time in the history of war, armies from two separate continents were landing simultaneously upon the shores of a third. At Algiers the resistance was slight and good progress was made, the town capitulating by the evening of the 8th. The fighting at Oran was more intense, both on land and sea, but by noon on the 10th the defenders surrendered and another valuable base passed into Allied hands. The all-American landings in the area of Casablanca had to be fought through in the face of a strong French resistance but, also by the 10th, all was over there as well. Admiral Darlan, representing the Vichy Government in North Africa, broadcast on that day an order to all French forces in North Africa, to cease fighting, and as their arms were laid down, the vast strategic area fell under Allied control.[16]

Landings, however, can only be the prelude to further exploitation, and it was in the follow-up to "Torch" that the decisive thrust could alone be made. As more and more men made their way ashore, so their eyes turned towards the eastward, where Tunis lay as a glittering prize that could solve for good and all the burning problem of Malta. Poor and inadequate roads in the North African hinterland had already indicated the need to capture the harbours of Bougie and Bone, farther to the east, as supply ports for the advancing armies. They were duly taken by assault from the sea on 11th and 12th November respectively, but ashore it was taking longer to concentrate the land forces than had been hoped. This was especially true of the air forces, because of difficulties in organising forward airfields, and there were many naval losses from enemy bombers at Bougie before adequate fighter protection became available over the port.

The physical difficulties of a land advance, allied to administrative difficulties in getting the armies quickly on the move, deprived Operation "Torch" of its full fruit. The French in Tunisia, too, were no more helpful to the Allied cause and, indeed, showed far less spirit than those in Algiers, Oran, and Casablanca. While the latter took up arms in an attempt to keep the Americans and British out, the former stood by passively and watched German and Italian troops, brought in by sea and air, occupy their soil.

Tunis, so much to be desired for its geographical command of the Sicilian Narrows, the deathbed of so many supply ships for Malta, was the true goal of Operation "Torch". As soon as it could be got away, a small advance force from Algiers made for the port at top speed. Axis forces, landed in Tunisia, had the same target in view. The British party just failed to win the race, and by so narrow a margin that even token resistance by the French in Tunisia to the Axis occupation might have made all the difference. But not even token resistance was forthcoming, and its lack condemned the Allies to six months of bitter fighting before at last the great prize fell.[17]

Operation "Torch", brilliant alike in its detailed planning and its smooth execution, stands out as the great turning-point in the war in Europe, the prelude to a vast strategic plan involving a succession of momentous operations of a similar nature. But it did not stand alone. Nearly 2,000 miles away to the east the enemy had already suffered crushing defeat and was reeling back across the desert in headlong flight. Farther eastward still, on the snow-covered plains around Stalingrad, the Russian armies too opened an offensive that was soon to end with the surrender of a field-marshal, 16 generals, and 46,000 men, gaunt, half-starved survivors of a German army of 200,000. The circle of Allied power around the Axis, already beginning to close in, now started to move inexorably, swiftly, towards the day of decision. Allied sea power, stretching its long fingers around the world, had both held the ring and set the stage for offence. It had made possible the great movements of men and munitions across the oceans, had carried them to their battle-fields, had brought them their weapons, had supplied their needs in every possible commodity of war. The fruits of its great endeavour were now ripening for the harvest, and there was the scent of victory in the air.

# Chapter 11

## ATLANTIC AND ARCTIC VICTORY

"THE U-boat attack of 1942", wrote the Prime Minister, "was our worst evil."[1] Figures provide at best but an arid commentary on the fortunes of this battle of the oceans, but in 1942 they reached so staggering a total that their very immensity reflects vividly the danger in which the Allies stood throughout that difficult year. U-boats alone sent to the bottom 1,160 ships of a total tonnage of 6,266,215 tons. Other causes—aircraft, mine, raider, E-boat, and unknown causes—added another 504 ships of 1,524,482 tons to the U-boat total.

On the same side of the 1942 picture was the growth in numbers of operational U-boats. In spite of the best that could be done by the Allied anti-submarine forces, the German operational U-boat strength grew from 91 in January to 196 in October, to 212 as the year came to its close, and reached a peak of 240 in April, 1943. The outlook was bleak indeed.

With the institution by mid-1942 of full convoy along the United States coast and in the Caribbean area the second "happy time" of the U-boats came to an end. They left those lucrative hunting-grounds and concentrated mainly in three areas, in mid-Atlantic beyond the range of shore-based aircraft from Britain, Iceland, and Canada; off the north coast of Brazil; and around the hump of Africa, where they could expect to meet the convoys to and from Freetown, in Sierra Leone. And in those areas they continued to make hay while the sun still shone for them.

There was still little that could be done to stop them. With the switch, in the late autumn of 1942, from the defensive towards a more offensive policy, with the great assault convoys for Operation "Torch" traversing the oceans, with the call for every available carrier to provide fighter cover over the landing-beaches, the long-foreseen answer to the U-boats was inevitably postponed. It was a situation that was particularly galling to the naval authorities charged with the conduct of this particular battle.

By the late summer of 1942 the first of the new family of escort carriers, ordered the previous year, came into service. She was the *Avenger*, and it has already been shown in an earlier chapter how she proved her worth on the Russian convoy route. In her and her sisters, of which six were in service by the end of the year, lay the final and decisive element in anti-U-boat warfare. It was not in surface escort alone, nor in air escort alone, that the true answer lay; it lay in the combination of the two along the whole length of a convoy route. Until the very long-range aircraft made their appearance in sufficient numbers in 1943, only the escort carrier was able to close those dangerous air-gaps in mid-ocean where the U-boats were still able to reap their grim harvest. Here, free from interference by patrolling aircraft, the "wolf-packs" could gather and swamp the surface escort by sheer weight of numbers.

Admiral Pound, the First Sea Lord, foresaw this withdrawal of the U-boats from the American seaboard to the Atlantic air-gap and lamented the lack of "single control, based on a single, unified strategy"[2] as between American and British escort policy. The British escort vessels sent over to assist the United States Navy in the institution of convoy along their coasts were still being retained in those waters and at the moment there seemed little chance of their release to reinforce their hard-pressed sisters in mid-Atlantic. Later, that "single, unified strategy" which Admiral Pound so earnestly desired was brought into being with electrifying success, but it took time to fructify.

One of the great difficulties which faced the mid-Atlantic escorts was that of time. The hunting of a U-boat to full destruction is more often than not a lengthy affair, needing a minimum of three or four ships. A convoy, however, cannot stand still in mid-ocean while its escorts engage in protracted hunts, and it became a delicate matter of decision as to the right moment to break off a hunt and rejoin the convoy. As a result, many promising attacks had to be broken off before completion, and many U-boats which might reasonably have been sunk, had time allowed, lived to fight another day.

It was to try to solve this particular problem that support groups were introduced into the Atlantic picture in September 1942. Their main function was to reinforce a normal escort group as soon as indications of a "wolf-pack" attack became apparent, and thus provide the necessary hunting element without suffering the simultaneous anxieties of close convoy protection. The first of the support groups, under the leadership of Commander F. J. Walker, was at sea during the third week in September, but other events were to intervene and delay the full fruition of this move. As with the long-awaited escort carriers, so with this first support group. Both were taken from the Atlantic convoy scene to shepherd the great "Torch" convoys down to their landing-beaches on the African shore. The carriers were required not only to provide anti-submarine air escort *en route* but also to give fighter cover over the beaches for the assaulting troops. It was for that reason that their allocation to the Atlantic battle, for which they were originally intended, was so long delayed.

In this situation there lay a strategical gamble of far-reaching importance. As 1942 began to fade towards its close it was becoming ever more apparent that the Atlantic was to assume a steadily increasing importance in Allied strategical plans. The preliminary planning for the final act of invasion in the European campaign, long recognised as a necessity to bring about the climax of final victory, was already well advanced. The build-up of force for this invasion was given the code-name "Bolero", and it rested squarely on the ability to bring ships safely across the North Atlantic. There was even more depending now on the outcome of the Atlantic battle than the vital imports on which Britain depended for her life and existence. If "Bolero" was to be successful, if the forces of invasion were to be concentrated for the future adventure of the

Normandy beaches, then the U-boats must first be defeated. There was no other way which could make that essential operation possible.

Throughout 1942 the losses in merchant shipping piled up alarmingly, outstripping the Allied capacity of replacement. The majority of them were independents, or stragglers from the convoys, always the most fruitful targets of the U-boats. Indeed, of the total shipping losses in 1942 attributable to U-boats, very nearly four-fifths of the ships sunk were sailing without escort.

As the year turned, the high rate of loss caused by the U-boats continued—203,000 tons in January, 1943, when wild weather in the Atlantic hampered the U-boats to some extent, 359,000 tons in February, 627,000 tons in March. And by the end of March, as mentioned above, the U-boat strength had risen to 240, of which no fewer than 112 were at sea. Highly trained, their morale fostered by success, they were able to dictate, by the very nature of their warfare, the conditions in which the battle was being fought. The first five months of 1943 saw them making their supreme effort against the convoys in mid-Atlantic, in the ocean gap which was still not covered by air escort. And even in this all-out attack, when they concentrated against the convoys, nearly half of their successes came from the independently routed ships.

It was the climax of the Atlantic battle, the crucial moment of decision from which one or other of the combatants would slide to defeat. Yet it was a "moment" to be measured in months rather than days, a "decision" that would not show itself in sudden defeat but rather as the start of a descending slope that led to the abyss. On that grim, groping struggle, fought out in the ocean wastes, a struggle largely unseen and unheralded in the clash of battle, rested the final destiny of mankind. The prize to the winner was no less than the key to final victory.

To this battle, especially during the savage U-boat onslaught of the autumn of 1942, the scientists contributed the fruits of their skill. They designed a very short-wave radar set which could reflect from smaller objects at sea and against which the existing type of German radar search receiver was of no value. These were fitted to many of the surface escorts during the second half of 1942. They led to far more contacts with attacking U-boats and to more wariness in the enemy submarine commanders in making their attacks. The new radar set was also designed for use in Coastal Command aircraft, but other priorities in the Royal Air Force made it slow to arrive.

To Liverpool, in November 1942, came Admiral Sir Max Horton as Commander-in-Chief, Western Approaches, relieving Admiral Sir Percy Noble in the main operational direction of the Atlantic battle. Admiral Horton was himself a submarine officer of high distinction, and so brought to his new task an intimate knowledge of submarine ways and habits. From Admiral Noble he inherited a command in which most of the groundwork necessary for ultimate success had already been done, both in the formation and training of the escort groups and in the organisation of a smooth-running machine. The great drawback against which Admiral Noble had to struggle had been the shortage in operational strength, the constant need to scrape the barrel for every ship capable of taking over the duties of an escort. To his successor, Admiral Horton, was to fall the task of gathering in the harvest from the seed so ably sown by Admiral Noble.

"Our shipping situation has never been tighter",[3] wrote the Naval Staff at the end of 1942. This was, if anything, an understatement, for the year ended with a net loss of a million tons of shipping and a severe contraction in the total of imports in comparison with 1941. Equally important in the wider sphere was the fact that Operation "Bolero", the build-up for the invasion of north-west Europe, was falling seriously into arrears. Less than one American division had reached Britain instead of the five which should by then have arrived.

This forbidding state of affairs had been brought into being, in part at least, by the withdrawal from the Atlantic of the United States escorts in June 1942. The need for this was to free American destroyers for American coastal convoys, for the projected invasion of North Africa, and for the Pacific war. By February of 1943 the division of escort forces with the North Atlantic convoys was

British, 50 per cent., Canadian, 48 per cent., and United States 2 per cent. At a convoy conference in Washington in March 1943, held between the naval authorities of Britain, Canada, and the United States, it emerged that the Americans proposed to withdraw entirely from all trade convoy duties in the North Atlantic.[4] The extra burden, if relatively slight, yet came at a distressing moment, when the battle was at its fiercest and when the British and Canadian escort forces were stretched to their utmost. The American withdrawal was absorbed by Britain and Canada in a partnership that grew ever more close and harmonious, and was shortly to be crowned by staggering success.

While the convoy conference was still sitting in Washington, one of the biggest, and indeed most disastrous, convoy battles of the war was fought out in the Atlantic. Two convoys from Halifax—one fast, of twenty-five ships, and one slow, of fifty-two—were concerned.[5] The fast convoy was located by the enemy early in its passage and soon eight U-boats were in contact. They sank twelve ships out of it during attacks over the next three days. Some hundred miles ahead was the slow convoy, also sighted and reported by U-boats. The concentration against it merged with that against the fast convoy as the two closed up until finally it became one great battle with some twenty U-boats swamping the defence and causing heavy damage. The loss from the two convoys was twenty-one ships of 141,000 tons. Only one U-boat was sunk from the many counter-attacks, to make the defeat an even harder one to bear.

Beyond the darkness of this March battle, however, the dawn was beginning to break. The end of March saw, at long last, the release of the escort carriers from Operation "Torch" and their introduction to the vital Atlantic theatre. It saw, too, the reappearance of the support groups and their challenge to the U-boats' supremacy. Finally, it saw President Roosevelt taking a hand in the distribution of the very long-range Liberator aircraft,[6] and ordering some to the North Atlantic to help to fill the chronic gap. Twenty of them were in operation in the North Atlantic by the end of March, and forty-one by mid-April; still far too few to cover the needs, but yet an encouraging start.

At the beginning of May another convoy battle was fought, to demonstrate only too clearly the supreme value of the support group and continuous air cover. An outward-bound convoy[7] was held up and to some extent scattered by a severe storm in an area south-west of Greenland known to contain a heavy concentration of U-boats. This was the situation for which the support groups were designed, and two were ordered out from St. John's, Nova Scotia, to augment the convoy's escort. The heavy weather delayed them and, before they were able to join, five ships of the convoy were sent to the bottom by a pack of twelve U-boats during the night of 4th/5th May. Four more were sunk during daylight attacks on the 5th, but during these attacks *U.192* was sunk by the corvette *Pink*.

That night, with the support groups at last with the convoy, the U-boats met for the first time with the full force of the new counter-measures. They continued to attack the convoy, but with no success. The corvette *Loosestrife*, however, chased and sank *U.638*, the destroyer *Vidette* hit *U.125* with her "hedgehog" and sent her to the bottom, the destroyer *Oribi* rammed and sank *U.531*, and the sloop *Pelican* gained a contact on *U.438* and hunted her to final destruction. Two more U-boats were sunk by very long-range aircraft in the vicinity of the convoy, *U.710* by Coastal Command and *U.630* by the Royal Canadian Air Force. It was a bitter defeat for the U-boats, and made even more bitter by the fact that two more boats, *U.659* and *U.439*, collided in the darkness and were both lost.

That this victory was no flash in the pan, but in fact the turning-point in the battle, was proved by the experiences of the convoys which followed. The next fast convoy lost three ships, but its escorts sank three U-boats in exchange; out of the slow convoy two ships were sunk at a cost to the enemy of two U-boats destroyed and some others seriously damaged. Of the next pair of convoys the slow reached Britain with all its vessels intact, while in its wake lay the corpses of *U.954*, *U.258*, *U.209*, *U.273*, and *U.381*. The fast convoy also arrived intact, leaving behind it *U.752* on the ocean bed.

The overall figures were even more staggering and portray vividly the effect of a fully integrated and properly constituted convoy system brought into being by the support groups and the closing of the mid-ocean air-gap. From the time the system came fully into being it took only five weeks to drive the U-boat fleet, then at the height of its power, to seek for less hazardous waters, and it mauled them badly in the process. The relative losses in North Atlantic and U.K. waters in April were 245,000 tons of shipping and 15 U-boats; in May, 165,000 tons and 40 U-boats; in June, 18,000 tons and 17 U-boats; in July, 123,000 tons and 37 U-boats.

Simultaneously, Coastal Command were employed on their own offensive in the main U-boat transit areas. These were the southern route across the Bay of Biscay and the northern route through the Iceland-Shetlands gap. Aircraft fitted with the centimetric radar, Leigh lights, and shallow-set depth charges were able to harass the U-boats on their way to the patrol areas in the Atlantic, and in the two months of April and May they sank no fewer than thirteen of them. Although, in terms of aircraft hours flown, these offensive patrols were not so productive as the air operations in the vicinity of the convoys, they were able to take advantage of a tactical error on the part of the U-boat Command, and their victims added to the new sense of discomfiture which the enemy submarine commanders were experiencing.

It was hardly surprising that the U-boat morale cracked under these staggering defeats, though it would perhaps be equally true to remark that it was surprising that British morale had not cracked under the consistent hammering of the previous year and a half. The battle had never ceased throughout that long period; it had instead grown in intensity and savagery from the two years of Atlantic fighting that had preceded it. Now, though it still called for the same watchfulness and effort, the same endurance and endeavour, it was being waged against a foe who had not only lost the initiative but also some of the will to press home his attacks to the ultimate.

On the cold, analytical plane this victory in the Atlantic battle may be laid at the door of the support group, the continuous air escort, the centimetric radar and the other new weapons which the scientists provided. But the victory went much deeper than that. Its real foundations lay securely based upon the courage and fortitude of the men who manned the escorts, the merchant ships, and the aircraft, their refusal to accept defeat when it stared them in the face, their constant endeavour and relentless pursuit of the enemy when the odds were most heavily weighted against them, their endurance and courage which fortified them to return again and again to the vast battlefield. British naval history, in its span across the centuries, boasts a galaxy of jewelled victories that shine across the years with the bright lights of courage, endurance, sacrifice, and achievement. In the years that lie ahead, when at last the true appraisal can be made, it is probable that no jewel in the naval crown will shine with so brilliant a glow as will this long battle fought across the oceans of the world.

In the whole concept of grand strategy in the European campaign the Atlantic stood as the fundamental battle which had to be won as the pre-requisite of victory. It was, as always, the task of maritime power to make possible the decisive thrusts of land and air power which alone could administer the *coup de grâce*. The problem differed nothing in theory, little in practice, from those which had confronted Britain throughout all her wars of the past—to deny to the enemy the riches of the world that lay across the oceans, to gain for ourselves the ability to move our transports and our merchant ships to those areas where the land battles were to be fought. In the dark days of 1940 and 1941 this traditional task had been made more difficult by the state of numerical weakness in which the Navy had stood in 1939. Yet throughout those grim years the ring around the Axis had been held at sea and every effort by the enemy to break through had been foiled by the natural resilience of sea power. The ring now was being contracted, and as the endless convoys streamed across the Atlantic, securely guarded at last, so the speed of contraction grew. In Britain, in North Africa, in Russia, in the tiny island of Malta, the sea-borne supplies of fighting men, of guns and tanks and aircraft, of petrol and oil fuel, of the raw materials of war, piled up in threatening array. All were carried by sea, guarded against attack by the maritime forces of the Allies, and their safe arrival at their various destinations was eloquent of the coming offensive. The great victories that lay ahead, in which the Allied armies and air forces were to shatter the final resistance of the enemy, were made possible only by the full opening of the sea routes to the all-essential shipping; ever the traditional task of the Navy in war. The oceans' doors were now fully opened. So it was that history repeated itself in the overall pattern of war. By mid-1943 the main task of the navies in the West had been accomplished, and it was the turn of the armies and the air forces now to go in and win the victory.

As in the Atlantic, so also in the Arctic, though the problem there was complicated by surface-ship strength. In spite of Hitler's tirade to Raeder of 6th January, 1943,[8] which resulted in the latter's resignation, Doenitz, the new Commander-in-Chief, had persuaded the Fuehrer, and incidentally himself as well, that capital ships still had a useful part to play in German naval strategy. As one result of this, the *Scharnhorst* was sent up to the far north to reinforce the *Tirpitz* and *Lützow*, even though Hitler was still sceptical. "Even if it requires six months [to force an action in the far north]," he said to Doenitz, "you will then return and be forced to admit that I was right."[9] In fact, it was ten months before Doenitz was called upon to explain to his Fuehrer how it was that the big ships had failed yet again.

The reason for the delay was the temporary cessation of the convoys to North Russia. By the beginning of April the Arctic night begins to pale into the long summer twilight in which both U-boats and aircraft could operate around the clock. The beginning of April also saw the moment of crisis in the Atlantic, when every escort was needed to stave off disaster. By holding back the Russian convoys seventeen more destroyers were freed for the Atlantic battle. Superbly trained in anti-submarine warfare, they formed the hard core of the new support groups and it was their contribution to the Atlantic battle which so largely turned the scale in May, June, and July.

Yet the concentration of German heavy ships in northern Norway was nonetheless a threat which the Home Fleet could not ignore. Although throughout the summer there were no Russian convoys for them to attack, they were admirably poised for a sudden break-out into the Atlantic. The Home Fleet, weakened by the despatch of two modern battleships to the Mediterranean for further operations there, was brought temporarily up to strength by the arrival of two United States battleships at Scapa, and on Admiral Tovey fell the duty of making certain that the enemy ships did not escape. After 8th May this duty fell to Admiral Sir Bruce Fraser, who relieved him as Commander-in-Chief.

The three German ships remained obstinately at anchor in their northern sanctuary and defied every effort to reach them. The Royal Air Force heavy bombers had not the necessary range to reach Altenfjord with a large bomb load and to return; the Fleet Air Arm was too heavily engaged elsewhere for carriers to be spared for such an operation. An attack by submarine was out of the question, for any attempt to penetrate by normal craft the long, defended fjord would be suicidal. It was a naval problem old as time, often solved in the past by the release of fireships with a favourable, onshore wind. A modern version of the fireship offered little prospect of success, and it seemed that only a new and novel weapon could hope to penetrate the heavily defended and inaccessible anchorage.

The new weapon was evolved in 1941, with just such a contingency in mind, and two prototypes carried out successful trials in 1942. On 12th May of that year a contract for six of them was placed and they were delivered to the Navy in January 1943. Known as X-craft, they were tiny submersible boats of thirty-five tons displacement with an overall length of 51 feet. They carried a crew of three officers and one engine-room artificer, were capable of diving to a depth of 300 feet, and carried as their armament two detachable saddle charges, each containing two tons of Amatex (a particularly powerful explosive) which were dropped on the bottom under the target and fired by clockwork time-fuses. Their crews were all men who had volunteered for "special and hazardous service".

The training for this desperate adventure was as thorough and as detailed as possible. Reconnaissance aircraft had photographed the German anchorage in Altenfjord and the conditions were reproduced as faithfully as possible in the Scottish Loch Cairnbawn, even to the extent of providing Home Fleet battleships protected by nets designed as nearly as possible to duplicate those protecting the German ships. By the end of the summer the chosen crews were so fully trained as to justify good hopes of success, and D-day for the actual operation was fixed for 20th September, when there would be just sufficient moonlight to assist the X-craft in their intricate navigation up the fjord.

To reach their operational area the X-craft were towed by normal submarines and were provided with two crews each, one to make the passage and the other to carry out the attack. On 10th September the Flag Officer Submarines, Rear-Admiral C. B. Barry, arrived at Loch Cairnbawn to inspect the crews; on the 11th the operational crews embarked in the six towing submarines—the *Thrasher*, *Truculent*, *Stubborn*, *Syrtis*, *Sceptre*, and *Seanymph*—and late that evening the little expedition sailed. They had over 1,000 miles to go.

Two of the X-craft broke adrift during the long passage to the north; one was recovered and a new tow passed, the other was never seen again. The troubles of the first, however, were not over, for on the following day her side charges flooded and had to be jettisoned. As they detonated on the bottom they did so much damage to the X-craft that her crew had to be taken off and the vessel sunk.

That left four, and by 19th September the towing submarines made their landfall successfully and had transferred the operational crews. On the evening of D-day, 20th September, the four X-craft, their crews "in great spirits and full of confidence", were slipped to continue their voyage alone. They quickly disappeared into the darkness as they steered to the southward towards the entrance of Altenfjord.

They crossed the German minefield guarding the fjord on the surface and successfully reached the entrance of the small Kaa Fjord at the head of Altenfjord, in which the *Tirpitz* lay, guarded by her nets. In the original plan three X-craft were detailed to attack the

*Tirpitz*, two the *Scharnhorst*, and one the *Lützow*. The four that had now reached the end of their journey contained all three allocated to the *Tirpitz* and one whose target was the *Scharnhorst*. This last was *X10*, which suffered such a series of mishaps that in the end she had to return without making her attack.

The other three were *X5*, *X6*, and *X7*, and by the evening of the 21st they had reached their waiting position off Bratholme Island, opposite the entrance to Kaa Fjord. They spent the first half of the night there charging their batteries, making good defects which had occurred during the passage, and dodging the German traffic. Ahead of them, moored close under the overhanging cliffs, lay the *Tirpitz*. Already they had come some 1,200 miles; there remained only six more to cover before they came to grips with their enormous opponent.

Shortly after midnight the first of the midgets crept out of her waiting position, dived to periscope depth, and proceeded on her desperate venture. The others followed her shortly afterwards. The sky was dull and overcast and a fresh breeze was whipping the surface of the sea into white horses. It was the sort of weather for which a submarine officer prays, and hopes were very high as the three tiny craft nosed their way in past the elaborate harbour defences.

Of the three midgets which, on this dark morning of 22nd September, set out to cripple the *Tirpitz*, none returned, and the story of their attack is pieced together from the survivors' memories and the German records. Two at least, after tremendous difficulties, forced their way through the nets and laid their charges under the great battleship—*X6*, whose captain and crew were taken prisoner by the *Tirpitz* when she was finally scuttled alongside the target, and *X7*, similarly sunk after the charges had exploded. From her crew the commanding officer and one other escaped. Of the third, *X5*, little is known. Half an hour after the explosion she was sighted by the Germans outside the *Tirpitz*'s anti-submarine nets and sunk by gunfire and depth charges. There were no survivors, and it will now never be known whether she had already reached the *Tirpitz*, laid her charges, and was on the way out, or whether she was still trying to get through the nets on her way in.

There remains the German account. Until seven o'clock on the morning of the 22nd all was quiet. The hands had been called, the normal day watches set, and work about the ship carried out in the usual daily routine. Seven minutes later, "a long black submarine-like object"[10] was sighted and reported to the officer of the watch. It was thought to be a porpoise, but was in fact *X6*, which was inside the net defence but had run aground when her compass had failed.

Five minutes later the alarm was raised on board the *Tirpitz* with a vengeance. *X6*, in getting clear of the shore, broke surface once again about thirty yards abeam of the ship and this time was correctly identified. Divers were sent down to examine the hull for limpet mines, and orders were given to raise steam and proceed to sea "in order to leave the net enclosure before the time-fused mines detonate".[11] These orders were cancelled a few minutes later when a second midget, which was *X7*, was sighted, the first intimation that more than one craft was involved in the attack. The picture that this sighting presented in the German mind was of a number of small submarines lurking in the fjord, an idea that was strengthened an hour later when a third (*X5*) was sighted just outside the nets. It was decided to keep the *Tirpitz* within the net defence and to try to minimise the damage by swinging her away from the charges before they exploded. It was during the course of this operation that they went up.

The explosions below her hull lifted the 45,000-ton battleship some feet out of the water. All the lights in the ship went out, the fire extinguishers on the bulkheads were wrenched from their housings and started belching foam, the decks were covered with broken glass from scuttles and mirrors. The whole ship was in an uproar. This, however, was all only minor damage. Far more serious was the fact that all three main engines were out of action, the rudders and steering engine were severely damaged, and some hundreds of tons of sea water had entered the double bottoms through flooding. The German Naval War Staff considered that the *Tirpitz* would be out of action for six months at the least and that she might, in fact, never regain operational efficiency. In point of fact she never did, but that is a story to be told later.

Of the twelve men who manned the three X-craft which attacked, six survived to tell the tale, all of them as prisoners-of-war. The commanding officers of *X6* and *X7*, Lieutenant D. Cameron, R.N.R., and Lieutenant B. C. G. Place, R.N., both received the award of the Victoria Cross for this gallant attack, the remaining surviving officers were decorated with the D.S.O., and the engine-room artificer with the C.G.M.[12] In his final despatch to Their Lordships the Flag Officer Submarines wrote: "In the full knowledge of the hazards they were to encounter, these gallant crews penetrated into a heavily defended fleet anchorage. There, with cool courage and determination, and in spite of all the modern devices that ingenuity could devise for their detection and destruction, they pressed home their attack to the full. It is clear that courage and enterprise of the very highest order in the close presence of the enemy was shown by these very gallant gentlemen, whose daring attack will surely go down to history as one of the most courageous acts of all time."[13]

This crippling of the *Tirpitz* came just in time to take some of the anxiety off Admiral Fraser's shoulders when the Russian convoys were restarted in November. They sailed with the same pattern of escort as had proved so effective in the later convoys of 1942, a strong, close escort of destroyers and corvettes, a covering force of cruisers to see the convoys right through to their destination, and a distant cover of the Home Fleet to guard against a sortie by the enemy's heavy ships. With the *Tirpitz* now out of action and only the *Scharnhorst* to guard against, only part of the Home Fleet was required for this duty and no longer the whole of it.

The December convoy, JW 55, was sailed in two portions, A and B, each consisting of nineteen merchant ships. The first half, JW 55A, left Loch Ewe on 12th December and reached the Kola Inlet in north Russia without mishap. During its passage the Commander-in-Chief took the opportunity of taking his heavy support force right through to Russia in order to establish personal contact with the Russian naval Commander-in-Chief. On the conclusion of this visit he returned with his ships to Iceland to refuel before covering the second half of the convoy.

Admiral Fraser was convinced that the successful passage of JW 55A, and incidentally of the November convoy, would tempt the enemy out to attack JW 55B. As a result he laid his plans for the second convoy on the assumption that it would lead to an action with the *Scharnhorst*. As with JW 55A, he provided the distant cover with his flagship the *Duke of York*, the cruiser *Jamaica*, and the destroyers *Savage*, *Saumarez*, *Scorpion*, and the Norwegian *Stord*. Close cover was provided by Vice-Admiral Burnett with the cruisers *Belfast*, *Norfolk*, and *Sheffield*, while the convoy itself had a close escort of fourteen destroyers, two sloops, and a minesweeper.

The Commander-in-Chief's plan of action, in the event of an encounter with the *Scharnhorst*, was, first, to close the enemy to within 12,000 yards and illuminate him with starshell; second, to form the four screening destroyers into two subdivisions and send them in to make torpedo attacks, and third, to keep the *Jamaica* in close support of the *Duke of York* but with freedom to open the distance if heavily engaged. So certain did Admiral Fraser feel that the *Scharnhorst* would come out that he practised several night-encounter exercises with his ships, culminating in a final one after sailing from Iceland, with the *Jamaica* playing the part of the *Scharnhorst*. He also stressed in a final meeting of all the commanding officers, that "every officer and man must be doubly sure that he knew his night action duty".[14] Seldom, since the days of Nelson, can a squadron so highly trained for one particular operation have put to sea.

On the German side the planning was less specific. Grand Admiral Doenitz, remembering his interview with Hitler of the previous February, was anxious to make good his assurances on the value of the capital ship in convoy operations. He reasoned that since two convoys had already reached Russia unscathed, a third would be less prepared for trouble. In fact, as shown above, the exact opposite was the case, and it was because of the safe passage of the first two that Admiral Fraser expected, and was fully prepared for, an attack on the third. At a meeting with Hitler on 19th December, Doenitz informed the Fuehrer that the next convoy to Russia would be attacked by the *Scharnhorst*,[15] and it was therefore almost entirely for this political reason of convincing Hitler that Doenitz, as soon as he knew that the convoy was at sea on 22nd December, ordered the *Scharnhorst* and five destroyers to prepare for the operation.

The convoy was already being shadowed and reported by aircraft, and as a result of these reports a patrol line of eight U-boats was formed west of Bear Island in order to intercept the approaching merchant ships. The German aircraft succeeded in maintaining contact with the convoy throughout the 23rd and most of the 24th. They lost touch late that day, but by 9 a.m. on Christmas Day *U.601* had reported that she was in contact. From then on the submarine continued to shadow, sending in constant signals of the convoy's progress, and just after 2.0 p.m. on Christmas afternoon the German Naval Staff ordered the *Scharnhorst* and her destroyers to sea. Five hours later they moved down the fjord, and as they emerged from the shelter of the land they found a tumultuous sea running. Rear-Admiral Bey, in command of the operation with his flag flying in the *Scharnhorst*, reported at 9.0 p.m. that the destroyers were being badly handicapped by the heavy weather, leaving to the Commander-in-Chief the decision whether in these conditions the operation should continue. That night Doenitz took the decision. If the destroyers could not remain at sea, the *Scharnhorst* was to go on alone. Admiral Bey received this signal at 2.0 a.m. on the 26th, and as a result continued his course to the northward. The *Scharnhorst*'s die was cast.

From Iceland came the *Duke of York*, *Jamaica*, and their four destroyers. Admiral Fraser sailed just before midnight on the 23rd, steering to the eastward towards Bear Island. The destroyers, battered by the heavy seas, had difficulty in keeping up with the two larger ships and the speed of the fleet was reduced to fifteen knots.

At about the same hour on the 23rd the three cruisers of the close support force sailed from North Russia, having safely delivered the first half of the convoy. These were the *Belfast*, flying the flag of

Vice-Admiral R. Burnett, and the *Norfolk* and *Sheffield*. Between the two support forces was the convoy, with its close escort of destroyers and sloops.

On Christmas Day the weather, already stormy, became worse, even the *Duke of York* finding it very uncomfortable as she steamed into it. For the destroyers, of course, it was even heavier going but they kept up gallantly in the wild weather.

In the very early hours of the 26th the Commander-in-Chief received the signal for which he had been waiting. In the Admiralty the Operational Intelligence Centre, alert as ever to any changes in the enemy's wireless traffic, deduced from the number of signals sent that an important movement was taking place in the far north. Just after 3.0 a.m. a signal went out to Admiral Fraser appreciating that the *Scharnhorst* was at sea, and it was received in the flagship half an hour later. The *Duke of York* increased speed to twenty-four knots, and in the south-westerly gale which was blowing the destroyers had great difficulty in avoiding broaching-to in the heavy sea. The flagship's bows were almost constantly under water.

By 7.30 a.m. the three forces were all converging on the convoy, the *Scharnhorst* and her destroyers steering north, Admiral Burnett and his cruisers steering north-west, and the Commander-in-Chief, still a long way to the west, steering east-north-east at his best speed. At that same moment, Rear-Admiral Bey detached his destroyers to form a line of search for the convoy. They steamed away from the *Scharnhorst*, leaving her by herself to fight the last battle of her career.

An hour later the first contact was made. The *Belfast*, steaming up with the *Sheffield* and *Norfolk* to join the convoy, got an echo on her radar at about eighteen miles range, and the cruisers closed rapidly. Three-quarters of an hour later the *Sheffield* reported the enemy in sight and the *Belfast* opened fire with starshell.

The first intimation received by the *Scharnhorst* that British forces were in her neighbourhood was when the starshell burst above her, lighting up the Arctic night with a dull yellow glow. A minute or two later she was hit by an 8-inch shell from the *Norfolk* which burst in her fore-top, causing many casualties and shattering her fore radar set. A second shell burst on her forecastle. She was now steering south-east and, increasing speed to thirty knots, she drew rapidly clear to the southward with the three cruisers in chase but unable to catch up with her.

It was at this moment that a signal was received on board the *Scharnhorst* from Admiral Doenitz, exhorting her to strike a blow for the German troops on the Eastern front by destroying the convoy. She altered course again to the north-east and by so doing sealed her fate. Admiral Burnett, rightly assuming that she was trying to work round the convoy from ahead, made straight for the merchant ships to give them extra protection. This meant losing contact temporarily with the enemy, though he was confident of regaining it later when the *Scharnhorst* returned to the attack.

The loss of contact placed the Commander-in-Chief in a dilemma. The time was fast approaching when the destroyers with the *Duke of York* would either have to turn back, because of fuel shortage, or go right through to Russia. It was quite possible that the *Scharnhorst* had already abandoned the operation, especially as German aircraft were in contact with the *Duke of York* and had certainly reported her position. If the *Scharnhorst* were on the way home, then Admiral Fraser could not catch her. But a few minutes after noon his doubts were set at rest. The *Belfast* was once again in radar contact, fifteen minutes later the *Scharnhorst* was in sight from the *Sheffield*, and in another five minutes was once more being hit. Four destroyers, detached from the escort of the empty ships returning from Russia, had now joined the cruisers and were ordered to attack with torpedoes. In the very heavy sea that was running they were unable to close the range sufficiently though all of them opened fire with their guns.

This second engagement decided Admiral Bey to abandon the operation and he set course for home. But already he was too late. His second attempt to find the convoy had given Admiral Fraser time to work far enough to the east to cut the *Scharnhorst* off, and in the *Duke of York* hopes of action were growing into certainties. It was time for Admiral Fraser to put his plan of battle into operation, and he disposed his destroyers in two subdivisions, one on either bow, to be in readiness to attack with torpedoes.

As the *Scharnhorst* steered south-east she was shadowed continuously by Admiral Burnett's cruisers, and a series of position reports kept Admiral Fraser fully informed of the enemy's movements. At 4.15 p.m. the *Duke of York*'s radar picked up the *Scharnhorst* at a range of twenty-three miles, and from that moment Admiral Fraser knew he had her at his mercy.

Half an hour later the *Belfast*, still shadowing from the north, illuminated the target with starshell. The *Duke of York* followed suit, and as the great guns of the flagship swung on to the target the gunnery officer wrote in his report: "At first impression the *Scharnhorst* appeared of enormous length and silver grey in colour."[16] As the 14-inch guns fired their opening salvo the range was no more than 12,000 yards.

As was the case earlier in the day, Admiral Bey was again taken completely by surprise. His first knowledge of the presence of a British battleship was the *Duke of York*'s shells landing on the *Scharnhorst*'s quarterdeck. He at once altered course to the north to try to escape, found the *Belfast* and *Norfolk* there, and swung round to the east, increasing to full speed.

The hunt was now on, and all ships settled down to chase the flying enemy. At 5.15 p.m. Admiral Fraser sent his destroyers off to carry out their part of the plan. But in the very heavy sea that was running they found it difficult to gain on the *Scharnhorst*. To Admiral Fraser, watching anxiously the progress of the four destroyers as they crept up so slowly, it seemed for a moment as though the *Scharnhorst* might yet escape out of the trap. Everything now depended on the destroyers.

The *Duke of York* was still firing at the flying *Scharnhorst* and at 6.20 p.m. hit her aft. This must have damaged her considerably, for she reduced speed. It gave the destroyers their chance and they began to forge ahead rapidly to reach good firing positions. Admiral Bey must have known then that his ship was doomed, for he sent at that moment a signal to Hitler: "We shall fight to the last shell";

but as yet that knowledge was denied to the British ships. To them it was still touch and go.

Between 7.50 and 7.55 p.m. both sub-divisions of destroyers succeeded in making their torpedo attacks. Closing right in to a range that varied between 3,500 and 1,800 yards, between them they hit her four times. Although under heavy fire from the *Scharnhorst*'s secondary armament, they pressed their attack home to almost point-blank range.

The battle was now approaching its end. The *Duke of York* and *Jamaica*, which had ceased fire while the destroyers went in, now opened up again and hit the *Scharnhorst* repeatedly. Her speed dropped right down until she was almost stationary, the target of a gruelling fire. Battered by gunfire, crippled by the four torpedoes from the destroyers, resistance was almost at an end. Admiral Fraser ordered the *Jamaica* and *Belfast* to finish her off with torpedoes. As they closed in and fired, the four destroyers which had been attached to Admiral Burnett's cruisers also arrived on the scene. Between the cruisers and destroyers, seven torpedo hits were claimed. The *Scharnhorst* took a heavy list to starboard and was obviously near her end.

"By now all that could be seen of the *Scharnhorst* was a dull glow through a dense cloud of smoke which the starshell and searchlights of the surrounding ships could not penetrate. No ship therefore saw the enemy sink, but it seems fairly certain that she sank after a heavy underwater explosion which was heard and felt in several ships at about 19.45."[17] So wrote the Commander-in-Chief in his despatch. When the *Belfast* went in three minutes later to make her second attack, the wreckage strewn on the water told its own tale.

The darkness, the heavy weather, and the icy water of the Arctic afforded little chance of survival to the unhappy crew of the *Scharnhorst*. Though the destroyers searched for an hour, no more than thirty-six were rescued from a total complement of very nearly 2,000.

So perished the pride of the German Navy. Even if Hitler, when informed of the loss of this fine ship, could say in effect "I told you so", he must at the same time have felt the strands of the net closing in upon him. For these were reckoned to be German waters, dominated by German aircraft and U-boats, and by the heavy ships of the German Fleet. The defeat of the *Scharnhorst* was a sorry blow to German naval pride, and no doubt Doenitz had an uncomfortable half-hour explaining to his Fuehrer the reasons for this new disaster.

The ripples of this defeat reached farther than the immediate waters in which the *Scharnhorst* met her end. The morale of the enemy at sea, already beginning to crumble under the Allied onslaught in the Atlantic against the U-boats, dropped rapidly away. One more milestone along the road to victory had been passed, one more sea route—and that right under the nose of the enemy—made safer for the merchant ships to carry to the fighting fronts yet more of the weapons of war. Throughout the Third Reich the first faint breaths of the chill wind of defeat were beginning to blow, and their icy fingers were prophetic of approaching doom.

# Chapter 12

## VICTORY IN THE MEDITERRANEAN

WITH the great two-pronged Allied attack from east and west safely launched in North Africa and making good progress, the Prime Minister of Great Britain and the President of the United States met in conference at Casablanca on 14th January, 1943. With the two war leaders were their respective Chiefs of Staff, the area Commanders-in-Chief, and the Chief of Combined Operations. The purpose of the conference, so far as the Mediterranean was concerned, was to decide the strategic policy to be followed after the final defeat of the enemy in North Africa.

The problem presented few difficulties. The basic requirement for future operations in this theatre was the safety of through communications by sea in the Mediterranean. Only with that guarantee could the true flexibility of maritime power be used to mount the next assault; it remained, as ever in the past, the cardinal requirement for any extension of the war into Europe. And that Europe was to be the next objective none could possibly doubt.

Already, as Mr. Churchill and Mr. Roosevelt studied the question, much had been done to make the answer clearer. Malta, for so long hanging on a frail thread of existence, had been relieved in mid-November 1942 by the unmolested arrival of a convoy of supply ships from Port Said. Four more convoys followed at short intervals, all of them arriving without mishap. The supplies which they unloaded marked not only the end of the long months of siege but also the emergence of the island, for the first time in the Mediterranean war, as a really secure base from which future operations could be launched.

Inevitably, as they studied the problem of the all-essential sea communications, the eyes of the two war leaders fell upon the narrow channel in the central Mediterranean, that eighty-mile stretch of water which divided Cape Bon, in Tunisia, from Marsala, in the south-western corner of Sicily. Those waters were already strewn with the wrecks of many fine ships, Allied and enemy alike, victims of the need to force through supplies to Malta on the one side, to Rommel on the other. It needed no expert eye to realise that the capture of Sicily would make those waters safe for Allied shipping. And of equal importance in the strategic development of the war was the value of Sicily as a base for future operations against Italy. The decision to invade was quickly taken and the Commanders-in-Chief of the sea, the land, and the air were charged with the preparation of detailed plans. To the assault was given the code-name of Operation "Husky" and a provisional date fixed for the moonlight period of June. As events turned out it had eventually to be advanced to the corresponding period in July.

Commanding-in-Chief at sea was Admiral Cunningham, who had returned to the Mediterranean to conduct the naval side of Operation "Torch" as Naval Commander Expeditionary Force. On 20th February he resumed his more famous title of Commander-in-Chief Mediterranean, and Admiral Harwood, who had relieved him at the end of the previous March, became Commander-in-Chief Levant, and responsible only for the eastern Mediterranean. With the change in title came also a change in command area, giving to Admiral Cunningham naval dominion over Malta and the Tunisian ports, from which the invasion of Sicily would be largely mounted. As his Deputy Commander-in-Chief, Admiral Cunningham was given Admiral Sir Bertram Ramsay, and it was into his well-tried hands that the Commander-in-Chief placed the responsibility for the organisation and training of the invasion forces.

Meanwhile, of course, the naval battles of the North African campaign had still to be fought. The advances of both the British 8th Army from Alamein and the Anglo-United States armies from

French North Africa were in a sense amphibious, requiring continual support and sustenance from the sea as they progressed along their respective coasts. This support and supply were the responsibilities of the two Inshore Squadrons, one at each end of the Mediterranean. Military supplies of all sorts were brought up by sea under the escort of the Inshore Squadrons and landed, sometimes across the beaches, sometimes in ports which had first to be cleared and made workable after heavy demolition by the retreating enemy. Channels into these ports were swept by the minesweepers of the two squadrons, and much of the work was done under frequent attack by U-boat and aircraft. Throughout the campaign there could be no let-up, no easing of the burden, for the momentum of advance on shore depended on the supply by sea. General Montgomery paid his tribute to this work of the Navy when he signalled: "Without the safe conduct of tanks, petrol, and other munitions of war to Tobruk, Benghazi, and Tripoli, the 8th Army would have been unable to launch the offensive."[1] That the 8th Army's offensive was not only launched but maintained with undiminished momentum throughout reflects in part the exemplary and tireless work of the Inshore Squadron.

Of equal importance with the supply of our own armies was the stopping of supplies to the enemy's. Everything that Rommel required, petrol for his tanks, shells for his guns, food and clothing for his troops, had to come by sea, ferried across the narrow waters of the Sicilian Channel. Even in the days of Axis dominion over those waters, when their ships, aircraft, and U-boats made the movement of any Allied ship hazardous in the extreme, Rommel's supply convoys had been often shattered by attack from the air, from the surface, and from below the surface. Control of those sea areas had now slipped from the Axis grasp. It was firmly held by the Mediterranean Fleet, assured by two cruiser squadrons—the 15th (*Cleopatra*, *Orion*, and *Euryalus*) based at Malta, and the 12th (*Aurora*, *Penelope*, *Dido*, and *Sirius*) based at Bône—by a growing force of destroyers and motor torpedo boats and gunboats, and by two submarine flotillas, the gallant 10th which still operated from Malta and the 8th now based at Algiers. Command of the air above these waters was in the hands of eight R.A.F. and three Fleet Air Arm bomber and torpedo-bomber squadrons operating from Malta, while fighters flew from the new bases gained during the advance along the North African coast. Behind them all, a guarantee of immunity from sudden attack by the main Italian Fleet, lay Force H, now commanded by Vice-Admiral Willis, and built up to a strength of two 16-inch battleships (*Nelson* and *Rodney*), one fleet carrier (*Indomitable*), and twelve destroyers. With such a force, sea command of the Sicilian narrows was virtually absolute.

As the two advances, from east and west, developed, the pressure against the enemy's supply convoys was intensified. The acquisition of new bases ever nearer the area of conflict enabled the smaller warships, the motor torpedo boats and gunboats, to be used against them, and sweeps against Axis shipping were carried out by night and day. The margin of success jumped to new heights, and of every three ships which left Italy to run the gauntlet of British maritime power, only one succeeded in reaching Tunisia. It was this crippling loss of vitally-needed supplies which in the end sapped the Axis ability to fight and brought Germany and Italy down to defeat in North Africa.

By 8th May the Allied grip had so tightened that the end was in sight. Ashore, the armies were entering Bizerta; at sea, destroyers and light coastal craft had established a close blockade of Cape Bon. The traffic to be stopped now was in the opposite direction. A quarter of a million soldiers, reduced to their last narrow strip of shore, were waiting to be taken off. There were, perhaps, memories of Dunkirk, of Greece, and of Crete in Admiral Cunningham's mind on that morning of 8th May when he made a signal to his ships: "Sink, burn, and destroy. Let nothing pass."[2]

Nothing passed. The main fleet of Italy, which might have risked a sortie to cover an evacuation, remained in its harbours. The few ships that tried to make their way home were quickly sunk, the few men who hoped to escape in small boats were soon rounded up and taken prisoner by the watchful British warships. The Axis defeat in North Africa was complete and absolute, and a vast army of the enemy was gathered in to swell the prisoner-of-war cages.

As the noise of battle died away in North Africa in this mass surrender, thoughts of the next step to be taken occupied all men's minds. Already the plans for the invasion of Sicily were well advanced. Under the watchful eyes of Admiral Ramsay the ships and the men were training and exercising. The operational plan was a massive one, involving in the initial assault some 3,000 ships, 160,000 men, 14,000 vehicles, 600 tanks, and 1,800 guns.

Operation "Torch", the invasion of North Africa during the previous November, had been a demonstration of planning at its best. Armies had crossed the oceans from different continents, converging on to their target beaches with consummate accuracy and brilliant timing. A vast quantity of weapons and stores was landed with the men, and with it all the priceless element of surprise had not been lost. Operation "Husky", now to occupy the centre of the strategical stage, was planned with the same brilliance and owed much of its success to the lessons learned in North Africa.

An elaborate deception plan was put into operation with the object of making it appear that Sardinia and Greece were to be the scenes of the next Allied landings. False information was allowed to fall into Spanish hands by means of papers on a body floated ashore from a submarine on to the Spanish mainland. It was staged to give the appearance of being the result of an air crash, and it was virtually certain that such papers would find their way into the hands of German agents. Though this plan did not deceive Mussolini, it certainly induced Hitler not only to reinforce the Balkans but also to pay less attention to the defence of Sicily than he might have done.[3] Exercises to test the adequacy of the planning and to accustom troops in the use of assault craft were carried out in Egypt to focus attention upon Greece as the probable target. Transports and supply ships were assembled at bases in Great Britain, the United States, and North Africa, widely enough separated to disguise the true objective. As the time ripened for the assault, the convoys carrying the invasion forces from these distant bases were brought without loss across the oceans, their arrivals timed to fall exactly together in order to achieve that measure of local surprise which in all seaborne invasions constitutes so vital a factor of success. During the early morning of 9th July, D-day minus 1, they all converged in the waters south of Malta.

Facing Admiral Cunningham, in addition to the purely naval side of mounting the assault, was an unknown quantity of impressive importance, the possible reaction of the main fleet of Italy. All experience of naval operations in the Mediterranean so far had shown an Italy reluctant to employ her fleet offensively, even in view of the self-evident failure of her alternative policy of reliance on light craft, submarines, and aircraft. This new operation, however, was something different, something far more vital to the whole existence of the country. Sicily was a bastion of the European fortress, its successful defence a pre-requisite of immunity from attack on the mainland itself. There was but one course of action open to Italy, the concentration of her naval power to force a conclusion with the assaulting armada. Failure to do so would permit the tide of attack to roll on with gathering strength until the whole of Italy herself was engulfed.

To counter this possibility, Force H was augmented to six battleships, two carriers, six cruisers, and twenty-four destroyers, and sailed under the command of Vice-Admiral Willis to cover the landings. The main fleet of Italy remained passively in port. Force H, not unexpectedly, attracted the attention of U-boats and aircraft, and both the carrier *Indomitable* and the cruiser *Cleopatra* were damaged by torpedoes. But it was not too heavy a price to pay for the immobility of the Italian battleships and cruisers, for it was on their absence from the field of battle that the success of the invasion hinged. With a determined attack they might have had it in their power to break up the assault; instead, they let the chance go by default and in doing so sealed their own ultimate fate.

During the afternoon of 9th July the weather began to break. There had been a succession of fine, hot days with an unruffled sea, promising perfect weather for the operation. But now, with the convoys approaching Sicily and the landing-craft with the assault troops on board already at sea, a freshening north-west wind began to raise a short and choppy sea. In such conditions an assault landing over the beaches was certain to be difficult, but the operation now was too far advanced to permit of postponement. It was realised that the heavy seas would not only slow the landing-craft down but also drive them down to leeward, but any difficulties in navigation should be easily overcome through the presence off Sicily of four submarines—the *Unruffled*, *Unseen*, *Unison*, and *Unrivalled*—which had been sent out in advance to lay navigational buoys off the beaches and themselves to act as markers for the assault shipping.

The landings were made in two sectors—British troops on the beaches around the south-east corner of the island, United States troops on beaches farther to the west. Shortly after 2.30 a.m. on the morning of the 10th the first landing-craft touched down on the British beaches and the men scrambled ashore. They were no more than twenty minutes late on the planned time, a triumph of seamanship in view of the unexpectedly heavy sea which had not only slowed them down but had also added materially to the difficulties of navigation in the unwieldy craft.

Lying out beyond the assault craft, the monitor *Erebus*, the cruisers *Uganda*, *Mauritius*, and *Carlisle*, and the destroyers *Eskimo*, *Nubian*, and *Tartar* supported the troops with their guns, engaging the fixed batteries ashore. Under their accurate fire the opposition to the landings was slight and the troops gained a substantial foothold without undue difficulty. Within a few minutes of the first landing the success signal was seen by the ships lying off, to be followed by others as each beach was consolidated. By the end of an hour all the beaches in the eastern sector had reported a successful landing[4] and the invasion was off to a flying start.

Farther to the west the United States landings were in some cases meeting with rather more opposition. At a few of the beaches the men were put ashore almost unopposed, enabling the assault troops to capture their initial objectives ahead of schedule. At others they had to fight their way ashore against determined resistance. Here, as the sun rose to light up the scene, American cruisers were enabled to close the beaches and to bring their guns into action to hold, and break up, the enemy's counter-attacks. In one case they were employed against German tanks with devastating effect.

As the hours of D-day passed, it became possible to recognise all the symptoms of success. The armies had been put ashore almost exactly as planned, every beach was securely held, and excellent progress was being made inland as the advancing troops linked up on their objectives. A fine start, too, had been made with the unloading across the beaches of the essential supplies to maintain the troops ashore, still with little or no reaction from the enemy. Such opposition as there was came only from the German forces in the island; that of the Italians was obviously half-hearted. It was a most encouraging sign.

By 11th July, twenty-four hours after the initial landings, the whole south-eastern corner of Sicily was firmly in Allied hands, and the main part of the Navy's task in the operation was over. It was for the ships now to serve the needs of the Army, supporting them by shore bombardment as required,* sustaining them by the landing of reinforcements and supplies, and making small-scale amphibious assaults behind the enemy's lines when necessary to maintain the speed of the land advance. This last requirement, it is true, was only carried out by the Americans in their sector, and by its use and its success they proved that they had little to learn in the correct use of sea power. In his report of the operation Admiral Cunningham drew attention to the value of these United States amphibious tactics and regretted that the British 8th Army had no occasion to make use of this priceless asset of sea power and flexibility of manœuvre.[5] In his opinion it might have saved much time and much costly fighting.

Operation "Husky" came to a triumphant end on 17th August when the British and United States armies met in Messina after a campaign that had lasted no more than thirty-eight days. The gain was a very real one, more, in fact, than the successful conquest of an important bastion of the European mainland. Its occupation reduced considerably the threat to Mediterranean convoys from the

* On one of these occasions the twenty-eight-year-old battleship *Warspite*, in order to reach the bombarding position, made a good 23½ knots with paravanes streamed over a period of five hours. Admiral Cunningham signalled: "Operation well carried out. There is no question that when the old lady lifts her skirts, she can run."

air and altogether freed them from the chance of surface attack. At the same time it effectively cut all Italian coastal traffic between the east and west coasts, for the Straits of Messina, through which it had to pass, was now dominated by Allied guns. The naval base at Reggio, opposite Messina, was rendered untenable, while those at Taranto, Brindisi, and Trieste now had no communication by sea with those at Naples and Genoa.

For Italy the Allied conquest of Sicily spelt disaster. Her whole system of naval defence now lay shattered and in ruins; her will to fight, already tested almost to extinction by the military collapse in Tunisia in May, crumbled away in this new defeat in July and August. On 25th July, with the fighting in Sicily still in progress, Mussolini was deposed. On the 26th the Fascist party was dissolved. The end, for Italy, was in sight even before the triumphant Allies stood in Messina and gazed across the narrow straits at the Italian shore, no more than 4,000 yards away.

This capture of Sicily from the sea stands out as an example of the value of maritime power in enabling an attack to be launched on the perimeter of a hostile territory. The experience gained at sea in this tremendous operation was to stand the naval planners in good stead when, less than a year later, it was to be repeated in an even greater assault on the European coastline. The lessons of "Torch" were used to good purpose in the mounting of "Husky", and "Husky" was to prove the model for "Overlord".

"Of the navies", wrote Admiral Cunningham in his report on the invasion,[6] "I can only say that I never wish to command better, and I count it a great honour that through the person of Vice-Admiral Hewitt [U.S.N.] I was privileged to command so large and efficient a force of the United States Navy. Both the Western Task Force, under Admiral Hewitt, and the Eastern Task Force, under Admiral Ramsay, performed their unaccustomed tasks in a manner befitting the highest traditions of any fighting Service."

As the guns in Sicily fell silent with the victory, the Prime Minister and the President of the United States were again meeting in conference, this time at Quebec. Their meeting was given the code-name "Quadrant", and its purpose was to evolve a full offensive strategy in Europe and a limited offensive strategy against Japan.[7]

The two statesmen met in an atmosphere rich with promise. As they studied the situation maps of the European campaign they could mark the turning of the tide and its encouraging flow in the Allied favour. The maps showed them a North African coastline from which the enemy had been completely eliminated, a Malta freed at last from the Axis siege, a Sicily firmly in Allied hands, an Italy which had discarded its dictator and was palpably on the brink of surrender. Farther east the maps showed a Russia fully recovered from the initial shocks of the German assault and growing massively in power. There, too, the wind of victory was beginning to blow, faintly as yet but with promise of developing into a gale.

But it was at the Atlantic map that the two statesmen could look with the greatest satisfaction, for it was there that the decisive victory had been won. For the first time since 1940 the Western Allies could justifiably feel themselves masters of that ocean, and in that mastery lay the key to the future operations now to be put into force. The mounting toll of U-boat losses, the dwindling tonnage of merchant shipping sunk, and the still growing strength of the sea and air escorts promised a safe and sure foundation on which to build the edifice of final victory in the West.

Encouraging as were all these signs, no one in Quebec in August 1943 had any illusions as to the task which still faced the Allies. Somehow, somewhere, and at not too distant a date, British and American soldiers, backed with all the power of modern weapons, would have to clamber out of the sea upon the mainland of western Europe. The build-up across the sea, both in men and material, would have to be faster and more powerful than the German capacity to reinforce across the land. The assault phase of Operation "Husky" gave proof that such an operation was technically and materially possible, but with the added experience gained from the raid on Dieppe almost exactly a year previously the British Chiefs of Staff now made it a condition of the proposed assault that the operation must be capable of being sustained for at least three weeks without the use of a great port.[8] It was on that basis that continued planning was agreed. When one looks back now in the full light of actual performance, the accuracy of the British condition is uncanny. Cherbourg, the first major port to fall into Allied hands, was captured exactly twenty-one days after the launching of the assault.

The "Quadrant" Conference fixed the target date for the proposed landing, to which was given the code name "Overlord", as 1st May, 1944; and at the same time approved an outline plan drawn up by Lieutenant-General F. E. Morgan, who had already been appointed as Chief of Staff to the Supreme Allied Commander (designate) for the assault. General Morgan was authorised to proceed with the detailed planning and to make full preparations for launching the greatest amphibious operation of all time.

The Combined Chiefs of Staff also laid down at the "Quadrant" Conference the strategy to be followed in the Mediterranean. Its main function, after the elimination of Italy as an Axis partner, was to tie down as many German divisions as possible in that theatre in order to give a relatively greater chance of success to the more vital operation across the Channel. The military requirements in the Mediterranean set out by the Combined Chiefs of Staff were:

1. The elimination of Italy as a belligerent.
2. The seizure of Sardinia and Corsica.
3. The maintenance of unremitting pressure on German forces in northern Italy.
4. Offensive operations in southern France against the enemy with the object of creating a diversion in support of "Overlord".

In this link between "Overlord" and the proposed Mediterranean operations the Combined Chiefs of Staff made clear their blueprint for victory in the West. Within its framework the task of the Navy was plain. It was to retain and consolidate the command of the oceans so hardly won from the enemy, to use that command to transport across the seas the men and the weapons required for the assaults, to put them ashore in their assaulting positions, and to support and maintain them there until the foothold was won and consolidated. This, indeed, was but the traditional task of maritime power, the age-old means by which Britain had so often won her wars in the past.

The implications of the Combined Chiefs of Staff's directive regarding Mediterranean strategy were not difficult to appreciate. Sicily was but a stepping-stone to the first of their requirements, the unlatching of the door which led to the Italian mainland. Nor was that unlatched door left long before being forced open. On the morning of 2nd September a heavy naval bombardment of enemy positions south of Reggio was the herald of a military barrage fired across the Straits of Messina before dawn on the 3rd. Beneath its cover a host of landing and other craft of the Royal Navy crossed the Straits, touching down on the beaches between Reggio and Catona and landing units of the British 8th Army on the Italian mainland. There was no opposition and no casualties, for the Italians were too dispirited to fight and the Germans were already pulling out towards the north.

While the 8th Army was making this first lodgement in the "toe" of Italy, plans for a more ambitious project were already far advanced. The unexpectedly rapid progress of the Sicilian campaign had, during its course, given some promise to a belief that an opportunity was being created to strike a really damaging blow while the enemy was still disorganised from defeat.[9] This was the moment, wrote General Marshall, Chief of Staff of the American Army, on 18th July, "for bold action and justifiable risks", an opinion with which the British Chiefs of Staff were in cordial agreement.[10]

The prize at which the Mediterranean planners now aimed was the port of Naples, some 150 miles ahead of the initial 8th Army landing near Reggio. To the operation was given the code name "Avalanche", and the interval between its first conception and its execution was no more than seven weeks. The assault landing was to be made by the United States 5th Army, commanded by General Mark Clark and comprising one British and one American corps. Joint British and United States naval forces were under the direct command of Vice-Admiral Hewitt, U.S.N., while the essential air cover over the beaches was to be provided by Royal Air

Force and American fighters operating from Sicilian airfields, temporarily augmented, until the capture of an airfield ashore, by naval fighters from the carriers *Unicorn*, *Battler*, *Attacker*, *Hunter*, and *Stalker*, sent out from Britain to reinforce the Mediterranean Fleet for this operation.

Some thirty miles south of Naples lies the small port of Salerno, once the capital city of the Lombard princes and the scene of their many battles against the Saracen invaders. In its day it had been sacked by Charlemagne, had fallen before the siege catapults of Robert Guiscard, had finally been burned to the ground by the Emperor Henry VI. That had been 750 years ago, and since then the little town had dwelt in peace, its importance as a port declining as that of Naples grew. Now, once more, it was to be thrust into the arena of war.

The choice of Salerno as the scene of assault was based on three factors: that its beaches were good, that there were no strong, fixed coast defences, and that it was the nearest point to Naples within reach of fighters based on Sicily. A disadvantage was a mountainous bottleneck north of the town on the road to Naples, but that was held not to outweigh its other military attractions. There was one more drawback, not perhaps appreciated to the extent to which it might have been, in that the advantages of Salerno as an assault area were every bit as apparent to the enemy as to the Allies. They, too, could appreciate the value of Naples and work out the maximum range of Allied fighters operating from Sicilian airfields. They carried out an anti-invasion exercise on those very beaches a few days before the Allied assault.

In preparation for the assault the submarine *Shakespeare* was sent to patrol off Salerno with the task of carrying out beach reconnaissance and of plotting the position of enemy minefields reported in the area. The information she gained was of the greatest importance to the assault forces. As they neared the shore just before midnight on 8th September she acted as a beacon to guide them in and steered them clear of the minefields. Most of the convoys involved in the operation had been sighted from the air during their approach and heavily attacked, but of the 700 ships engaged no more than one was sunk. There had been a time, and not so long since, when the *Luftwaffe* dominated the Mediterranean skies, when its planes wreaked havoc among warships and merchant ships alike. On this occasion it was strangely ineffective although, as events were to develop, it still had one strong card to play.

As was the case in Operation "Husky", Force H stood by to prevent any interference by the Italian Fleet. The carrier force under the command of Rear-Admiral Vian, consisting of the *Unicorn*, *Battler*, *Attacker*, *Hunter*, and *Stalker*, lay off well to seaward to augment the air cover over the beaches during the early stages of the assault. In the original planning it had been expected that the capture of an airfield ashore at Montecorvino would allow shore-based fighters to take over this duty after the first two days, but the bitter German opposition held up its early capture and Admiral Vian's carriers had to remain.

The assault craft, on their way in to the beaches during the early hours of the 9th September, met with a mixed reception. The British landing on the northern beaches, closely supported by heavy gunfire from the sea, was achieved without undue loss. On the southern beaches the Americans decided to dispense with such gun support and their landing was fiercely opposed. They had great difficulty in establishing themselves ashore, a difficulty which was exacerbated by a failure to get the follow-up supplies quickly off the beaches and into the hands of the fighting men. By the end of the day, however, the northern beachhead was securely held, although one main objective, the Montecorvino airfield, had not yet been taken. In the American sector the situation was less secure.

The need for Force H soon disappeared. Italy, with her morale gone and her country in a state bordering on chaos, was known to be on the brink of defeat even before the first landing on the mainland at Reggio. On that day, 3rd September, she asked for terms of surrender; on the 8th it was announced that an armistice had been signed. With its signature her fleet was no longer hostile, and the removal of that threat made it possible to withdraw the heavy ships of Force H to Malta, from where they could very soon be recalled if required to support the men ashore with heavy gunfire.

For four days the grim fighting ashore continued with little change in the situation, the ships in Salerno Bay doing what they could to support their comrades on the beaches. But the enemy was bringing up reserves, and on the evening of 13th September launched a powerful counter-offensive down the dividing line between the British and American sectors. Aided by a strong force of armour, they broke through to the coastal strip and the situation ashore became one of crisis. Admiral Hewitt signalled to Admiral Cunningham, appealing for more naval support. The response was swift and effective. The cruisers *Euryalus*, *Scylla*, and *Charybdis* were ordered to Tripoli to embark additional troops and transport them to Salerno at maximum speed. The *Warspite* and *Valiant* from Force H were ordered back into the assault area to add the might of their 15-inch guns to the naval bombardment, and Admiral Cunningham offered to send in addition the *Nelson* and *Rodney*, each with nine 16-inch guns, should they be needed. The cruisers *Aurora*, *Penelope*, *Mauritius*, and *Orion* were also made available for shore bombardment. At the same time the Allied air forces redoubled their efforts to seal off the attack by heavy bombing of the German lines of communication.

For two days the crisis at Salerno continued, the troops ashore holding on precariously to their narrowing foothold. But the growing might of the naval bombardment as more and more ships went in held the enemy's penetration at bay and effectively cut his reinforcement route. The fire of the two battleships, lying at times little more than a mile off shore, was devastating in its accuracy. By nightfall on the 16th it was not only evident that the enemy had shot his bolt but also that the whole operation was going to prove a success.

On that day patrols of the 5th Army, probing south from Salerno, made contact with those of the 8th Army moving north from Reggio. The whole length of that coastline was now under Allied control and the Salerno beachhead had been relieved. A few days later the great port of Naples was safely gathered in.

For a time Operation "Avalanche" had been touch and go, but its ultimate success amply justified all the risks which had been taken.

When it is considered how great were the difficulties in planning so massive an assault within the short time available, and how stubborn and skilful the German resistance, it can be appreciated that a great prize was won at a cost which, though heavy for the Army, was comparatively light for the Navy and almost negligible for the Air Force. "Once again", wrote Admiral Hewitt, "the decisive factor was the application of sea power supplemented by air power. Under the gruelling fire of long-range naval guns the German penetration was sealed off, and on the 16th the surviving German elements withdrew."[11]

The most serious naval losses were caused by a new air weapon which the enemy used for the first time at Salerno. It was a winged bomb, controlled by radio from an attendant aircraft. The American cruiser *Savannah* was hit and severely damaged by one of these bombs on the 11th, and two days later H.M.S. *Uganda* shared her fate and had to be towed back to Malta. On the 16th, in the course of her bombardment of enemy positions ashore, the *Warspite* was attacked by three of these radio-controlled bombs simultaneously. Two were near-misses, but the third penetrated her decks and burst in a boiler room. The damage was extensive, and shortly after the explosion she found herself with all steam cut off and some 5,000 tons of water on board. Although nearly unmanageable, she eventually reached Malta three days later under the tow of four tugs.

Great as was the achievement at Salerno, an even greater, and infinitely more dramatic one had taken place almost at the same moment as the first landing-craft touched down on the beaches there. The surrender of Italy on 8th September meant also the surrender of her fleet. The bulk of it lay at Spezia, with a second force at Taranto and units at Genoa and Trieste. In accordance with the terms of the armistice the squadron at Spezia, consisting of the battleships *Roma*, *Italia*, and *Vittorio Veneto*, six cruisers, and eight destroyers, left harbour in the early morning of the 9th, bound for Allied waters. They were ordered to proceed to the westward of Corsica and then alter course to the southward for the coast of Africa, where they would be met by Allied warships.

Shortly after midday they had reached the point at which they were to alter course. Out of the afternoon sky swooped a flight of German aircraft armed with their new radio-controlled bombs. The *Italia* was hit and damaged, but not so severely as to bring her to a stop, and she continued on her course to the southward. The *Roma*, too, was hit, and in her case the wound was mortal. She was set on fire and sank twenty minutes later with heavy loss of life, including that of Admiral Bergamini, the Commander-in-Chief. One cruiser, the *Regolo*, and six destroyers remained behind to pick up survivors, and then proceeded independently to the Balearic Islands where they gave themselves up to the Spanish authorities for internment. The remaining ships steamed south towards Africa and were later met by British warships which escorted them to Malta. Admiral Cunningham, flying his Union flag as an Admiral of the Fleet in the destroyer *Hambledon*, was at sea to witness their arrival off the African coast.

From Taranto, direct to Malta, came the two older battleships, *Andrea Doria* and *Caio Duilio*, two cruisers, and one destroyer. The Commander-in-Chief reached Malta in time to accept the full surrender; to realise in this dramatic occasion the triumphant culmination of all his patient toil and inspired leadership in these historic waters. One can, perhaps, sense the feeling of pride with which, on 11th September, he composed his famous signal to the Secretary of the Admiralty: "Be pleased to inform Their Lordships that the Italian Battle Fleet now lies at anchor under the guns of the fortress of Malta."[12]

It was the traditional naval phraseology, but behind the laconic wording lay three years of courage, devotion, and endeavour, and one more justification of the age-old national belief that salvation and success in war can be founded only upon the rock of maritime power.

The surrender of the Italian Fleet, although it removed at one blow the major naval adversary in the Mediterranean, by no means meant the end of naval operations in those waters. German U-boats were still at large and there were a number of minor German warships to threaten Allied movements. There were still many small-scale actions to be fought in the Adriatic and in the waters around

Greece and the Dodecanese Islands where enemy posts still held out. There were a number of small amphibious assaults to be carried out on both coasts of Italy, all of them designed to speed the advance of the Allied armies and air forces up the Italian mainland. And still in the future lay the two major assaults from the sea in 1944, at Anzio in January and in the south of France in August, both of them following very much the same pattern as the successful landing at Salerno. With it all there remained the burden of seaborne supply to the armies and air forces ashore, their tanks and guns and ammunition, their food and clothing and essential stores. All these tasks, and others like them, were part of the Navy's fundamental duty, a natural corollary of the control of the Mediterranean seaways, so hardly secured in battle.

It was in this way that the Mediterranean war was finally won. The pattern of that victory ran true to form, guided by an overall strategy hallowed by three centuries of experience. As in past wars, so in this, with the power exercised upon the seas producing those conditions in which the final, vital blows could be struck on land. It had cost many bitter battles, many losses, many anxious moments of stress, before control of the Mediterranean had been won, but the winning of it gave to the Navy the ability to carry the armies and the air forces to their battlefields and to sustain them throughout the brunt of their actions. It was, as ever in the history of war, the forces based upon land whose task it was to drive home those last, devastating blows upon the enemy that alone could win the final victory. It was the mastery of the seas, with the flexibility in attack which it brought in its train, that gave to the land forces the opportunity to win their battles.

The campaign in the Mediterranean made many naval reputations. Admiral Somerville will be remembered for his inspired handling of Force H, Admiral Vian for his brilliant action in driving off the Italian Fleet at the Battle of Sirte when it had his Malta convoy at its mercy, Admiral Troubridge and Admiral McGrigor for their sterling work in the Sicily landings, Commodore Oliver for his brilliant handling of the crisis at Salerno, Captains Agnew, Mack, and Stokes in their sturdy attacks against Rommel's convoys in the dark days of 1941 and 1942, the naval pilots at Taranto and Malta, the destroyer and the submarine captains whose endless endeavours contributed so much to the victory. There were a host of others. And though he made his greatest claim to fame in Home waters, one remembers, too, Admiral Ramsay and his meticulous planning for the invasions of North Africa and Sicily.

But above them all stands the figure of the great Commander-in-Chief, Admiral Cunningham, whose inspired leadership never failed to sustain the spirit of victory in the men he so ably led. To his relentless tenacity in holding the eastern Mediterranean throughout those pregnant months when defeat was staring us in the face, to his unfailing grasp of the essential meaning of maritime power, to his courage in adversity and his brilliance in victory, was due the ultimate triumph of the Mediterranean Fleet.

At the height of his fame he was called home from the Mediterranean, the scene of his great triumph. Other, more important, work was awaiting him, for in London the First Sea Lord lay dying.

# Chapter 13

## THE LIBERATION OF EUROPE

EARLY in October 1943 the resignation on account of ill health of Admiral of the Fleet Sir Dudley Pound as First Sea Lord was announced. He died on Trafalgar Day, less than three weeks later, worn out by the heavy burden he had carried for over four years. If, on rare occasions, his judgment had been at fault, if he had been, perhaps, too prone to intervene from his Admiralty office in the conduct of operations at sea, yet throughout those long, critical years he had steered the Navy faithfully through the shoals of war. When the shadow of death compelled him to relinquish the helm he could see a Navy that had weathered the earlier storms of adversity and could take comfort in the knowledge that it was now set fair upon the course to victory.

To succeed him as First Sea Lord came Admiral of the Fleet Sir Andrew Cunningham. His work in the Mediterranean was done and his energies were now to be directed to the solution of the naval problems of a wider sphere. Among the many preoccupations which faced him in his new office two were outstanding. The first was the continuing preparation for the forthcoming invasion of north-west Europe, the other was the naval contribution to be made in the Pacific in the war against Japan.[1]

The elimination of the Italian Fleet in the Mediterranean in the summer of 1943 had permitted the reinforcement of Admiral Somerville's fleet in the East Indies, but Admiral Cunningham wanted more than this. The brunt of the naval war was being borne in the Pacific, and it was towards that ocean that the new First Sea Lord was now looking. His desire was to see a British Fleet in action there alongside the ships of the United States, and taking a share in what had been so far largely an American theatre of operations. It was a desire that, at first, commanded little support. There was an influential body of naval opinion in the United States, led by Admiral King, the American Chief of Naval Operations, which was distinctly hostile to any appearance of a British Fleet in Pacific waters, and Admiral Cunningham's first task was to remove that prejudice so far as possible. Such a fleet could not, of course, be assembled in the Pacific until the verdict in Europe was beyond all possible doubt, but Admiral Cunningham was determined, if it lay within his power, to see British warships in action there.[2]

More immediate, however, and therefore more pressing, was the forthcoming Operation "Overlord", now reaching the stage where it was taxing the ingenuity and skill of planners of all three Services. One of Admiral Cunningham's first duties was to recommend to the Prime Minister and to the Combined Chiefs of Staff an officer for the position of Naval Allied Commander-in-Chief for the invasion. His choice was virtually automatic; one name stood out above all others. Admiral Ramsay's brilliance at this type of work had been startlingly apparent in the North Africa and Sicilian assaults, and all were agreed, United States leaders as well as British, that there was no man better qualified for the task. There was, too, something of poetic justice in the appointment. In the dark days of 1940 it had been Admiral Ramsay who had planned and carried out Operation "Dynamo", the evacuation of the British Expeditionary Force from the shores of France around Dunkirk. Now he was to plan to put an invasion force back into France and in so doing to see the wheel turn full circle.

Operation "Overlord" depended for its success upon many essential pre-requisites, all of them bound up in the overall strategic plan. Its ramifications stretched far beyond the particular area of the Channel where it was to be staged. They reached east to Russia and south to Italy, where heavy fighting on both these fronts absorbed so much of the German military strength. They reached to central

Germany, where the combined bomber offensive of the Royal Air Force and the United States Army Air Force was draining off a large proportion of the enemy's fighter strength. They reached, too, across the Atlantic to Canada and America, from where came many of the men and the munitions with which the assault was to be made. Finally, for an instant or two, they reached up into the Arctic, where a latent threat to the Atlantic shipping called for naval action.

It is not easy to pick on any one of these essential pre-requisites as of more vital importance than any other, though they all depended in the ultimate analysis on domination at sea. By the end of 1943 this domination was virtually absolute and, as the year drew to its close, the Navy had many good reasons for rejoicing.

As already described, the German battle-cruiser *Scharnhorst* had been sunk in the Arctic on 26th December by the guns and torpedoes of the Home Fleet. Two days later another, though smaller, action gave equal cause for satisfaction. A German blockade runner, the *Alsterufer*, had been intercepted by the Royal Air Force while approaching the Bay of Biscay and had been sunk by bombs. Already at sea in the Bay was a strong force of German destroyers which had been sent out to escort her in. Also at sea in the Bay were the British cruisers *Glasgow* and *Enterprise*, the latter Canadian manned. They were ordered by the Commander-in-Chief, Plymouth, to intercept, and shortly after noon on the 28th the enemy were sighted from the *Glasgow*'s bridge. There were ten all told, and four of them were the big Narvik-class destroyers of 2,400 tons. There was a heavy sea running in the Bay, and the sky was grey and overcast.

Boldly handled, these ten destroyers should have had the two British cruisers at their mercy. But instead of going in to the attack they tried to escape at full speed to the south-eastward, and in the long-range, running fight which developed some of them were hit and damaged. Finally, to split the gunfire of the cruisers, they divided into two forces, six of them continuing their south-easterly course, the remaining four trying to double round to the north-west. The *Glasgow* and *Enterprise* turned westward in pursuit of the latter group and sank three of them before they were lost to sight in the winter darkness.

The action, in the general pattern of the war at sea, was relatively unimportant except in one interesting aspect. It reinforced vividly an impression that was gaining ground, that the German will to fight at sea was declining. It had first become apparent as early as November, 1939, when the *Scharnhorst* and *Gneisenau*, after sinking the *Rawalpindi*, had run from the cruiser *Newcastle*. In April, 1940, they had done the same thing when they encountered the *Renown* off the Norwegian coast. Even the *Bismarck* and *Prinz Eugen*, in May, 1941, had run from the *Prince of Wales* when they could have had her at their mercy. It was equally apparent, too, in the Arctic at the end of 1942 when the *Hipper* and *Lützow*, during their attempt to attack Convoy JW 55B, had allowed themselves to be driven off by a much weaker force of destroyers and cruisers. It was also noticeable in the Atlantic that, after their heavy defeat in May and June of 1943, the U-boats were becoming more reluctant to press home their attacks against the convoys. And now this action in the Bay of Biscay was telling the same tale. There appeared to be more in it than pure coincidence, and as a result it was not surprising that the New Year of 1944 found the Navy in optimistic mood.

The sinking of the *Scharnhorst* and the successful action by the *Glasgow* and *Enterprise* were both encouraging, but of far deeper significance was the continuing ascendancy over the U-boats in the Atlantic. During the third quarter of 1943 no fewer than 71 of them had been destroyed; in the fourth 53 had been sent to the bottom, to bring the total for 1943 up to 237. This was a rate of loss that no Navy could afford without a serious drop in morale, and by the end of the year Doenitz, under the smart of this defeat, was forced to withdraw the U-boats from their Atlantic hunting-grounds. The other side of the picture was, if possible, even more encouraging, for during the last three months of the year only three British merchant ships, totalling less than 15,000 tons, had been sunk in the North Atlantic. And of these three ships the U-boats could claim only two, and one of those was lost through hitting a U-boat-laid mine off the Canadian coast.

The battle against the U-boats had been intensified by every possible means throughout 1943. While the main killing areas were always around the convoys, a useful addition to the total was made by Coastal Command aircraft operating across the U-boat transit routes from their Bay of Biscay bases to their Atlantic operating areas. This transit route was considered by the Chiefs of Staff as the "trunk" of the Atlantic menace, its roots lying in the Biscay ports and its branches spreading far and wide, to the North Atlantic convoys, to the Caribbean, to the eastern seaboard of America, to the sea lanes along which the faster merchant ships sailed without escort.[3] To strike effectively at the trunk, it was thought, would cause the branches to wither. It was, perhaps, a part of the answer in that some U-boats were sunk, but it was by no means the whole of it. Taking the U-boat war as a whole, it remained true that, in terms of aircraft/hours flown and aircraft losses for each U-boat sunk, success in the Bay offensive was achieved only at a cost some ten to twelve times greater than in similar air operations around the convoys.

Nevertheless, in the summer of 1943, three factors combined to give a greatly increased rate of U-boat loss in the Bay of Biscay. The first was a grave error of tactics by Admiral Doenitz when, between 1st June and 31st August, he ordered his U-boats to cross the Bay on the surface and fight back with their anti-aircraft weapons. The second was his acknowledgment of defeat around the convoys when, on 23rd May, he withdrew most of the U-boats from the Atlantic and as a result increased their density in the Bay. The third was some excellent forecasting of U-boat movements by the Submarine Tracking Room in the Admiralty. These three factors gave the airmen of Coastal Command their great chance, and they made the most of it.

The virtual immunity of North Atlantic shipping from submarine attack during the autumn and winter of 1943 and the early months of 1944 was a vital factor in the build-up for "Overlord". Considerable numbers of American and Canadian troops were coming across the Atlantic to play their part in the coming assault, and huge quantities of essential weapons and stores were brought over in the holds of merchant ships. Their uniformly successful arrival was a reflection of the sound basis of convoy protection evolved through the years of painful experience. Effective maritime power, exercised through its twin elements of surface and air protection, converted each convoy into a task group with formidable killing capabilities, a fact which the U-boats bold enough to join battle with them discovered to their very great cost. The price for each convoyed ship sunk in the North Atlantic between September 1943 and the eve of "Overlord", a mere twelve in all, was no less than six U-boats, or seventy-two in all. The true answer to the U-boat, which lay in combined surface and air escort and support to all threatened convoys, had been apparent for a long time but had been sadly delayed in execution by the difficulties which Coastal Command experienced in obtaining sufficient very-long-range maritime aircraft. These difficulties had, however, been overcome by May 1943, though not entirely by adequate numbers so much as by working the available aircraft and their crews to the limit of their capacity.

The Atlantic victory was fundamental to "Overlord", and without it the invasion of north-west Europe could never have been mounted. The whole success of "Overlord" depended on the ability of the Allies to maintain unchecked the flow of men and materials from Canada and the United States, both for the initial assault and for the subsequent build-up of the forces engaged. American wishes to invade in 1942—when they agreed that they would be unable to contribute men, supplies, or shipping to the venture—and again in 1943, an operation much in their minds and one which they pressed strongly with the British Chiefs of Staff, failed to take fully into account the North Atlantic situation. It is perhaps a long cry from the Atlantic convoys to the beaches of Normandy, but without the security of the first, success on the second would have been impossible. It is not always recognised how closely the two were bound together and that it was the long, hard, and tireless work of the escort crews, both surface and air, that really gained the key to the continental door.

Operations in the Arctic, too, played their part. Early in 1944 it became known in the Admiralty that repairs to the *Tirpitz*, damaged in the midget submarine attack of the previous September, were approaching completion. It was not considered likely that the enemy would use her operationally against the Russian convoys, but there was a possibility that she might return to Germany, be refitted there, and sent out as a last, desperate gamble to harry the Atlantic shipping.[4] Memories of the *Bismarck* and the trouble she had caused made it advisable to try to damage the *Tirpitz* once more.

She still lay up in the north of Norway in Kaa Fjord, her berth strongly protected by anti-submarine nets, by anti-aircraft guns on board and also mounted in the surrounding hills, by flak ships moored in the fjord, and by smoke-generating apparatus. She was beyond the range of heavy bombers based in Britain, and attempts by the Royal Air Force to hit her from temporary bases set up in north Russia were failures. The task was then handed over to the Fleet Air Arm which, with its greater flexibility, might well command success.

Considerable thought and training were given to the operation, a full-scale bombing and firing range being constructed at Loch Eriboll, in conditions as similar as possible to those which would be found in Kaa Fjord. Barracuda bombers from the *Victorious* and *Furious*, and Wildcat, Hellcat, and Corsair fighters from the *Pursuer*, *Searcher*, and *Emperor*, were trained energetically over this range throughout the weeks preceding the attack.

In order to minimise the risk of U-boats finding and attacking the carriers, it was decided to synchronise the operation with the passage of an outward-bound convoy to north Russia, which was certain to draw the U-boats to the eastward of Bear Island. Such a convoy was due to leave on 27th March and it was arranged to attack the *Tirpitz* eight days later, on 4th April, by which time the convoy would be well into the Barents Sea, east of Bear Island, having taken the U-boats with it.

The main force of carriers, accompanied by cruisers and destroyers, sailed from Scapa on 30th March. Two days later, so well was the convoy proceeding and so favourable the weather for air operations, the Commander-in-Chief Home Fleet advanced the attack by one day, altering the prearranged flying-off position to one closer to the Norwegian coast. By increasing to full speed the carrier force was able to join forces with the Home Fleet during the afternoon of 2nd April, and there the battleship *Anson*, flying the flag of Vice-Admiral Moore, and the *Victorious*, which had sailed with the Home Fleet, were detached to join the main carrier force for the attack. Course was set for the new flying-off position, due to be reached at 4.15 a.m. the following morning. This was zero hour for taking off.

"By 3.0 a.m. on 3rd April it appeared that everything was in our favour. So far as we knew we had not been sighted, and flying conditions were perfect for putting the operation into effect. There was a light off-shore wind, and visibility was in fact so good that while landing on the strikes later we sighted the Norwegian coast at a distance of about fifty miles."[5] So wrote Admiral Moore in his official report. On board the carriers all was in readiness. The first strike of twenty-one Barracudas and forty-five fighters were in the air and formed up within twenty minutes of the first take-off. They flew in low over the water to avoid possible radar location, and at 4.57 a.m. they began to climb to 10,000 feet to cross the Norwegian coast. Coming in across the land they altered course to the eastward down the snow-covered valley which led to the head of Kaa Fjord. There lay their target, easily distinguishable in the clear light of early dawn, and they swooped down on to their unsuspecting quarry from the south-west.

The fighters, diving down into the cover of the hills, engaged the *Tirpitz* and the anti-aircraft batteries with their guns and "undoubtedly spoilt the *Tirpitz* gunnery".[6] They were followed down by the bombers, which attacked from heights of between 3,000 and 1,200 feet. Hits were scored immediately, causing heavy explosions and flames, and it was quickly evident that the *Tirpitz* was severely damaged. Exactly sixty seconds after the first bomb had fallen the attack was over and the aircraft were on their way back to the carriers. Only one Barracuda was missing; the remainder "returned in flight formation with a unanimous broad grin".[7]

Meanwhile, the second strike of nineteen Barracudas and forty-five fighters was on its way in. Although the *Tirpitz* was now surrounded by smoke, she was still easily visible from above. The same tactics were employed as for the first strike, and the same success was achieved with many hits observed. Again one Barracuda was shot down, the remainder all landing on successfully. By 8 a.m. the carriers and their covering forces were withdrawing from the area.

It had indeed been a red-letter day for the Fleet Air Arm. At a cost of two bombers they had effectively put out of action the only remaining battleship in the German Fleet. She had been hit by fifteen bombs, her decks had been ripped up, bulkheads shattered, and over 300 of her crew had been killed. She could, however, still steam, for no bomb had been able to penetrate the lower armoured deck of eight-inch steel.

Later in the year, as soon as she had been patched up, she steamed round the coast to Trömso, her fruitless days in the Arctic at an end. There she was just within range of the Royal Air Force and, on 12th November, Lancasters of the "dam-busters" squadrons reached her and sank her with six-ton bombs. By that time, of course, she was no longer a menace, for the invasion had been launched and in Europe the enemy was already on the run.

With the North Atlantic virtually clear of U-boats and with the danger of the *Tirpitz* making her appearance in that ocean removed by the bombs of the Fleet Air Arm, all was clear for "Overlord". Within that main operation, designed "to undertake operations aimed at the heart of Germany and the destruction of her armed forces",[8] was another, known as Operation "Neptune", which was the naval side of "Overlord". And it was "Neptune" that now held the centre of the naval stage. It was to prove the most massive combined operation of the war, and as such its planning was equally massive.

It was, too, beset by difficulties from the start. In General Morgan's original plan the landing was to be made on a three-divisional front, in accordance with the maximum forces allotted to him by the Combined Chiefs of Staff.[9] General Eisenhower, appointed to the post of Supreme Commander early in 1944, and General Montgomery, selected to command the combined British, Canadian, and United States armies during the initial fighting, both asked for an assault on a wider front. From three divisions assaulting from the sea the plan was stepped up to five divisions. The Combined Chiefs of Staff noted their agreement,[10] but failed to indicate the sources from which the increase in shipping and assault craft would come.

This threw an added burden on the Navy, for each additional division required a naval assault force to put it ashore, now making a total of five assault forces in all. The wider front also naturally called for an increased number of escorts, minesweepers, and bombarding ships. Some of this requirement was met by heavy drafts on the Atlantic convoy escorts, the Home Fleet, and the Mediterranean Fleet, as well as by holding back reinforcements destined for the Far Eastern Fleet, but even these could not fill the whole bill. Admiral King, when asked to provide American warships to fill the deficiency, professed himself unable to do so, and for a time the full operation swung in the balance. It was not until 15th April, only seven weeks before D-day, that Admiral King relented. Then he bettered the requirement and promised more ships than were actually needed.

More difficult still of solution was the problem of assault craft. Here, again, there were differences of opinion between London and Washington. It was, perhaps, not easy for the United States authorities, remote from the scene of conflict and unaware of the dislocation that a well-placed bomb in a shipbuilding yard could cause, to realise the difficulties and shortages which existed in Britain. Admiral King's eyes, too, were wandering away from Europe. Although there had been ready agreement, on the grand strategical level, that Germany was the prime enemy and that her defeat must take precedence over that of Japan, it was the Pacific war which was now engaging all Admiral King's attention. There need, indeed, have been no problem in the supply of assault craft for "Neptune" except for the fact that almost the whole of American production in those vessels went straight to the Pacific.

An effort to meet part of the deficiency was made in Britain by postponing for three months the completion of one fleet carrier, four destroyers, and fourteen anti-submarine frigates, in order that the manpower thus engaged might be devoted to the building of assault craft. But even that was not enough to fill the gap. More stringent remedies still were required. "Overlord" was postponed for a month from its initial target date of 1st May in order to obtain the use of one more month's construction, and the complementary landing in the south of France was put back for three months so that the assault craft in the Mediterranean might be brought home for "Neptune". It was with the contribution made by these two delays that "Neptune" was at last mounted on its new and larger scale of assault.

Of increasing importance as the planning developed was the problem of follow-up and supply. The vagaries of English Channel weather were well appreciated in Britain, and since the initial landings and the subsequent maintenance must necessarily be over beaches, the need for calm water was only too obvious. In any operation of such importance as this it was manifestly impossible to gamble on a long, settled spell of weather; therefore steps had to be taken to protect, so far as was humanly possible, the landing-beaches from the caprices of Æolus, the father of the winds. Odysseus knew him from bitter experience as a god with whom it was unwise to trifle; the British planners of "Neptune" were not prepared to run the same risks as Odysseus.

It was planned to provide sheltered water off the five assault beaches by means of an artificial breakwater composed of block-ships, brought across the Channel under their own steam and scuttled in line. These five breakwaters were known as "Gooseberries", the individual ships comprising them as "Corncobs". Two obsolete battleships, two cruisers, and fifty-five merchant ships were used for this purpose. Two of these "Gooseberries", one off the British beaches and one off the American, were then to be developed into artificial harbours. The "Gooseberries" were to be prolonged and turned shorewards by sinking prefabricated caissons of steel and concrete known as "Phoenix", to form two harbours each the size of Dover. In all, 213 caissons were required, of which the largest were 200 feet long, 55 feet wide, and 60 feet high.

Inside these two harbours were floating piers, consisting of articulated steel roadway supported by pontoons, and with specially designed pierheads, anchored to the ground by four legs to keep them in position but free to float up and down with the tide. These piers could deal with all shallow-draft vessels engaged in supply, enabling them to be discharged at all states of the tide. For larger ships an extra breakwater to seaward of the harbours was provided, composed of heavy steel floating structures known as "Bombardons", cruciform in section and each 200 feet long and 25 feet high.

This whole assembly was known as a "Mulberry". They were designed and built in Britain, and in all amounted to the prodigious total of nearly 2,000,000 tons of concrete and steel. With the exception of the original "Corncobs", which proceeded under their own steam, each section was towed across the Channel by tugs and fitted together on the far shore in the manner of a jig-saw puzzle. It was a vast and remarkable undertaking, British both in conception and execution, and although in the end only one of the two planned "Mulberries" became fully operational, it played a prodigious part in the smooth flow of men and materials needed to sustain the campaign. The second "Mulberry", constructed off the American beaches, came to grief in the exceptionally heavy weather which followed the landings.

The full naval plan for "Neptune" embraced some 7,000 ships of all types and sizes. Of these just over 1,200 were warships, ranging from battleships to midget submarines. More than 4,100 landing ships and craft were required to put the armies ashore, a further 735 auxiliary ships and 864 merchant ships were needed to sustain them there. So great an armada required a vast detail of planning to ensure exact and orderly movement of all the ships within their operational areas.

"Neptune" was, above all, a combined operation of all three Services in which it is impossible to consider the naval side without reference to the equally vital tasks of the air and land forces. A great amount of preparatory work was done by the Royal Air Force and the United States Army Air Force in making the assault possible, for an overriding necessity of a successful invasion was complete air mastery over the assault area. This was achieved partly by the wearing down of the *Luftwaffe* in day and night air operations over France, the Low Countries, and Germany, and partly by a sustained attack on enemy radar posts and early warning systems. This, however, was not all. Another requirement for success was the Allied need to build up their forces on the Continent faster than the enemy could reinforce his, and in this, too, the air forces were to play a vital part. Between mid-April and the first week in June they carried out the "Transportation" plan, bombing rail centres, marshalling yards, repair shops, engine sheds, and the like. Although it was not possible to stop all railway traffic, enough damage was done to slow it up very considerably. As D-day approached, this attack was broadened to include important bridges, road and rail, leading to the battle area.

Another task of the airmen, in this case of Coastal Command, was the patrol of the south-western approaches to the Channel in an anti-shipping and anti-submarine role. Similar anti-shipping patrols were flown over the southern North Sea and anti-U-boat patrols over the northern exit to the Atlantic. It was an endless, day-after-day, night-after-night task, often unrewarding in terms of ships or U-boats sighted, yet it helped to keep clear the crucial stretch of sea over which the armies were to be carried. The German Admiral commanding in western Europe, Vice-Admiral Krancke, noted that his ships "were almost invariably attacked from the air as soon as they left harbour and suffered numerous hits . . . darkness provided no relief".[11]

Thus it was that the way was made safe for the launching of invasion. By the end of May everything possible in the way of preparation for the greatest adventure of the war had been done. Even the day had been selected. In compliance with Army requirements for conditions of landing a date had to be chosen on which the tide would still have three hours of rise at the time of sunrise, with a good moon on the preceding night to aid the airborne troops in finding their objectives. Three days in June fulfilled these varied requirements, the 5th, 6th, and 7th. On 23rd May a signal was sent from General Eisenhower's Headquarters to the operational Commanders-in-Chief. When deciphered it read: "Exercise Hornpipe Bigot Halcyon Y plus four." Hornpipe meant "Overlord". Bigot was a code word used to express the highest degree of secrecy, Halcyon indicated D-day, and Y had been fixed as 1st June. The signal thus fixed D-day as 5th June.

With this decision made, Operation "Neptune" began to get into its stride. Ships waiting in the northern ports of Britain put to sea to start their long voyage to the shores of Normandy. They were the "Corncobs" to form the breakwaters and those of the bombarding ships which were lying at Scapa and in the Clyde. On 2nd June two midget submarines slipped out of Portsmouth Harbour to identify and lie off the narrow beaches on the other side and, on the morning of D-day, to act as markers for the assault convoys. On the 3rd the bombarding force for the American beaches sailed from Belfast, and the first assault convoys set out from the West Country ports of Dartmouth, Brixham, and Salcombe. The whole intricate naval plan was slipping into gear and accelerating as the hours before D-day dwindled.

Out in the Channel on 3rd June the wind began to increase, knocking up a choppy sea. Low cloud swept across the sky, typical forerunner to a Channel storm. The assault convoys already at sea were soon making heavy weather of it and many of the soldiers on board were beginning to suffer from seasickness. As the day advanced, the weather grew steadily worse and the meteorologists on the Supreme Commander's staff were pessimistic. That night a worried General Eisenhower consulted his sea, land, and air commanders, but decided to delay any postponement decision until the following morning. The ships at sea continued their passages towards France, and more and more assault craft were manned and loaded and put to sea as the momentum of Operation "Neptune" gathered force.

Early on the Sunday morning of 4th June General Eisenhower was again in conference with his commanders. The forecast made by the meteorologists on the preceding day was confirmed, if anything the weather would get worse still on the 5th. It could be ignored no longer, and D-day was postponed for twenty-four hours, with the prospect of a still further postponement if the weather experts were to be believed.

So far advanced now was Operation "Neptune" that this postponement could not fail to cause extreme difficulty. Convoys at sea were recalled and directed to sheltered anchorages; warships were ordered to reverse course for a period but to remain at sea. By nightfall on the 4th every convoy, with one exception, had been accounted for and was either back at anchor or on the way home. The exception was an assault convoy of 128 tank landing-craft with nine escorts. It had not received the postponement signal and was still heading for the beaches at the base of the Cotentin Peninsula, which it would reach at dawn on the morning of the 5th. It was finally stopped by a naval aircraft sent out from Portsmouth, and was ordered to return and refuel.

All through Sunday the weather grew worse. The Admiralty issued a gale warning to shipping in the Irish Sea during the morning, and outside General Eisenhower's headquarters at Portsmouth, when the Allied commanders met again that night, a boisterous wind and driving rain indicated a rough and stormy night in the Channel. Yet, surprisingly enough, the report of the weather experts was reassuring. It was forecasted that the storm would clear by the Monday morning and that the ensuing fair weather would last at least over the Tuesday. General Eisenhower decided to hold another meeting at four o'clock on Monday morning and, if the forecast were still favourable, to hold to Tuesday, 6th June, as D-day. But for Admiral Ramsay the decision was a more difficult one. To arrive at the beaches across the Channel during the early hours of 6th June meant that the first naval movements must start at once. It meant that he had to risk the weather, and as soon as he reached his own headquarters he gave the order for Operation "Neptune" to proceed.[12]

It was as well that he did so, for at the meeting on Monday morning the meteorologists confirmed their opinions of Sunday night. While the weather would be by no means ideal, it would be possible. At 4.30 a.m. General Eisenhower gave the order to go ahead and the whole force of invasion swung once more into action. From every port on the south coast of Britain, and from some on the east, a stream of ships and assault craft flowed continuously into the waters of the English Channel. The men on board, soldiers and sailors alike, were on the whole quiet and thoughtful but in good heart, for all doubts were now at rest. This was the great adventure for which they had been so assiduously trained. The endless exercises were over; and this was invasion.

There was a disturbed sea still running in the Channel with a fresh wind blowing, but as the hours of 5th June passed the wind began to drop and the sea to moderate. Nevertheless, there was still a good deal of seasickness, though even this could not damp the ardent spirits of the men. Admiral Vian, commanding the eastern task force which was to support the British landings, was full of praise for the men. "Their spirit and seamanship", he wrote, "alike rose to meet the greatness of the hour, and they pressed forward in high heart and resolution; there was no faltering and many of the smaller craft were driven on until they foundered."[13]

Every possible precaution had been taken. Down to the south-west, squadrons of Coastal Command were on patrol to guard against any influx of U-boats into the assault area. Over the convoys flew an umbrella of fighters, while further squadrons of Coastal Command carried out anti-E-boat patrols. Ahead of the convoys were flotillas of minesweepers, clearing the approach routes for the assault craft and their support squadrons.

As the ships swept on in the darkness towards their goal on the opposite coast of the Channel the troops on board could hear overhead the roar of engines of the transport aircraft, some towing the gliders of the airborne divisions, others laden with parachute troops for their drop on to objectives ashore. They were followed by a great fleet of heavy bombers on their way to pound the coastal batteries. It was a heartening sound as the small assault craft laboured in the acute discomfort of a heavy sea. Finally, as the first light of a grey dawn began to tinge the eastern horizon, two dim green lights were sighted ahead, marking the British beaches. The time was a minute or two after five o'clock.

The green lights were shown by the midget submarines *X20* and *X23*, which had lain submerged off the Normandy coast since their arrival there during the night of 3rd June. They had sailed before the postponement of the operation, and the endurance of their crews as they lay submerged in the extreme discomfort of their tiny craft for twenty-four hours longer than had been expected was beyond praise. The lights that they showed, visible only from seaward, led in the British bombarding squadrons to their allotted anchoring positions.

As the dawn came up on the morning of the 6th it became possible for the naval commanders of the assault forces to make an appreciation of the night's work. In the assault convoys there had been a few casualties because of the stress of weather, but they were remarkably few and in general the convoys were arriving punctually and accurately in their planned positions. Overhead, even at this early hour, a swarm of fighters gave effective air cover; others, unseen from the ships, ranged over northern France beyond the immediate target area to harass any enemy movements. The whole scene was a most heartening one for the assault troops, for almost as far as the eye could see the surface of the sea was covered with thousands of Allied ships and craft, while the skies above were filled with Allied fighters. So overwhelming a concentration of power could hardly fail to command success.

Behind all the men, all the ships, and all the aircraft which formed the assault force on this June morning, there lay the long battle of the oceans, whose success alone had made possible the conditions of overall superiority in which they could gather in such huge numbers off the beaches of Normandy. Here was to be seen the climax of all the years of bitter fighting at sea; and here was proof of the ability to transfer the victory won in the oceans into its final decisive phase of a victory won across the land.

Even more extraordinary, perhaps, was the fact that tactical surprise had been achieved. During the night it had seemed impossible that so great a concourse of ships moving towards the invasion beaches, their numbers running into thousands, could have escaped observation. Even the minesweepers, which had been at work off the French coast during the night, had done their task unchallenged. Yet there was the evidence, almost unbelievable perhaps but none the less true, lying before the eyes of the naval commanders as they looked out in the dawn over the waters. There lay the ships of the invasion fleet and the enemy had shown no single sign of activity.

At 5.30 a.m. the guns of the bombarding squadrons opened fire on the coastal fortifications. At the same time a heavy bombing attack by American day bombers was directed upon the same targets. The coastal fringe of Normandy erupted into a sheet of flame, behind which the assault craft made for the shore. In the van of the invasion force were landing-craft carrying amphibious tanks, support craft specially armed with naval guns ranging from 4.7-inch downwards, others with rockets, followed by further assault forces of infantry, artillery, and engineers. With them went the special parties of seamen and Royal Engineers whose task it was to clear the underwater obstructions, most of them with mines attached, with which the enemy had strewn the beaches. This was one of the reasons for stipulating a state of half-tide for the initial assault, for at high water these obstructions were covered and their removal wellnigh impossible.

As the invasion craft neared the water's edge the rocket assault craft, known as "Hedgerows" and manned by Royal Marines, closed in. Each could fire a thousand 5-inch rockets within the space of ninety seconds. In the three British sectors some 20,000 rockets were fired, and in the two American about 18,000. They curved away from the assault craft to deluge the beaches in a devastating burst. Destroyers, moving in close to the shore, added to the din of explosion with the fire of their 4.7-inch guns as they sealed the flanks of the landings. The first wave of landing-craft touched down in France and the soldiers waded ashore in the wake of the tanks.

Wave after wave followed. There was a good deal of opposition at first, for the bombardment from sea and air, indescribably heavy as it had been, had not silenced every enemy weapon. It was not, however, sufficiently heavy to hold up the landing, and the remaining beach defences were either overrun by the advancing troops or subdued by direct fire from guns already ashore or from supporting ships at sea.

On the British beaches as a whole the landings were accurate and successful, though inevitably here and there unforeseen difficulties held up for a time the break-out from the beaches. Individual calls for supporting fire from the ships increased as the day wore on, and they did much to subdue those enemy strong-points which were still holding out against the initial assault. But as the sun rose higher in the sky on this morning of 6th June there was room for sober satisfaction on the way that all three Services, combining together in this massive operation, had carried through their initial tasks. There was, however, still a long way to go before the beachhead could be called secure.

The American landings farther west were not so uniformly successful. On one of their two beaches they were virtually unopposed and the leading troops made good progress inland, though held up in places by flooded fields ashore. But on the other beach there was considerable confusion. The assault craft bunched badly on the way in, the amphibious tanks were given so long a swim to the shore that most of them foundered before reaching the beach, and the troops as they landed were met with a withering fire from the German defenders which pinned them down among the breakers. Confusion was made worse by the launching of succeeding waves of assault craft while the first was still bunched off the beach, until the whole became a milling mass in which little semblance of order remained. Wind and tide, both strong, added to the difficulties, and a lack of adequate training by the assault-craft leaders led to many errors in navigation.[14]

Yet out of chaos, order finally emerged. With much gallantry small parties of American soldiers, braving the heavy fire and the mine-strewn beach, broke through the defence into the open country beyond. They were then able to work round and to silence the German posts and so make easier the landings of the follow-up troops.

Thus it was that the great assault was made. In spite of difficult conditions of wind and sea some thousands of ships and craft, some large but many very small, had been navigated across a hundred miles of Channel and brought to their journey's end with remarkable accuracy and precision. During this first day, which included the breaking down of Hitler's much vaunted "Atlantic Wall", more than 130,000 men were landed from the sea, together with their equipment and stores. That was surprisingly good, but more surprising still was the almost complete absence over the landing-areas of the *Luftwaffe*, a fine tribute to the overwhelming command of the air won by the British and United States Air Forces. And most surprising of all, perhaps, was the fact that a vast concourse of ships could cross the narrow waters of the Channel and still achieve tactical surprise. Land, sea, and air commanders kept returning to that extraordinary fact, still hardly able to believe that it had really been accomplished.

Only in one aspect did the landing cause some apprehension, and that was in the losses of the landing-craft. The beach obstacles, laid with such thoroughness by the enemy along the half-tide mark, had caused many casualties as the craft went in. As the tide rose during the morning the task of removal had to be postponed except for the labour of some naval frogmen able to continue the work under water. Later in the morning, with the falling tide exposing them again, full work on their removal was resumed. It proved a tremendous and dangerous job, for the enemy had not lacked thoroughness in the preparation of these seaward defences. They were mostly made of steel and concrete, and the majority of them had fused shells or mines attached. But by the end of the day the work was completed and the assault craft could now come in to the beaches without fear of their bottoms being ripped out or shattered by explosions.

For the next seven weeks the naval bombarding forces, or a proportion of them, remained in the assault area ready to fire at call on objectives as required by the armies. But the greater naval task now was to organise and transport the follow-up formations and their supplies, a constant procession of men and materials arriving to nourish the momentum of invasion. Until the Mulberry Harbour came into operation on 9th July everything had to be landed over the beaches, with the exception of very small numbers of men through the little harbours of St. Laurent and Arromanches. The 500,000th man, the 77,000th vehicle, and the 150,000th ton of stores were all landed on 15th June, nine days after the initial landing, and on 6th July, exactly one month after D-day, the millionth man stepped ashore. Eight days later the millionth ton of stores and the 250,000th vehicle were landed. This rate of build-up would have been even greater had it not been for a gale which blew in the Channel from 19th to 21st June and reduced landings to a trickle. It is figures such as these which, perhaps, best illustrate the immensity of the naval task.

All the time that this great cross-Channel movement of men and weapons and supplies was going on, the invasion area had to be sealed off from attack by the enemy. It was from the west that the heaviest threat was expected, for it was in the Biscay ports that the main concentrations of U-boats and destroyers lay. The waters of the western approaches to the Channel were covered by no fewer than ten escort groups of destroyers, frigates, and sloops, while the sky above was patrolled by the maximum strength which Coastal Command could muster for the occasion. As the U-boats moved up in their bid to dislocate the maritime movements across the Channel, they met the full force of this anti-submarine shield. Many were sunk and more damaged, in spite of their new "Schnorkel" fitting which enabled them to make the whole passage submerged with only the top of the breathing tube above water. No more than four or five managed to slip through, and they achieved little before they were themselves rounded up and sunk.

The main forms of naval opposition used by the enemy were motor torpedo boats and mines; later in the operation "human torpedoes", long-range circling torpedoes, and explosive motor-boats made their appearance. They all had a few successes, but the whole opposition was on too small a scale materially to affect the operation. The elaborate Allied defensive arrangements at sea, with day and night patrols of destroyers and motor torpedo boats, gave the enemy little chance to organise any serious opposition in the invasion area. At best it was hardly more than spasmodic. The greatest nuisance, perhaps, was caused by a new type of mine, known as the "Oyster", actuated by the pressure wave of a passing ship and unsweepable by any existing method.

This tremendous superiority in the Channel, both on sea and in the air, gave to the armies ashore their golden chance, in the words of the directive to General Eisenhower, to "enter the continent of Europe and, in conjunction with other United Nations, undertake operations aimed at the heart of Germany and the destruction of her armed forces".[15] That they seized that chance and made the most of it is now a part of history and beyond the scope of this account. Nourished across the seas by an increasing volume of supplies and armaments, they overcame in fierce fighting the initial crust of German opposition and then swept away across Europe in an electrifying dash towards Germany, through France, Belgium, and Holland. And in that advance, they captured the great prize of Antwerp, a valuable modern port, virtually undamaged, and through which the burden of military supply could be channelled for yet further operations towards the east.

The armies' bound forward inevitably brought in its train a similar move forward for the Navy. Isolated pockets of resistance in the coastal towns were subdued by the guns of the fleet, the blocked harbours were cleared by naval port parties as soon as they were captured, and the offshore waters were swept clear of mines. Work of this nature extended westward as well as eastward as the coasts of France were liberated from the enemy's hold. All through these naval movements to east and west there was opposition from small enemy units, including a number of midget submarines. Though it could not affect the expanding British hold on these continental waters, it yet had a considerable nuisance value and caused many losses in small craft.

Antwerp, which had been captured on 4th September, remained unused as a supply port for some weeks, in spite of its obvious value as such. The military operations to capture the bridges across the Lower Rhine by airborne assaults at Eindhoven,

Nijmegen, and Arnhem held up the clearance of Antwerp, a delay which enabled the Germans to reinforce the east bank of the River Scheldt in considerable strength and which was to cost the Navy a savage and bloody battle. The port itself lies some thirty-five miles up the River Scheldt, the entrance to which is commanded on the eastern side by the islands of South Beveland and Walcheren. During the last week in October the Canadians, assisted by a British amphibious landing on the south coast, pushed into South Beveland and by the end of the month were in control of the whole island. There remained Walcheren. Only with its capture could the great port of Antwerp be used. The low-lying island, its centre protected from the sea by high banks, had been extensively fortified by the Germans and its guns commanded the waters of the Scheldt estuary, effectively barring them to the entrance of Allied ships. The protective dyke had been breached by Royal Air Force bombers in an earlier attack at West Kapelle, on the western side of the island, and as a result most of the interior of the island was under water.

A three-pronged attack on Walcheren was planned for 1st November. The Canadians in South Beveland were to attack across the causeway which linked the two islands, while an assault crossing of the Scheldt was to be made by Royal Marines, directed on Flushing. But the main operation for the capture of the island was to be a Royal Marine Commando landing, mounted from Ostend and directed on West Kapelle, where the breach in the dyke gave a good chance of getting ashore.

The attack on Flushing, supported by artillery from the south bank of the Scheldt, got away to a good start and by noon, after four hours of fighting, the Royal Marines had a firm bridgehead on the island. By the following afternoon they had occupied half of Flushing and were clearing the dock area. The whole of the town was in their possession by the evening of the 3rd.

The West Kapelle assault was a much more serious proposition, for there lay the main weight of the German defences, centred on several batteries of 6-inch guns, well protected in concrete emplacements on the sea wall. A naval support force, comprising the battleship *Warspite*, and the monitors *Roberts* and *Erebus*, was provided for heavy bombardment of the German defences, while the assault craft of the Royal Marine Commandos were also accompanied by a close-support squadron of twenty-five converted landing-craft variously armed with guns and rockets. A heavy air attack on the German batteries, together with close air support of the landing, was also to have been provided but had to be cancelled on the morning of the assault because of fog over the airfields. This was doubly unfortunate, for it also deprived the bombarding ships of air spotting for their fall of shot.

As it approached the island under the lowering grey skies of a typical November morning, the assault force was heavily engaged by the enemy batteries. In order to draw this fire away from the Royal Marine Commandos, the close-support squadron stood in to point-blank range, their guns and rockets firing. Every enemy battery that could be brought to bear was concentrated on them. Their casualties were tremendous, and of the twenty-five landing-craft engaged in the support role no fewer than fourteen were lost. By their gallantry and determination in pressing home this attack they drew the brunt of the enemy's fire, and the Commandos were able to get ashore in their tank landing-craft without undue difficulty or loss.

All through the day the heavy ships of the bombarding squadron carried out intermittent unobserved fire on the batteries, nine of them being engaged by this means. Some were silenced, but in the prevailing conditions it fell to the Royal Marines ashore to deal with the majority, and this they did in exemplary fashion, though it called for much savage and bitter fighting.

By 3rd November most of the opposition in Walcheren had been overcome, though spasmodic opposition continued in some areas for a further two days. The importance of Walcheren did not lie, however, in the possession of the island but in the waters which it controlled, the waters which led to the port of Antwerp. As soon as the last German battery was silenced on 3rd November, the mine-sweepers gathered in the estuary and began their task of clearing a channel to Antwerp. A small force of them reached the city during the afternoon of the 4th, having detonated six ground mines on the way up. On the 5th they began the systematic sweeping of the docks and the river, both known to be extensively mined. For three weeks they were engaged on this difficult and intricate task, to see their reward on the 26th in the safe arrival at Antwerp of three coasters from England. Two days later a convoy of eighteen Liberty ships sailed up the Scheldt in perfect safety and berthed in the port. Thenceforward Antwerp became the main supply base of the Allied armies, sustaining them through the winter campaign along the left bank of the Rhine and, in the spring of 1945, in their crossing of the Rhine and their advance through Germany.

The port was kept open only with difficulty. E-boats, operating from Dutch bases, made continual forays into the estuary, occasionally attacking ships but more often engaged in minelaying. One- and two-men midget submarines were also sent into these waters to attack Allied shipping, though with little success and considerable loss to themselves. The battle to keep the estuary open and the merchant ships moving steadily up to the port was continuous, for the Germans never gave up their efforts to dislocate this vital seaborne traffic.

All through these closing months of 1944, and, indeed, until the end of the war, the naval pressure on Germany was increased. Sweeps along the Norwegian coast and inside the Norwegian Leads were carried out at frequent intervals whenever the weather was favourable, making the movement of enemy supply ships almost impossibly hazardous. Far and wide ranged British warships in their search for the enemy, keeping him always on the run, always uncertain and apprehensive of the next attack. And almost daily the margin of naval superiority grew, even though a substantial portion of the fleet, as the war in Europe drew towards its inevitable end, was sent to reinforce British squadrons in the Far East.

On the morning of 1st May, 1945, ships of the Home Fleet left Scapa to carry out what proved to be their last offensive operation of the European war. Their main targets were the U-boat depot ships at Kilbotn, to the north-west of Narvik. Two cruisers—the *Norfolk* and *Diadem*—three escort carriers—the *Searcher*, *Queen*, and *Trumpeter*—and five destroyers were engaged, all under the command of Vice-Admiral McGrigor, and they reached the flying-off positions on the morning of 5th May. Conditions were perfect as the Avengers and Wildcats went in from the carriers. The depot ship *Black Watch* was hit with eight bombs and exploded in a sheet of flame, a nearby tanker was destroyed, and *U.711*, discovered under way at Harstad, was sunk. Well satisfied, the ships turned for home and were still at sea when they received the signal announcing the unconditional surrender of Germany. As they came in sight of the coast of Britain on the night of the 8th the lights in the houses were shining out to sea.

In waters nearer home the closing months of 1944 and the first four months of 1945 had seen a recrudescence of the U-boat warfare. The adoption of the Schnorkel breathing-tube had brought to the U-boats two great advantages: the ability to charge their batteries while still submerged and the elimination of the danger of discovery by radar, for the top of the Schnorkel tube was too small a target to reflect a recognisable radar return. With this protection, it was mainly in the waters around Britain that they now sought their victims.

It was a move that cut both ways. The seas around the British coasts are strewn with wrecks, every one of which provided an asdic echo. With so large a measure of naval and air superiority there was no difficulty in providing a reasonable number of anti-submarine groups and Coastal Command squadrons to cover the area, but their task was made the more difficult by the asdic echoes from wrecks. Each one had to be examined and classified as non-submarine before being abandoned. From the air the task was equally difficult, for radar could no longer give the answer and a Schnorkel was not easily distinguished by eye. But the U-boats, too, had their difficulties, for the problem of moving large numbers of ships in confined waters in the face of a heavy concentration of U-boats was handled by Admiral Horton, Commander-in-Chief Western Approaches, with supreme skill. All the knowledge and experience gained during the anti-submarine war was distilled into a brilliant solution of the problems of this little inshore campaign.

The waters of the Western Approaches, from the Minches down to the Fastnet Rock, were divided into three areas, in each of which a support group operated. Two, or even three, convoys were amalgamated into one, and sailed as required. Not only did this reduce the density of shipping in these waters, it also increased the numbers of escorts available for each convoy and as a result made protection from attack more certain. There were, in addition, the three support groups in their areas. As each convoy entered an area, the support group augmented the escort and took the convoy down to the next area, where it was handed over to the next support group. It was a system that provided, at one and the same time, the maximum protection to the convoys and the minimum number of targets to the U-boats.

There was little that the U-boats could do. The density of air cover forced them to lie on the bottom (they usually chose a wreck alongside which to lie) and to rely on a hydrophone watch to warn them of an approaching convoy. More often than not they found, when coming to periscope depth to investigate, that the convoy was too strongly guarded or had already passed out of range. They had their successes in an occasional ship sunk on the British doorstep; they had their losses when, from time to time, they were discovered and sunk. Throughout the period the exchange rate remained at approximately one U-boat destroyed for every merchant ship they sank.

But for them, too, the time was running out, although they never gave up trying. During April 1945 the tonnage sunk by U-boats in the Atlantic and in the coastal waters of Britain was the heaviest since the previous August. On the reverse side of the picture was the fact that the number of U-boats destroyed during April, and during the first eight days of May, reached record totals. It was, perhaps, an overstatement when, as late as 17th April, 1945, the Secretary of the United States Navy, in evidence before a Congressional Committee, said: "The German submarine menace round the British Isles is now very serious, because the enemy is trying to cripple the supply lines to Europe."[16] Nevertheless, they created a problem right up to the end, even though they must have recognised, as April drew to its close, that the capacity of Germany to continue the fight was to be measured now only in days. The last two merchant ships to be destroyed by the U-boats were sunk in the Firth of Forth on the night of 7th May, the very last night of hostilities. The last U-boat to be sunk was *U.320*, destroyed off the Norwegian coast by a Coastal Command Catalina on the morning of the same day.

It was fortunate for the Allies that the war ended when it did, for the new design of U-boat with long endurance and high underwater speed, on which the enemy was pinning high hopes, was approaching operational use. Its advent would certainly have posed a difficult problem for the anti-submarine forces, and one to which at the time there was no certain answer. Although, of course, it had come far too late to influence the course of the war at sea, it could certainly have made a considerable nuisance of itself in operations against Allied shipping had it ever appeared at sea.

Under the terms of the surrender, U-boats at sea were ordered to surface, to report their positions, and to proceed by fixed routes to prescribed ports. Every eight hours these orders were broadcast both in plain language and in the U-boat cipher by the German authorities. Early on the 9th the first U-boat complied and was ordered to a Scottish port. Others followed until, by 1st June, the seas were reckoned to be clear. A couple of U-boats were still unaccounted for, but in the end they too made belated surrenders, one at Mar del Plata, Argentina, on 10th July, the other at the same port on 17th August. This last U-boat, *U.977*, had been off Norway when she heard the surrender signal but had made the long journey to Argentina, much of it below the surface, in order to avoid surrendering to the Allies. It made no difference, for at the end Argentina, too, had declared war on Germany and the U-boat was promptly handed over to the United States Navy.

The end in Europe came quietly, almost with a sense of anticlimax for having been so long apparent from the scale of the Allied victories in Germany. It would be an over-simplification to suggest that the Allies were carried to victory on the back of their maritime power, although in the final analysis it was maritime power that made possible the Allied victory. The apparent paradox can be explained by the fact that, in modern war, the true exercise of maritime power depends nearly as much upon the exertions of land and air forces as it does upon naval. The pattern of sea power is so closely interwoven with air and land power that often the boundaries between them merge into each other.

It had been a remarkable campaign, showing a reversion from the continental strategy of 1914–18 to the traditional maritime strategy of an island nation. The evil days of the First World War, with vast armies locked in close combat and with casualties counted in the millions, had given way to the wiser concept of utilising the resilience of sea power, now backed with air power, to the limit of its usefulness. It had been at times a desperately close affair, and there had been periods when the control of the oceans, on which the whole edifice of Allied strategy stood, had looked like slipping from the Allied grasp. Those storms, however, had been weathered, and as the naval strength at sea grew, so the grip upon the Axis had been tightened. It was as though an invisible barrier had been thrown around the Axis powers, maintained by the maritime forces of the Allied nations and cutting off Germany and Italy from the outside world. And gradually, with the growing Allied strength at sea, that barrier had been moved ever closer in until, behind its shield, the armies had been launched on their chosen battlefields to finish off the job.

It was the end of a chapter in European history. Once again, as so often in past campaigns, the Navy had emerged from its ordeal to see its work crowned by overwhelming victory on land. But the Navy's work was not finished yet. Even as the guns in Europe grew silent, naval eyes had already turned to the East. There, across the oceans on the other side of the world, the curtain was up for the final act of another great drama. Two British Fleets were already there to play their part in the action and, with the downfall of Germany, more ships were on the way.

# Chapter 14

## THE SETTING OF THE RISING SUN

THE vast Japanese advance of 1942 had brought in its train dominion over a wide area of south-east Asia and over the chain of islands running down towards Australia. Java had fallen into their eager grasp after the defeat of Admiral Doorman's hastily assembled squadron in the battle of the Java Sea on 27th February, 1942. In April they completed their conquest of Burma, and their raid into the Indian Ocean during that same month proved that they had as yet little to fear from the newly constituted British Eastern Fleet under Admiral Somerville.

So far their strategy had been supremely successful. Based initially upon surprise and political deceit, they had been able to follow up their first outstanding success at Pearl Harbour with an advance so swift that it swept the Allies off balance and gave them no chance to recover it. Each new step forward was preceded by the capture or construction of airfields, so that all through their long march forward there was ample cover from land-based aircraft for the Japanese assault forces. To this simple strategy the Allies, disorganised by defeat, had no answer.

It was at this stage of the campaign that the Japanese first began to run into difficulties. They had made their great gains with ridiculous ease, but to consolidate them was another matter. The Japanese plan was to deny to the Allies those bases in the Pacific from which offensive operations might be possible against them, and it was in the execution of this plan that Japan took her first steps along the downward path. It was basically unsound in that it stretched the new "empire" far beyond the capacity of Japanese sea and air power to maintain, and thus opened the door to Allied initiative.

This expansion in search of an outer defence line led the Japanese northward to the Aleutian Islands, eastward to Midway Island, and southward through eastern New Guinea and the Solomon Islands. Two landings were made in the Aleutians, yet although they led to much spasmodic fighting in the icy and foggy waters of the northern Pacific, they had small effect on the campaign as a whole. To neither side did these inhospitable islands prove of much value.

Midway, however, had been a very different affair. There, as described on p. 253, four Japanese carriers had been sunk, the *Soryu*, *Kaga*, *Akagi*, and *Hiryu*, and with them went most of the Japanese hopes of holding the Americans at bay.[1] This was the turning-point in the Pacific War, reversing completely the strategic situation in that ocean. It did more than save Midway Island as an important American base, for it brought to an abrupt end the Japanese offensive phase and thereafter placed them squarely on the defensive. Four carriers, 250 naval aircraft, and 100 well-trained pilots were a crippling loss to the Japanese, all the more so as they formed the backbone of the striking force on which Japan relied to repulse American attacks on her new "co-prosperity sphere". Japanese industrial capacity was already so strained that replacement of the four lost carriers was beyond their powers; that of America so flexible that, a little over a year later, more than fifty carriers were in commission.

The battle of Midway had repercussions, too, far away to the south, where the Japanese were setting up their defensive outposts in the Solomon Islands. This was an area vital to both sides. To the Japanese it was a doorway to New Caledonia, Fiji, and Samoa, with all that that meant in the threat to Allied supplies; to the Allies it was the first stepping-stone in the planned offensive through New Guinea to the Philippines. Moreover, it was a position of great strategic importance, for it lay close to the main supply route between the United States and their forward bases in New Zealand and Australia. In Japanese possession the Solomons could prove an impossible bar to progress; as an Allied base the vital shipping on the main supply route would be safeguarded.

As at Midway, the Japanese played into Allied hands. During their rapid advance southward at the outbreak of the war their strategy had been wellnigh faultless, making certain of local air superiority before bringing forward their assault and occupation forces. But in the case of the Solomons they were in a hurry. They had an air base at Rabaul, in New Britain, some 700 miles from Guadalcanal, but it was too far away to provide cover for its initial capture. The Japanese troops leapt ahead of their air support, and it was that which gave the Allies their chance. The loss of the four carriers at Midway was now to cost the Japanese dear.

The Allied decision to attack in the Solomons was taken only just in time, for Japanese airfields were under construction both in Bougainville, halfway between Rabaul and Guadalcanal, and at Guadalcanal itself. Had that at Guadalcanal been in use—and it was within a few hours of completion when American troops landed on 7th August, 1942—the result might have been very different.

The key to the Solomon Islands campaign was this Guadalcanal airfield. It was captured by an American amphibious force at the outset and United States aircraft were operating from it within two or three weeks. It was successfully defended against persistent and bitter attacks launched with all the ferocity and suicidal courage for which the Japanese were noted. It was defended, moreover, in spite of a severe naval defeat on the second night of the campaign, which for a time forced the withdrawal of all Allied shipping from these waters.

This was the battle of Savo Island, fought on the night of 8th/9th August. It had been widely thought in the United States, and promulgated in many Intelligence reports, that the Japanese were inexperienced in night fighting. The United States Pacific Fleet itself had no night-fighting instructions and was ignorant of the techniques and tactics. It may be that this faulty assessment of the enemy, coupled with their own lack of experience, produced less than the requisite watchfulness at sea during the dark hours. But whatever the cause, any suggestions that the Japanese were incapable of night action were very quickly removed after the battle.

The transport anchorage off Guadalcanal, from which the American soldiers and their supplies were landed on the island, was guarded from seaward by four United States and two Australian heavy cruisers, together with a few American destroyers. During the hours of darkness these ships withdrew from the immediate anchorage area and patrolled the approaches to it north and south of Savo Island. On the evening of the 8th Rear-Admiral Crutchley, in command of the cruisers and with his flag flying in the *Australia*, had been called to a conference with the American admiral. In his absence the other five cruisers—H.M.A.S. *Canberra* and the United States cruisers *Chicago*, *Vincennes*, *Quincy*, and *Astoria*—were carrying out the night patrol off Savo Island. They were in two divisions, covering adjacent patrol areas.

Unseen, and totally unexpected, a Japanese squadron of seven cruisers steamed down between the two divisions. They passed within 500 yards of the American destroyer *Blue*, which was on radar patrol, without being sighted by her. The first intimation of their presence was a salvo of torpedoes fired at the *Canberra* and *Chicago*. Almost immediately afterwards the *Vincennes*, *Quincy*, and *Astoria* came under heavy and accurate gunfire. They were all set on fire and sunk. The *Canberra*, too, was blazing and sank an hour or so later. Of the five Allied cruisers, only the *Chicago* escaped to reach port, badly damaged by a torpedo hit.[2]

In this one blow the Allied command of the seas around Guadalcanal had been lost. The inevitable result was the withdrawal of the ships of the amphibious forces, leaving the American marines already ashore without naval support. For a time supplies could only be carried to them by destroyers operating at night, and that they managed to hold out, and eventually to win their long and bitter battle, is remarkable testimony to their fortitude and endurance.

For six months the Japanese continued their efforts to regain the vital Guadalcanal airfield. It was not until the first week in February 1943 that they finally owned themselves beaten and withdrew the last of their men.

This American occupation of the Solomons, so dearly bought,

enabled them to proceed with the great series of offensive moves which was to lead in the end to the downfall of Japan. It was based entirely on maritime power, which is the modern combination of control at sea and of the air above it, and it stands out, perhaps, as the classic example of a great campaign won by the flexibility in attack which this command of the sea and air brings in its train. The vastness of American production and the prodigality of supplies of all types with which they sustained their great forces in the Pacific gave them the ability to fight for and to win the control of the oceans on which their chosen strategy depended.

Two main axes of advance were followed. One, under the overall command of General MacArthur, was directed north-westward with its ultimate goal in the Philippine Islands. The second, under Admiral Nimitz, drove westward from Hawaii behind a screen of carriers. It cut across the line of the Japanese sea communications with their newly-won gains in the south, and thus complemented General MacArthur's advance by permitting him to by-pass Japanese outposts in the certain knowledge that American sea and air power could deny them the supplies on which they depended. This by-passing strategy, advancing north-westward towards the Japanese home islands in a series of great forward bounds, had the inestimable advantage of short-circuiting the necessity of a long, slogging battle up the chain of Japanese-controlled islands. It did not matter that strong enemy bases were left unattacked in the rear, for the overwhelming United States sea power in the Pacific made sure that they would perish of attrition by cutting off their supplies.

The vast distances in the Pacific over which the Japanese war was fought called for a new technique in the art of keeping fleets at sea. This was achieved by the Americans with the provision of an extensive fleet train which formed, in effect, a floating base a hundred miles or so behind the scene of operations. By thus giving to the warships facilities for repair, re-fuelling, re-ammunitioning, and even recreation in the vicinity of battle, the fleet could remain at sea and carry out offensive operations for periods of from six to eight weeks without the need of shore bases. It was a practice that was followed by the British Pacific Fleet when it made its appearance in those waters, though its fleet train, for economic reasons, had to be far less elaborate than that of the Americans.

It was, however, in the Indian Ocean, where British naval strength was predominant, that the main British contribution to the defeat of Japan was eventually made. The loss of Singapore and the

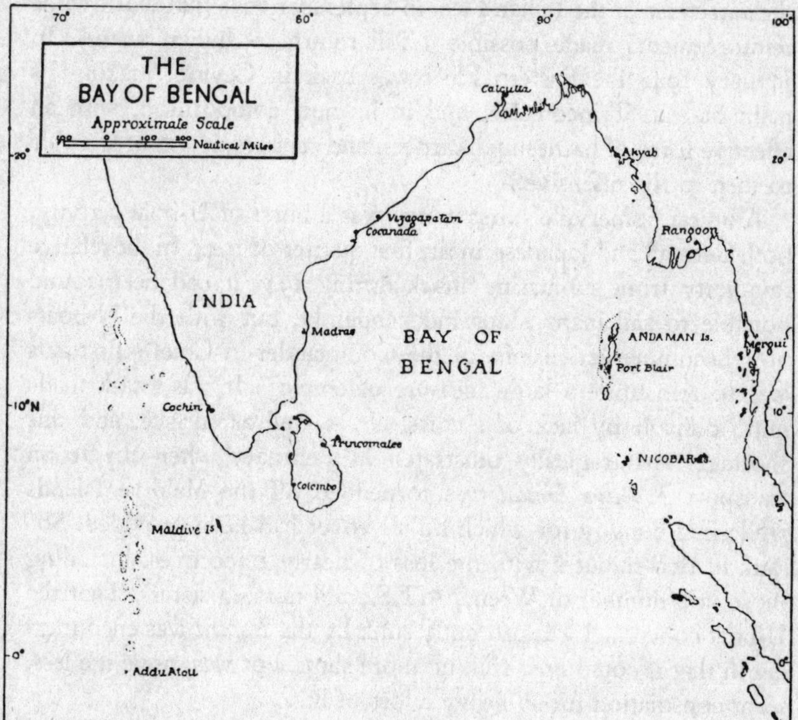


Japanese occupation of Burma in 1942 had deprived the British Eastern Fleet of all its bases in the Indian Ocean with the exception of Colombo and Trincomalee, in Ceylon. Even these bases had to be given up after the Japanese raids in April 1942 which resulted in the sinking of the carrier *Hermes* and the cruisers *Cornwall* and *Dorsetshire*. Admiral Somerville had then withdrawn the fleet to

Kilindini, and the Japanese had been left in unquestioned command of the Bay of Bengal.

The return of British sea power into these eastern waters could be made only by stages as and when ships became available from the more important European theatre. The capture of Diego Suarez, in Madagascar, had eased the situation, it is true, but it was not until the surrender of the Italian Fleet in September 1943 that worthwhile reinforcements made possible a full return to Indian waters. In January 1944 the Eastern Fleet was back in Ceylon, making its main base at Trincomalee, and in its new composition, with an effective force of battleships, carriers, and cruisers, it was at last able to turn to the offensive.

Admiral Somerville's first worry was a burst of U-boat activity, both German and Japanese, in the first quarter of 1944. In the relative immunity from submarine attack during 1943 it had been found possible to sail many ships independently, but with the U-boats now becoming active, one of the Commander-in-Chief's first acts was to reinstitute a large measure of convoy. It was a task made more difficult by lack of escorts, air as well as surface, and this shortage was tragically illustrated in February when the troop transport *Khedive Ismail* was torpedoed off the Maldive Islands while in a convoy for which no air cover had been provided. She sank in two minutes with the loss of nearly 1,300 lives, including those of a number of Wrens, A.T.S., and nursing sisters. That the U-boat concerned was promptly sunk by the *Petard* was encouraging in that it could now sink no more ships, but was, none the less, scant consolation for so heavy a loss of life.

The heavy rate of sinkings in the Indian Ocean continued until March, and was made all the harder to bear by many cases of sickening atrocity on the part of Japanese submarine commanders. Lifeboats full of survivors were frequently machine-gunned, and sometimes deliberately rammed and sunk. In one case the crew of a merchant ship was lined up on the U-boat's casing and massacred with swords, crowbars, and hammers. Admiral Somerville, faced with these reports and the impossibility of finding additional escorts from his own slender resources, pressed the Admiralty on several occasions for reinforcements. Few, however, could be spared, for at home the demands for Operation "Overlord", the invasion of North-west Europe, were growing almost day by day. Some, scraped together by cutting commitments in the Mediterranean and the Atlantic, did reach Admiral Somerville by the end of March, but they still left him woefully short.

It was, in fact, a particularly anxious time, for large numbers of troops and considerable cargoes of supplies were being carried across the Indian Ocean to reinforce the 14th Army in Burma, now building up for a major offensive. It was a fortunate turn of events that, from the end of March, the submarine onslaught dwindled away for a few months to almost negligible proportions. It was caused partly by the sinking of three enemy tankers used for refuelling U-boats at sea, partly by successful counter-attacks which sank three of the six German U-boats operating in the area, and partly by the destruction in the Atlantic of two supply U-boats on their way to the Indian Ocean. They had been carrying replenishments of the new "Gnat" acoustic torpedoes and their failure to reach their destination did much to bring the submarine campaign to an end.

The growing strength of the fleet in the Indian Ocean, coupled with a temporary reinforcement from the United States Pacific Fleet, was a portent of more offensive operations in this area. On 19th April Admiral Somerville opened the programme with an air strike on the island of Sabang, a diversion whose object was the holding of Japanese air and surface forces in the area while the American attack on Hollandia, in Dutch New Guinea, was developing. With the main fleet engaged as a covering force, aircraft from H.M.S. *Illustrious* and U.S.S. *Saratoga* inflicted severe damage in the dockyard area almost without reply from the enemy. One American Hellcat fighter was lost, the pilot being recovered by the British submarine *Tactician*. Two Japanese merchant vessels were sunk, three others damaged, and twenty-seven enemy aircraft were claimed as destroyed, twenty-four on the ground and three in the air. A second strike by the Eastern Fleet on Surabaya a month later was equally successful. The same two carriers took part, and the damage on this occasion included the complete destruction of the oil refinery at Wonokromo.

An even more ambitious operation took place on 25th July, when Admiral Somerville took the whole Eastern Fleet back to Sabang for a bombardment of the Japanese shore defences. As the fleet approached the enemy base, fighters from the *Illustrious* and *Victorious* attacked the airfield to silence any possible opposition and caught the Japanese aircraft on the ground. Four battleships, seven cruisers, and ten destroyers then closed the land from the northward and opened fire shortly after dawn at ranges which varied from 18,000 to 3,000 yards, virtually point-blank with naval guns. An inshore force of three destroyers and the Dutch cruiser *Tromp*, under the command of Captain R. G. Onslow, entered the harbour to add to the damage with their close-range fire. The whole of the dockyard area was heavily hit, and both the wireless and the radar stations were put out of action.

British submarines, too, were active, ranging into the Straits of Malacca, in the coastal areas off Burma, around the Andaman Islands, and even farther afield in the waters of the Dutch East Indies. Apart from an extensive junk traffic carrying supplies to Japanese troops there were few worthwhile targets, although in January 1944 the *Tally Ho* sank the cruiser *Kuma* off Penang. But if the targets were small individually, they were large enough in the aggregate to play an appreciable part in the gradual strangulation of Japanese seaborne supply.

All these operations in the Indian Ocean, none of them particularly noteworthy perhaps, were nevertheless closely linked with the land operations against the Japanese in Burma. The defeat of the Japanese offensive on the Manipur front against India in April and May 1944 had presented the Supreme Commander, Admiral Lord Louis Mountbatten, with a chance which he was quick to seize of striking a blow of real force at the enemy. The Japanese had thought that the breaking of the monsoon would give them the opportunity of withdrawing their broken troops unmolested, but they had reckoned without the 14th Army—incidentally the largest single army in the world—and also without modern medical science which was able to hold at bay the toll of sickness in tropical climates. When the Japanese offensive was broken and turned in mid-May, the 14th Army were quickly on the enemy's heels, and in a series of shattering blows threw the Japanese back across the Chindwin River with terrific losses. The 14th Army itself forced crossings of the river in November and December. Mandalay was now within range, and Admiral Mountbatten decided that its capture should be attempted without delay and the advance continued beyond it to Rangoon.

It was at this point that the Eastern Fleet's long task in the Indian Ocean became fully apparent. Poor roads and an insufficient railway system made air supply of the Army essential if it were to maintain the momentum of its advance beyond Mandalay to Rangoon. Indian bases were too far away for such supply and the only alternative was an air supply base in the Arakan Peninsula. This called for the capture of the Akyab airfields, which in its turn meant an amphibious assault in conjunction with an offensive thrust by land. And for that it was necessary to have complete maritime control over the Bay of Bengal and also over the sea area bounded by the Andaman and Nicobar Islands, the Tenasserim and Kra coasts, and the northern end of Sumatra.

This, indeed, was what the Eastern Fleet had achieved in its operations during 1944, though it is but true to point out that this control was gained more by lack of Japanese naval reaction than by any hard fighting at sea in the Indian Ocean. It is equally true to add that, throughout the Burma campaign, the overwhelming share of the fighting fell upon the land and air forces. The Navy's role was always secondary throughout, its main responsibility being the safe passage of reinforcements and supplies and the denial of the waters of the Indian Ocean to Japanese naval incursion. With the Japanese Navy so fully occupied in the Pacific, the danger of raids into these British-controlled sea areas was remote.

A change in the command of the Eastern Fleet took place in August 1944, when Admiral Sir Bruce Fraser arrived from the Home Fleet to relieve Admiral Somerville. It proved to be little more than a temporary command, for three months later he was selected to command the newly-formed British Pacific Fleet, being relieved in the Indian Ocean by Admiral Sir Arthur Power. With this second change in command, the name of the Fleet itself was altered to the East Indies Fleet in order to avoid any confusion with the British Pacific Fleet farther east.

Planning for the amphibious assault on Akyab began in November 1944, and was given the code name "Talon". It was approved by Admiral Mountbatten at the end of the month,[3] but was in fact overtaken by the rapidity of the Army's advance ashore. By 27th December it was learned that the Japanese were preparing to evacuate Akyab, and a new plan, with the code name of "Lightning", was made for the landing. The assault went in just after dawn on 3rd January, 1945, and the troops were put ashore without opposition. Both the port and the airfields were quickly occupied.

The naval forces engaged in the Arakan campaign were then given two further tasks. The first was the landing and maintenance of troops at different points along the coast in order to cut off the retreating Japanese, the second was the capture of Ramree and Cheduba Islands, about 80–100 miles farther south, where the facilities for airfields were better than Akyab. At the same time a considerable force of coastal vessels penetrated into the intricate network of waterways, or chaungs, along the Arakan seaboard, shooting up Japanese seaborne supplies and cutting their escape routes.

None of this work could have been done without the labours of small naval parties known as Combined Operations Pilotage parties. Their duty it was to explore and chart the labyrinth of mangrove swamps and tidal streams in which the coastal craft carried out their operations. Without their work many of the small amphibious operations could never have been carried out, but at the same time it was dangerous work and "involved stealing up the chaungs in canoes during the night or in the mist of early morning to sound for depth, and marking the channel with buoys. It meant climbing ashore at low tide up the slimy banks to reconnoitre beyond them, the prospect of assault across the firm (or flooded) paddy-fields. At any bend or confluence the chaung might be mined or ambushed. Indeed, the whole distance of this jungle water-maze was a sniper's paradise."[4] It might well have been added that it was a paradise for crocodiles as well.

The easy capture of Akyab was followed by a number of small landing operations down the coast. In one or two cases there was some opposition, usually silenced by a bombardment from supporting cruisers and destroyers. The main difficulties were rarely, however, the extent of any Japanese reaction so much as the intricate navigation required to bring the landing-craft to their selected beaches. That all the landings were carried through with great accuracy and with negligible casualties was a measure of the preparatory work performed by the Combined Operations Pilotage parties. To them, probably, the major credit was due.

As more and more of the Arakan coast fell into British hands, the planning for the assault on Ramree Island took on a new urgency. This was the largest operation carried out by the Navy in Burma and involved the landing of one division of the Army, some 23,000 men, on the northern beaches of the island. Although the Japanese garrison on Ramree Island was thought only to number about 1,000 men, and although it was known that the enemy's naval forces consisted only of a few motor gunboats, prodigious forces were assembled for the assault, including the battleship *Queen Elizabeth* for bombardment purposes.[5] In addition, the escort carrier *Ameer*, the cruiser *Phœbe*, and seven destroyers accompanied the landing and assault craft. Seven days before the landing took place a small party of soldiers was put ashore from two motor-launches in the vicinity of the assault beaches. They were successfully re-embarked three nights later after having made a complete reconnaissance of the harbour.[6]

The troops were landed on their beaches on the morning of 21st January against minor opposition which was quickly overcome. By the end of the day over 7,000 men were ashore as well as 120 vehicles and 70 tons of stores. During the following days the build-up went on rapidly, continuing until 12th February, by which date 23,091 men, 679 vehicles, and 9,233 tons of stores had been put ashore in the island. That so considerable a force, both on land and at sea, should be used to capture an island defended by 1,000

Japanese without air or naval support appears surprising. As events turned out, the proposed airfields on Ramree were not ready for the transport aircraft, with which it was hoped to supply the 14th Army, until 15th May, by which time Rangoon itself had been occupied and the whole campaign was virtually over.

The assault on Rangoon on 2nd May followed much the same pattern as on Ramree Island. Once again overwhelming power was deployed at sea and on land, only to discover that the city had already been evacuated by the Japanese, and that British prisoners-of-war had released themselves and taken over its administration. The landings all went very much as planned, though in the circumstances it proved little more than a demonstration of navigational skill in bringing the large convoys of assault and landing-craft safely up the river in darkness.[7]

These naval operations in Burma, all of them in general support of the Army, were of relatively minor importance. In the case of every assault from the sea the battle had already been won in advance by operations of the Army ashore, with the result that opposition to the landings had been reduced to a minimum. Yet the campaign is of some interest as illustrating the ability of the Navy to operate on a significant assault scale—that is, of landing up to one division in amphibious operations—even in such a maze of uncharted waters as the chaungs and swamps of the Arakan coast.

It had been agreed by the Combined Chiefs of Staff[8] in 1943 that operations in the South-east Asia area should be conducted in support of the main offensive in the Pacific, leaving the Indian Ocean as a somewhat subsidiary area of naval importance. The chief duty of the East Indies Fleet, therefore, became more of a holding and trade protection force than a main fighting fleet, although during 1944 it was augmented temporarily by the ships destined eventually for the Pacific. Support for the Pacific operations had taken the form during 1944 of naval strikes against Japanese war potential, such as the Fleet Air Arm attacks on the Andaman Islands and Sabang, and this policy was continued in early 1945 by similar attacks against Japanese oil installations in Sumatra. By the beginning of the year a considerable carrier force, comprising the

*Indomitable*, *Indefatigable*, *Illustrious*, and *Victorious*, had been assembled at Trincomalee under the command of Rear-Admiral Vian. It was, in fact, destined for the Pacific Fleet, but before proceeding to Australia Rear-Admiral Vian carried out three strikes during January in the East Indies command area. These were against the oil refinery at Pangkalan Brandan on 4th January, at Palembang on the 24th and again on the 29th, when the refineries on both banks of the river were severely damaged. All three were successful, but were in essence no more than "tip and run" raids.

By mid-1944 the Japanese Navy, on the full defensive in the Pacific, had virtually abandoned any pretence of control in the waters around Burma, leaving those seas bare of targets. Such seaborne traffic as did attempt to use the Malacca Strait and the Java Sea was severely harassed by the British submarines on patrol there.

Yet occasionally a target made a reluctant appearance. On 10th May the submarines *Statesman* and *Subtle*, on patrol in the Malacca Strait, both reported a Japanese cruiser escorted by a single destroyer. Neither was able to get within range for an attack. The *Subtle* sighted her again on the 12th, missed with an attack at long range, but reported her position to the Commander-in-Chief. A considerable force of ships, engaged in carrying out diversionary attacks to cover the troop convoys to Rangoon, were in the vicinity and Admiral Power ordered them to search for her. She was sighted again on the 15th by an aircraft from the carrier *Shah*, shadowed from the air, and damaged in a bombing attack by three Avengers later in the day.

The nearest ships to her were the five destroyers of the 26th Flotilla, the *Saumarez*, *Venus*, *Vigilant*, *Virago*, and *Verulam*, at the time about eighty-five miles away. Increasing speed to twenty-seven knots they searched along a bearing calculated on her farthest-on position and shortly after midnight found her by radar. The destroyers shadowed her in the darkness for a short period while preparations for the attack were made, and then went in, simultaneously but independently, to fire their torpedoes from different bearings at very close range. It was in all respects a model destroyer attack and the cruiser was hit eight times. She was the 10,000-ton

*Hagura* and she sank almost at once. Her escorting destroyer, the *Kamikaze*, was severely damaged by gunfire but succeeded in making good her escape in the darkness.

With the occupation of Rangoon the war in Burma was virtually over. The Burmese R.N.V.R. took over the duty of cutting the Japanese escape route east of the Irrawaddy River and of landing small parties of troops for mopping-up purposes, but these on the whole were very minor operations. There was virtually no fighting, and the final Japanese surrender on 14th August came as little surprise. Throughout the campaign it had been so much more the battle on shore which had proved the decisive factor that the operations at sea in the Indian Ocean played a very secondary part in the victory. Once the command of the seas had been obtained, and by 1944 it was no longer being challenged by the Japanese, the ultimate victory was assured.

The decision to send a British fleet into the Pacific was approved in principle by the Combined Chiefs of Staff late in 1943,[9] a decision which entailed considerable forward planning before the ships could arrive. Some British units, notably submarines and the fast minelayer *Ariadne*, were already operating in Pacific waters, while many Australian ships were also engaged there. Admiral King, the American Chief of Naval Operations, in commenting on the decision, proposed that any British fleet should be self-supporting, a suggestion which not only entailed a considerable build-up of stores in Australia but also called for the provision of a fleet train of supply and repair ships of all kinds that could sustain the fleet at sea for long periods without the need for a return to shore bases. The Americans had already perfected this new principle of naval war for operations in areas where distances were so vast, but to the British it was a new departure in naval planning. The Admiralty sent a naval mission to Washington in February 1944 to study the logistics of American task forces in the Pacific and to make recommendations as to the best way of maintaining the proposed British Fleet in Pacific waters. Rear-Admiral Daniel, leading the naval mission, very quickly reached the decision that the only way to do so was to adopt the American method of the fleet train.

The British Pacific Fleet came formally into being on the morning of 22nd November, 1944, when Admiral Fraser hoisted his flag as Commander-in-Chief first in the gunboat *Tarantula* and later in the battleship *Howe*. In her he sailed for Australia on 2nd December, the first capital ship of the new fleet to arrive in Pacific waters. Vice-Admiral Sir Bernard Rawlings, his second-in-command, followed a few days later in the *King George V*, while the carriers, under Rear-Admiral Vian, arrived in Australia, following their strike on the oil installations at Palembang, early in February 1945.

By the New Year of 1945, the American advance in the Pacific had reached the Philippine Islands and had cleared Leyte of the enemy. Troops were also ashore and mopping-up in Mindoro Island. On 9th January they invaded Luzon, the largest island in the Philippine group, landing in the Lingayen Gulf, north of Manila Bay. Manila itself, capital of the Philippines, was captured a month later. Admiral Fraser, who was present at the Lingayen Gulf action as a spectator, had there his first experience of the Japanese Kamikaze suicide bombers and, among other ships sunk or damaged as a result of their attacks, saw the cruiser *Australia* survive five hits by them. It was a good augury for the coming actions of the Fleet in the Pacific, revealing as it did the strength and staunchness of British shipbuilding. So far as carriers were concerned, Admiral Fraser's confidence proved to be fully justified.

With the capture of the Philippines the naval war in the Pacific entered its final phase. During February 1945, United States Marines landed on the island of Iwojima in the Volcano Islands, and no more than 750 miles from Tokyo. It took a month of desperate fighting to subdue the fanatical Japanese, over 20,000 of whom fought to the death. Iwojima stands out as an action fought in the great tradition of the United States Marine Corps, the élite of the American armed forces, a battle in which, as Admiral Nimitz wrote with justifiable pride, "uncommon valour had been commonly displayed".

There was now one more step to make before the home islands of Japan were brought within range of invasion. This step was to the Ryukyus, the group of islands which stretch between Japan and

Formosa. The target in this group was Okinawa, the largest of the islands, and the assault date was fixed as 1st April.

The assault against Okinawa was also the signal for the first appearance of the British Pacific Fleet upon the operational stage in these distant waters. It was not engaged in the main attack, but had the task of neutralising Japanese airfields in the Sakishima group of islands just south of the Ryukyus. The fleet, accompanied by its fleet train, sailed from the Caroline Islands on 23rd March, with two battleships, four fleet carriers, five cruisers, and eleven destroyers. On 26th March it was in its operational area and made the first of a series of attacks on the airfields and installations in the islands. For sixty-two days, with a break midway of eight days at Leyte for taking on additional stores, the fleet remained at sea, being nourished at intervals in a refuelling area by the fleet train.[10] This was something new in the British Navy, a technique now being practised for the first time, and the success of the operation put to rest some doubts expressed by American naval officers as to the British ability to operate for long periods at sea in this Pacific manner. It had, of course, been normal American practice in this great ocean over the past two years.

Inevitably the fleet, and especially the carriers, attracted the attention of Japanese suicide bombers. The *Indefatigable* was hit at the base of her island superstructure on the morning of 1st April, but was operational again by the afternoon. During the second series of strikes in May, the *Formidable* and *Indomitable* were both hit in Kamikaze attacks on the 4th, while the *Victorious* and, for the second time, the *Formidable* were hit on the 9th. In each case the damage proved to be only temporary and all ships were operational again within a matter of hours, a state of affairs that compared favourably with American carrier experience. With them a hit on the flight-deck by a suicide bomber put the carrier out of action for a long period, for they had not adopted the British practice of fitting armoured flight-decks in their carriers.

Enemy resistance on shore in Okinawa came to an end on 21st June, and with it the last hope of Japanese survival perished. Already, in point of fact, Japan was a defeated nation, although, through the stubbornness of her leaders, she still refused to accept the fact. In the three and a half years during which she had been engaged in war the greater part of her fleet and nearly the whole of her merchant fleet had been wiped out. It was, indeed, the loss of the merchant shipping which created the conditions for Allied victory and which drained the life-blood from her industry and armed forces. In all, 88 per cent. of Japanese shipping was sunk, and of that, British, United States, and Dutch submarines sank two-thirds. By the beginning of 1944 the situation was beginning to look bleak; a year later and it was black indeed. Cut off from imports from her original conquests in Malaya and the Dutch East Indies, a tottering national economy was bolstered only by trade across the Sea of Japan with China. In mid-1945 this last line of communication with the outer world was threatened. On 9th June American submarines began to dominate even these closed waters, and in the course of the next eleven days they sank twenty-seven ships. This rate of sinking dwindled after the first onslaught, not from any falling-off in skill or lack of forceful tactics on the part of the submarine captains but entirely because Japanese ships were no longer there to be sunk.

More vulnerable even than Great Britain—that other island nation in the West—to a war of attrition at sea, Japan's economy lay in ruins. As late as June 1945 she still had as many as two million unbeaten troops in the field. She still had a host of men willing and eager to hurl themselves to death in suicide aircraft. They were all of no value to her now, for the soldiers faced starvation for lack of supplies, the aircraft remained on the ground for lack of fuel. Japan had now come to the end of the road.

British submarines, both of the Pacific and East Indies Fleets, played their part in this sea blockade. For the most part their prey consisted of small coasters and junks, to which the Japanese were now reduced, though occasionally fortune smiled upon them in the shape of a more dramatic target. These, however, grew progressively rarer as the Japanese were driven farther and farther back into their home waters. Such a target was seen through the periscope of the *Trenchant* on 8th June, and all the more welcome for appearing in the narrow and confined waters of the Banka Strait, off Sumatra.

She was the 10,000-ton cruiser *Ashigara*, and she sank in half an hour after being hit by five of the *Trenchant*'s torpedoes.

More dramatic still was an echo, in the waters around Singapore, of the midget submarine attacks which had crippled the *Tirpitz* in the fastness of her Norwegian fjord in 1943. Four British midget submarines were allocated in July to the United States Seventh Fleet in the Pacific. Their tasks were to cut cables and to attack Japanese heavy cruisers as they lay in the Johore Strait, leading to Singapore. They sailed, each in tow of a British submarine, on 27th July; the D-day for their operations was the 31st.

The cable-cutting operations were performed by a diver from the midget submarines working on the sea bed. On her D-day *XE4* cut both the Saigon–Hong Kong and Saigon–Singapore cables, returning with one foot's length of each cable she had cut as a proof of her success. *XE5* was less successful, though she spent four days and nights searching in the defended waters of Hong Kong for the cable from there to Singapore.

The attack on the cruisers was also carried out on the 31st. *XE1*, towed by the submarine *Spark*, whose target lay at the entrance to the naval yard, was delayed in her passage up the Johore Strait by several encounters with surface craft. As a result she was too late to reach the cruiser she was to attack and to make her return passage in daylight. She was thus forced to come back with her task unattempted. *XE3*, towed by the *Stygian*, had better fortune. Lieutenant I. E. Fraser, R.N.R., her commanding officer, took her up the forty miles of the Johore Strait outside the swept channel and successfully slipped past the trawler guarding the boom gate. Two hours later Fraser sighted his target, the 10,000-ton cruiser *Takao*, lying close inshore.

She was anchored in such shallow water that *XE3* had to push her way along the bottom to reach her without breaking surface. Once alongside, Fraser discovered that there was insufficient water beneath her keel for *XE3* to penetrate, except for a small space midships. Even there, the depth of water was insufficient for *XE3* fully to open her hatch. Her diver, Leading Seaman Magennis, managed to squeeze himself through the narrow space available, only to discover that the cruiser's bottom was so encrusted with barnacles that the limpet mines which *XE3* carried would not stick. For three-quarters of an hour he was engaged in scraping off the barnacles and in fixing the limpets, tied in pairs by a line under the *Takao*'s keel. After the withdrawal Magennis, although exhausted by his previous dive, again left the midget submarine to clear a limpet carrier which had failed to release and fall clear.

*XE3* made the return journey down the Strait and a successful contact with the *Stygian* to reach Brunei, in Borneo, in safety. Behind her she left a wrecked and useless *Takao*. Both Lieutenant Fraser and Leading Seaman Magennis were awarded the Victoria Cross for their notable skill and gallantry.

It was while these British midget submarines were carrying out their tasks around Singapore and Saigon that the Pacific Fleet was again called to action, this time in the final battle of the campaign. The home islands of Japan were now under constant attack, both by carrier-borne aircraft of the British and United States fleets and by land-based Super-Fortress bombers from the newly captured airfields in Okinawa. The British Pacific Fleet sailed from Sydney on 6th July to take part in this last battle, and on the 17th aircraft from the carriers *Formidable*, *Victorious*, and *Implacable* raided targets in the Tokyo area. From that day until the end, the air war upon Japan was continued in a crescendo of devastation. The little that remained of the Japanese Fleet was destroyed in a carrier raid on the naval base of Kure that lasted from 24th to 28th July, and among the major casualties in these attacks were the battleships *Haruna*, *Hyuga*, and *Ise*, and the carriers *Amagi* and *Katsuragi*. Many others—cruisers, destroyers, and submarines—were sunk at their moorings.

This was the knock-out blow, the virtual end of the Japanese Fleet. For a few days more the nation lay prostrate beneath the blows of the air forces, both maritime and shore-based. Japanese feelers for a "liberal" peace treaty were put out on 28th July, but the Allied Powers could have no mercy on a foe whose treachery and whose savage disregard of the human decencies had been so evident from the start of hostilities. After due warning had been given,

Japanese cities were heavily bombed one by one, and the mounting tale of destruction grew.

On the morning of 6th August, a lone American aircraft, flying high, dropped the first atomic bomb ever to be used in war. It exploded above Hiroshima, and devastated four square miles of the centre of the city. Three days later a second atomic bomb fell on Nagasaki. It destroyed the industrial centre of the town, which contained among other installations the great Mitsubishi steel works. On the 10th Japan proclaimed her readiness to accept unconditional surrender subject to an understanding that would leave intact the prerogatives of the Emperor as a sovereign ruler, and five days later the surrender was proclaimed to the world.

The collapse of Japan, so much sooner than had at one time been anticipated, was not brought about by the use of the atomic weapons or by the entry of Russia into the Far Eastern War against Japan on 8th August, though both these reasons were put forward as "face-savers" by the Japanese Prime Minister. The first inkling of a Japanese willingness to accept defeat had come on 11th July with a request to Marshal Stalin from the Japanese Government that Russia should mediate in the war. That had been followed by the demand for a "liberal" peace on the 28th. But long before either of these dates Japan had been brought to a desperate state by the inexorable pressure of Allied sea power in the Pacific. Dependent on food and raw materials from overseas for her existence, with her fleet sunk and her sea power gone, she had but a single choice between surrender or a slow but certain death.

It had been a remarkable campaign, and its ending was no less remarkable. Japan's home army was still strong and unbeaten, and at the close of the war she had twice as many combatant aircraft as on the day she had first launched her attack at Pearl Harbour. Only her fleet had been defeated. Because of that, because Japan was a maritime nation that depended for her all on the retention of her sea power, she had no alternative but to surrender. Her unbeaten army and her still strong air force were valueless when her shield of sea power was shattered.

The war in the Pacific was a triumph for the United States Navy.

Although British fleets operated both in the Pacific and in the Indian Ocean, although Australia, New Zealand, and Holland contributed naval squadrons, although the French battleship *Richelieu* took part in the Indian Ocean strikes against Japanese installations, the vast burden of this sea and air war was borne by the United States. It was they who, by their ingenuity and application, overcame the difficulties of operating at vast distances from their bases, who evolved the technique of keeping their great fleets at sea for months at a time. Placed beside their effort in this ocean, the contribution of Britain was small indeed. Yet, in viewing the war at sea as a whole, the balance swung not unevenly. If, in the Pacific, it was the United States who played the leading role at sea, in the Atlantic and the Mediterranean it had been Britain and Canada whose ships had carried the greater share of the burden.

With the final surrender of Japan on 15th August the great task was over. Allied sea power, exercised in every ocean in the world, had once again, as it had so often done throughout the centuries, laid the foundations of inevitable victory. As all the fighting came to an end, the navies, armies, and air forces were brought slowly home for release, reorganisation, and redeployment for occupation duties. The tasks of war now lay behind them. Ahead, the tasks of peace stretched into a sombre and uncertain future, for high in the sky above the ruins of Hiroshima and Nagasaki there now hung a vast question mark. The whole pattern of war had changed in the flashes of those two atomic explosions, and at the time no man could tell their implications for the naval future.

# References

## ABBREVIATIONS

| | |
|---|---|
| A. | Admiralty Air Branch Paper |
| A.M. | Admiralty Out Signal |
| B.S. | Battle Summary |
| C.C.S. | Combined Chiefs of Staff, Meetings and Papers |
| C.O.S. | Chiefs of Staff Committee, Meetings and Papers |
| G.H.S. | German History Series |
| G.M. | General Out Message |
| J.S.M. | Joint Staffs Mission |
| M. | Admiralty Military Branch Papers |
| R.O. | Admiralty Record Office |
| S.W.C. | Supreme War Council |


*Chapter 1*

1. *Hansard*, 12th November, 1936, col. 1144.
2. German Air Ministry Q.M.G. Dept.
3. Air Ministry S.38173, Part 3.
4. C.O.S. 727.
5. C.O.S. 797.
6. W. S. Churchill. *The Second World War*, Vol. I, p. 305.
7. A.M. 1420/31.

*Chapter 2*

1. C.O.S. (39) 102. S.W.C. 1st meeting.
2. W. N. Medlicott, *The Economic Blockade*, Vol. 1, p. 88.
3. C.O.S. (39) 102.
4. S.W.C. (39) 1st meeting.
5. A.M. 1409/5th October.
6. B.S. 26, pp. 8, 40. M.013217/39.
7. Commodore S.A.D. 1200/12th December.
8. Weichold, *Report on German Operations*.
9. *Ibid.*, paras. 39, 40.
10. Supp. L.G. No. 37989. 17th June, 1947.
11. C.O.S. (39) 127.
12. S.W.C. (39) 4th meeting.
13. Fuehrer Conferences. Report by C.-in-C. Navy, 10th October, 1939.
14. *Ibid.* Report by C.-in-C. Navy, 12th December, 1939.
15. S.W.C. (40), 2nd meeting.
16. S.W.C. (40), 1st meeting.
17. See ante, ref. 4.
18. C.O.S. (40) 270.
19. C.O.S. (40) 216(5).
20. S.W.C. (40), 2nd meeting.
21. Fuehrer Conferences. Reports by C.-in-C. Navy on dates mentioned.
22. See T. K. Derry, *The Campaign in Norway*, p. 51.
23. 2210/13th April; 1027/14th April.

24. Vice-Admiral W. Wegener, *Die Seestrategie des Weltkrieges*, p. 49.
25. A. Carton de Wiart, *Happy Odyssey*, p. 174.
26. *London Gazette*, 8th July, 1947. Supplement No. 38011, para. 10.
27. Log of *Scharnhorst*, 6th June, 1940.
28. Capt. T. H. Troubridge. Report of Proceedings, H.M.S. *Furious*.
29. See ante, ref. 27.

*Chapter 3*

1. A.M. 2325/3rd May.
2. A.M. 2249/7th May.
3. C.O.S. (40) 133rd meeting.
4. M. 011883/40.
5. Ministry of Shipping, T.O. 9436/40. (See Transport Dept.)
6. A.M. 1944/22. R.O. Case 5458.
7. Lord Gort's second Despatch, para. 44.
8. A.M. 1857/26. R.O. Case 5458.
9. V.A. Dover to Admiralty 1344/3rd June.
10. A.M. 1910/26.
11. For operations at Oran, see M.016021/40, A.0742–6/40.
12. A. 0789/40.
13. C.O.S. (40) 543; W.P. (40) 256.
14. A.M. 1840/5th July to C.-in-C. H.F.
15. M. 013582/40 of 20th July, 1940.
16. Fuehrer Conferences, C.-in-C. Navy, 20th June, 1940.
17. See especially Fuehrer Conferences. C.-in-C. Navy. 19th September, 1940; 12th October, 1940.
18. C.O.S. (40), 206th meeting, minute 5.
19. C.O.S. (40) 422.

*Chapter 4*

1. See Fuehrer Conferences, July–September, 1940.
2. Fuehrer Conferences. Report of C.-in-C. Navy, 11th July, 1940.
3. Convoys S.C. 2 and H.X. 72.
4. Convoys S.C. 7 and H.X. 79.
5. C.O.S. (40) 183.
6. Telegram to C.-in-C. Middle East annexed to C.O.S. (40) 521.
7. See, e.g., C.-in-C. Navy's report to Hitler, Fuehrer Conferences, 6th September, 1940.
8. Ciano's Diplomatic Papers, p. 402.
9. Directive No. 18, Fuehrer's Headquarters, 12.11.1940.
10. C.O.S. (40) 344.
11. O/20568 Cipher 25/9 to War Office.
12. Directive No. 22. Fuehrer Conferences, 11th January, 1941.
13. C.O.S. (41), 7(o), and Annex II; see also C.O.S. (41) 22.
14. Naval Conference at Merano, 13th and 14th February, 1941.
15. Message from German N.L.O. Rome to Italian Naval Staff 19th March, 1941.
16. Admiral Iachino, *Gauda e Matapan.*
17. T.O.O. 2326/28 from C.-in-C.
18. 3rd Supp. to L.G. 29th July, 1947, No. 38031.
19. A.M. 2118/1/4/41.

*Chapter 5*

1. Adm. tel. 114.
2. Adm. tel. 982/15th April. F/Libya/1, p. 167.
3. F/Libya/1, p. 169.
4. Adm. tel. 64. F/Libya/1, p. 182.
5. Signal 1436/22.
6. Fuehrer Conferences, Directive No. 25.
7. C.O.S. (41) 42. Minute 2, Confidential Annex.
8. Official Despatch No. 38293, p. 3049.

9. C.O.S. Signal 101, 10th May, 1941.
10. Wavell to Prime Minister, 18th May, 1941. See W. S. Churchill, *The Second World War*, Vol. III, p. 250.
11. C.O.S. (41), 189th Meeting, minute 2 and Annex. F/Crete/1, p. 153.
12. Telegram 68366.
13. Telegram 0/67808. F/Crete/1, p. 164.
14. Telegram 035. F/Crete/1, p. 166.
15. 1305/29. F/Crete/1, p. 170.
16. For examples of these, see S. W. Roskill, *The War at Sea*, Vol. I, pp. 446–7.
17. Viscount Cunningham of Hyndhope, *A Sailor's Odyssey*, p. 389.
18. Telegram No. 229, 17th June, 1941.
19. G.M. 16656.
20. C.O.S. (41), 220th Meeting, minute 7.
21. No. 97404: Hist. (B) 5 (Final) No. 70.
22. Report of Lieut.-Gen. Laverack, *Operations of 1st Australian Corps in Syria.*

*Chapter 6*

1. Fuehrer Conferences, Report by C.-in-C. Navy, 14.11.1940.
2. C.O.S. (41) 284.
3. 600–900 tons, 15–16 knots.
4. 1,300–1,500 tons, 20–24 knots.
5. *Hansard*, H. of C. Debates. 10.12.1940.
6. *The R.A.F. in Maritime War*, Vol. II, pp. 419–39.
7. In January 1941 the average number of surface escorts with a trade convoy was 1·8, a year later the figure was 4.5.
8. For the full directive, see W. S. Churchill, *The Second World War*, Vol. III, pp. 107–9.

*Chapter 7*

1. Commander G. A. Rotherham, R.N. The pilot was Lieut. (A) N. N. Goddard, R.N.V.R. In his official despatch after the action the C.-in-C. remarked: "This skilful and determined reconnaissance is deserving of the highest praise, as is the initiative of Captain Fancourt (C.O. of R.N.A.S. Hatston) in ordering it."
2. See German account of this operation, published in Fuehrer Conferences, pp. 201–13.
3. A partial German reconnaissance of Scapa Flow in the afternoon of 22nd May reported four battleships, six cruisers, and several destroyers present.
4. H.M.S. *Prince of Wales*, Signal log.
5. H.M.S. *Prince of Wales*, Report of Proceedings (M.011222/41).
6. Commander R. F. Jessel, *The Bismarck Operation—The German Aspect.* R.U.S.I. Journal, February 1953, p. 18.
7. *Ibid.*, p. 20.
8. C.-in-C. H.F. 1047/25th May.
9. A.M. 1924/25.
10. Captain D.4. Report of Proceedings (M.08780/41).
11. P.G. 20418 (German Staff report on operation "Rheinübung").
12. Supp. to L.G. 14th October, 1947, No. 38098, paras. 92, 93.
13. Fuehrer Conferences. Report of C.-in-C. Navy, 17th September, 1941.
14. F.O. U-boats, *Reports of Convoy Operations* (*Second Series*), PG. 30943, pp. 9–11.
15. War Diary of German Naval Staff, Pt.C4 PG.32173, p. 139.
16. *Ibid.*, Pt. A, 22nd November, 1941.

17. *The Pearl Harbour Operation*, p. 15. See S. E. Morison, *The Rising Sun in the Pacific*, p. 95.

*Chapter 8*

1. Fuehrer Conferences. Report of C.-in-C. Navy, 12th January, 1942.
2. *Ibid.*
3. A.M. 1252A/3rd February, 1942.
4. Dover Letter 145/211, F. 42, 16th February, 1942.
5. Full reports are in M.02189/42.
6. Full reports of the destroyer actions are in M.02228/42.
7. *The Times*, 14th February, 1942.
8. Supp. to L.G., 20th February, 1948, No. 38214, Narrative, para. 1.
9. *Malay Invasion Naval Operations* (Japanese monograph, No. 107).
10. Log of messages received at Singapore. C.-in-C. E.F. 741/4724 in M.01512/42.
11. Report of Flight-Lieutenant T. E. Vigors, R.A.F. C.-in-C. E.F. 730/4742 in M.0251/42.
12. "Abdacom" Directive to Supreme Command, attached to *Despatch of Supreme Commander* (H.M.S.O. 1948).
13. *Ibid.*, p. 1.
14. U.S. Combat Narrative, *The Java Sea Campaign*, p. 52.
15. W. S. Churchill to F. D. Roosevelt. 5th March, 1942.

*Chapter 9*

1. "The war . . . is coming very close to home. . . . We have, accordingly, extended our patrol in north and south Atlantic waters." At the end of his broadcast the President declared an unlimited national emergency.
2. Report of C.-in-C. Navy. Fuehrer Conferences, 12th December, 1941.
3. S. E. Morison. *U.S. Naval Operations in World War II. The Battle of the Atlantic*, I, p. 126.
4. In an interview to a German war correspondent. Translated in *Monthly Report, A/S Command* (October 1942), p. 16.
5. S. E. Morison, *op. cit.*, I, p. 41.
6. First Sea Lord papers, Vol. 16.
7. German Naval Staff Study, PG. 32615, p. 39.
8. Monthly A/S Report, April 1942.
9. Report in M.08720/42.
10. Report in R.O. Case 8285.
11. Report in M.011161/42.
12. *Ibid.*
13. R.O. Case 7607.
14. C.O.S. (42) 28 (o).
15. C.-in-C. H.F. Report. M.050801/42.
16. Log of *Tirpitz* (G.H.S. 4, p. 104).
17. *Ibid.*
18. Sir D. Pound to Adm. King, 18th May, 1942. First Sea Lord Papers, Vol. 18.
19. A.M. 2111/4/7/42 and A.M.2136/4/7/42.
20. G.H.S./4, pp. 213–15.
21. Diary of Luftflotte V.
22. Report of Proceedings, H.M.S. *Obedient*, in M.052714/43.
23. M.052901/43.
24. Fuehrer Conferences, Report of C.-in-C. Navy, 6th January, 1943.

*Chapter 10*

1. *Campaigns of the Pacific War*. U.S. Strategic Bombing Survey.
2. Secret Information Bulletin No. 1. *Battle Experience from Pearl Harbour to Midway*.
3. Report of Flag Officer Commanding Force F, M.09213/42.

4. *Ibid.*
5. Remarks of the C.-in-C. Plymouth on Operation "Chariot", M.05386/42, Enclosure 1.
6. Report by Commander R. E. D. Ryder, M.05386/42, Enclosure 2.
7. *Ibid.*
8. S. E. Morison, *History of U.S. Naval Operations*, Vol. II, p. 15.
9. W. S. Churchill, *The Second World War*, Vol. IV, p. 404.
10. Report on the Dieppe Raid by Combined Operations H.Q.
11. M.051641/42, para 42.
12. See his telegrams to President Roosevelt, *The Second World War*, Vol. IV, pp. 475–87.
13. C.O.S. (42) 41.
14. Governor and C.-in-C. Gibraltar to War Office, 28.9.42.
15. Report in M.052138/42.
16. Admiral Cunningham's Despatch and Enclosures in M.053475/43.
17. See General Eisenhower's Despatch in M.01167/46.


*Chapter 11*


1. W. S. Churchill, *The Second World War*, Vol. IV, p. 110.
2. First Sea Lord Papers, Vol. 24. Sir D. Pound to Sir A. Salter. 13th July, 1942.
3. *Ibid.*, Vol. 21. Review by A.C.N.S.(T).
4. *Ibid.*, Vol. 26. Sir H. Moore to First Sea Lord.
5. H.X. 229 and S.C. 122.
6. J.S.M. 843, 29th March, 1943.
7. ONS. 5.
8. Fuehrer Conferences, Report of C.-in-C. Navy, 6th January, 1943.
9. *Ibid.*, 26th February, 1943.
10. Log of the *Tirpitz*.
11. *Ibid.*
12. The full British account of this attack is in M.054868/43, M.05578/44, and No. 1098/S.M. 04351.
13. Supp. to L.G. No. 38204, 10th February, 1948.
14. C.-in-C.'s Despatch in M.01881/44.
15. Fuehrer Conferences. Report of C.-in-C. Navy, 19th December, 1943.
16. Gunnery narrative, H.M.S. *Duke of York*, in M.01881/44.
17. C.-in-C.'s Despatch in M.01881/44.


*Chapter 12*


1. General Montgomery to C.-in-C. Levant, 14th April, 1943.
2. C.-in-C. Mediterranean, 1215 A/8th May.
3. See Fuehrer Conferences. Report of C.-in-C. Navy, 14th May, 1943, para. 1.
4. Admiral Ramsay's report in M.054931/44.
5. M.044 89/44, para. 42.
6. *Ibid.*, para. 48.
7. John Ehrman, *Grand Strategy*, Vol. V, p. 1.
8. *Ibid.*, p. 8.
9. NAF 265, 181233 July.
10. C.O.S. (W) 717, 211040.
11. File A 16–3/011, Serial 0010 (Report of Vice-Admiral Hewitt, U.S.N.).
12. C.-in-C. Mediterranean 1038 B/11th September.


*Chapter 13*


1. Viscount Cunningham of Hyndhope, *A Sailor's Odyssey*, p. 585.
2. *Ibid.*, p. 598.
3. C.O.S. (W) 587, 211420Z, April 1943.

4. M.056731/44, Appendix III.
5. Admiral Moore's report in 2nd B.S. 128/026 of 10th April, 1944.
6. Report of strike commander in H.M.S. *Furious* 02524Z of 5th April, 1944.
7. H.M.S. *Victorious* 0137/6206 of 5th April, 1944.
8. C.C.S. 304/12, 12th February, 1944.
9. C.O.S. (43) 416 (O).
10. C.C.S. 465/1.
11. Admiralty F.D.S./3/53, P.G. 32100 (Krancke's Diary).
12. ANCXF Report, Vol. 1, p. 46.
13. *Ibid.*, Vol. II. Report of Naval Commander Eastern Task Force.
14. *Ibid.*, Vol. III, Report of Naval Commander Force O.
15. C.C.S. 304/12, 12th February, 1944.
16. Mr. James Forrestal. *The Times*, 18th April, 1945.

*Chapter 14*

1. For details of this battle see M. 051642/42 (Official report by C.-in-C., U.S. Pacific Fleet) and N.I.D. 0052799/47 (The Midway Operation B.I.O.S./ Jap. Docs./1602).
2. Reports in M.051784/42, M.052067/42, and M. 04229/43.
3. M.059855/47, pp. 137–8.
4. M.04956/45.
5. In his despatch (M.059855/47, p. 143, para. 368) Admiral Mountbatten says that H.M.S. *Queen Elizabeth* was required as he had learned that the Japanese were placing guns in caves overlooking the beaches.
6. M.3524/46, pp. 46, 47.
7. Full report in M.09253/45.
8. C.C.S. 417.
9. *Ibid.*, Annex II.
10. See Supp. to L.G., No. 38308, of 1st June, 1948.

# INDEX